The Soviet Suppression of Academia

The Soviet Suppression of Academia

The Case of Konstantin Azadovsky

Petr A. Druzhinin
Translated by Sarah Vitali

BLOOMSBURY ACADEMIC
LONDON • NEW YORK • OXFORD • NEW DELHI • SYDNEY

BLOOMSBURY ACADEMIC
Bloomsbury Publishing Plc
50 Bedford Square, London, WC1B 3DP, UK
1385 Broadway, New York, NY 10018, USA
29 Earlsfort Terrace, Dublin 2, Ireland

BLOOMSBURY, BLOOMSBURY ACADEMIC and the Diana logo are trademarks of
Bloomsbury Publishing Plc

First published in Great Britain 2022
This paperback edition published 2024

Copyright © Petr A. Druzhinin, 2022

Petr A. Druzhinin has asserted their right under the Copyright, Designs and Patents Act,
1988, to be identified as Author of this work.

English language translation © Sarah Vitali 2022

Cover image: Sculptures Of Victims Of Gulag And Stalinist Repressions, Art Muzeon
Sculpture Park, Moscow, Russia Monument by Evgeny Chubarov at Muzeon Park of Arts ©
ЦПКиО им. М. Горького Photography: Nikita Cherepov, Moscow

All rights reserved. No part of this publication may be reproduced or transmitted
in any form or by any means, electronic or mechanical, including photocopying,
recording, or any information storage or retrieval system, without prior permission
in writing from the publishers.

Bloomsbury Publishing Plc does not have any control over, or responsibility for,
any third-party websites referred to or in this book. All internet addresses given in this
book were correct at the time of going to press. The author and publisher regret any
inconvenience caused if addresses have changed or sites have ceased to exist, but can
accept no responsibility for any such changes.

Every effort has been made to trace copyright holders and to obtain their permissions
for the use of copyright material. The publisher apologizes for any errors or omissions
and would be grateful if notified of any corrections that should be incorporated in future
reprints or editions of this book.

A catalogue record for this book is available from the British Library.

A catalog record for this book is available from the Library of Congress.

ISBN: HB: 978-1-3501-3613-7
PB: 978-1-3503-3320-8
ePDF: 978-1-3501-3614-4
eBook: 978-1-3501-3615-1

Typeset by Deanta Global Publishing Services, Chennai, India

To find out more about our authors and books visit www.bloomsbury.com
and sign up for our newsletters.

Contents

List of illustrations	vi
Author's acknowledgements	vii
Translator's acknowledgements	viii
Glossary and list of frequently used abbreviations	ix
Note on Russian names	xi
Introduction	1
1 Beginnings	7
2 The blitzkrieg	15
3 Awaiting trial	25
4 The three pillars of accusation	45
5 *Ex ungue leonem*	53
6 Justice	63
7 A prisoner of conscience	71
8 Russian truth	89
9 Life in *khimia*	107
10 The Kolyma saga	135
11 The start of a long road	159
12 The journalist	169
13 The retrial	173
14 The aftermath	189
15 Rehabilitation	195
16 The heart of the matter	205
17 Proof	209
18 The aftermath	229
Conclusion	235
Notes	239
Bibliography	244
Index	251

Illustrations

Note: The images are placed between chapters 9 and 10.

1. Konstantin Azadovsky with a group of East German tourists
2. Yefim Slavinsky and William Chalsma
3. Konstantin Azadovsky seeing Yefim Etkind off at Pulkovo Airport
4. Portrait of Konstantin Azadovsky by Anatoly Belkin
5. Kama Ginkas, Daniil Ginkas, Genrietta Yanovskaya, Roza Yanovskaya and their dog Jeff
6. Konstantin Azadovsky in Aida Khmeleva's flat
7. Lidia Brun-Azadovskaya
8. Joseph Brodsky
9. Prison photo of Svetlana Lepilina
10. Svetlana Lepilina's prison badge
11. Prison photo of Konstantin Azadovsky
12. Azadovsky's prison card, issued before his release
13. Soviet prison gate
14. Kolyma highway in summer
15. Susuman city centre, Magadan Oblast
16. Svetlana Lepilina's Gorky Automobile Plant pass
17. Brass signet ring made by prisoners at the Susuman camp as a wedding gift to Konstantin and Svetlana
18. Mikhail Feiginzon, doctor at the Susuman prisoners' hospital
19. Baptist Anatoly Redin at work in the camp
20. Svetlana Lepilina's certificate of conditional release
21. Konstantin Azadovsky's certificate of release
22. Konstantin Azadovsky after his release
23. Konstantin and Svetlana Azadovsky
24. Kuibyshevsky District Court in Leningrad
25. Azadovsky at his court hearing on 12 August 1988
26. Kuibyshevsky District Court in Leningrad
27. Konstantin Azadovsky and Sergey Zilitinkevich during a court recess on 12 August 1988
28. Yury Shchekochikhin and Konstantin Azadovsky during a court recess on 12 August 1988
29. Konstantin Azadovsky during a court recess on 12 August 1988
30. Konstantin Azadovsky and Galina Starovoitova
31. Konstantin Azadovsky, Svetlana Azadovskaya and Sergey Dovlatov
32. Joseph Brodsky, Konstantin Azadovsky and Maria Sozzani with her daughter Anna

Author's acknowledgements

I would like to express my sincere thanks to the following people for their unstinting help with both advice and materials: Nadezhda Azhgikhina, Anatoly Belkin, Yakov Gordin, Yury Kleiner, Alexander Lavrov, Tatyana Pavlova, Yefim Slavinsky and Gabriėl' Superfin.

I would also like to express my gratitude to the late Arseny Roginsky (1946–2017), former chairman of Memorial, who provided invaluable comments on the original Russian manuscript. Additionally, I would like to thank Alexander Sobolev, a Russian literary historian whose many years of friendship and aid have helped to make this book a reality.

I also owe a great debt of gratitude to the heroes of this book, Konstantin and Svetlana Azadovsky. They have been generous in sharing their experiences and have provided me both with materials and with detailed answers to what were, at times, difficult questions.

Finally, I would like to thank my Russian publisher, Irina Prokhorova, for giving this project her heartfelt support, for waiting so patiently for the manuscript and for doing everything in her power to make sure that the Russian edition of this book appeared with her prestigious Moscow publishing house, *Novoe Literaturnoe Obozrenie* (New Literary Observer).

The English-language version of this book would not have existed without the advocacy of Professor Vera Tolz (University of Manchester); I am deeply grateful for her tireless help and support. I am especially thankful to Sarah Vitali, the translator of this book.

Translator's acknowledgements

I would like to sincerely thank Petr Druzhinin for entrusting his project to me and for being such an excellent collaborator. I would also like to thank Andrei Zorin for putting us in contact.

I am extremely grateful to Claude Green and Daniel Green for their thoughtful comments on this manuscript and to Philip Redko, Maria Vassileva, Lynn Vitali, Jacob Yunis and Ksenia Zanon for generously offering their time and expertise. My thanks as well to the editorial team at Bloomsbury Academic, Rhodri Mogford, Laura Reeves and Emma Tranter, and to our copy editor, Joseph Gautham.

Finally, I would like to thank Konstantin and Svetlana Azadovsky for sharing their incredible story and for answering my questions.

Glossary and list of frequently used abbreviations

This glossary has been composed with the help of Vasili Mitrokhin's *KGB Lexicon* and Mark Galeotti's 'A Glossary of Russian Police & Security Service Acronyms and Abbreviations'.

Big House	Saint Petersburg police and KGB (now FSB) headquarters
blatnye	professional criminals who live by a 'thieves' code'
CPSU	Communist Party of the Soviet Union
'D' measure	covert search
DGOR	group operational cultivation file
DON	operational surveillance file
DOR	operational development file
druzhina	Voluntary People's Guard
druzhinnik	member of the *druzhina*
Fifth Directorate	Directorate of the KGB concerned with 'ideology and dissidents'
FSB	Federal Security Service, the main successor agency of the KGB
Glavlit	Main Directorate for the Protection of State Secrets in the Press, the main Soviet censorship body
Gorlit	see Lenoblgorlit
GU MVD	see GUVD
GUVD	Main Internal Affairs Directorate, the police command of a major city
ITK	Corrective Labour Code OR Corrective Labour Colony, depending on context
KGB	Committee for State Security, the main Soviet security agency from 1954 to 1991
khimia	conditional release from incarceration with mandatory labour
Komsomol	All-Union Leninist Young Communist League
Lubyanka	Central headquarters of the KGB, now FSB, in Moscow
Lenoblgorlit	Leningrad Oblast Directorate for the Protection of State Secrets in the Press, the local censorship body

LO	Leningrad Oblast
MVD	Ministry of Internal Affairs
NKVD	People's Commissariat for Internal Affairs, predecessor of the KGB
oblast	administrative region within Russia and the former Soviet Union
OGPU	Joint State Political Directorate, predecessor of the KGB
OP	operational collection file
OVIR	Visa and Registration Department
propiska	residency permit
RSFSR	Russian Soviet Federative Socialist Republic
RUVD	District Directorate of Internal Affairs
'S' measure	audio surveillance
UPK	Criminal Procedural Code
UUR	Directorate for Criminal Investigation
UVD	Internal Affairs Directorate
zone	general term used to refer to corrective labour camps and colonies

Note on Russian names

Russian names consist of a given name, a patronymic derived from one's father's name, and a surname. In formal or polite contexts, a person will be referred to by their first name and patronymic. For example, Konstantin Azadovsky would be addressed as Konstantin Markovich. Russian given names often spawn a multitude of nicknames; for example, in this book, Svetlana Lepilina is referred to variously as Sveta, Svetlanochka, Svetochka, Svetka and Svetulik.

A list of the main recurring figures in this book is given here.

The family

Konstantín Márkovich **Azadóvsky** – the protagonist of our story. Referred to affectionately as **Kóstya**.

Svetlána Ivánovna **Lepílina** (later, Azadóvsky) – Konstantin Azadovsky's partner, later his wife. Referred to affectionately as **Svéta**, **Svetlánochka**, **Svétochka**, **Svétka** and **Svetúlik**.

Lídia Vladímirovna **Brun** – Konstantin Azadovsky's mother.

Mark Konstantínovich **Azadóvsky** – Konstantin Azadovsky's father, a pioneering Russian folklorist and victim of the 1949 anti-cosmopolitan campaign.

The police

Captain Olég Nikoláevich **Artsibúshev** – the police officer who detained Lepilina and led the search of Azadovsky's flat.

Lieutenant Yevgény Emílyevich **Kaménko** – the police investigator responsible for investigating Azadovsky and Lepilina's cases.

Lieutenant Nikoláy Nikoláevich **Khlyúpin** – a police officer present at the search of Azadovsky's flat. Found the narcotics that had been planted on Azadovsky's bookshelf.

The KGB

Víktor Ivánovich **Arkhípov** – a KGB operative present at the search of Azadovsky's flat.

Yúry Alekséevich **Bezvérkhov** – the KGB deputy department chief responsible for Azadovsky's DOR.

'Hassán' – a Colombian KGB agent posing as a Spanish mathematics student studying abroad in Leningrad. Gave Lepilina hashish and other contraband. Code-named **'Baryte'**.

Alexánder Valentínovich **Kuznetsóv** – the KGB criminal intelligence investigator in charge of Azadovsky's DOR.

Pável Grigóryevich **Pozdéev** – the KGB specialist called in to assist in the search of Azadovsky's flat. Also known by his pen name, Pável **Krenyóv**.

Vladímir Vladímirovich **Shlémin** – a KGB operative present at the search of Azadovsky's flat.

The lawyers

Ilyá Mikháilovich **Bréiman** – Lepilina's defence lawyer in 1981. Encouraged her to plead guilty in a bid to reduce her sentence.

Semyón Aleksándrovich **Khéifets** – Azadovsky's first defence lawyer. Refused to represent Azadovsky in court shortly before his trial.

Savély **Ryazánovsky** – Azadovsky's defence lawyer during his 1981 trial.

Natálya Borísovna **Smirnóva** – Azadovsky's defence lawyer during his 1988 retrial.

The rest

Vadím 'Fíma' **Rózenberg** – Azadovsky's cellmate in Kresty who encouraged Azadovsky to send a note to Lepilina through the unofficial prison post. A KGB informant and agent provocateur.

Yúry Petróvich **Shchekochíkhin** – a Moscow-based investigative journalist who wrote extensively about the Azadovsky Affair. Later became a liberal politician. Died under mysterious circumstances.

Zinaída **Tkachyóva** – Lepilina's communal flatmate. Assisted in the investigation against Lepilina in order to take over her rooms.

Introduction

To us fell the great honour
Of living in a time of change . . .

Boris Grebenshchikov[1]

In the late Soviet period, certain ideas became entrenched in the minds of Soviet citizens: that, after the death of Stalin, life in the USSR was mostly prosperous (or, at any rate, much better than life in the West); that the government took care of everyone; that the USSR had an excellent educational system; that Soviet academia was well funded and flourishing; and that citizens were free to do anything they liked – as long as they stayed within the confines of the law. Such rosy beliefs about the late Soviet period are insistently repeated in Russia to this day: in the press, on television, on the internet and especially in school textbooks. This elaborate campaign of disinformation has achieved its aim: the USSR in the 1970s and 1980s is not generally associated with totalitarianism, either at home or abroad. In other words, a doctored version of history has almost entirely eclipsed what actually happened; to quote George Orwell's *1984*, 'The past was erased, the erasure was forgotten, the lie became truth.'

Fewer and fewer witnesses to that 'wonderful era' remain, and, as they pass on, they take with them their deeply held antipathy towards the Soviet past. More recent generations, whose world view has been shaped by modern myths of Soviet greatness, tend to regurgitate the propagandistic thesis that things were good in the years leading up to the collapse of the Soviet Union.

But were they?

This book tells the story of the criminal prosecution of prominent philologist and translator Konstantin Azadovsky. In the process, it offers insight into the well-oiled machine that was used to oppress the Soviet intelligentsia in the waning days of 'developed socialism'.[2] Azadovsky was a polymath and gifted scholar, but he wasn't a dissident. This is an important distinction: though there were plenty of openly political cases during this period, this wasn't one of them.

Azadovsky's story is, first and foremost, the story of an individual doing battle against the Soviet state. Over time, many high-profile figures (from bureaucrats to academics and cultural luminaries) became involved in his struggle, and this private criminal case turned into a notorious show trial, a microcosm of an era that many now view as 'prosperous'.

The adversarial relationship between the Russian state and the academic and cultural sphere (commonly referred to as the 'intelligentsia') has deep roots, dating back to the eighteenth century. This rift continued – and occasionally worsened – during the Soviet period. Throughout the twentieth century, the Russian and Soviet cultural elite contributed a distinct note of dissonance to the thunderous chorus being sung by the builders of communism. The state viewed this dissonance as hostility, while the intelligentsia saw themselves as the nation's voice of conscience. The totalitarian regime was unwilling to accept any failure to conform; free-thinkers were dealt with, usually in short order.

For many years, the state employed a universal and effective strategy: one part of the intelligentsia could be frightened into submission, while the other could be bought. Incentives came in many forms: from medals and the opportunity to occupy certain posts, to trips abroad, official cars and dachas. Intimidation came in different forms as well: people could be tried in 'comrades' courts'[3] or they could be arrested, prosecuted and sent to prison or the camps. These practices were used to maintain the country's tenuous balance.

However, even under totalitarian conditions, the Russian intelligentsia has the remarkable ability to foster individuals who cannot be intimidated or bought. This small subset of the population functions like yeast, eventually rousing even politically loyal segments of society into action. The Soviet Union made examples of such upstarts to keep the intelligentsia in their place: they were not to take too much pride in their intellectual mission. As Lenin famously wrote, the intelligentsia 'are not [the country's] brains, but its shit'.

The Khrushchev Thaw unleashed free-thinking tendencies within society, upending the conception of the social contract that had prevailed during Stalinist times. The so-called 'sixties generation' entered the historical scene. This generation hadn't experienced the degrading, mortal fear of mass arrests. These young people hadn't lived through a time when someone they knew would be arrested nearly every day. As a result, they became much bolder than their parents. An increasing number of talented, educated young people dared to dream of scholarly and literary freedom, of maintaining contact with colleagues abroad. At the same time, the Soviet ruling elite began interpreting discussions about 'bourgeois' human rights and civil freedoms as a threat to state security.

In 1967, in an attempt to purge the country of 'liberal bourgeois propaganda', the KGB's Fifth Directorate was formed. This directorate dealt with 'ideological sabotage' and was designed to keep a tight rein on free-thinkers and dissidents within the intelligentsia; such individuals could be prosecuted and imprisoned under articles 70 ('anti-Soviet agitation and propaganda') or 190-1 ('systematic circulation . . . of false statements which defame the Soviet state or social system') of the Russian Soviet Federative Socialist Republic (RSFSR) Criminal Code.

Around the same time, the state developed new, unspoken rules of conduct, which would remain in force throughout the 1970s and 1980s. If a scholar or independent artist wished to enjoy a free and relatively comfortable existence in the USSR, they would have to give dissidents a wide berth; in more extreme cases, they would be obliged to demonstrate their loyalty to the state, which might mean secretly collaborating with the KGB.

On the one hand, the Azadovsky Affair illustrates how this unspoken compact could be broken by the state. Because there was no clear, universal line demarcating which behaviours were and were not allowed, individual citizens were left to negotiate this boundary for themselves; Azadovsky, for one, seriously misjudged the limits of permissible behaviour. On the other hand, sometimes even unreserved submission to the regime wasn't enough. Sooner or later, even free-thinkers who had mastered the art of assimilation would give themselves away. Even if they didn't publicly advertise their views, there was an army of secret informants dedicated to unearthing their subversive thoughts. At that point, they would be left with little choice: they could either 'repent' and become a cog in the machine or they could be mercilessly crushed by it.

This book tells the story of one such free-thinker whose life was torn apart by the Soviet regime.

Konstantin Markovich Azadovsky came of age in the late 1950s–early 1960s, and when this period of thaw gave way to the Era of Stagnation,[4] he didn't know how to keep his head down. However, his arrest and the arrest of his future wife, Svetlana Lepilina, in 1980 sent shockwaves through society. After all, he had stayed away from politics; his life was wrapped up in teaching and scholarship. He was head of a department of foreign languages, his work was published in scholarly journals and his behaviour appeared circumspect: he didn't seem to have violated the government's unwritten rules.

The Azadovskys' story wouldn't be any less tragic if they had been convicted of ideological offences rather than criminal ones, but ideological cases would have been more straightforward and in keeping with the times. However, no political or ideological charges were brought against them: Konstantin and Svetlana Azadovsky were convicted and sentenced under Article 224 ('unlawful possession of narcotics').

But then something happened that no one could have predicted: several years after the Azadovskys had finished their sentences, they were officially declared victims of political repression. This admission was made possible, first and foremost, by the breakdown of the Soviet system in the late 1980s; it also came as a direct result of the unprecedented, quixotic battle Azadovsky had waged throughout the decade. Azadovsky had made it his mission to investigate the cases against himself and his wife; not only did he discover undeniable evidence that they had been set up, but he uncovered the names of those responsible.

The Azadovsky Affair was, at its core, a political matter: the trumped-up criminal charges against the couple were ideological persecution in disguise. It was nearly impossible to expose this kind of fraud in the Soviet Union. However, thanks to the tectonic shifts that were occurring at this time, both in the country and in the world at large, Azadovsky was able to expose the conspiracy against him and catch a glimpse of the KGB's inner workings in the process.

One of the main reasons why the KGB's involvement in this case eventually came to light was the fact that the people behind it had acted with utter impunity. Though the state security organs had undergone a number of name changes over the years (they were known variously as the Cheka, the OGPU, the NKVD, the NKGB, the MGB, the MVD and the KGB), this sense of untouchability had pervaded Soviet law enforcement since the days of the Red Terror.[5] It has exerted considerable influence on the course of Russian history, and its legacy continues to this day.

It would be disingenuous to suggest that Azadovsky accomplished this mammoth task all on his own. On the contrary, he received a great deal of help from his friends and colleagues. Some of his champions, including the poet Joseph Brodsky and the writer Sergey Dovlatov, are known the world over.

But how did two 'common criminals' wind up at the epicentre of such a high-profile social and political event? This is the question that lies at the heart of this book.

* * *

This book, which was originally written and published in Russian in 2016, is the result of careful documentary research. Though it draws on a variety of sources, access to certain types of documents was limited; the archives of the Russian security services are still closed to historians researching the latter part of the twentieth century.

A number of the documents cited in this book first appeared in the Russian and international press. I am grateful to Yefim Slavinsky (1936–2019), a former employee of the BBC World Service, for providing me with a wide range of materials. The majority of the documentary evidence for this book comes from criminal case files, complaints and responses to complaints, internal reviews, internal KGB documents and so on. A complete list of the over 300 documents consulted appears at the end of the Russian version of this book.

For the most part, these documents became accessible in the 1990s, after Azadovsky copied them out and sent them to be kept in various archives. The largest collection of documents related to the Azadovsky Affair is located at the Research Centre for East European Studies at the University of Bremen, where they form part of Azadovsky's papers (nos. 1–255). This collection was invaluable to the writing of this book. Another key set of documents was the collection of Azadovsky's papers kept in the archives of Memorial, a Moscow-based historical, educational and human rights advocacy society; this archive also contains a number of documents that were useful for putting the Azadovsky Affair into the context of the Soviet human rights struggle during the 1970s and 1980s.

Konstantin and Svetlana Azadovsky were themselves an invaluable resource. Though the official documents related to their cases were, for the most part, located in the aforementioned archives at the time of this book's writing, the Azadovskys' personal papers, and, most notably, their correspondence with each other, were kept in the couple's personal archives. These documents are currently being transferred to the State Archive of the Russian Federation.

This project would not have been possible if the Azadovskys hadn't managed to copy out the bulk of their criminal cases and other legal documents when they had the chance. Later on, the originals were sent to various archives, and many of them have become inaccessible in the intervening years. During the writing of this book, Azadovsky submitted official requests to court archives on my behalf. However, none of the documents were available: some of them had been destroyed when they reached the end of their retention period, while others had been lost. In keeping with the patterns of official behaviour described throughout this book, Azadovsky was informed in 2015 that the Information Centre of the Saint Petersburg and Leningrad Oblast Main Internal Affairs Directorate (GUVD) did not contain any information regarding his criminal prosecution, nor did it possess the criminal files themselves; all records related to his case had been destroyed at the end of their retention period. It was as if none of it had ever happened: the trial, the imprisonment, the rehabilitation, the Azadovskys' shattered lives...

The very fact that I was able to review so many of the documents related to this case was an incredible stroke of good luck. Like other state and agency archives, the KGB archives are off-limits to researchers studying the persecution of scholars (and the intelligentsia more broadly) in the 1970s and 1980s. This is particularly true of cases that took place in Leningrad.

As for the archives of 'The Big House' (as the Leningrad KGB headquarters are colloquially known), all of its operational files seem to have been destroyed en masse in 1989–91. It is unlikely that the files that managed to escape destruction will be made available to historians in the coming decades. Finally, access to the internal KGB documents related to Azadovsky's case (which are probably still held in the archives of the Saint Petersburg and Leningrad Oblast KGB's Inspection Directorate) are also restricted, on the grounds that they 'contain information on the operational activities of state security agencies'. In accordance with a resolution passed by the Interagency Commission for the Protection of State Secrets in 2014, the KGB's archival materials from the 1970s and 1980s will be closed until spring 2044 at the earliest.

The KGB remains shrouded in secrecy and myth, and agency archivists live in fear of losing their jobs for accidentally granting access to something they shouldn't. The conditions for scholarship would be better if agencies had continued to conform to the original standards that were set for them, which called for files to be declassified after thirty years, at which point they would be sent to the national archives. However, this is not the path that Russia has chosen: on the contrary, the government has pursued increasingly strict secrecy policies. There are resources like the Mitrokhin Archive, which comprises detailed notes made by the defector Vasily Mitrokhin, a former senior archivist in the KGB's foreign intelligence archive. This vast and invaluable source on the history of Soviet intelligence is now held at the University of Cambridge and is also available online. However, the fact that the security services' archives are sealed means that fewer archival historians are choosing to research late twentieth-century Russian political history.

Nevertheless, several legitimate paths remain open to researchers interested in documents related to the Soviet security services.

First, a significant number of KGB documents were published in the 1990s in various collections and monographs on academic history.

Second, after the collapse of the USSR in 1991, some post-Soviet states (like Lithuania and Ukraine) proved far more liberal in their approach to KGB and CPSU documents than Russia. A number of secret documents – including memoranda issued by KGB headquarters – were disseminated to affiliate offices in the Soviet republics. Thus, one can fill in some of the gaps in the Russian sources using documents from other countries' archives. This method has proved particularly effective with regard to KGB instructional materials, as well as terminological dictionaries issued by the KGB and MVD, etc.

Third, many historians and journalists who were granted access to KGB, Ministry of Foreign Affairs and Central Committee documents in the early 1990s had the wherewithal to order a number of copies for their work; for the most part, these copies are still accessible. For example, the Dmitry Volkogonov papers, now held in the US Library of Congress, comprise copies of over 10,000 documents from the KGB Central Operational Archive, the archive of the OGPU/NKVD's Foreign Department, the Politburo archive and other depositories. In the Soviet Union, most of these materials were classified as top secret; many remain classified to this day.

Fourth, opportunities occasionally arise for historians to view copies (or excerpts of copies) of the investigative files of people deemed victims of political repression. These copies were made in the late 1980s and 1990s, when it was easier for historians and the relatives of repressed individuals to gain access to such documents. Many copies are kept in the Memorial Society Archive, as well as in other archives, most of which are located outside of Russia; many documents are also held in private collections.

Using the methods listed above, I have been able to reconstruct a detailed picture of the Azadovsky Affair despite having limited access to state-controlled archival materials.

1

Beginnings

Konstantin Azadovsky was born in Leningrad on 14 September 1941, on the seventh day of the infamous Siege.[1] His father, Mark Azadovsky (1888–1954), was a renowned scholar of literature, ethnography and folklore, while his mother, Lidia Brun (1904–84), worked at the Russian Public Library (now the National Library of Russia). In March 1942, after surviving the Siege's most difficult winter, the family was evacuated to Irkutsk in Eastern Siberia, where Mark Azadovsky was from. They remained there until the end of the Second World War.

However, in August 1946, a new war broke out in the USSR, this time on an ideological front. The Central Committee's campaign against prominent writers Anna Akhmatova and Mikhail Zoshchenko marked the beginning of a movement to stamp out 'apolitical attitudes' among the Soviet intelligentsia. A year later, a campaign was launched against 'grovelling before the West'. This campaign took a particular toll on literary scholars and historians who dared to put Jewish literature on an equal footing with the products of ethnically Russian culture. The sheer scale of the crackdown, both on individual scholars and on entire scholarly traditions, called to mind the Great Terror (1936–8).[2]

Konstantin's father was singled out as one of the leading representatives of 'harmful cosmopolitan ideology'.[3] In 1936, he had dared to argue that Alexander Pushkin, Russia's national poet, had borrowed plots from the brothers Grimm to use in his own fairy tales. In the 1930s, his work had been treated as a scholarly discovery; in 1949, it was regarded as an ideological crime. Mark Azadovsky was accused of 'libel against Russian culture and the great Pushkin' and was excoriated both at party meetings and in print.

These accusations of cosmopolitanism were only a pretence: at the time, 'cosmopolitanism' was a code word used to persecute Jewishness. The national campaign against cosmopolitanism came down particularly hard on the professors of Leningrad State University, including Mark Azadovsky. As punishment for his 'ideological errors', he was removed from his leadership position in the folklore department and expelled from the Academy of Sciences; his works were no longer published. Having lost his livelihood, he was forced to write 'for the desk drawer'. Years later, the texts Mark Azadovsky wrote would be recognized as seminal works of Russian scholarship. He died of a heart attack in November 1954.

And so, at the age of thirteen, Konstantin Azadovsky was left without a father. A gifted child, he was determined to study hard and live up to his father's legacy. His mother, who was of German extraction, spoke German with him from an early age. He grew up surrounded by German; he studied Spanish in school, and in university he mastered English and French.

In autumn 1958, he enrolled in the German section of Leningrad State University's philological faculty, where he spent the next five years immersed in his studies.

Azadovsky had shown a keen interest in poetry starting in his school days, and, as a university student, he befriended the younger generation of Leningrad poets, including Joseph Brodsky, Dmitry Bobyshev and, later on, Viktor Krivulin, Oleg Okhapkin and other underground poets. Through his friend Gennady Shmakov, he became acquainted with Marianna Kuznetsova, a ballerina at the Kirov Theatre (now the Mariinsky Theatre). Kuznetsova periodically hosted gatherings of 'open-minded young people' in her company housing: the guest lists would include people like Mikhail Baryshnikov and Joseph Brodsky.

Immersed in Leningrad's bohemian art and poetry scenes, Azadovsky became part of the so-called second culture.[4] He showed genuine literary talent: in fact, two of his poems were erroneously included in Brodsky's first collected works, which were published in 1992. These poems had been written in December 1964, while Azadovsky was visiting Brodsky in exile in Norinskaya.

However, Azadovsky's primary literary interest was translation, of both poetry and prose. While still in secondary school, he had participated in translation seminars led by the prominent translators Yefim Etkind and Elga Linetskaya. In university, he began publishing translations from German and Spanish; he gained a reputation in literary circles for his translations of Rainer Maria Rilke. His translation of 'The Love and Death of Cornet Christopher Rilke', which circulated in samizdat,[5] was particularly well received. Brodsky, who often gave nicknames to his friends and acquaintances, dubbed Azadovsky 'the Cornet'.

Later on, Azadovsky began writing academic works on literary history, establishing his lifelong scholarly interest in the history of Russian poetry and the connections between Russian and German literature.

But poetry wasn't the only thing on Azadovsky's mind: more pressingly, he had to find a way of earning money to supplement his meagre student stipend. Not only did he have to support himself, he had to help his mother, too. And so, when he was offered a summer job interpreting for foreign tourists in spring 1960, he eagerly accepted. Fresh out of his second year of university, he was excited by this opportunity to travel around the country and come in contact with contemporary spoken German.

In 1963, Azadovsky graduated from university with honours. However, he was not offered a place in any postgraduate programme, and the only job he could find was teaching in the foreign languages department of Leningrad State Pedagogical Institute (now Herzen State Pedagogical University of Russia). A year later, on top of his teaching duties at the institute, Azadovsky enrolled in evening classes on art history in Leningrad State University's history faculty. In spring 1969, he received his second undergraduate degree. By this time, he had managed to enrol in full-time postgraduate studies in Herzen's foreign literature department. His advisor was Naum Berkovsky, one of the leading Germanists in the Soviet Union. In autumn 1969, Azadovsky was finishing up his PhD thesis on the works of Franz Grillparzer and waiting to learn the date of his defence.

However, earlier that year, in spring and summer 1969, an incident had taken place that would severely hinder Azadovsky's career. An account of this incident appears in the diary of Azadovsky's colleague, Alen Zhmaev (1934–87), who would be fired for political reasons shortly thereafter. In an attempt to maintain some level of secrecy, Zhmaev replaces Azadovsky's first name with that of his father; however, it is obvious who the story is really about:

> I was approaching the institute, humming a tune, when I was stopped by Anna Sergeevna [Romm – a professor and leading specialist in contemporary English literature – P.D.]. Oh, the look on her face – it was as if it had suddenly crumpled!
> 'Have you heard?'
> 'What?' I asked, not anticipating anything good.
> 'It's Mark,' she said in a barely audible sigh.
> Mark was the department's pride and joy. Even in its heyday, the department had never seen a postgraduate student like him. Berkovsky himself took the time and trouble to read his thesis. Mark's translations from three different languages were published in handsome editions, and he never failed to give copies to Lvovich [Aleksey Grigoryev, professor and department head]. The old-timers in the department would swoon listening to Mark expound upon some abstract theme, while Anna Sergeevna probably wondered why her daughter had to be such a hopeless case: as things stood, she didn't stand the slightest chance of ensnaring this dazzling young man. Naum Yakovlevich [Berkovsky], who never praised anyone and who couldn't bear for others to be praised in his presence, said of Mark: 'He is an exceptionally well-read young man. One might even call him an educated one.'
> To top it all off, Mark had an excellent pedigree. He came from a line of well-known Leningrad philologists. . .
> 'What about Mark?' I mouthed. 'Is it politics?'
> Anna Sergeevna nodded. In a barely audible voice, she added:
> 'And even worse . . . drugs.'
> A group of drug users had been arrested, and Mark had been called as a witness. He wasn't accused of any wrongdoing. . . . But the hopes we had all cherished of him working in our department had been dashed forever.

Zhmaev is referring to the notorious 'Slavinsky Affair', in which Azadovsky found himself entangled. Yefim Slavinsky (1936–2019) was an English-language specialist and a close friend of Azadovsky's. He did, in fact, 'light up' on occasion; what's more, he did so not just with other young Russians, but with foreigners as well. This was extremely reckless behaviour. Unsurprisingly, the investigation characterized Slavinsky's flat as a 'den of debauchery' and painted all of his guests as 'drug users'. Leningrad critic Viktor Toporov later wrote, 'The charges brought against Slavinsky were, though factually accurate, wildly exaggerated: he was prosecuted – and convicted – not for the drugs, and still less for his politics, but for his extensive contact with foreigners and for his lifestyle in general.'

Azadovsky's flat was searched at 6.30 am on 1 June 1969 (early-morning searches remain common practice in Russia to this day). Though it was officially a narcotics search, the police saw fit to seize nearly everything from Azadovsky's desk. The confiscated items included Azadovsky's medicines and prescriptions, his notebooks, his correspondence with foreigners, slips of paper with telephone numbers on them, lists of seminar participants, foreign magazines (which ranged from *Die Spiegel* and *The New Yorker* to *Esquire* and *Playboy*), 'extended-play records of foreign manufacture' and foreign editions of the works of Anna Akhmatova and Osip Mandelstam. Even newspaper clippings were swept up in the raid.

Slavinsky was arrested that same day. But stitching Azadovsky up proved to be more difficult: he was known as a serious-minded young man, and besides, at the time, drug use was not yet punishable by law.

However, it wasn't just Slavinsky who found himself in hot water, as is evidenced by this excerpt from the official recommendation issued to the rector of the Pedagogical Institute by the Leningrad Investigation Directorate on 12 August 1969:

> During the investigation, it was established that Konstantin Markovich Azadovsky, a postgraduate student in the foreign literature department, was among those who visited Slavinsky's den of debauchery. On numerous occasions, Azadovsky attended illicit gatherings in Slavinsky's privately rented room and smoked a narcotic substance, hashish. Moreover, Azadovsky brought individuals who were not drug users to Slavinsky's illicit gatherings with the aim of habituating them to drug use. To this end, in 1968, he brought US citizen L. Leighton to Slavinsky's room, where Slavinsky gave him hashish. In 1967, Azadovsky brought V.I. Demin, an actor employed at the Mossoviet Theatre [to the room] and, together with Slavinsky, convinced him to take drugs by giving him a hashish cigarette. During a search of Azadovsky's flat, officials seized a white powder that Azadovsky had obtained in a narcotics deal with US citizen Phillips in 1969. Pornographic American magazines and books with anti-Soviet content were also seized from Azadovsky's flat.
>
> Azadovsky conducted himself in a cowardly manner during the investigation, denying obvious facts for fear that he would be held responsible for his actions. Azadovsky faces no criminal charges. However, by keeping pornographic and anti-Soviet literature in his home and attending illicit gatherings for the use of narcotics (namely, hashish), Azadovsky has exhibited behaviour that is incompatible with his future professional duties. As someone who leads a dissolute lifestyle, Azadovsky cannot be trusted with the education of young people. Now that you have been informed of these circumstances, I request that you discuss Azadovsky's behaviour and institute measures of social pressure[6] against him. I request to be informed of the measures taken within one month's time.

The rector, Alexander Boborykin (1916–88), was shaken by this message; he immediately notified the Investigation Directorate that Azadovsky was no longer registered as a postgraduate student at the institute. Boborykin's reaction was humane by the standards of the day. He could have expelled Azadovsky with a so-called wolfish character reference, which would have made it impossible for Azadovsky to teach anywhere at all. But Boborykin let Azadovsky off as lightly as possible. He approved a laconic entry in Azadovsky's employment history book: 'Completed postgraduate studies'. Such a statement wouldn't prevent him from finding work.

The records from Slavinsky's trial completely contradict the assertions made by the police: witnesses testified that Azadovsky 'took a negative view of drugs and had never smoked so much as a cigarette'. As for the 'white powder' discovered during the search, it turned out to be aspirin.

Slavinsky's trial took place 24–29 September 1969.[7] The fact that the Investigation Directorate sent its recommendation to the Pedagogical Institute before the trial had even begun shows that Azadovsky's guilt was considered a foregone conclusion. There is nothing surprising about this: in the USSR, there was no expectation that a person would be presumed innocent until proven guilty.

It is worth noting that the police pressure on Azadovsky – threats, harassment and so on – did not yield the desired results: at no point during the investigation or trial did Azadovsky give testimony that could be used against Slavinsky. He remained undaunted by the searches and interrogations. In fact, the experience only seemed to make him stronger. Zhmaev writes:

'Because I'm not guilty,' Mark said, 'it's impossible for me to vindicate myself. "Your name has figured in a trial" – that's all it takes. The rector has washed his hands of me. He took one look at my exculpatory papers and said: "I understand, and I believe you, my boy, but we have to wait for things to settle down." "For what to settle down?" I ask. "Why, the trial, the drugs, the press." So I'm waiting for things to settle down. I figure, two years from now, give or take, I'll be able to return to Leningrad. But when I see people I know on the street, their eyes practically pop out of their heads: "Didn't they throw you in jail?"'

'Did they return the things they took from you?'

'None of it. But you can't exactly ask for it back! ... .You have to understand, things are only straightforward where common criminals are concerned: if you steal something, you go to jail; if you didn't do it, then get back to work. But the situation with the intelligentsia is terrible. THEY understand that the real evil is up here.' Mark pointed to his high, handsome forehead. 'They couldn't care less what you write in your articles. They know that something up HERE isn't as it should be. And they only have one job: to recast your consciousness. They'll haul you in, hold you in preliminary detention, arrange simultaneous witness questionings, do whatever they want with you, all with just one goal: to force you to think differently. To destroy your individuality. Destroy your brain. Make your brain so supple and submissive that you start to hate sedition, so that the very sight of, say, a samizdat publication causes you not just to recoil, but to automatically leap into action, selling out your closest friend. [They want to] stamp out your dignity. Prove that you aren't a member of the intelligentsia, you're just a piece of shit like everybody else. Drive the very idea of individuality out of your head. And when you start to see them as your friends, when you go to them of your OWN volition, they'll treat you with kindness, and help you out, and set you up in some institute even if your character reference says that you've slit little children's throats.... They kept me in that chair for 20 hours at a time. But I kept telling myself: you have dignity. You do! You'll get out of here, you'll be with other people, you don't want to be ashamed to look them in the eye afterwards.... Do you know what Berkovsky said? "After a while," he said, "this will be the only romantic episode in your biography."'

These words suggest that Azadovsky had developed strong opinions about life in the Soviet Union before 1969: they show a clear contempt for official doctrine, a deep antagonism towards enforced morality and a keen understanding of the criminal justice system's role in society. And Azadovsky wasn't alone: his views were more or less typical of the younger generation of the Leningrad intelligentsia.

And so, thanks to the rector, Azadovsky was removed from the institute without incurring any official restrictions that would prevent him from working in higher education. But he was faced with a pressing question: What next? Slavinsky's trial had made a considerable splash in Leningrad, and the KGB was still monitoring his friends: no university in Leningrad would risk hiring Azadovsky even on a casual basis. And so, Azadovsky set off for Petrozavodsk, a haven for persecuted members of the Leningrad intelligentsia. Just an overnight train journey away from Leningrad, Petrozavodsk offered pariahs like Azadovsky the chance to find work. However, very few people went there by choice. With the help of his friends and acquaintances, Azadovsky found a place as an English teacher at the Karelian State Pedagogical Institute. At first, things were difficult: his intensive workload didn't afford him many opportunities to visit his mother, who had remained in Leningrad.

Gradually, the furore surrounding the case died down, and, a year and a half later, Azadovsky's defence at the Leningrad State Pedagogical Institute was allowed to go ahead. In June 1971, Azadovsky was granted his degree, which gave him the leverage he needed to attain the rank of docent. At this point, he could even consider moving back to Leningrad: The only question was, how? It wasn't easy to find teaching work there, even for someone with a PhD. Luckily, an opportunity arose at the Vera Mukhina Higher School of Art and Industry (now the Saint Petersburg Art and Industry Academy). With the support of Zoya Tomashevskaya (daughter of noted Pushkin scholar Boris Tomashevsky), Azadovsky became head of the department of foreign languages in autumn 1975.

This marked the beginning of a fruitful five-year period in Azadovsky's career. His research focused on authors including Stefan Zweig, Thomas Mann and, of course, Rainer Maria Rilke. Equally impressive was his work on the history of early-twentieth-century Russian poetry, and, in particular, his writings on Russian Symbolism. It was during these years that he penned his seminal works on Alexander Blok, Valery Bryusov and Nikolay Klyuev. Around the same time, in the mid- to late 1970s, Azadovsky was laying the groundwork for his second thesis, on representations of the 'Russian soul' in European culture in the late-nineteenth to early-twentieth century.

These years were also a time of material prosperity: as a department head, Azadovsky received a relatively high salary, and he earned additional income as a translator. He was one of very few literary scholars in Leningrad who owned a car, a Zhiguli: at the time, this was an exclusive luxury item. However, Azadovsky was far from the top of the university's food chain. Though he refrained from outright criticism of the Soviet regime, he also didn't join the Communist Party, despite pressure from above. Azadovsky's family history and his own personal experience had shown him that the relative academic freedom and material comfort he enjoyed were no more than a veneer. Having attained a certain status within Soviet society, he knew that it was imperative, if not to follow all the rules of that society, then at least to be circumspect in the ways in which he broke them. The Slavinsky trial and the search of his flat in 1969 had taught him a great deal. He had learned to be cautious and not to give anyone reason to suspect him of involvement in 'anti-Soviet' activities.

And, in fact, Azadovsky wasn't a dissident. In the 1970s, Moscow was the centre of the dissident movement. It was home to the Moscow Helsinki Group and *A Chronicle of Current Events*; it was the site of sensational trials against nonconformists, as well as the struggle of Jewish 'refuseniks' to gain permission to emigrate from the USSR.[8] The dissident movement in Leningrad was far less robust. The local authorities nipped any nonconformist activity in the bud, even though most Leningrad dissidents would be considered harmless by Moscow standards: their activities were largely limited to hosting small gatherings in one another's kitchens, reading one another's poetry and mounting semi-official art exhibitions.

It is unlikely that the KGB's interest in Azadovsky was sparked by his passion for poetry and painting. It is more likely they took issue with the company he kept: Azadovsky often accompanied friends and acquaintances to the airport as they emigrated from the USSR. He also maintained contact with academic colleagues who had come to the USSR from capitalist countries. The KGB was particularly interested in such foreigners: most of them were kept under constant surveillance. Azadovsky's 'contacts' would provide the impetus for much of what happened later.

'Non-conformity' had always come naturally to Azadovsky, though he didn't approve of the 'sex, drugs and rock-and-roll' lifestyle that dominated the young dissident circles of Leningrad and Moscow. At the same time, having come of age in a time of political thaw, he didn't share the fears of his parents' generation, which had witnessed the Great Terror. He said what he thought, and he didn't cosy up to people he didn't like; he often came across as ambitious, even arrogant. He hoped to receive his higher doctorate[9] and join the Writers' Union. He felt bolstered by his talent, his relative freedom and his material success. Unfortunately, none of this would protect him from what lay in store.

2

The blitzkrieg

2.1 Svetlana

Azadovsky met his future wife in 1975. They lived in the same building on Zhelyabov Street. Svetlana Lepilina was different from the women Azadovsky knew from Leningrad's philological and poetic circles. She had little interest in scholarly discussions; she was sincere, emotional and kind. She was also a beauty, crowned with a full head of flaxen hair. Originally from Bryansk, Lepilina had moved to Leningrad in 1970. She married soon after, and was widowed in 1974. By the time Azadovsky and his mother moved to a flat on Vosstaniya Street in 1978, he and Lepilina were already in a committed relationship.

Autumn 1980 was a difficult time for Azadovsky: he had had a falling-out with Lepilina over the summer, and problems had begun to arise at the Higher School of Art and Industry. Azadovsky's five-year term as department head was coming to an end. Elections for the position had originally been scheduled for early autumn, but were unexpectedly moved to December. Neither Azadovsky nor his colleagues seriously doubted that he would retain his position, but, nevertheless, the uncertainty was wearing.

At the same time, fear had been gnawing at him for several months: he had a growing suspicion that he was being watched. It was the year of the Moscow Olympics, so his fear of surveillance was not at all far-fetched, especially since he and Lepilina openly associated with foreigners. In fact, their belief that they were being monitored by the local KGB was confirmed more than once that year. That autumn, a friend of Azadovsky's was called down to the Big House for a 'preventative conversation': some of the questions involved Azadovsky. Unable to shake his anxiety, Azadovsky went through his flat to make sure it contained no samizdat materials; he was afraid of an unannounced search.

On the evening of 18 December 1980, Azadovsky was at home, waiting for Lepilina. He was unaware that she was planning to meet a foreigner after work. Lepilina had a remarkable knack for making friends with people from all walks of life – a talent that annoyed Azadovsky no end.

On this occasion, she was trying to help a Spanish student called Hassan. Hassan had come to study in Leningrad for a semester and had often struggled, both with his health and with the austerity of everyday life in the Soviet Union. Genrietta Yanovskaya and Kama Ginkas, world-renowned theatre directors and the Azadovskys' friends, describe the scene in the following manner:

[Svetlana] and Kostya[1] weren't legally married, but they had been dating for several years. She was a very open-hearted person, she made friends very easily.... She happened to meet a Spanish mathematics student somewhere: he was in Russia for the first time, didn't understand anything, felt completely at sea. Right away, she threw herself into helping him. Later on, when he fell ill, she would bring him medicine. Finally, it came time for the very grateful Spaniard to leave the country. Sveta[2] met up with him to say goodbye. They even spent some time in a café. First, he asked her to change some dollars for rubles: he claimed that he needed to go to Moscow and that he didn't have any other money. She said that she didn't have any money with her and suggested that he stop by their place. At the time, Kostya lived not far from the Moskovsky Railway Station. 'No, no, that's all right, I'll figure something out.' Then he walked her part of the way home, urging her to accept some jeans and asking for help the whole time. He had brought medicine [into the country] for someone, but hadn't managed to meet them, so he asked her to pass the medicine along on his behalf. They said their goodbyes.

As Lepilina entered the courtyard of the Azadovskys' building, she heard a shout: 'Citizen, halt!' One man dressed in a police uniform seized her by the elbow, while another blocked her path. A man and a woman in civilian dress appeared beside them. Lepilina tried to maintain her composure, but she was afraid. She was still carrying Hassan's parting gifts: imported jeans and two packs of cigarettes. If they were discovered, she would be asked where she had got them, which would lead to uncomfortable questions. Agitated, Lepilina dropped her bag and its contents spilled out onto the snow. The officers gathered everything up and hauled her off to the nearest police point.

There, the contents of the bag were dumped onto a table. Standing around it were the two police officers, Artsibushev and Matnyak, and the two civilians, who turned out to be members of the *druzhina*, the Voluntary People's Guard.[3] Fortunately, neither the jeans nor the cigarettes raised any questions. But then Lepilina saw Matnyak examining a small foil packet. It was this little packet that served as the catalyst for everything that happened next.

'Even without laboratory analysis, this clearly isn't medicine', Matnyak said. The conversation took a sharp turn.

A woman ordered Lepilina to undress: she was forced to strip naked in front of everyone. When the search yielded no results, she was allowed to put her clothes back on.

At this point, practically distraught, Lepilina was led back out onto the street, where a black car was idling. It was a Volga, the kind of car associated with high-ranking officials and the security services. The scene was like something out of a spy film: Lepilina was put into the backseat with a person flanking her on either side. Artsibushev, as the highest-ranking officer, sat in front. As they waited for the driver, Artsibushev turned to Lepilina and said, rather excitedly, 'You've gone and got yourself three years!'

The car set off towards the district police station on Krylov Alley. There, the situation grew even more dire: the *druzhina* volunteers were asked to act as witnesses, and an official investigation was opened. The police examined the contents of the foil packet and declared that Lepilina had been carrying hashish. This assertion was later confirmed by laboratory analysis.

Lepilina tried to explain that the packet had been presented to her as medicine, but to no avail. Finally, she began to realize the gravity of her situation: she was going to be prosecuted. That very evening, Major Zamyatkina of the Kuibyshevsky RUVD's Directorate for Criminal Investigation (UUR) opened criminal case no. 10196 against her: Lepilina was being charged under Article 224, paragraph 3, of the RSFSR Criminal Code, which pertained to the unlawful acquisition and possession of narcotic substances.

Lepilina's interrogation went on until midnight. Her protestations – that she had never used drugs and that she didn't understand what was going on – were met with laughter. The search witnesses had already confirmed that the packet belonged to Lepilina, so the police didn't bother dusting it for fingerprints. The officers had opened the packet at the police point and its contents had been transferred into an envelope before being sent for laboratory analysis. Zamyatkina didn't seem particularly concerned with where the drugs had come from. Though Lepilina was unable to provide certain basic details about her Spanish acquaintance (including his surname), she did tell the police where he studied, the name of the hostel where he was staying and the fact of his imminent departure. These details would have been more than enough to locate him, but the police made no attempt to track Hassan down: not then, not ever.

By contrast, Zamyatkina seemed very interested in where Lepilina had been heading: why, for example, she had been walking through the courtyard of No. 10 Vosstaniya Street. Lepilina's response, that it was a public thoroughfare, didn't satisfy her. Lepilina realized what was happening and did her best to avoid getting Azadovsky mixed up in this affair. Then Zamyatkina changed tactics: she asked if Lepilina knew anyone who lived in the building. Lepilina mentioned the Azadovskys, but clarified that she had been on her way home.

At this point, Zamyatkina declared, 'The authorities know all about you!' She proceeded to do everything in her power to trick Lepilina into admitting that she had, in fact, been heading to flat 51 to see Azadovsky. But Lepilina sensed that something was off: Zamyatkina seemed all too eager to include the fact of Lepilina and Azadovsky's 'cohabitation' in her interrogation report. Lepilina stood firm, and, no matter how hard she tried, Zamyatkina was unable to get what she needed from her. The interrogation ended. Lepilina was led to a holding cell.

But the investigator's work wasn't done. A few minutes later, Zamyatkina began interrogating Zinaida Tkachyova, who lived in Lepilina's communal flat. Tkachyova and her son had been making Lepilina's life a living hell for years. It is unclear how Zamyatkina first learned of Tkachyova, but a police car had been sent to fetch her before Lepilina's interrogation was even over.

Unlike Lepilina, Tkachyova eagerly latched on to everything Zamyatkina said. She signed off on an interrogation report that contained statements like, 'Yes, Lepilina cohabitates with Azadovsky! Yes, she's practically never at home! Yes, they are cohabiting partners who share a joint household.'

Lepilina couldn't sleep that night. She saw now that Hassan had given her narcotics, claiming they were medicine. But why? Who was behind it? And why were they asking so many questions about Azadovsky? Lepilina was overcome by panic. She spent the night crying in the holding cell, practically out of her mind with fear.

Azadovsky also had trouble falling asleep. He had been waiting all evening for Lepilina to call. Unable to reach her, he started to worry. He finally drifted off long after midnight.

Zamyatkina wasn't sleeping, either. It was already past midnight, but there wasn't any time to lose. Now that Tkachyova had provided information linking Lepilina to Azadovsky, Zamyatkina could ask the Prosecutor's Office for permission to search Azadovsky's flat. In the small hours of the morning, she put in a call to Kuibyshevsky District Deputy Prosecutor Sergey Zborovsky, who immediately authorized the search. At around one or two in the morning, Artsibushev arrived at Zborovsky's home with a search warrant for him to sign.

Lepilina had served her purpose. She had been caught red-handed with drugs, criminal proceedings had been initiated against her and there was clear evidence of her wrongdoing. The rest was a formality.

On the afternoon of 20 December, Investigator Yevgeny Kamenko asked Lepilina who ought to be informed of her arrest. Lepilina requested that he contact her friend Zigrida Vanag. Kamenko telephoned Vanag, informed her that Lepilina had been detained for possession of narcotics and requested that she bring a toothbrush, soap, towel, linens and so on for her friend. Vanag and her husband, Yury Tsekhnovitser, were the first of Lepilina's friends and family to find out what was going on.

At this point, Lepilina was in an extremely fragile mental state. A terse police report from 20 December records an attempted suicide. A note about Lepilina's 'suicidal tendencies' was added to her criminal file. Later on, she was taken under guard to the infamous Kresty Prison: Leningrad Pretrial Detention Centre no. 1.

Even under the best of circumstances, prison processing can be extremely upsetting; however, the prison made sure that Lepilina's experience was especially traumatic. During the standard personal search, the inspector gave orders for Lepilina's head to be shaved on the grounds that 'long hair might lead to unsanitary conditions'. This order was carried out on the spot.

It is unclear whether this measure was taken at the inspector's initiative or whether it was an order issued from above. In any case, it served its purpose: Lepilina felt humiliated and demoralized.

Only two months later, when she was presented with the official case against her, would Lepilina learn that, while she was being held at the police station on 20 December, the officers who had detained her had been searching her home. They left her flat with quite a haul, which is reflected in the list of items seized during the search. For the most part, these items were connected to her passion for French; more importantly, many of them were meant to prove her relationship with Azadovsky.

2.2 The search

On the morning of 19 December, Azadovsky was awakened by the doorbell and a woman's voice calling 'Telegram!' This turned out to be one of Azadovsky's neighbours, who had been recruited to take part in the police operation. Upon opening the door, Azadovsky was greeted by six people in civilian dress; four introduced themselves as police officers, while two of them were there to act as search witnesses. The incursion was led by Captain Artsibushev, who presented Azadovsky with the search warrant and his official ID, which showed that he was part of the GUVD's Fifteenth Department, which dealt with drug-related crimes.

This wasn't the first time Azadovsky had been confronted with 'postmen' bearing search warrants. However, this document struck him as odd. It incorrectly referred to Lepilina as Azadovsky's 'cohabiting partner' and its overall premise seemed dubious. Azadovsky refused to sign it, a fact that was noted by the two search witnesses.

Meanwhile, his 'guests' were making themselves at home; from the way they moved around the flat, Azadovsky began to suspect that they already knew its layout. For example, instead of starting with Azadovsky's mother's room, which was closer to the entrance, they made a beeline for Azadovsky's room, which was further down the hall. This room was a sort of academic lair: it was fitted with floor-to-ceiling bookshelves and littered with manuscripts; mountains of books and papers were piled on his desk.

The 'narcotics' search began with an examination of Azadovsky's bookshelves. Later on, in an official complaint to the Central Committee, Azadovsky wrote:

> The operatives conducting the search were interested only in my library, my academic and literary works (in manuscript form), my personal papers, correspondence, etc. No one was looking for drugs. None of the operatives even touched the prescriptions or drugs (my mother's medicines) that were present in the flat. No part of the flat (with the exception of my room) was examined, or, if it was examined, then not in any detail. My car was not searched, though I myself suggested it.

By nine in the morning, the police had already managed to cull an impressive pile of foreign publications. But then they made a discovery they hadn't been expecting: a collection of photographs depicting early-twentieth-century Russian poets. Artsibushev anxiously telephoned for assistance. After hanging up, he explained that someone else would be joining them: 'a colleague, a specialist'.

However, before they had time to arrive, a key piece of evidence was 'found' in Azadovsky's study. According to testimony given by Azadovsky in 1988:

> I was standing by a window, looking out onto the street; there was a bookcase between the two windows. [Lieutenant] Khlyupin was examining my books. Suddenly, I looked away from the window and over at Khlyupin, and in that moment, I saw a packet wrapped in foil near Khlyupin's hands, on a shelf about five up from the bottom; I asked Khlyupin rather sharply (in my typical manner), 'What have you got there?' At which point Khlyupin became confused and embarrassed and faded into the background, as it were; Artsibushev intervened, saying, 'That's exactly what we're about to find out, what you've been keeping on that shelf.' The packet was transferred onto the desk and unwrapped: it contained a reddish-brown substance that gave off a spicy odour (I don't doubt that it was, in fact, hashish). In short, I realized what was going on and immediately said to Khlyupin that they had planted the drugs: 'You probably took that from your pocket,' I said. This statement is the reason why pockets are repeatedly mentioned

in [the search witness] Konstantinov's testimony, why he stubbornly insists that he is sure that none of the police officers placed a hand in their pockets for two whole hours. The operatives conducting the search barely reacted to my exclamations; the search continued, and Artsibushev began explaining to me (with no small measure of satisfaction) that everything was coming together, everything was adding up. He said that Lepilina had been detained the day before, that he had been the one to detain her, that she had had drugs in her possession, too, and that she had even tried to get rid of them as she was being detained. Now that drugs had been found in my place, too, he said, I was looking at three years, and he said plenty more besides. The search continued until about two in the afternoon. In addition to the drugs, a bag belonging to Lepilina was seized, along with its contents. Later on, Artsibushev explained to the GUVD's Investigation Directorate that he had taken it because he needed to prove [my] connection with Lepilina. Apart from the drugs and the bag, eight printed publications were seized, along with two fliers and twenty-three photographs. I refer here only to the items recorded in the search report; I won't bother mentioning the things that aren't reflected in official documents, though there is a great deal about this case that isn't reflected in official documents.

By the time the specialist arrived, the search had already reached its climax. Azadovsky looked flustered, while the officer's colleagues appeared calm and triumphant. The new arrival, who didn't show an ID of any kind, poured oil on the flames by making comments as he looked over the photographs. At one point, the telephone rang. Azadovsky instinctively went to answer it, and one of the police officers roughly shoved him aside. Incensed by this behaviour, Azadovsky demanded that it be recorded in the search report. Thus, Artsibushev was forced to write down his impulsive colleague's name: Lieutenant V.I. Bystrov.

What happened next? According a later document, Khlyupin 'not only became confused, he got so worked up that he stopped taking part in the search altogether: "God forbid I should find something else."' The bookcase he had been searching wasn't subject to further scrutiny, nor were the rest of the bookshelves (according to official documents, the flat contained 12 bookcases of varying widths, holding 7,000–8,000 volumes in total). The kitchen, bathroom, toilet, Azadovsky's mother's room and most of the corridor were also left untouched. In other words, the search was effectively limited to Azadovsky's desk, some piles of papers and a single bookcase. All told, this task took nearly six hours. Towards noon, the operatives began wrapping things up. The 'anti-drug crusaders' were clearly in a hurry.

Azadovsky didn't back down: he continued to accuse the police of planting drugs in his flat; however, he was powerless to do anything more. According to the internal MVD *Guidance for Investigators*, 'a search's success is determined by the quality of the planning that goes into it.' Clearly, the search of Azadovsky's flat had been well planned, and it was, indeed, a success.

In the search report, the witnesses give testimony meant to discredit Azadovsky's allegations. One of these witnesses was Azadovsky's neighbour, G.S. Makarov, who was clearly frightened by the situation. By contrast, the other witness, D.A. Konstantinov ('a *druzhinnik* who happened to be in the area'), bustled about, taking books down from the shelves; when he found one that might be deemed 'politically harmful', he would take it over to one of the police officers.

> <u>D.A. Konstantinov</u>: ... I was observing the police, and I distinctly saw the officer examining the bookcase between the windows take a pile of books down from the shelf, look at the books and let out a shout. At that point, he took a foil-wrapped packet from the space where the books had been and put it on a shelf. The other operatives went over to him immediately, and I saw the packet close up. By the looks of it, I was convinced that the packet must have been kept somewhere carefully; at any rate, it hadn't been in someone's pocket or else it would have been crumpled. Moreover, the police had not put their hands in their pockets for an instant. The packet was unwrapped in my presence, and I saw with my own eyes the reddish-brown substance, which gave off a spicy odour.
>
> <u>G.S. Makarov</u>: ... I wasn't observing the officer who was examining the bookcase between the windows. I heard that some kind of packet had been found. ... This packet was lying on a shelf in front of the books; when the search was just getting started, the packet hadn't been there. The officer showed us the place [where he had found it], on the left side of the bookcase, behind the books. Azadovsky immediately started saying that the packet had been planted.

The next day, Inspector Khlyupin's testimony was added to the case file:

> On 18 December 1980 my colleague Artsibushev invited me, along with two search witnesses, to help carry out a search of citizen Azadovsky's flat. ... I selected several books from the shelves, pulled them down, quickly flipped through the pages without reading them and then put them back in their place. I examined several books this way, then I reached the fourth shelf from the bottom and began pulling books out from right to left and examining them. I had already taken down the last few books from the left and examined them; I was getting ready to put them back when I saw a foil-wrapped packet lying in the space where the books had been. I really was somewhat confused, but then I took the packet, placed it on the next shelf up and asked, 'What is this?' At that point, Azadovsky was standing next to the shelf by the window, watching me. He immediately started shouting that I had taken the packet out of my pocket and planted it on the shelf. The packet was unwrapped, and there was a reddish-brown substance in it ...
>
> After I found the packet, the search went on for about four hours more; after all of Azadovsky's objections had been registered, we continued examining the books. He kept making comments that had nothing to do with the search, taking issue with all sorts of things, and I really was in a hurry to get to work; I had my own matters to attend to, and I told Artsibushev that I could sign the report, since the search was already finished, and go.

Soon afterwards, the 'guests' left, taking their host with them. According to the search report, at 2.00 pm Azadovsky was 'detained on suspicion of having committed a crime' and escorted to the Twenty-seventh Police Station. As Artsibushev handed Azadovsky over to the police investigator, Lieutenant Kamenko, he commented, 'I don't like all this. I'm just following orders.'

Kamenko coolly informed Azadovsky that he was facing charges under Article 224, paragraph 3 of the RSFSR Criminal Code: 'unlawful acquisition and possession of narcotic substances without intent to sell'. Such crimes were punishable by up to three years' incarceration. According to the Criminal Procedural Code (UPK), a decision had to be taken at this point regarding Azadovsky's pretrial restrictions: whether he would be put in pretrial detention, required to submit a signed acknowledgement of travel restrictions, etc. These measures would require the approval of the chief of the District Investigation Directorate, Lieutenant Colonel I. Sapunov.

Sapunov, however, was reluctant to sign off on Azadovsky's arrest: the evidence against him was too weak. There were no fingerprints on the foil, no witness testimony, no record of Azadovsky ever having used drugs; in short, they had nothing.

How could they be certain that the drugs belonged to Azadovsky if his partner had been detained with the same kind of packet the evening before? Wasn't it possible that the drugs belonged to her? Why hadn't a statement been taken from Azadovsky's mother? Why had the packet been unwrapped right away, before it could be dusted for fingerprints? Why didn't Khlyupin say anything when he first saw the packet? Why did he move it from one shelf to another?

Azadovsky thought that he might be released at this point. However, it quickly became apparent that his case was being monitored from above. Azadovsky and Makarov overheard snatches of Sapunov's telephone conversations from the corridor. Alongside numerous unprintable expressions, Sapunov was heard repeatedly saying: 'How am I supposed to put him away? There's no evidence!'

That evening, in an attempt to add to their meagre store of evidence, the investigator took Azadovsky's coat and suit jacket; they were returned to him a half hour later. Azadovsky only learned why this had occurred later on, while reading his case file. As it turned out, at 10.00 pm, the investigator had conducted a 'search of the contents of the pockets of the coat and suit jacket', during which he seized 'waste particles' weighing a total of 0.22 grams. Soon afterwards, laboratory analysis confirmed that these 'waste particles' contained traces of hashish. This evidence was obtained in violation of procedural norms; nonetheless, it was added to the case file.

One episode in particular illustrates the strangeness of the circumstances surrounding Azadovsky's arrest. After he had been taken to the station, the police officers began arguing over what to do next; Azadovsky was asked to leave the room and wait in the corridor. For a while, he sat there listening to the officers bickering with one another. But then he realized that he was alone: he wasn't under guard, and he wasn't wearing handcuffs either.

He walked calmly down the corridor until he reached the stairs, then he went down to the ground floor and exited the building. He walked down Krylov Alley until he reached Sadovaya Street. There was a telephone booth on that corner, and he had some change. First, he called his mother. He reassured her as best he could and advised her to wait and see how things developed. Then he called his work: the departmental assistant, Yelena Krichevskaya, picked up the phone. He told her he would not be in for several days. Lepilina, alas, was not in a position to take calls.

Azadovsky considered his next move. If only he knew where Lepilina was, it would make his decision much easier. But Artsibushev had said that she had 'already made her confession'. What could she possibly have confessed to? What was going to happen to her?

A wild thought entered his head: he could go to the train station and get on the next train to Moscow. He could go to the Prosecutor General's Office and submit a petition about the planted drugs, the illegal search, Lepilina's detention. . .

But before long, practical considerations brought him down to earth. Would he be able to make it to Moscow? Who could he stay with if he did? Where would he get the money for a ticket? He couldn't go home for it. In any case, Azadovsky hadn't given up hope that he would be allowed to go home once he had signed an acknowledgement of travel restrictions.

In the end, Azadovsky decided to return to the station to avoid making matters any worse. Just then, he ran into his friend Vadim Zhuk (now a well-known actor and poet). Azadovsky explained the situation and asked Zhuk to inform their mutual friends, Boris Rotenshtein and Genrietta Yanovskaya.

After returning to the station, Azadovsky remained alone for another half hour. Finally, Kamenko called him into his office. He waved some papers around, saying, 'It has come to our attention that you were involved in a narcotics case in 1969.' At this point, Azadovsky was presented with an arrest warrant. Fixing him with a meaningful stare, Kamenko said, 'It's not about drugs, it's about . . . your contacts.'

Azadovsky spent the night of 19 December (and the two nights that followed) in a holding cell. On 22 December, a prisoner transport vehicle arrived and Azadovsky was taken under guard to Kresty, where Lepilina was already being held.

3

Awaiting trial

3.1 Books and photographs

Though the authorities had ostensibly come to Azadovsky's flat in search of drugs, they showed far greater interest in his books and papers. The books they seized were mostly foreign editions of works whose authors were considered subversive by the Soviet state. However, it was the photographs that captured the police's attention – probably because the search hadn't turned up any literature that was actually banned. If the police had found any 'anti-Soviet propaganda' – anything by Alexander Solzhenitsyn or Andrey Sakharov,[1] for example – it might have been a different story, but the police hadn't found anything like that. What they *did* find was a collection of early-twentieth-century photographs.

Not long before the search, Azadovsky's photograph collection had grown considerably larger. His friend, the poet and collector Mikhail Baltsvinik (1931–80), had taken his own life that April; before his death, he had been compiling a photo gallery of twentieth-century writers and poets, mostly by taking pictures of originals held in personal archives. Acting on Baltsvinik's wishes, his widow had given the entire collection (some 2,500 photographs) to Azadovsky.

Fantastical rumours began circulating in the wake of Azadovsky's arrest: one story held that some foreigners had offered him money for this remarkable collection, and that, if the Leningrad authorities hadn't intervened, it might have been smuggled to the West. But Azadovsky had never intended to export the photographs. In the 1990s, when it would have been perfectly legal to send Baltsvinik's collection abroad, Azadovsky donated it to the Anna Akhmatova Museum in Saint Petersburg, where it remains to this day.

The operatives conducting the search culled twenty photographs from the collection. For the most part, these photographs showed famous Russian poets who either committed suicide (like Sergey Yesenin) or found themselves on the receiving end of a Bolshevik bullet (Nikolay Gumilyov and Nikolay Klyuev). Some of them featured the writers' dead bodies or coffins (in the cases of Sergey Yesenin, Alexander Blok and Vladimir Mayakovsky). But why had these photographs been seized in the first place? It is possible that, at the time of the search, the authorities hadn't yet decided what charges to bring against Azadovsky; they might have been considering Article 190-1 ('systematic circulation . . . of false statements which defame the Soviet state or social system'). Lyudmila Petrova, Baltsvinik's widow, later reported that KGB operatives came to her home in 1981, demanding a statement asserting that Azadovsky had obtained the photographs illegally. If this had been the case, the photographs could certainly have been used as evidence against him.

3.2 Resistance

Because of Azadovsky's status within Leningrad's intellectual community, his arrest could hardly go unnoticed; his friends' shock was only compounded by the absurdity of the charges levelled against him. They decided to join forces to raise public awareness of the situation and expose the political motivations behind it. And their efforts weren't in vain: soon enough, this petty narcotics case came to be seen as an example of the Soviet regime's persecution of dissidence (though, it bears repeating, Azadovsky himself was not a dissident).

Later on, an international community of scholars and writers would rally in Azadovsky's defence. In the beginning, though, he relied on the support of his immediate circle of friends, who had banded together immediately after his arrest. Their strategy was simple. Genrietta Yanovskaya writes:

> Kostya's lawyer, Zoya Toporova, and other people with ties to dissident culture explained our plan of action to me in no uncertain terms: if we wanted to save Kostya, there had to be constant buzz around his case; that way, they wouldn't do anything [bad] to him. We had to keep moving all the time, like you do in the frost so you don't freeze.

Even now, with the benefit of hindsight, it is difficult to say what the best course of action would have been. Another strategy commonly employed in that era was to lie low and await the court's decision; that way, the court might decide not to treat the case as political. However, considering how aggressive the investigation of Azadovsky's case had been from the beginning, it is plausible that they might have 'found' even more evidence to bolster the charges against him.

A small group of activists within this circle (Yanovskaya, Vanag and Alexander Lavrov, among others) compiled a document giving background information on the case, which was subsequently sent to Moscow. After just ten days, on 31 December 1980, an item about Lepilina and Azadovsky's arrests appeared in the underground dissident publication *A Chronicle of Current Events*.

In January 1981, when it became clear that this hadn't been some kind of mix-up, the same group sent a summary of the situation to Western media outlets, most notably Radio Free Europe/Radio Liberty. This summary was used in news programmes on Voice of America, the BBC and Deutsche Welle and was paraphrased in the foreign press. It was also reproduced in *Samizdat Materials*, a prominent Soviet dissident publication based in Munich.

In late January–early February 1981, another release appeared in *Samizdat Materials* outlining the reasons for these criminal proceedings:

In 1969, [Azadovsky] was called to testify in the case against Yefim Slavinsky, which was presented as a criminal case (Slavinsky was charged with possession and distribution of narcotics) despite its clear political motivation (the KGB was attempting to curb Slavinsky's extensive contact with foreigners). Because of Azadovsky's uncompromising stance during this trial, he was prevented from working in his field in Leningrad after finishing his postgraduate work at Leningrad State Pedagogical Institute, and he was forced to live in Petrozavodsk for a significant period of time. During his time as department head at the Leningrad Vera Mukhina Higher School of Art and Industry, Azadovsky had a colleague fired (by court order) for a breach of workplace discipline. This person, a certain Ravich, threatened to use his connections in the KGB to take revenge. In 1979, through no small expenditure of effort, Azadovsky got the courts to punish a certain Tkachyov, who had assaulted Azadovsky and Lepilina. Tkachyov also threatened to take revenge against Azadovsky by exploiting a personal connection: a relative of his was a captain in the Leningrad police. Azadovsky's arrest is viewed by the Leningrad intelligentsia as an attempt by the KGB to intimidate people it suspects of sympathizing with unofficial ideology. Azadovsky was probably made an example of for the following reasons: 1) he is well known in different intelligentsia circles (among writers, academics, etc.) in both Leningrad and Moscow; 2) he is well known in the West, and so his trial would allow the KGB to observe how the West would react to such a blatant provocation; and 3) the fact that Azadovsky has personal enemies and has already acted as a witness in a criminal trial makes it easy for the KGB to remain in the shadows, to avoid attracting public attention. It is fairly obvious that the KGB's desire to intimidate the intelligentsia is a response to the situation in Poland.[2] It is altogether possible that the case against Azadovsky is designed to remind people of the persecution of 'cosmopolitans' in 1949.

In early February 1981, Alexander Lavrov and Sergey Grechishkin (young literary historians affiliated with Pushkin House, part of the Russian Academy of Sciences) organized the publication of an open letter asking the city prosecutor to release Azadovsky from custody while awaiting trial. Its signatories were six venerable academics: Boris Bukhshtab, Lidia Ginzburg, Dmitry Maksimov, Viktor Manuilov, Isaak Yampolsky and Boris Yegorov. Addressed to Leningrad City Prosecutor Sergey Solovyov, this letter of support arrived at the City Prosecutor's Office on 11 February 1981. It characterized Azadovsky in glowing terms:

We know Azadovsky as a highly qualified specialist; as one of the leading authorities on the history of early twentieth-century Russian literature and on the connections between Russian and foreign literatures; as the author of several dozen seminal articles and other publications; and as a talented translator, both from numerous Western European languages and from languages of the peoples of the USSR. His creative endeavours have earned him fame among a wide readership.

The signatories asked for only one thing: a change in Azadovsky's pretrial restrictions.

Another letter in Azadovsky's defence was sent to the city prosecutor by his colleagues in the department of foreign languages. It is worth mentioning that this letter was signed by everyone in his department. Though Azadovsky wasn't the most easy-going of department heads, the blatant injustice of the charges he was facing inspired his colleagues to rally round him.

Despite various letters and petitions, Azadovsky wasn't shown any leniency. The criminal case against him proceeded without any major alteration – apart from the unusual fact that Azadovsky's case was severed from Lepilina's. On 17 January 1981, nearly a month after their arrests, Sapunov, chief of the Kuibyshevsky District Investigation Directorate, approved the following resolution:

> Having reviewed criminal case file no. 10196, Lieutenant Kamenko of the Kuibyshevsky District Investigation Directorate has established the following: on 18 December 1980, citizen Lepilina was detained in the courtyard of 10 Vosstaniya Street, and an illegal narcotic substance (hashish) was discovered in her bag. Lepilina's acquaintance K.M. Azadovsky resides in the aforementioned building, and so a search of his residence was carried out on 19 December 1980, during which a narcotic substance was discovered on a bookshelf: hashish, which Azadovsky had in his possession unlawfully. Thus, Azadovsky's actions give grounds to charge him under Article 224 of the RSFSR Criminal Code.
>
> In light of the fact that the investigation did not establish a conspiracy between Azadovsky and Lepilina to possess, acquire, or distribute narcotic substances and the fact that the crimes they have committed are entirely unconnected, in conformance with Article 26 of the RSFSR Criminal Procedural Code, I have resolved the following: that the materials in criminal case no. 10196 relating to Konstantin Markovich Azadovsky shall be severed from the present case.

In retrospect, it isn't difficult to understand the strategy behind the 'Azadovsky Affair', or why it had been necessary to detain Lepilina first. This clumsily executed circus had been devised solely to give the authorities 'legal' grounds to enter Azadovsky's flat. Once Azadovsky and Lepilina had been neutralized, the charges against them were separated into two cases, allowing the authorities to sidestep a number of investigative procedures that would have jeopardized their position. For example, if Azadovsky and Lepilina had been facing joint charges, they would, at the very least, have had the right to be questioned simultaneously. To the investigator, separating the cases might have seemed like the easiest way forward: this way, there would be less evidence, less publicity and less chance of facing unpleasant surprises at the trial. It is also possible that Kamenko was simply following orders from above.

Meanwhile, the City Prosecutor's Office made sure to answer the letters they received in Azadovsky's defence within the legally mandated time frame. A reply to the letter signed by the group of prominent scholars was sent to Azadovsky's mother on 26 February; it bore the signature of V.N. Tulchinsky, chief of the Department of Investigative Oversight. Of course, the academics' letter had been 'reviewed', but 'Preliminary investigation indicates that there are no grounds to alter the pretrial restrictions that have been imposed on your son, K.M. Azadovsky. At the present time, the criminal case against K.M. Azadovsky has been completed and sent to the Kuibyshevsky District People's Court for review.'

These letters made their way to the West, where they attracted widespread public attention after their publication in *Samizdat Materials*. This raises an important question: What was at stake for those who spoke out in Azadovsky's defence, and, specifically, for those involved in writing these letters and gathering signatures for them?

Viktor Toporov, who witnessed and, for a time, took part in the efforts on Azadovsky's behalf, later wrote that they largely went unnoticed; he suggests that this campaign was little more than a way for Azadovsky's friends to amuse themselves in the dreary Leningrad climate. But that is only one perspective. In fact, the circumstances took a serious toll on Azadovsky's circle. Some people encountered difficulties at work, and Zigfrida Vanag miscarried late in a pregnancy as a result of nervous strain.

3.3 Kresty and lawyers

When the prisoner transport vehicle took Azadovsky from Krylov Alley to Kresty Prison on 22 December 1980, he entered a completely different world: unfamiliar, alien and dangerous.

When Kresty was built in the late nineteenth century, its cells were intended to house individual prisoners; in the Soviet period, they held an average of four people each. The prison population could be double, triple and sometimes even quadruple what the building was meant to hold. The cell to which Azadovsky was assigned, cell 447, was occupied by six other people when he arrived.

This cell was located in the part of Kresty that housed the so-called first-timers: defendants awaiting their first trials and their first trips to the zone.[3] Though, theoretically, it was possible to receive a not-guilty judgement in the Soviet criminal justice system, in practice acquittals were vanishingly rare. Even if the defendant was obviously innocent, if they had already been arrested and put in pretrial detention, the chances of receiving a not-guilty judgement were practically zero. They might be given a suspended sentence or be sentenced to time served; they might be released directly from the courtroom after the judgement had been read. However, nothing could be allowed to discredit the Soviet judicial or law enforcement systems. This is true in Russia to this day.

Azadovsky was processed in the usual manner: first, he was subjected to a 'shakedown' (strip search), after which his personal belongings were taken for storage and he was taken to shower. Then he was issued a mattress and pillow (without bed linens, of course). Finally, he was escorted from prisoner intake to his future home: cell 447. His cellmates were mostly young 'hoodlums' (aged eighteen to twenty), but there were older men there as well. Azadovsky would spend nearly three months in this cell without receiving any news of Lepilina's fate or his mother's health. Not once was he taken for questioning during this time; it was as if he'd been forgotten. Each day, he expected to be called down to see either an investigator or a lawyer: his cellmates went in and out on an almost daily basis. But no – Azadovsky remained in an information vacuum.

In later years, Azadovsky spoke of his time in prison rarely and reluctantly. Little information is available regarding his incarceration. However, in 1993, on the 100th anniversary of Kresty's founding, several Petersburg academics were asked to share their views and, in some cases, memories of the institution. In an interview, Azadovsky said:

> My first impression was: how horrible! Everything there produced a feeling of horror: the atmosphere, the bare painted walls, the water pipes, the filth. In those conditions, every detail, every little thing could evoke only one sense in a 'newbie': a sense of horror.
>
> ... You can't ask a person to withstand such completely abnormal, amoral conditions, to bear a burden clearly not meant to fall on an average, normal person's shoulders. There are sensitive people, there are impressionable people, there are people who are physically weak. At the end of the day, as we know from George Orwell's novel, for example, there are ways of breaking anyone. All you have to do is find them. I saw many people who were broken in prison, broken in the zone. They harmed others. And they deserve our censure. But nevertheless, we must first ask ourselves: 'If I were told to sign something or else face five more years' incarceration, would I not falter, would I not break? If they started beating me, would I not break?' ... Fortunately, I never found myself in such a dire situation.
>
> ... There are only about a thousand cells in Kresty, I believe. And each cell contains four sleeping areas, four 'bunks'. So Kresty is intended to house four thousand people. Now, the cells I found myself in held from ten to sixteen people. This is probably difficult to imagine. I've never seen anything like it in films or in books. The question presents itself immediately: How do I sleep, how do I get one of the sleeping places, lie down on a mattress, lay my head down on a pillow and cover myself in a woollen blanket? There was a whole art to this, or, more accurately, a whole hierarchy. When you were just coming into a cell, and particularly when you were just coming into a cell for the first time, you never went straight to the privileged places, the ones on the bunks. The 'ascent through the ranks' began with a place on the floor, under a bunk. When I got to the cell, I was immediately told where my place would be, and it was a place for a first-timer. Then my 'ascent' began. Someone would be taken to trial or for transport and I would move up; I started building relationships with the other prisoners, I began to make my way into this system. But I spent my first days there (around Christmas, 1980) under a bunk, saying to myself: in this country, this is probably the right place for a person like you.

During his time at Kresty, Azadovsky maintained the position he had adopted during his first interrogation on 19 December 1980: he flatly denied having anything to do with drugs and continued to accuse Khlyupin of planting the packet of hashish in his flat. Azadovsky's cellmates were aware of his stance, which is probably why the police didn't bother interrogating him again. The police were kept well apprised of the conversations that went on in each cell by a network of snitches. A confession from Azadovsky would have been an investigator's dream: that's all they would have needed to convict him.

It was during his time in Kresty that Azadovsky had his first meeting with a lawyer. His friends had gone to great lengths to secure the services of Semyon Kheifets (1925–2012), a venerable Leningrad lawyer who was already a legend in his field.

However, Azadovsky had only one meeting with Kheifets, on 18 February 1981. This was a key part of the process known as 'closing' a case, when a defendant reviewed investigation materials together with a lawyer. Kheifets arrived at the meeting with his assistant, Alla Kazakina, and he was brief. He didn't bring Azadovsky any news 'from the outside'; however, the petitions he had written to send to the court (mostly requesting access to materials necessary for the trial) struck Azadovsky as convincing.

Other detainees met their lawyers frequently, and Azadovsky's bunkmates would always come back not just with news, but with cigarettes and money as well. It had seemed that lawyers were not being allowed in to see Azadovsky, thus depriving him of his right to a defence. And when he finally was allowed access to legal counsel, the meeting ended in bitter disappointment: Kheifets brought no news of Lepilina, and his assistant only mentioned in passing that she had fully confessed her guilt. Kazakina also said something like: 'She's trying to protect you, too: she gave testimony.' This statement aligned with what Artsibushev had said on 19 December. During this same meeting, Azadovsky learned that his case had been severed from Lepilina's, which made very little sense. And Azadovsky wasn't informed of one crucial fact: Lepilina's court date had already been set, and her trial was scheduled to take place the following day, 19 February 1981.

Of course, Azadovsky wasn't the only Soviet prisoner to be purposefully kept in the dark as a demoralizing tactic. But he hadn't fully grasped that the fact he hadn't been called in for further questioning or allowed regular meetings with his lawyer was not just an unfortunate coincidence, but a tried-and-tested tactic of Soviet law enforcement. The dissident and human rights advocate Vladimir Bukovsky writes:

> The investigator's main weapon is the average Soviet citizen's ignorance of the law. From the day of their arrest to the end of their investigation, a citizen is kept isolated from the outside world; they see a lawyer only after the case against them is complete. They aren't given any law-books, though what good would law-books do them? How are they supposed to know what they should and shouldn't say, what rights they have, what rights they don't?

And actually, to those familiar with this sort of case, the fact that Kheifets had agreed to defend Azadovsky was a troubling sign. Kheifets wasn't just a famous lawyer; he was a lawyer with 'clearance'.

To explain the Soviet system of 'clearance', I will refer to a description written by defence lawyer Dina Kaminskaya (1916–2006). Kaminskaya defended high-profile 'enemies of the Soviet state' including Vladimir Bukovsky (1967), Yury Galanskov (1967–8) and Anatoly Marchenko (1968); she was subsequently stripped of her law license and forced to leave the USSR in 1977.

> According to current legislation, all lawyers are permitted to try any criminal or civil case in any court in the country. However, in practice, the rights of lawyers and defendants are being violated by the government itself. I am referring here to the system of 'clearance'.
>
> Essentially, cases that have been investigated by the KGB (nearly all political cases, as well as cases related to illegal exchange transactions, cases involving foreigners and certain other categories of cases) can be argued only by lawyers who have received special permission to do so.
>
> Even experts in Soviet jurisprudence would be unable to find any reference or allusion to this system in Soviet law.
>
> Both the Criminal Procedural Code and the Statute on Advocacy are built on the principle of complete equality among collegium members. Neither experience nor ability should grant an individual any advantage regarding their right to speak in any court on any case, nor should these factors affect the payment they receive. In fact, such inequalities do exist, and they are based solely on a lawyer's political reliability. 'Clearance' acts as a formal marker of such reliability.
>
> The collegium's presidium determines the number of lawyers to be granted clearance, subject to the KGB's approval. (In Moscow, clearance has been given to about 10 per cent of all practising lawyers, which is to say, to 100–120 individuals.)
>
> Clearance is always granted to all members of the collegium's presidium and all heads and secretaries of party organizations based at legal consultancies. Clearance will also be given to three to four rank-and-file lawyers at each consultancy, usually party members. For several years, I also had such clearance (I was probably not the only non-party member to be given clearance, but I cannot recall any others).
>
> It is important to emphasize that a lawyer's clearance to work on cases investigated by the KGB is not the same as the ordinary clearance required to access classified documents, which is issued to all Soviet citizens working in sensitive sectors. They are not the same because the majority of cases requiring a lawyer with clearance do not contain any classified information or documents; often, these cases are even tried in public proceedings.
>
> A state that maintains such strict control over public statements of a political or ideological nature could hardly give an unvetted lawyer free rein to speak in a public court of law. I was stripped of my clearance fairly quickly. And not for divulging classified information (which, incidentally, I had the opportunity to do on more than one occasion): I was stripped of my clearance because I failed to demonstrate political obedience.

A fuller portrait of Semyon Kheifets emerges from the memoirs of Mikhail Ruvimovich Kheifets (1934–2019, no relation). Mikhail Ruvimovich was arrested in 1974 and prosecuted under Article 70 of the RSFSR Criminal Code for writing the introduction to a samizdat edition of the collected works of Joseph Brodsky, preparing copies of Andrey Amalrik's essay 'Will the Soviet Union Last until 1984?', and other activities of this type. He was sentenced to four years in corrective labour camps and two years of exile; he emigrated to Israel after his release in 1980. He writes:

> In the camps, [lawyers with clearance] are called 'pocket lawyers' because they're in the KGB's pocket: they take the prosecutor for your case out of one pocket and your defence lawyer out of the other. The KGB uses these lawyers . . . to carry out the kinds of sensitive missions that their own ham-fisted agents aren't capable of managing. It is precisely this role – as the KGB's doormat – that Kheifets (with whom I unfortunately share a surname) played in the trial of my friend Vladimir Maramzin. . . . He persuaded him to 'sincerely repent' and 'rebuff the West': the investigators couldn't have done a better job themselves. But Kheifets is one of the better ones: in exchange for political services rendered to the government, he's able to knock significant time off his clients' sentences; the others don't even ask for that, they're just happy to be praised by their contemptuous KGB masters. . .

Kheifets had been involved in high-profile political trials for many years, and his former clients levelled criticisms against him similar to Mikhail Ruvimovich's. When the philologist Mikhail Meilakh (another Leningrad 'political type') was arrested in 1983 for possession of banned literature, he was 'lucky' enough to get Kheifets as a lawyer. Several years later, he wrote: 'The lawyer Kheifets appeared on the scene (you couldn't even call him a "conscience for hire" because he didn't have one).' As for the 'help' Kheifets gave him, Meilakh observed, 'He's completely useless as a lawyer; as far as I could see, he was only good for bringing in news of the outside world.' In Azadovsky's case, he didn't even do that.

The Parisian publication *La Pensée Russe*, to which Maramzin was an active contributor at the time, couldn't possibly have known exactly how and why Kheifets had come to defend Azadovsky. However, it came to the following conclusion: 'The fact that S. Kheifets has been assigned as Azadovsky's lawyer proves once again that this case is being run by the state security apparatus.'

Back in his jail cell after the meeting with Kheifets, Azadovsky began turning the situation over in his mind. How could he find out what was happening to Lepilina? What did they mean, 'She gave testimony . . . she's trying to protect you'? Really, it could mean only one thing: Lepilina had considered the circumstances, weighed all her options and was now attempting to take the blame for the crimes he was accused of. Her goal seemed to be to clear him of any possible wrongdoing, to force the courts to free him.

But was his guess correct? How could he find out the truth? Would it be possible for him to make contact with Lepilina? She was very close, in the women's section of Kresty. Such thoughts gnawed at him ceaselessly, oppressing and tormenting him. What could he do?

One of his cellmates helped him to find a solution.

His name was Vadim Rozenberg, but his cellmates called him Fima; he had been arrested either for theft or for fraud. He was intelligent, sharp-tongued and charming. His pragmatic style made for a welcome change from the 'childish prattle' of the others. And so, he and Azadovsky soon became friends. Rozenberg really did try to provide him with moral support: he was an active listener, gave Azadovsky tips on navigating the system and offered sound advice. Practically speaking, he was the only person Azadovsky had to talk to: the rest of his cellmates came from completely different backgrounds. Placing a potential confidant like Rozenberg in Azadovsky's cell was a clever and, of course, premeditated tactic; however, Azadovsky didn't know that at the time.

Azadovsky didn't share everything with Rozenberg: he kept his thoughts about his case to himself, didn't name names and didn't lay out all the facts. And Rozenberg didn't insist on any of that. He did make it clear, though, that he would be happy to help Azadovsky if the need arose. And his communication skills were excellent, as Azadovsky frequently observed. Rozenberg had no trouble conversing with the 'chow slingers' (prisoners assigned to serve food in the canteen) or the guards, and it was through them that that 'kites' (personal messages) were sent and received. More than once, Azadovsky saw Rozenberg facilitate his cellmates' correspondence: 'kites' were dispatched and responses arrived. It didn't occur to him that this might be a show put on for his benefit.

Azadovsky was much more concerned about a different type of 'friendly' behaviour. In a complaint to the Central Committee dated 15 February 1982, he wrote: 'I have been assigned to a cell with specially selected prisoners, and one of them, V.G. Rozenberg, constantly and deliberately attempts to incite me to behaviour punishable under Article 121 of the Criminal Code.' This was the article criminalizing sodomy, which carried a serious punishment: up to five years' incarceration. Like the earlier incident with the photograph collection, this was an attempt on the authorities' part to tack extra charges on to Azadovsky's case. If Azadovsky had taken the bait, he would have also been tried under Article 121, which would have made life in the GULAG extremely difficult.

Leningrad-based professor and world-famous anthropologist Lev Klein (1927–2019) was arrested pursuant to this article on 5 March 1981. He later wrote of Azadovsky: 'The arrested man's colleagues were certain that the drugs had been planted in his flat during the search. At the same time, during questioning, many of his male friends were pressured to admit to having had sexual relations with him.' Therefore, it seems likely that Rozenberg was part of a plan to incite Azadovsky into criminalized behaviour. This particular tactic was probably chosen because Azadovsky wasn't legally married.

Rozenberg was constantly being pulled out of the cell for what he referred to as 'interrogations'; afterwards, he would return to the cell and feed Azadovsky tantalizing bits of information, mostly regarding Lepilina. On one occasion, Rozenberg claimed to have learned from a female guard he knew that Lepilina had gone mad. Another time, he mentioned that the interrogator had asked him questions about his cellmates, showing a particular interest in Azadovsky. Rozenberg proceeded to ask Azadovsky what exactly he had done: though he was being charged under Article 224-3, the kinds of questions they were asking were related to Article 70 ('treason against the motherland'). Meanwhile, Azadovsky tried to disentangle what was true from what might have been designed to trip him up. One day, in early March 1981 (as the investigation was drawing to a close), Rozenberg even confessed that they had 'had him up against a wall', forcing him to sign some sort of testimony.

Every day, in addition to agonizing over what might be happening to Lepilina and his mother, Azadovsky speculated as to the true motivations behind his case. At first, he dismissed the thought that he might have been arrested for political reasons: after all, he wasn't involved in any dissident activities. But no matter how he racked his brains for answers, he couldn't find anything in his behaviour that could have led to a criminal case. There were only two incidents he could think of, and both of them were extremely trivial. The first had taken place a year before, when one of his subordinates, M. Ravich, was fired at Azadovsky's insistence. Ravich, who had a drinking problem and a reputation for shirking his professional duties, also happened to have the support of the Higher School's Party Bureau. After a trial determined that Ravich's firing had, in fact, been lawful, Ravich vowed to Azadovsky that he would 'take revenge for his entire life'. The second incident involved A. Tkachyov, the son of Lepilina's flatmate Zinaida Tkachyova. One day, Tkachyov got drunk and picked a fight with Azadovsky, who wound up in medical clinic. Azadovsky filed a petition against him, but Tkachyov's police connections made it difficult to bring him to justice. Eventually, Tkachyov was convicted of hooliganism and put on probation.

These were petty interpersonal conflicts; there was nothing political about them. And yet, in the first months after his arrest, Azadovsky was certain that one of them must be the motivation behind the present case. Of course, this would have been a rather complicated way of taking revenge; it would have been much easier to hit him over the head with a pipe outside his building (this wasn't a rare occurrence at the time, and it yielded maximal results for minimal effort). But Azadovsky, a suspicious person by nature, remained convinced for a long time that either Ravich or Tkachyov had used their connections with the authorities to bring about his present misfortune.

3.4 A note for Svetlana

Azadovsky couldn't stop thinking about what might have happened to Lepilina. On the one hand, he was certain that she didn't use drugs and that she would never have kept drugs in her possession; on the other hand, he knew from his arrest warrant that she had been detained with drugs on her person in the courtyard of his building. There were so many questions. How had she ended up with the drugs? What could she have said during questioning to make them show up the next morning at his flat?

He began piecing together the scraps of information that – thanks to Rozenberg – he had been able to glean from the chow slingers and the unofficial prison post. He learned that Lepilina had been broken, that she was on the verge of going mad and that she had given a full confession in which she claimed to have hidden drugs in Azadovsky's flat without his knowledge.

This last piece of information came as a serious blow. But as he processed this new information and pieced it together with what he already knew, he began to see his situation in an entirely different light. If he and Lepilina had been arrested as accomplices, but she was planning to take all of the blame, then the judge would have no choice but to declare him not guilty. Was that really what was happening? How could he find out? He had to make sure that they were questioned simultaneously.

And so, on the same day as his meeting with Kheifets, Azadovsky wrote a petition to the warden of Kresty and sent it through the unofficial prison post; this petition was accompanied by a request that it be passed along to the chief of the Kuibyshevsky District Investigation Directorate, as per standard prison procedure. The letter was sent through the 'hatch', the opening in the cell door through which chow slingers delivered bowls of food and guards collected correspondence. It read:

> Today, 18 February 1981, during the closing of the criminal case brought against me under Article 224, paragraph 3, I learned about the testimony of my acquaintance, Svetlana Ivanovna Lepilina, who is also being held in the pretrial detention centre.
>
> Lepilina has testified that the narcotic substance found in my flat was hidden there by her without my knowledge. Additionally, on numerous occasions throughout autumn 1980, Lepilina wore the coat belonging to me in which 0.2 grams of hashish was found.
>
> Because Lepilina's testimony significantly changes the case against me, I request to be questioned simultaneously with her.

Azadovsky thought he had finally grasped the logic behind what was happening: having already confessed to the packet of hashish that had been found on her person, Lepilina had decided to go one step further and claim she was responsible for the packet discovered in his flat and the particles found in his jacket, which she occasionally wore. Despite her deep depression, Lepilina had realized the gravity of the situation and was trying to save him. She knew that there was no way she could avoid a guilty judgement: she had been caught red-handed with drugs on her person. What's more, Lepilina needed Azadovsky to be freed, both so that he could help her and so that Azadovsky's mother could receive the care she needed.

Obviously, Lepilina's confession completely undermined the charges against Azadovsky. After all, she claimed to have been using his flat as a hiding place without his knowledge. This was very upsetting, of course, but it meant that the authorities would have no choice but to set him free.

Such were the thoughts swirling around in Azadovsky's head as he paced back and forth in his cell. Things became even more confusing when Rozenberg returned from another round of questioning to inform him that Lepilina's trial had already taken place, and that she had been sentenced to a year and a half. Rozenberg had ostensibly received this information from an investigator familiar with the 'Azadovsky Affair'. There was no reason not to believe Rozenberg, and, in any case, there was no reason for him to lie: if it was a lie, it would be found out eventually. However, if it was true, then a year and a half would have been a long sentence for a first-time conviction on the charges Azadovsky knew about for certain. That could mean only one thing: Lepilina had claimed responsibility not just for the drugs discovered on her person, but for the ones linked to Azadovsky as well.

Azadovsky was now consumed by the thought of his imminent release. Every day, he expected to be called down from his cell to be questioned 'in light of the changed circumstances'. Every day, he mentally prepared himself to speak to the investigator.

And every day he asked himself an increasingly tortuous question: What could be taking so long?

Finally, Azadovsky landed on an answer: they were trying to conceal the fact that Lepilina had taken all the blame on herself. Since their cases were being tried separately, at this point the investigator's main task was to hide Lepilina's testimony from Azadovsky's judge and prosecution. With each passing day, Azadovsky became more convinced that he and Lepilina would not be questioned simultaneously.

Something else that had puzzled him was now becoming clear: why his case had been severed from Lepilina's, against all common sense and legal logic. Now he understood: it was easier to deal with them separately. Could they stop this blatant miscarriage of justice in its tracks? If so, how? They would need evidence no court could ignore: for example, a written statement from Lepilina. If he could present such a document to the court, he could petition for Lepilina to be called as a witness in his trial.

A new plan began to take shape. It wasn't perfect, but it would have to do. Rozenberg came up with the following strategy: Lepilina's birthday was on 16 February, so they would put together a small present for her. Inside would be a note asking her to confirm what was happening. According to Rozenberg, this kind of package wouldn't be hard to send. And, though he admitted that the plan involved some risk, he offered to help Azadovsky by asking a female guard he knew for help.

And so, Azadovsky assembled a small care package for Lepilina: a piece of soap, a pencil and several hard candies. This present might have seemed meagre by the standards of the outside world, but in prison these were luxuries. Before giving the present to Rozenberg, Azadovsky wrote a note to Lepilina, which said:

> Tuzik [Azadovsky's nickname for Lepilina], my darling! Our cases have been severed, it seems, to brush aside your testimony, which demonstrates my <u>total</u> innocence. What are we to do?
>
> They clearly want to put me away for three years. So: don't back down from the testimony you gave in December, especially <u>in court</u>. I am currently demanding that we be questioned simultaneously, and I will demand that you be allowed to give testimony in court (for my case). The only thing that can save me is the steadfastness and consistency of your testimony.
>
> When they ask how I know about your testimony, I'll tell them that I found out through the chow slingers. I asked them to send you my greetings, and you told me about your testimony in reply. That was sometime in January.
>
> Just in case you aren't allowed to speak in my defence, I need to have a note from you in my possession. Write a letter to me saying how and why you hid the foil packet of hashish on the bookcase between the windows (on the fourth shelf up) and when you wore my <u>coat</u>.
>
> Remember, <u>after</u> the trial, your testimony won't be able to make any difference. And that's what they seem to be counting on.
>
> And so, I need a letter from you – your confession – to use as a document, as evidence.
>
> My infinitely dear, my good and unhappy Tuzik. I think of you every day and every night. No matter how many years they give us, no matter where we are – I

will always be with you. If I am released, I will find you right away. Hold on, my darling. I'm all right: in good health and good spirits.

These little things are for your (belated) birthday.

I eagerly await your reply.

(When you write, tell me where you were detained: on the street, in the courtyard, or in the entryway; did you say you were on your way to flat 51?)

In principle, Azadovsky knew that sending such a letter was a risk. But he also knew that it was his only chance to obtain compelling proof of his innocence. Moreover, he considered the letter's contents to be harmless, especially for Lepilina: after all, her trial had already taken place. All he asked was for her to confirm her own testimony. The clarifications regarding the coat and the foil packet were intended to look like reminders, but they were, in fact, vital questions: if Azadovsky's case went to trial, the judge would certainly ask where she had put the packet and when exactly she had worn the coat.

Looking back, what can be said about this gambit? At the time, Azadovsky was thoroughly misinformed; moreover, he was demoralized. However, to his credit, he tried to act despite the hopelessness of his situation. He had anticipated the potential twists and turns his case might take; he was hoping that a letter from Lepilina would allow him to scupper the case if the prosecution claimed the drugs were his. Then they would have no choice but to refer the case for further enquiry. That was his reasoning at the time: needless to say, it was naïve and incorrect. His first mistake was sending a note that could easily be used against him. His second was daring to think he was capable not only of playing the game, but of winning it. He would later look back on this moment with chagrin.

Azadovsky's note remained unanswered. His appeal to the Investigation Directorate was also met with silence. However, several days later, the investigator finally called him down to review the indictment against him. Azadovsky refused to sign it. From the very beginning, he had refused to sign anything, hoping that this would demonstrate his unyielding refusal to admit to any wrongdoing. Generally speaking, this strategy didn't act in a defendant's favour: on the contrary, it served as a black mark against them. In this instance, Azadovsky's refusal to sign was inconsequential. He finally realized that conviction was inevitable.

The investigator allowed Azadovsky to review the materials gathered during the investigation. There were documents from the Slavinsky trial, as well as the petition Azadovsky had filed asking to be questioned simultaneously with Lepilina. Azadovsky also learned that Investigator Kamenko had reviewed all of Kheifets's petitions and, predictably, denied them.

Now all Azadovsky could do was wait for his court date, which was scheduled for 16 March 1981.

On the eve of the trial, Azadovsky was dealt yet another blow: his lawyer, Kheifets, had refused to represent him in court. This development was both unexpected and baffling. Regardless of Kheifets's motivation, the very fact of his refusal would count as a strike against Azadovsky. Because it followed so closely on the heels of Azadovsky's denial of wrongdoing, it would look as if Kheifets had decided that his client's case was hopeless, that he was powerless in the face of such overwhelming evidence. This was all despite the fact that, according to Article 51 of the UPK, 'a lawyer may not refuse to defend an accused person who has been taken on as that lawyer's client'.

In fact, what had happened was this: upon returning from Kresty, Kheifets had asked Zigrida Vanag, who had hired Kheifets on Azadovsky's behalf, to come down to his office. When she arrived, he informed her that he would be stepping down from the case. He told her that it smacked of KGB involvement and that the police were barely involved. Taken aback, Vanag tried to persuade him to stand by his client, but Kheifets firmly replied that he could not and would not do so. To add insult to injury, the law office refused to refund the fee Vanag had paid in advance to secure Kheifets's services.

Vanag found Azadovsky another lawyer: Savely Ryazanovsky (b. 1925). Another well-known Leningrad lawyer, Ryazanovsky would later be named to the Presidium of the Saint Petersburg Lawyers' Collegium, and, like Kheifets, awarded a Fyodor Plevako gold medal.

Ryazanovsky visited Kresty the day before Azadovsky's trial was scheduled to begin. He introduced himself to his client and explained that Kheifets had refused to represent him. Then they discussed the details of the upcoming trial. Like Kheifets, Ryazanovsky wasn't particularly forthcoming: he did, however, tell Azadovsky about a letter written on his behalf by prominent Slavonicist Mikhail Alekseev. He said that he saw nothing unlawful about Azadovsky's actions, that the investigation had been biased and that he would make this fact the cornerstone of Azadovsky's defence. This gave Azadovsky a glimmer of hope.

3.5 Lepilina's trial

Lepilina's trial took place on 19 February 1981.

As in Azadovsky's case, the investigative team had decided to supplement the evidence it had against her. During a search of Lepilina's room on 20 December, 'Traces of a reddish-brown substance were discovered in the pocket of a jacket belonging to [Lepilina]. These traces were later sent for laboratory analysis and found to be narcotics.' The total weight of these 'traces' was 0.06 grams. This evidence was clearly meant to show that the four grams of hashish seized upon Lepilina's detention was part of a larger pattern.

Investigator Kamenko also made sure to obtain a negative character reference for Lepilina; such references sometimes played a decisive role in sentencing. In a document dated 27 January 1981, an employee from the Office of Housing Operations wrote (as it later turned out, from dictation):

> [Lepilina] occupies three rooms of a four-room [communal] flat. Complaints have been made about Lepilina's domestic behaviour to the local police inspector. For a long time, she did not work. She has brought strangers to the flat and held orgies there that lasted until morning. She has bothered other building residents. She has not been tried in a Comrades' Court.

Prior to her trial, Lepilina was presented with her indictment and permitted to review the case against her. In his zeal, Kamenko had escalated the charges against her: instead of charging Lepilina under Article 224-3 ('unlawful acquisition and possession of narcotic substances without intent to sell'), he had interpreted her 'crimes' as occurring on separate occasions, allowing him to charge her under Article 224-4. Thus, instead of a maximum of three years' incarceration in a corrective labour colony, she was facing up to five.

Like Kheifets and Ryazanovsky, Lepilina's lawyer, Ilya Breiman (1929–83), was a well-known attorney hired by Lepilina's friends on her behalf. He had 'clearance' and had taken part in numerous political trials. His defence strategy was based on a fundamental tenet of Soviet (and Russian) justice: the admission of guilt. This method had its advantages, particularly if the defendant was already in custody awaiting trial. In the USSR, the assumption was that an innocent person could never be incarcerated, and so pretrial detention was considered additional evidence of a person's guilt. Therefore, those willing to confess were shown greater leniency than those who stubbornly refused to 'admit what they had done'.

Lepilina, however, had not yet admitted any kind of guilt. Meanwhile, the evidence against her consisted of only two items: the drugs found in the foil packet and the 'traces' discovered in her jacket pocket. However, the packet hadn't been dusted for fingerprints, and, what's more, both the seizure of the contents of Lepilina's jacket pockets and the search of her rooms on 20 December had been carried out in violation of the UPK: neither Lepilina nor a representative from the Office of Housing Operations had been present. It also emerged that Tkachyova, Lepilina's flatmate and the mother of A. Tkachyov, had participated in the search. Not only did she act as a search witness, but, with the police's permission, she claimed some of Lepilina's things as her own. Several years later, this would become a serious point of contention.

Tkachyova had once thought highly of Lepilina; for years, she had even tried to set her up with her son. Her behaviour during the investigation can best be explained by the following circumstance. At the time, Article 306-5 of the RSFSR Civil Code decreed:

> In the case of a conviction carrying a sentence of more than six months' incarceration or exile within or outside the Soviet Union, if the convicted person has no family members currently residing in their living quarters, the residential lease agreement is considered invalid from the moment the sentence comes into force.

In other words, a sentence of more than six months would mean that Lepilina was out on her ear. In that case, Tkachyova would have legal grounds to lay claim to the other three rooms of the four-room flat. Lepilina's cellmates explained this to her. They also informed her that, in addition to her housing, Lepilina stood to lose her *propiska*, the document that granted her the right to live in Leningrad.

Up to this point, Lepilina had been planning to maintain her innocence during the trial. But then her case was taken over by Breiman, whose professional style was described by Vladimir Bukovsky thus:

A lawyer can only help [their client] in criminal cases. In political cases, as a rule, the lawyer is there to help the KGB. They have been assigned by [the KGB], or, in official terms, 'allowed' by them. And if the investigative team, the snitches within the accused person's cell, the witnesses and the accused's own ignorance of the law aren't enough to get Citizen X to confess, that's where the lawyer comes in. They'll use examples not only from law-books, but from their own personal experience to show that sincere repentance will act as a mitigating circumstance.

And that is exactly what happened. First, Breiman dismissed Lepilina's desire to take responsibility for the narcotics that were being pinned on Azadovsky. Knowing perfectly well who and what stood behind this case, Breiman spoke of Azadovsky with annoyance, claiming that he had dragged Lepilina into this mess. Then, he explained to her in no uncertain terms that denying her guilt wouldn't do her any good: not only would the court not believe her, but they might insist on trying her not under Article 224-4 ('repeated possession'), but under Article 224-1 ('with intent to sell or sale'). This was a serious crime: it carried a maximum sentence of up to ten years' incarceration.

If Lepilina were to 'do the right thing', which is, to say, confess to the possession of narcotics for personal use, then it would be easier for Breiman to defend her, or at least to get some of the charges against her thrown out: after all, the traces of drugs found in her jacket had been obtained through a serious violation of the UPK. If that evidence were deemed inadmissible, the charges against Lepilina would fall under Article 224-3, which carried a maximum sentence of up to three years. Because this was her first offence, if she confessed her guilt, she would be given either a suspended sentence or the minimum sentence permitted by law, in which case she would be eligible to apply for parole in several months' time. It was also possible that she might receive a very light sentence indeed: up to one year of community service.

And so Lepilina confessed her guilt under Article 224, paragraph 3 of the RSFSR Criminal Code. In 1988, during Azadovsky's retrial, Lepilina testified:

> When Breiman came to the closing of the case against me, I seized onto him like a drowning man clutches at straws. I trusted in him completely, and while he was preparing me for the trial, he said: 'There's nothing for it, you'll have to confess your guilt. There's nothing you can do to help Azadovsky anyway; his case is being handled by the KGB, so his number is up.' Breiman told me that if I confessed my guilt, then maybe 'I would get six months and I could keep my flat,' and so I confessed my guilt in court. The testimony I gave in court was a false confession; incidentally, given the condition I was in at the time, I would have confessed to anything, signed anything. In that moment, I began to feel profound indifference towards everything that was going on.

It should be noted that, within the context of the Soviet judicial system, Breiman was absolutely right. Their line of defence worked: Lepilina managed to avoid the maximum sentence. Breiman's skilful exposure of the investigation's glaring procedural violations led to a modification of the charges Lepilina faced; the court was even moved to issue a special ruling on the investigative team. In later years, Lepilina characterized Breiman as someone who understood that she was innocent and sympathized with her plight. He was, however, powerless to change the overall course of events.

Lepilina's trial was presided over by People's Judge V.V. Lokhov; the prosecutor was V.A. Pozen. The judgement, which was issued on 19 February 1981, reads as follows:

> The court has examined the case against Svetlana Ivanovna Lepilina (born 16.02.1946, from Bryansk, of Russian ethnicity, not a party member, with secondary-level education, a widow, no children, worked as a typist at the S.M. Kirov Palace of Culture in Leningrad, resides in Leningrad, 13 Zhelyabov Street, flat 60, no prior convictions, in custody since 18.12.80) for committing a crime under Article 224, paragraph 4 of the RSFSR Criminal Code, and it has
>
> ESTABLISHED
>
> Lepilina's guilt in the unlawful acquisition and possession of a narcotic substance without intent to sell.
>
> ... In addition to Lepilina's own confession, the following evidence was used in establishing Lepilina's guilt: 1) the testimony of witnesses O.A. Petrov and L.V. Mikhailova, who participated in Lepilina's detention on 18.12.80 at around 18.20 in the courtyard of 10 Vosstaniya Street, Leningrad ... 2) materials from Lepilina's case file: the report recording Lepilina's detention and the seizure of a narcotic substance from her; the results of the forensic chemical examination; and an expert report attesting to the fact that the substance seized upon Lepilina's detention was a homemade narcotic substance.
>
> ... The court has stricken the charges against Lepilina related to the acquisition and possession of 0.06 grams of a narcotic substance and tried her under article 224-3 rather than 224-4 for the following reason: the investigative team has not presented, and the court has not received, evidence of Lepilina's guilt in that episode. Lepilina herself has declared that she has no explanation whatsoever for how 0.06 grams of a narcotic substance came to be found in the pocket of her jacket and that she can only guess as to how this occurred. The 0.06 grams of narcotics found in Lepilina's jacket pocket clearly indicates that the pocket once contained a larger amount of the narcotic substance that was suitable for use; the quantity that was found was small and the form in which it was found would not have been suitable for use. Furthermore, the court is mindful of the fact that the warrant used to search Lepilina's place of residence renders the evidence discovered in that search inadmissible, as the document does not comply with legal requirements and the search was carried out in violation of the requirements laid out in the RSFSR UPK for such a document.
>
> In determining Lepilina's sentence, the court has taken into account the nature of her crime and the level of public danger that it poses, as well as information regarding her character. Considering the considerable public danger posed by Lepilina's crime, the negative character reference provided by her place of residence and the compromising information contained in the reference issued by Lepilina's workplace, the court finds it necessary to sentence Lepilina

to incarceration, though not for the maximum period allowable by law, as the court finds it possible to take into account the fact that Lepilina has not previously been charged with any criminal offence, that she has confessed to her actions and that the character reference from her workplace was, for the most part, positive.

Taking into consideration both the nature of Lepilina's offence and the information provided about her character, the court does not find it possible to charge her under Article 224-2 of the RSFSR Criminal Code. In accordance with Articles 300–303 of the RSFSR UPK, the court

FINDS:

Svetlana Ivanovna Lepilina guilty under Article 224, paragraph 3 of the RSFSR Criminal Code and sentences her under the same article to incarceration for a period of ONE year, SIX months, to be served in a minimum-security corrective labour colony. Lepilina's sentence will be considered to have started on 18 December 1980. Lepilina is to remain in custody as per her pretrial restrictions.

However, this judgement fails to provide a full picture of the court proceedings. For example, it omits the fact that the account given by Vladimir Matnyak, the officer who detained Lepilina, was contradicted by witness testimony. In his first report, Matnyak recorded that he 'saw a woman walking down the street quickly, looking over her shoulder, visibly nervous, and that seemed suspicious to me'. However, the statements made by O.A. Petrov and L.V. Mikhailova on the day of Lepilina's detention tell a very different story. Their testimony was read aloud in the courtroom:

Witness Petrov: On 18 December 1980, as part of the city Komsomol operative detachment [a youth affiliate of the *druzhina* – S.V.], I participated in a raid of known gathering places for drug users in central Leningrad. At around 18:20, Inspector Matnyak of the Fifteenth Department of the Leningrad Oblast UUR GUVD, with whom we were conducting the raid, asked me and L.V. Mikhailova, another member of the city operative detachment, to help him detain a female citizen, whom he would point out. In the courtyard of 10 Vosstaniya Street (by the door), we detained a female citizen wearing a short fur coat, dark trousers and a light knitted hat, who later turned out to be S.I. Lepilina.

Witness Mikhailova: On 18 December 1980, as part of the city Komsomol operative detachment, I participated in a raid of known gathering places for drug users in the neighbourhood around Moskovsky Railway Station. At approximately 18:20, Inspector Matnyak of the Fifteenth Department of the Leningrad Oblast UUR GUVD, with whom we were conducting the raid, asked us (I was with citizen O.A. Petrov, another member of the operative detachment) to aid in the detention of a female citizen in the courtyard of 10 Vosstaniya Street by the door, which she was preparing to enter. We detained a female citizen dressed in a white knitted hat, a short fur coat and dark trousers, who as it turned out, was citizen Lepilina.

This testimony seriously undermined the version of events put forth by Matnyak and Artsibushev, who insisted that Lepilina's detention hadn't been premeditated. This glaring inconsistency would have been obvious to everyone in the courtroom, including the judge, Lokhov. However, since Lepilina had already confessed, Lokhov chose to gloss over this contradiction. As Breiman had predicted, he changed the paragraph under which Lepilina was charged and let her off with a relatively light sentence. Given the circumstances, Lepilina (along with everyone else) felt that it could have been worse: her sentence was only half of what Artsibushev had predicted on the day of her detention.

Lepilina and Azadovsky's friends were in attendance at the trial. As she was being led out of the courtroom, Lepilina told them: 'Don't believe anything that happens here.'

That same month, a release about the court proceedings was published in samizdat. It ends with the following plea: 'S.I.L still has the chance to appeal to the City Court. Naturally, any kind of publicity around her situation might affect the City Court's decision.' The hope that publicity might help Lepilina's case was, of course, naïve. At that time, statistically speaking, the probability of a ruling being altered on appeal was about 1 per cent. Despite this fact, after consulting with Breiman, Lepilina applied for resentencing; predictably, the sentence was upheld by the Collegium on Criminal Proceedings of the Leningrad City Court.

The judgement came into effect, and Svetlana Ivanovna Lepilina was transported to minimum-security corrective colony US 20/2 in the town of Ulyanovka in the Tosnensky District of Leningrad Oblast.

4

The three pillars of accusation

Azadovsky spent 5 March 1981 in Kresty, reviewing the case against him. He learned that the investigation had ended on 12 February, which made him wonder: What had they been doing for the past three weeks? Even more shocking were the documents appended to his file: their contents took his breath away.

Azadovsky's character was to be assessed using three main documents: 1) the expert report on the books seized from Azadovsky's flat; 2) a typescript of an article from *Leningrad Pravda*; and 3) the character reference issued by Azadovsky's workplace.

4.1 The censors' findings

The expert analysis issued by the Leningrad Oblast Directorate for the Protection of State Secrets in the Press (Lenoblgorlit, or Gorlit) gives an ideological appraisal of the books seized from Azadovsky's flat. It was dated 22 December 1980 and signed by the directorate chief, Boris Markov (1915–2006).

Gorlit's primary mission was to screen books, journals and newspapers before they were sent to the printers, with the aim of preventing ideologically 'dangerous' or 'harmful' materials from appearing in print. However, they also provided expert analysis of seized works.[1] As a rule, such reports were commissioned by the KGB; these documents were in particularly high demand during the 1970s. The requests would arrive along with the materials for evaluation, and would typically indicate only the quantity of items that had been sent and the number of the criminal case to which they corresponded. Though this process was anonymous – the censor wouldn't know who the materials belonged to – the very fact of the request, and the fact that it was coming from the KGB, meant that the censor had little choice but to furnish a report condemning the materials. The KGB invariably got the answer it was looking for.

The materials seized from Azadovsky's flat on 19 December 1980 were sent for expert analysis that same evening. By 22 December, Gorlit had issued its findings, which were marked 'For Official Use Only'. The report contained the following entries:

1) Photograph of an unknown image with politically harmful content; the image shows fascist leaders, the anti-Soviet dissident Solzhenitsyn, and other despicable figures. Unfit for publication and dissemination in the USSR.

2) Italian-language album titled *Capolavori dell'arte*, which contains lewd sketches and drawings. Unfit for import and dissemination in the USSR.
3) *Tsvetaeva*, a photobiography. Printed by the anti-Soviet publishing house Ardis in 1980; contains photographs of the authors [Nikolay] Gumilyov, who was executed for his participation in a White conspiracy in Kronstadt, and [Vladislav] Khodasevich, who emigrated from the USSR and engaged in anti-Soviet activities abroad. The introduction to this album, written by Carl R. Proffer, is full of libellous inventions regarding Tsvetaeva's fate and the reasons for her death after returning to the Soviet Union. The album contains commentary written by the malicious anti-Soviet traitors Vladimir Nabokov and Nadezhda Mandelstam. Unfit for publication and dissemination in the USSR.
4) *My Home is Language*, a book by Igor Burikhin. Printed by the French anti-Soviet publishing house Third Wave in 1978. Contains poetry with religious propaganda. The introduction to this volume contains malicious attacks on the KGB. Not published in the Soviet Union, unfit for publication and dissemination.
5) *Before the Sunrise*, a book by Mikhail Zoshchenko. Printed by the anti-Soviet publishing house Inter-language Literary Associates (USA-West Germany) in 1967. An abridged version of this work was printed in the journal *October* in 1948. The current version has not been published in the Soviet Union; it is unfit for publication and dissemination. The book also contains an advertisement for books by the malicious anti-Soviet authors Abdurakhman Avtorkhanov, Raymond Aron, Joseph Brodsky, Nikolay Berdyaev, Gleb Struve and others.
6) German-language pamphlet titled 'Sammlung Luchterhand', published in West Germany. Advertises books by anti-Soviet authors Alexander Solzhenitsyn and György Lukács. Unfit for import and dissemination in the USSR.
7) German-language pamphlet titled 'Reihe Hanser', published in West Germany. Advertises books by Mao. Unfit for import and dissemination in the USSR.
8) *The Salt Barn*, a book by Boris Pilnyak. Printed in the United States, undated. Chapters of this novel were published in the USSR in the journal *Moscow*, issue no. 5, 1964. The book's cover cites an item from *The New York Times* that gives a biased account of Pilnyak's life and works. Unfit for import and dissemination in the USSR.
9) German-language copy of *Wir* (*We*) by Yevgeny Zamyatin, published in West Germany, 1975. The novel *We* is a malicious tract against the Soviet state. Not published in the USSR. Unfit for import and dissemination.
10) *Letters to Berberova and Khodasevich*, a book by the anti-Soviet émigré Zinaida Gippius. Printed by the anti-Soviet publishing house Ardis in 1978. Not published in the USSR. Unfit for import and dissemination.

The censorship issued this report, and the investigator included it in Azadovsky's criminal case. However, there was no record of who commissioned the report, and so it was hard to say how it came about. This was a clear violation of Article 184 of the UPK, which decreed, 'Having deemed expert analysis to be necessary, the investigator must write a statement containing: the reason why the expert analysis has been commissioned, the surname of the expert or the name of the organization conducting the analysis, the questions that have been put to the expert and the materials that have been provided for analysis.'

Azadovsky's case file contained no such information. However, it did contain a revealing document composed by Lieutenant Kamenko on 12 February 1981:

> On 19 December 1980, various foreign publications of an anti-Soviet character were discovered and seized during a search of citizen Azadovsky's flat (10 Vosstaniya Street, flat 51). These malicious tracts against the Soviet state contained libellous inventions against the Soviet state and were unfit for import and dissemination in the Soviet Union.
>
> Given that the investigation has not established any incidents in which Azadovsky distributed these materials, and that the acquisition and possession of such publications does not constitute a crime, in accordance with p. 2, Article 5 of the RSFSR UPK, it has been
>
> RESOLVED
>
> not to charge Konstantin Markovich Azadovsky under Article 70 of the RSFSR Criminal Code.

4.2 Adventures over the abyss

The next document was meant to prove that the drugs found in Azadovsky's flat were not part of an isolated incident. As the guidance for investigators first issued in 1971 suggests, 'Information regarding the accused's past life and activities is essential to gaining a full understanding of them as a member of society.' This advice explains how Azadovsky's case file came to include the typescript of an article from *Leningrad Pravda* titled '"Intellectual Adventures" . . . over the Abyss' by I. Ivanov. Again, no explanation was provided for the article's presence in the case file; no one signed off on it and no one confirmed the veracity of its contents.

It was a long article about the Slavinsky trial that had been written in 1969, shortly after the judgement was announced. Its most relevant sections are reproduced in the following text:

> As previously reported in the press (*Evening Leningrad*, 5 June 1969), in early June UVD representatives detained Yefim Slavinsky, a person of no fixed occupation who hosted gatherings of young people in his flat for the purpose of using narcotics . . .
>
> As part of the investigation, UVD operatives questioned William Chalsma, a professor at Ohio State University (USA) who was in Leningrad on a research trip. Two other Americans, Professor Anthony Phillips of Columbia University and Professor George Gibian of Cornell University, were also implicated in this affair, but they managed to leave Leningrad before the investigation started. These individuals have been declared *personae non gratae* in the Soviet Union . . .

K. Azadovsky, a postgraduate student at the Pedagogical Institute, and Anthony Phillips, an American, were out for a springtime stroll on Vasilyevsky Island [part of Leningrad]. They wanted to have a heart-to-heart chat, but there was no place to do it: Azadovsky lived with his mother, who would only get in the way. At that point, Azadovsky suggested looking in on an acquaintance, a 'true member of the Russian intelligentsia'. What happened next is recorded in Slavinsky's testimony: 'When Azadovsky brought Phillips to my flat, he produced two large marijuana tablets and three small ones. Phillips gave me one of the large tablets, as well as the three small ones. He didn't ask me for any money. Phillips apparently gave the other large tablet to Azadovsky. I didn't see this myself, but Azadovsky told me that Phillips had given him a mescaline tablet.'

... Not content to write this story based on secondhand accounts, the author of this article spent nearly three hours talking to Slavinsky face to face in his prison cell, hoping to discern at least a spark of intellect within him. There was none. In his student days, Slavinsky had shown a modest talent for languages. His is extraordinarily well read. But he is shockingly spineless and lacking in willpower. Everything he says is taken from books, articles and pamphlets. Even when he tells stories from his own life in an attempt to justify his criminal activities, he is entirely incapable of exercising independent thought ...

Apparently, the people who were drawn into Slavinsky's illicit gatherings didn't realize they were walking on the edge of an abyss. In the wake of Slavinsky's arrest, panic spread through this community of 'intellectual risk-takers'. They naively admonished one another: 'Keep quiet! Don't tell the investigators anything! Stay strong!' But they told the UVD investigators everything they knew, mercilessly condemning and abusing one another ...

Many of them had cherished ambitions of 'making it' in academia, and were even close to receiving their doctorates. But now they are gripped with fear: institutions might refuse to hire candidates who have sullied themselves by associating with drug users. . . . The court did not make any special rulings in this case. Nevertheless, the institutions where these people studied and the establishments and organizations where they currently work must draw their own conclusions.

This article made a profound impression on Azadovsky. He knew for a fact that it had never been published – so how had it ended up in the criminal case against him?

At this point, a few words must be said regarding this article's authenticity. After Azadovsky's trial, some claimed that it was a fabrication cooked up by the Leningrad KGB. However, there is nothing to suggest it isn't genuine. Before his death in London in 2019, Slavinsky himself confirmed the article's authenticity in an interview with the author of this book. He explained that a person claiming to be a journalist had come to visit him in Kresty while he was waiting for the result of his appeal, and that they had had a lengthy conversation. Though it is possible that this person was, in fact, a journalist, his intimate knowledge of Slavinsky's case suggested that he had other professional responsibilities as well.

This article paints Azadovsky in a particularly dire light: he is portrayed as being far worse than Slavinsky's other 'morally bankrupt' friends. This is because Azadovsky, unlike the others, had refused to testify against Slavinsky.

It is important to note that, in 1969, drug use was not yet a criminal offence. Even if Azadovsky or the other witnesses had confessed to smoking hashish in Slavinsky's flat, they wouldn't have been treated as accessories to their friend's crime. However, from the very beginning, Azadovsky rebuffed the investigative team's attempts to get him to give incriminating testimony. This defiant stance was probably the source of the authorities' grudge against him. It is also worth pointing out that this article mischaracterizes Slavinsky's friends' behaviour: in fact, many of them acted with great decency and resolve. As a result, several of those involved were unable to find work in academia for a number of years; others emigrated from the USSR.

Another striking aspect of this story is its blatant vilification of the American professors involved. The reference to the fact that these professors had been declared '*personae non gratae*' has another, deeper meaning. Readers are meant to draw the obvious conclusion that these so-called scholars were actually CIA agents and that Slavinsky and Azadovsky's relationship with the Americans was a serious black mark against them.

The article's conclusion is clearly a swipe at Azadovsky: at that point, he was the only one of Slavinsky's close friends to be interested in an academic career. The statement 'But now they are gripped with fear: institutions might refuse to hire candidates who have sullied themselves by associating with drug users' suggests that the journalist might have known that Azadovsky was about to be expelled from postgraduate studies.

So why wasn't the article published that autumn?

Azadovsky was expelled in early September, so by the time it would have appeared in *Leningrad Pravda*, there wouldn't have been any point. More importantly, the publication of such an article would have represented a marked departure from official Soviet doctrine, which held that drug addiction did not and could not exist in a truly socialist country (which explains why, for such a long time, drug use wasn't punished under Soviet law). Geopolitical considerations would also have come into play: a new official policy had just been announced, one aimed at easing international tensions. In that moment, it would have been inappropriate to whip up anti-American sentiment. Moreover, the article presented Soviet youth in a negative light: it suggested that they were all too susceptible to drug use and liberal conversations.

Two questions naturally arise. First, who was the author of this article? The use of such an obvious pseudonym ('I. Ivanov' is the Russian equivalent of 'John Smith') suggests that the article might have been commissioned by the KGB. And the second, more important question is: Where had this article been for the past decade? One thing is for certain: it couldn't have been included in the criminal case against Slavinsky because it hadn't been written yet. Slavinsky himself only learned of its contents many years later, when he met Azadovsky in London. There is only one reasonable explanation: the article had been stored in the bowels of the KGB for over a decade, probably in Azadovsky's operational development file (DOR), and had resurfaced when they decided to press criminal charges against him.

4.3 The character reference

The third document to be examined in this chapter is the character reference issued by Azadovsky's workplace. First, it is worth saying a few words about the Soviet character reference as a genre. A workplace character reference couldn't be written by an individual; rather, it was composed via a special procedure. As a rule, references were written collectively and then discussed and voted on at trade union or party meetings. In other words, the entire collective was responsible for them. Practically speaking, this meant that an arrested person had very little chance of receiving a positive workplace character reference. And indeed, Investigator Kamenko had no trouble securing the kind of reference he needed to support the prosecution's case.

For five years, Azadovsky had served as head of the department of foreign languages at the Vera Mukhina Higher School of Art and Industry, where he taught German and English. When he first read his character reference, signed by the Higher School's rector, V.I. Shistko, its trade union leader, L.N. Babushkina, and its party organizer, V.Ia. Bobov, Azadovsky was stunned:

CHARACTER REFERENCE

K.M. Azadovsky has been employed at the Leningrad Vera Mukhina Higher School of Art and Industry as head of the department of foreign languages since October 1975. Since that time, K.M. Azadovsky has devoted a significant amount of time to artistic and scholarly tasks that are directly related to his doctoral thesis. He has not shown particular depth or initiative in his capacity as department head. Student performance in the department of foreign languages has not improved in this time. The department's level of ideological instruction is inadequate. In the permissive atmosphere cultivated by Azadovsky, there have been incidents of drunkenness and breaches of workplace discipline among the department's faculty members . . .

When it reviewed Azadovsky's application to be considered for the position of head of the department of foreign languages, the School's administration did not have at its disposal the facts and materials necessary to form a detailed picture of K.M. Azadovsky's character. However, the records currently in the administration's possession . . . testify to Azadovsky's lack of moral fibre. He often engages in drunken or debauched behaviour and forms casual acquaintanceships with foreigners. Azadovsky's behaviour has been discussed by the School's administration and the Party, but attempts to improve his moral character have not yielded the desired results.

Recognizing that Azadovsky's character went beyond the bounds of 'normal' disorderly conduct, the School's administration kept a close watch on Azadovsky's 'other side'. In an attempt to limit his undesirable influence on the staff, Azadovsky was put in a position that did not afford him the opportunity to propagate his views. Though a satisfactory report on Azadovsky's work was drafted by the institution's academic council in 1980, K.M. Azadovsky was not considered for another term as department head.

As Azadovsky demonstrated a few years later in court, this report was nothing but a pack of lies. And now it would be read out at his trial! Azadovsky couldn't understand how his colleagues could have signed their names to such a document. After all, only a year before, the School had written him a glowing character reference:

> [Azadovsky] has proved himself to be a capable young administrator who performs his official duties with great diligence. K.M. Azadovsky engages in significant research and often weighs in on questions of philology and literary history in print. He is respected by the staff. He is principled and of good moral character. He is politically literate.

Furthermore, the administration had already approved Azadovsky's reappointment for another five-year term. On 8 September 1980, his review was unanimously approved at a meeting of the School Council, and on 3 November 1980 his candidacy was unanimously approved by the School's search committee. However, the School was preparing for a change of rector, and so the schedule for Azadovsky's reappointment was never confirmed. And so, the question of Azadovsky's reappointment remained unresolved until the end of 1980, when Azadovsky found himself under arrest.

Azadovsky didn't find a single positive remark about himself or his work in the entire case file, despite its formidable length; it did, however, contain at least three seriously damning documents. They didn't prove his guilt under Article 224: the only direct evidence the investigators had on that count were the packet 'found' among his books, the traces of drugs 'found' in the pockets of his jacket and the laboratory analysis of these substances. But the aforementioned documents showed that Azadovsky was guilty of something far graver: possession of anti-Soviet books, involvement in the Slavinsky Affair and a general lack of moral fibre.

The criminal case against Azadovsky was loaded with materials that would have been better suited to Articles 70 or 190-1, which dealt with political crimes. Politically charged cases like this one often proceeded according to a pattern Bukovsky describes as follows:

> A political investigation isn't meant to solve a crime; it is meant, first and foremost, to gather compromising materials. Its mission is to explain how Citizen N, a seemingly Soviet person, who has been raised in a Soviet family and educated by the Soviet school system, has suddenly turned out to be so un-Soviet.

Azadovsky's investigation succeeded in this mission. It didn't matter whether the evidence was relevant to the crime he was charged with. The investigation had proved something more vital: Azadovsky's moral depravity, the corruption of his character, his alienation from the Soviet way of life, his incompatibility with Soviet society. Azadovsky might have been charged with anything: possession of narcotics, speculation or parasitism. It was all the same. The Soviet court of public opinion had no choice but to return a guilty verdict to protect society from the influence of this pariah.

5

Ex ungue leonem

After reviewing the case against him, Azadovsky was convinced that his investigation was not being run by the police. That is to say, the police may have been nominally in charge, but a more powerful agency was clearly pulling the strings.

In those years, the KGB's influence over the country's civic life was so pervasive and its reputation (rooted in the mass repressions of the 1930s) was so terrifying that people would have suspected KGB involvement in Azadovsky's case even if they didn't have anything to do with it. This perception was deliberately cultivated by the agency itself, and it was deeply ingrained in the mind of the average Soviet citizen.

Therefore, it is important to establish whether Azadovsky had legitimate grounds to believe that the KGB was behind this case or whether he was simply gripped by the persecution mania that was so widespread within the Soviet academic community.

5.1 Traces of KGB involvement in the criminal case

It was generally difficult to prove KGB involvement in a case because, as a rule, they didn't leave any evidence behind. This was particularly true of cases that were ostensibly being run by the police: no materials directly linked to the KGB were to be included in their files. This rule appears in a lengthy classified document titled 'Instructions on KGB Record-keeping Related to Criminal Cases and Individuals Charged with Crimes, Issued by the Council of Ministers of the USSR', which was approved by Yury Andropov on 9 August 1977; it is the only part of the text that appears in bold.

However, Azadovsky's criminal case file did contain a document indicating KGB involvement: the resolution issued by Kamenko on 12 February 1981 on the decision not to initiate criminal proceedings against Azadovsky under Article 70 of the Criminal Code. Avoiding such charges might seem like a good thing, especially since the article in question refers to 'especially dangerous crimes against the state' and carries penalties of up to seven years' incarceration. But the fact that this document appeared in Azadovsky's case file is telling: it shows that the case had been categorized as political. Any Soviet judge or prosecutor would have recognized this as a sign that the defendant wasn't to be shown any leniency.

The question arises: How had this document come to be included in Azadovsky's file in the first place? Article 70 dealt with the following activities:

Agitation or propaganda carried out with the aim of subverting or weakening Soviet power; the commission of separate, especially dangerous crimes against the state; the dissemination of slanderous inventions against the Soviet political and social system with that same aim; as well as the dissemination, production, or possession of such literature with that same aim.

Such crimes didn't fall under police jurisdiction: any criminal proceedings initiated under Article 70 were to be administered by the appropriate territorial arm of the KGB's Investigation Department. The resolution clearly indicates that the KGB considered – and rejected – the option of charging Azadovsky under Article 70 in connection with the books that had been found in his flat. This decision was probably taken due to a lack of evidence. Filipp Bobkov, chief of the KGB's Fifth Directorate (which dealt with 'ideological sabotage'), writes about the major changes that took place within the agency's territorial directorates in 1967, when Yury Andropov became KGB chairman:

> Andropov limited certain powers held by local leaders. In particular, this affected their ability to charge individuals under Article 70 of the RSFSR Criminal Code (anti-Soviet agitation and propaganda). Such a decision could only be taken with the Centre's approval. The accused's guilt had to be proved with hard evidence and documentary proof. Witness testimony and confessions on the part of the accused would only be considered as an explanation of [the accused's] actions.

This explains why, after receiving Gorlit's report on 22 December, the investigators spent a month and a half considering their next move. In all likelihood, the Fifth Directorate's Moscow leadership had reviewed the materials against Azadovsky and refused to sanction the police to charge him with a political crime; it is also possible that the Leningrad KGB, knowing how the centre was likely to proceed, had decided to refuse permission on its own.

However, the spooks left behind unintentional traces of their work. Upon careful examination, the censorship report from Gorlit reveals an unusual physical trait: on the first page of the document, in the upper right-hand corner, something has been stricken out using a razorblade and rubber. But because typewriters leave deep imprints (unlike, say, modern laser printers), it is possible to discern the two lines that the investigative team clumsily attempted to erase: 'Leningrad Oblast | Directorate of the USSR KGB'.

It is hard to say whether, at the time, Azadovsky would have preferred to be charged with a political offence or a criminal one. A narcotics charge would destroy his reputation; it would mark him as a common criminal. Being found guilty of a political offence would make him a criminal, too, but of a different kind. For Azadovsky, a Leningrad academic and a pedigreed member of the intelligentsia, it would be psychologically easier to be branded a political prisoner than a drug user.

Article 190-1 ('systematic circulation...of false statements which defame the Soviet state or social system') carried the same maximum sentence as the article under which Azadovsky was being charged: up to three years' incarceration. It was also an article that could be applied to practically any Soviet citizen: all the prosecutor needed was a single overheard conversation or undesirable anecdote. Why, then, had they chosen to prosecute Azadovsky for narcotics? They could have got him under Article 190-1 just as easily. Azadovsky couldn't understand.

But then the pieces started coming together in his mind. He remembered how, in autumn 1980, he had constantly felt like he was being watched, how he had lived in fear of raids. He thought about how long his reappointment as department head dragged on, how he hadn't been admitted to the Writers' Union. He came to see these 'coincidences' and bits of 'bad luck' in an entirely different light. He finally realized that a noose had been tightening around his neck throughout autumn 1980.

At the time, Azadovsky's friends had tried to reassure him, chalking his suspicions up to his innate mistrustfulness. As it turned out, however, Azadovsky was right: his suspicions proved to be justified.

5.2 Beyond the criminal case

In September 1980, Vladimir Shistko (whose signature was soon to appear on Azadovsky's character reference) approached Azadovsky in the corridor. Azadovsky was stunned to learn that Shistko had been approached by a KGB handler (every Soviet post-secondary institution had one). This person had insisted that Azadovsky was anti-Soviet, and that he had made anti-Soviet speeches in the presence of German tourists. He forcefully recommended that Azadovsky not be reappointed as department head. Shistko, however, was sympathetic to Azadovsky's plight, and so he offered him some advice: Azadovsky ought to join the Communist Party 'for immunity'. This wasn't the first time Azadovsky had received such a proposition, and he rebuffed it sharply. However, two weeks later, Azadovsky would come to appreciate the full weight of Shistko's words. An acquaintance of Azadovsky's, Natalya Isametdinova, called to ask if they could meet. When they were together, she tearfully recounted how she had been summoned from work to the local police station on 13 October 1980, several days prior. There, some people claiming to be from the Investigation Directorate had started interrogating her about 'Citizen Azadovsky', claiming that he was a covert enemy of the Soviet state. They broached the subject in a roundabout way, starting by announcing that Azadovsky's father had been an 'enemy of the people', 'part of a Zionist conspiracy who had been shot for his anti-Soviet activities'. They also said shocking things about Azadovsky himself: that he was a drug user, that he frequented illicit drug gatherings and, what's more, that he was a West German spy. They tried to get Isametdinova to confirm these 'facts'. When that didn't work, they attempted to force her into giving false testimony: they demanded that she write that she had entered into relations with Azadovsky while still a minor (this would have been a crime under Article 120: 'corruption of a minor'). Isametdinova refused. However, as she was leaving, the officers told her that 'Azadovsky is an enemy who should and shall be punished' and had her sign a non-disclosure agreement.

It is impossible to know who else might have been called in for similar conversations in autumn 1980. But in this case, the authorities had acted rashly. In their attempt to extract compromising materials on Azadovsky using threats, they had made the mistake of approaching someone who would tell him about it. But how many of Azadovsky's acquaintances might have signed such a document and never said a thing?

Later on, Azadovsky learned that the KGB continued its attempts to 'expose' him throughout the investigation. The agents involved were called Bezverkhov and Kuznetsov, and they worked for the Leningrad Oblast KGB. To this day, archival collections hold scraps of paper bearing their contact information: the agents gave these homemade business cards to people that they talked to in the hopes that they would call if they 'remembered' anything and decided to give testimony. Years later, Azadovsky would include copies of these 'business cards' in his petitions to the KGB. In a petition dated 1988, he wrote:

> In January 1981, one of the indicated operatives demanded (over the telephone) that Citizen M.G. Tsakadze, an actress working for Lenconcert, cut short her national tour and immediately return to Leningrad for the sole purpose of 'rewriting' the testimony she had given as part of the pretrial investigation for the Lepilina case. Bezverkhov and Kuznetsov spoke with Tsakadze on more than one occasion, bragging that the criminal case against us was only the beginning, that they were just giving the two of us (myself and Lepilina) a little 'scolding' 'for a start', etc.
>
> ... In January 1981, Bezverkhov and Kuznetsov went to see the widow of my acquaintance M.A. Baltsvinik, claiming that I was planning to sell the collection of photographs her late husband had left me to the West for fifty dollars, etc. The KGB agents' efforts to persuade [L.G.] Petrova into giving false testimony had only one aim: to 'prove' that I had contemplated a crime against the state.

Traces of KGB influence can also be seen in the rejection of Azadovsky's application to join the translation section of the Writers' Union. At the time, the selection process for this organization was extremely long and complicated, and it isn't hard to see why: union membership was seen as a mark of professional distinction, and being granted official status as a writer came with certain privileges. For one thing, it provided writers with a certain degree of immunity in case of conflict with a governmental institution. If Azadovsky had managed to join the Writers' Union, it would have created additional complications for the KGB: it was harder to neutralize a 'Soviet author' than a rank-and-file citizen.

In 1978, Azadovsky secured recommendations from three prominent writers (the scholar Dmitry Likhachyov, the translator Rita Rait-Kovalyova and the German professor Vladimir Admoni), and his application was approved by the translation section in the first round of the selection process. However, on 1 December 1980, the selection committee rejected Azadovsky's application: his bid for membership failed by a single vote. Apparently, the authorities' plan had already been set in motion.

In spring 1977, Lepilina received a call at work: 'This is a representative of the Leningrad KGB speaking. We need to see you today. We'll give you the details in person. Is the Summer Garden a convenient place for you to meet?' It wasn't, really, but it would have been handy for the agent: the Summer Garden wasn't far from the Big House. If they had called her into Leningrad's KGB headquarters, Lepilina might have been more suspicious and acted in a more guarded manner. The agent might have hoped that a meeting in the Summer Garden would throw her off her balance.

Lepilina arrived first; she was waiting for a couple of minutes before a man arrived and introduced himself. They entered the garden and slowly made their way along the Swan Canal. The conversation was light, with a hint of flirtation; the agent was polite. He delicately probed Lepilina about her past, about her deceased husband and, finally, about her relationship with Azadovsky.

Lepilina was frightened by the agent's intimate knowledge of her life. His questions became less innocuous. Was Lepilina sure that her friends could be trusted? Did she understand that the motherland might need her help someday? Did she know the ways in which Western intelligence agencies were working against the Soviet Union?

Lepilina asked the agent point-blank what he wanted from her. She wasn't involved in any objectionable activities, and she couldn't imagine why the KGB would take an interest in her. The agent acknowledged Lepilina's point, and even agreed with her. However, he explained that there were people in her circle who might slip up and do harm not only to themselves, but to the country, too; some of them had regular contact with foreigners and were thus at particular risk.

The agent invited Lepilina to meet him from time to time, to take a walk or go to a café. And perhaps, one day, he might ask her to tell him about someone in particular. Lepilina frankly replied that 'this offer wasn't for her' and that she 'wasn't the kind of person who could lead a double life, or who would want to'. Her answer was a firm no.

Upon parting, the agent asked Lepilina not to tell anyone about their conversation: 'It's important for your peace of mind as well.' A half hour later, she saw Azadovsky and told him everything.

In counter-intelligence terms, this meeting would be characterized as 'face-to-face contact with a recruitment target aimed at determining the candidate's fitness for intelligence work'. And on that beautiful spring day, the agent had learned that Lepilina was unfit for intelligence work. In all likelihood, that's exactly what the agent wrote in his report.

5.3 A mystery

But where had all this come from? Apart from having contact with foreigners, Azadovsky wasn't 'guilty' of anything. What's more, the foreigners with whom Azadovsky associated were mostly fellow philologists, specialists in Russian literature. Western journalists were extremely rare in Azadovsky's circle, and diplomats even more so. All the foreigners he knew had come to the USSR legally. They had received their visas through Soviet consulates and secured practical training placements in Moscow and Leningrad's universities and academic institutions in advance; they couldn't possibly pose a threat to the Soviet state. However, the security services suspected anyone studying Russian literature or the Russian language of working for Western intelligence; as a result, these agencies tried to monitor the contact these foreigners had with Soviet citizens.

This was probably what sparked the Leningrad KGB's interest in Azadovsky starting in the second half of the 1960s. At that point, he would have become a de facto 'contact of foreigners', as the KGB referred to Soviet citizens who 'have or have had contact with foreigners who have come to the Soviet Union from capitalist states'. The KGB was suspicious of practically anyone capable of forging ties with foreigners living in the USSR; philologists, who studied foreign languages and links between cultures, were considered particularly suspect.

Azadovsky wasn't aware of all this at the time – he couldn't have been. But as he groped for the true motivation behind his present misfortune, he became more and more convinced that it lay somewhere in his past. In his university years, he had worked as a guide and interpreter over the holidays. He was employed by the Sputnik Bureau of International Youth Tourism, an organization that had been founded in the late 1950s, during a period of thaw; it was the youth equivalent of Intourist. Though this job provided Azadovsky an excellent opportunity for language practice, it also required him to have contact with the KGB. In his journal from the 1960s, Alen Zhmaev writes:

> Morning found me on the workroom windowsill, in the shade of a geranium, in the company of a young woman from the German language department. We had had a real knees-up, but, as the miserly dawn approached, we sobered up along with it. My female companion had worked at Intourist for several years, and of course, I began enquiring about our attitudes towards foreigners. It was something I had wondered about for a long time, and this was my first opportunity to hear an answer straight from the horse's mouth.
>
> 'It's terrible!' she said. 'Simply terrible. Intourist is an official branch of the KGB. All of our guides are registered with them and we all sign documents saying that we'll report anything suspicious. Itineraries for foreigners are scheduled down to the minute. Say we're driving to a neighbouring city on a hot day and we pass a picturesque little village. If, for whatever reason, our guests want to stop, stretch their legs, lie on the grass, maybe drink a bit of milk, we, the guides are required to report in writing how long the coach was stopped for, who stepped away and for how long, whether additional questions were asked during the stop, etc. None of the visitors can be trusted: not the Communists, not the anti-Fascists. Maybe they're anti-Fascists where they come from, but here they're potential spies. We're required to catalogue everything about them: their questions, their observations, their interests, what they say about the places they're from – everything but their conversations about the weather and their admiration for Russian vodka.'

As an eighteen-year-old student signing up to work as a guide and interpreter for Sputnik in summer 1960, Azadovsky would have had only have a vague understanding of this situation. The Khrushchev Thaw had given Azadovsky's generation a relative sense of freedom and independence. Moreover, Sputnik was technically separate from Intourist. Azadovsky worked for Sputnik for two summers, once after his second year of university (1960) and once after his third (1961). Each stint lasted a little over a month. Azadovsky wasn't paid a salary, but he received free board and a per diem of several rubles.

It was in 1961 that he landed himself in hot water.

Finding himself at a southern resort with a group of West German tourists, Azadovsky allowed himself to relax, both literally and figuratively: he spent his days sunbathing and his evenings having heart-to-heart chats with the Germans. Soviet holidaymakers joined them for their lively evening meals. Various subjects would come up, and there were often debates about socialism and capitalism. In the heat of one such conversation, someone proposed a toast to capitalism. Azadovsky supported the toast and added something of his own. By the following morning, this incident had been reported to the appropriate quarters. As soon as Azadovsky arrived in Moscow with the tour group, one of Sputnik's directors called him into his office. The director informed Azadovsky of the report that had been made against him and announced that he was being dismissed. 'Why?' 'You have to be more careful what you say.'

Azadovsky found his own way back to Leningrad. Soon afterwards, he was called into the offices of Sputnik, where a man calling himself Nikolay Mikhailovich wanted to speak with him. After questioning Azadovsky about the incident at the resort, Nikolay Mikhailovich informed him in a gracious tone that the 'authorities' generally trusted him, and that they saw this offence as a mistake. He was invited to continue his work, but with Intourist rather than Sputnik.

The difference between working at Intourist and working at Sputnik was largely a matter of paperwork. All Intourist guides were required to submit reports after working with tour groups or individual tourists. It seems unlikely that all of them were under the KGB's thumb. Some were probably employed by the KGB as 'active reserve officers'; some, like Azadovsky, had yet to be recruited to the agent network; and some were only nominally connected with the security services.

Azadovsky began work at Intourist the following year, and the post came with a mountain of paperwork. He led tours for foreigners who had come to marvel at Leningrad's wonders. From time to time, the coordinator would call Azadovsky into his office to ask questions about one or another of the tourists. 'Did it seem like he knew Russian?' 'No, it didn't.' 'Did he try to wander away from the group?' 'No, he didn't.' And so on.

In summer 1962, Azadovsky was unexpectedly called in for a conversation with one of the heads of the Leningrad branch of Intourist. Azadovsky, he said, was now an adult (he was twenty years old at the time) and a citizen of the motherland. The world, he continued, was divided into two hostile camps, and every Soviet citizen was required to pick a side. He told Azadovsky that they trusted him, of course, but that this wasn't enough. He asked Azadovsky to confirm in writing that he, as an Intourist employee, would be willing to help the KGB. Naturally, this would only pertain to his work with foreigners: he wouldn't be asked to do anything else. There were several other people present at this meeting, one of whom was 'Nikolay Mikhailovich'.

This conversation contained no direct threats, only suggestions that it was 'important to think about the future'. He was also reminded of his membership in the

Young Communist League (Komsomol) and of the mistake he had made the previous year, which the KGB had been gracious enough to overlook. Bewildered, Azadovsky wrote down what was dictated to him.

After this incident, Azadovsky continued leading groups of German, Austrian and Swiss tourists through the city. He wrote reports after every assignment, just as before. Another summer passed. The work itself didn't change, and nobody bothered him.

But in autumn 1962, Intourist called him into their offices and began asking questions that had nothing at all to do with foreigners. They enquired about his Leningrad friends and acquaintances. He heaped lavish praise on everyone they asked about. The agents were clearly dissatisfied with his answers. They could tell that Azadovsky was dodging, that he was unwilling to cooperate.

As he left the building, Azadovsky finally realized that he had landed himself in trouble. He immediately informed the people he had been asked about that the KGB had taken an interest in them. He gradually came to the decision to leave Intourist to avoid further contact with the KGB. This was a considerable risk: he was in his fourth year of university, and he could have easily been expelled or drummed out of the Komsomol, which would have prevented him from enrolling in postgraduate studies or finding work in academia. To make matters worse, if he was expelled, he would be called up for military service.

But no one gave him any trouble. He and his mother moved to a new flat. He worked on his dissertation. For the first time, he began translating in earnest; he attended translation seminars at the Writers' Union. He had new teachers and new friends. He hoped that his unpleasant run-in with the authorities would simply be forgotten.

A few months later, however, they showed up in front of his building one morning. 'Nikolay Mikhailovich' approached him and asked him to get into a car. They drove to a building near Finlyandsky Railway Station and went up to a flat. There, two agents engaged Azadovsky in conversation. The tone was neither as calm nor as restrained as it had been a year earlier: they were clearly putting pressure on Azadovsky, making thinly veiled threats. The conversation lasted until nightfall; it seemed as if it would never end. Finally, both parties realized they would never come to an agreement. Azadovsky was deeply frustrated when he left. This feeling remained with him through the next day, and he relives it each time he passes by that building.

This feeling isn't difficult to understand. In those days, many young people (and not-so-young people) agreed to cooperate with the KGB. Whether or not this cooperation was voluntary, few found the inner strength and courage required to resist and break ties with it forever.

This conversation weighed on Azadovsky as he was writing his dissertation and later on when he was preparing for his state exams. He was afraid that they could come for him again; he would jump each time the telephone rang or whenever he saw a stranger standing underneath the archway of his building or at the door of his department. Right up until his graduation from Leningrad State University, he was waiting for the other shoe to drop.

'They let me finish university after all!' he thought to himself. Perhaps he had been lucky. Or perhaps KGB regulations had prevented the agency's operatives from dealing with him in such an obvious manner.

Over the years, this strange incident continued to haunt him. At first, he thought that there was nothing strange about it: he had been young, and they had wanted to feel him out or scare him. But in 1969, when his stubbornness during the Slavinsky trial brought misfortune down upon him, he remembered this incident. As Azadovsky lay in his prison cell, grimly reflecting on the direction his life had taken, he realized that this, too, was payback for his failure to cooperate.

6

Justice

On 10 March 1981, a surprise inspection took place in cell 447. A more cautious inmate might have acquiesced quietly, but Azadovsky reprimanded the guard. The guard said something to him, Azadovsky answered back, and, suddenly, he was struck hard in the head with the cell's metal door. Azadovsky received mild concussion and a nasty bruise; he was lucky to escape serious injury. He wrote petition after petition to the warden, requesting medical attention, a meeting with the prosecutor and that the abusive guard be brought to justice. He provided the names of his cellmates who had witnessed the incident and were willing to testify on his behalf. Finally, Azadovsky was taken to the infirmary, where the doctor diagnosed him with concussion and prescribed bed rest, along with a course of injections. Shortly afterwards, three days before his trial, Azadovsky was transferred to a different cell.

6.1 16 March 1981

For prisoners being held in pretrial detention, one's court date was (and still is) an incredibly trying experience. Russian professor and GULAG survivor Alfred Mirek (1922–2009) provides a vivid account of his own journey from the pretrial detention centre to the courthouse, which took place in 1985:

> Every morning except Saturdays and Sundays, between four and five in the morning, they would come around banging on the 'hatches'. The guard on duty would call out a surname; the person whose court date it was would supply the rest. The court date was communicated [to the prisoner] in advance, and preparations usually began the evening before: the prisoner would have to consider which mattress to take out with them, which bowl and cup . . .
>
> If they were going to the district court, where trials were usually finished in a single session, the inmates would take everything with them, both personal and state-issued items. If they were going to the city court, where trials lasted longer, inmates would take only the documents they needed for their trial, leaving the rest of their belongings behind in their cells.
>
> The time came for me to start making my own trips to the courthouse. This was a long and exhausting process: they would wake you up early and take you out of your cell; then you would have to wait for everyone to be called and rounded

up; then there was the line at the 'monkey cage', the cell where you turned in your mattress and other state-issued items. Finally, there was the 'kennel', the cell where they gathered all the people being taken to court. . . . They must have called them 'kennels' because they were gloomy and dark and usually packed with people, and the noise there was like something you might hear coming from dog cages being sent to the knacker's yard.

The prisoner transport vehicle would arrive, and escort guards would collect the prisoners waiting to be taken to different locations throughout the city. Prisoners would disembark at each District People's Court and be escorted to a small area set aside for defendants.

Azadovsky's first hearing at the Kuibyshevsky District People's Court was scheduled to begin at 1.00 pm; however, it was significantly delayed. There was a crowd milling about in the corridor; Azadovsky recognized some familiar faces as he was being led into the courtroom.

'All rise! The Court is now in session.' The young judge, Alexander Lukovnikov, took his place beneath the RSFSR crest. Azadovsky immediately presented a petition to have his court date changed on the grounds of ill health; he informed the court about the incident with the cell door. The judge summoned the doctor from Kresty. The very same doctor who had diagnosed Azadovsky with concussion several days before arrived, measured the defendant's blood pressure and testified in writing that 'Citizen Azadovsky is practically healthy' and was fit to take part in the trial.

This 'public trial' was a typical example of a Soviet kangaroo court: the defendant was disenfranchised, the judge and the prosecutor were in cahoots, the defence lawyer was consigned to a walk-on role and the outcome was determined in advance.

Around forty people had come to witness the proceedings, mostly Azadovsky's friends and acquaintances; however, the courtroom was packed, so most people were unable to get in. The writer Nina Katerli recalls the scene as follows:

> I remember that trial well. Or, rather, I remember what happened just outside the courtroom door, since I didn't manage to make it inside. I arrived early and was touched to see so many young people in the corridor: 'Students. They're worried. They've come to support their teacher.'
>
> However, just before the hearing was to start, the 'students' got up as if on cue and stood in a group, blocking the door. I had reached the door before them and was standing flush against it. But I didn't manage to make it into the courtroom. These 'students' had powerful elbows; I was pinned up against the wall, and, to ensure I wouldn't struggle, one of them pulled on my necklace so hard that I practically choked. And while he was strangling me, the whole gang of 'students' filled up the courtroom in an instant. I heard about the hearing and the judgement later on, from Yakov Gordin, who had managed to wangle his way into the courtroom by showing his Writers' Union membership card (I didn't have mine at the time).

These 'students' were, in fact, cadets from the police academy. They filled the courtroom, allowing almost no one else in. Only five of Azadovsky's friends managed to make their way inside: Yakov Gordin and Poel Karp showed their Writers' Union credentials, while Genrietta Yanovskaya and Kama Ginkas earned entrance with the phrase 'We're with you'; the art scholar Alyona Spitsyna slipped through unnoticed.

Packing the courtroom was a tried-and-tested strategy used mostly at dissident trials. The fact that it was used here is yet another indication that Azadovsky's case was politically motivated. The court comprised Judge Lukovnikov and two assessors, I.P. Ivanov and G.P. Zaporozhets. The prosecutor, V.A. Pozen, had also worked on Lepilina's case. Ryazanovsky served as Azadovsky's lawyer. V.I. Shistko acted as the 'civic accuser'.[1] Azadovsky was charged under Article 224-3: 'unlawful acquisition and possession of a narcotic substance without intent to sell'.

The notes of Poel Karp (b. 1925), a noted arts critic and translator of German literature who has lived in London since 1999, are extremely helpful in reconstructing the events of this trial. Karp writes:

> A crowd started gathering in the corridor as early as noon: some people there, the ones who knew the defendant personally, were mostly around forty years old; some were young men and women who were clearly part of a single group. The ranks of the latter gradually started to swell, spilling over towards the door. At around two, when the hearing was about to begin (it had been delayed by an hour), a dozen young people emerged from the room next to the courtroom, pushing members of the public out of the way, and occupied the front rows. Then they pushed together, leaving only a narrow passage for the crowd to come through; they allowed only their own to pass, blocking the rest. Two of them were standing at the doors, blocking them entirely. . . . Very few outsiders managed to make it into the courtroom, which could hold about forty people. When the courtroom was full, the police, who up until this point had been observing from the sidelines, resumed their responsibility to keep the peace, and they restored it in short order. The officers were exceedingly polite, and, in response to the public's requests to be allowed in, they replied, 'No seats!' or 'It's full!' . . .
>
> The defendant did not confess his guilt. He asked to postpone the trial because he had concussion. He claimed that, during a search of his cell on the evening of the 10th [of March], he had been hit on the head with an iron door. On the morning of the 11th, the prison doctor had diagnosed him with concussion and prescribed two weeks of strict bed rest – but the trial was scheduled for the 16th. The defendant asked for those responsible to be punished and gave the judge a list of his cellmates who would be willing to confirm his story. A recess was announced. After the recess, the judge announced that the doctor who had examined the defendant considered him fit to give testimony. The fact of the beating itself was neither discussed nor challenged. At the end [of the hearing], when the judge pronounced his judgement, he announced that the court was issuing a special ruling. Not only did he not read this ruling out, he did not even indicate who the ruling had been issued against, which was the only indication that it was, in fact, against the prison.
>
> The defendant challenged the civic accuser, prorector Shistko of the Mukhina Higher School. The reason was simple: in his capacity as chair of the search committee, the prorector had only just voted to reappoint the defendant to

another five-year term as head of department and asked him to consider joining the Communist Party; meanwhile, he came into the courtroom that day to present a character reference condemning the defendant's past. In the defendant's opinion, such behaviour was unprincipled. However, the prosecutor suggested that, if any lack of principle was to be found in the prorector's actions, it was on a highly personal level; because the accuser was present at the trial as a representative of society, his personal lack of principle was irrelevant. The challenge was dismissed.

The search of the defendant's flat on the morning of 19 December, which ended in his arrest, had been motivated by the detention of his cohabiting partner, Lepilina, on the evening of the 18th not far from his building; upon examination, Lepilina was found to be carrying a narcotic substance. The defendant objected to the phrase 'cohabiting partner'. Though he admitted that Lepilina had, in effect, been his common-law wife for several years (though even then they had lived separately, in neighbouring buildings), he claimed that their intimate relationship had ended in August. They remained friends; Lepilina kept her keys to the defendant's flat and continued coming over, frequently visiting the defendant's mother even in his absence. The defendant also asserted that he had repeatedly requested to be questioned simultaneously with Lepilina during the pretrial investigation; now he insisted that she be called to court as a witness. The court denied his petition.

In sum, according to the prosecution and the court, the discovery of narcotics on Lepilina's person was so directly linked to the defendant that an immediate search of the defendant's flat was warranted. The success of that search, which is to say, the discovery of narcotics in the defendant's flat, did not lead to the natural next step, a single case against the defendant and Lepilina. Rather, it led to the separation of their cases and, what's more, in defiance of any logical strategy for uncovering the truth, the prosecution and the court categorically refused to summon Lepilina even as a witness.

The charge was based on the fact that a police inspector had discovered a foil packet on a bookshelf during the search. This packet contained five grams of a brown substance, which expert analysis determined to be hashish. The inspector was summoned to court to testify as a witness, but he did not appear. He was, according to a police document, away on assignment. The court saw fit to review the case in his absence since he had given testimony during the pretrial investigation. During the trial, it emerged that this inspector had not been on the list of officers sent to carry out the search and had taken part at the invitation of another inspector who had been sent there.

According to the inspector's testimony, which was read out at the trial, after discovering the foil packet on the bookshelf, he moved it to the next shelf up, and then onto the desk, where it was opened. The defendant confirmed that the inspector did indeed move the packet from the shelf where it had first appeared to the next one up and from there onto the desk. However, he emphasized that he did not know where the packet had come from in the first place: it did not belong to him, and it had not been discovered when the books in front of it were removed;

rather, it appeared out of thin air. However, the defendant did not witness the inspector taking the packet out from his pocket or his sleeve.

The first witness claimed to have been asked to be a search witness by the metro station, where [the police] promised to show him a rare photograph of Yesenin during the search. The witness confirmed that, after the inspector discovered the packet, he moved it around on the same shelf and then took it over to the desk, where the packet turned out to contain a brown substance. The second search witness, who lived in the same building [as the defendant], testified that he saw the packet for the first time when it was on the desk, and that it contained a grey substance. The same witness reported that, before the police and search witnesses went up to the defendant's flat, they waited on the ground floor landing while one police officer went upstairs, rang the neighbours' doorbell and asked the woman who answered the door to ring the defendant's doorbell and say that a telegram had arrived for him. When the defendant opened his door, the police officers and search witnesses went up to his flat.

It also became evident during the hearing that the search was concentrated in the defendant's study; the rest of the flat, including the medicine cabinet, which contained narcotics used by the defendant's aging mother, remained largely unexamined. It also emerged that a fifth officer had been called in during the search to assist the other four operatives executing the search. This person paid special attention to the defendant's papers, but was not mentioned in the search report.

The prosecution presented to the court a note written by the defendant to Lepilina, who was being held in the same prison. The defendant did not deny the note's authenticity. According to the note, the defendant had learned about the testimony Lepilina had given at her trial, which had taken place earlier; [in this testimony] she apparently confessed that she had hidden the foil packet on the fourth bookshelf in the defendant's study, and the defendant asked her to stand by that testimony moving forward. Interpreting this note as an attempt to convince Lepilina to take the blame for possession of those narcotics, the prosecution asserted that such an attempt was sufficient evidence of the defendant's guilt. But the defendant would be just as likely to try to shift the blame to someone else if he had not committed the crime in question. By assuming that the defendant would only try to shift the blame for a crime that he had actually committed, the court accepted as given what the prosecution had a responsibility to prove. The note's somewhat agitated tone (though it should be noted that the text itself is full of endearments) more plausibly suggests that the defendant himself suspected Lepilina of using narcotics (her first husband died of narcotics poisoning [this claim, made by the prosecutor, was false: V. Lepilin died of food poisoning. – P.D.]) and that he was now implicitly reproaching her for the misfortune that had befallen him because of her actions. But no interpretation of this note, even one that takes the dimmest possible view of the defendant's moral character, would prove the defendant guilty in the least of narcotics possession. All [the note] does is point to the need for greater scrutiny of Lepilina and the defendant's attitudes towards narcotics; it should have served as additional motivation to call Lepilina to the stand. Judge Alexander Sergeevich Lukovnikov could barely contain his annoyance during the rest of the trial, and the heartfelt vehemence with which he pointed out that the defendant had begun the note with his own needs and only later wished his loved one a happy birthday indicates that the judge, who was young, but clearly not stupid, was well aware that this case lacked the evidence required to justify a guilty judgement.

The judge, prosecutor and civic accuser all talked at length about the defendant's moral character. The prosecutor even exclaimed, 'What can you say about the moral character of a person who has reached the age of forty without ever being married?!' While indicating his respect for the defendant as a scholar and a pedagogue, the civic accuser accused him of leading a double life, which manifested itself in his womanizing. Reproaches of this sort, which the defendant did not refute, created an atmosphere of [criminal] exposure in which no evidence of concrete guilt would be required. This feeling was exacerbated by multiple references to the defendant's involvement in the 1969 Slavinsky trial, during which he was listed as one of the people who had used narcotics; however, these allegations were not verified by the court at the time, as narcotics use was not criminalized until 1974.

The defence lawyer had taken this case just two days prior to the hearing. . . . The new lawyer asked for an acquittal, as his client's guilt had not been proved. He disputed the prosecutor's claim that a serious prison term was absolutely necessary in this case and pointed out that the law makes provisions for more lenient punishments under this article. However, he emphasized that he would not speak at length about potential punishments because the defendant was innocent and the charges against him were built on assumptions rather than evidence . . .

The lawyer performed a thorough analysis of the character reference issued by the Mukhina Higher School, noting that, if the document really did reflect the administration's opinion of the defendant, they could not possibly have recommended him for a second term as department head shortly before his arrest. However, they did recommend him, and his reappointment (like the reappointments of a number of other people in similar positions) had been delayed due to the arrival of a new rector, not for any other reason. The lawyer also pointed out clear distortions of fact [in the document], such as when the defendant was blamed for the gross disciplinary breaches of a colleague who was, in fact, fired at the defendant's insistence. This circumstance was confirmed using materials from the civil case brought by the colleague in an attempt to gain reinstatement. Then the judge, who had conducted himself more or less appropriately up to this point, cut the lawyer off sharply: 'I won't allow references to materials that were requested and denied by the court.'

In his final statement, the defendant repeated that he did not consider himself guilty. He said that he would not attempt to assert that the narcotics had been planted by the police, as he hadn't seen how this had been accomplished, and that he could not say whether the drugs belonged to Lepilina until they had been questioned simultaneously. However, he knew for certain that the narcotics and the foil packet did not belong to him, that he had not been hiding this packet on the bookshelf, that he had never used narcotics or kept them in his possession and that he had not used narcotics twelve years prior, when he was involved in the Slavinsky trial. Furthermore, the prosecution's assertion that the defendant would have been charged during the Slavinsky trial if the 1974 [narcotics] law been in place in 1969 was unjustified, given that there was no proof even then that he had used narcotics. 'I may have made many mistakes in my life,' the defendant said, 'but I did not associate with Slavinsky for the sake of narcotics; I had no need for them then and I have no need for them now. I don't know,' he continued, 'what to ask of the court, as my words here are all twisted against me. But I have to tell [the court] about my mother. The problem is not that her pension is 39 rubles, but that she is 77 years old. And so whatever sentence the court hands down will be on her, not me.'

After two hours of deliberation, the sentence was read out. It was exactly what the prosecutor asked for: two years' incarceration in a minimum-security facility. The judge repeated, 'The sentence may be appealed within a period of seven days' and asked the defendant: 'Do you understand? Seven days.' The convicted man nodded and was led out. As he shooed the public towards the exit, the court clerk crisply announced, 'Show's over, folks!'

In addition to what appears in these notes, there were two memorable outbursts in the courtroom. The first came from civic accuser Shistko, who shouted: 'Give him more! I ask the honourable court to give him more!' The second was from Azadovsky himself. As he was being led out of the courtroom, he cried out: 'Take care of my mother!'

6.2 The note, again

And so the note that Azadovsky had sent to Lepilina in prison resurfaced in court. Its reappearance was unexpected, and its reading was a triumph for the prosecution. According to the prosecutor, the note had been discovered by a prison guard in an internal exercise yard.

As soon as the prosecutor announced this new piece of evidence, Azadovsky understood what was going on. Because the note was read out on its own, without the petition Azadovsky wrote that same day, the prosecutor was able to present it as a means of putting pressure on Lepilina. This note was of a piece with the other evidence presented at Azadovsky's trial; in fact, there wasn't any hard evidence against him.

Azadovsky was upset; despondent, even. How could he, a forty-year-old scholar, a polygot with multiple degrees, have been tricked into making such a schoolboy error? And he had no one to blame but himself. He had gambled and lost.

Fima Rozenberg had turned out to be a snitch. Several years later, on 19 February 1985, Azadovsky would see his cellmate again, this time on television. He was in a documentary film titled *The Conspiracy Against the Soviet State*, about nonconformists who had ostensibly been planted in the USSR by foreign intelligence services. Produced in 1984, it is a typical propaganda film masquerading as a documentary. It introduces Rozenberg as a double agent who had served as a custodian of the 'so-called Solzhenitsyn Fund', which was founded in 1974 to aid the families of political prisoners. He is presented as an agent provocateur, which is precisely the role he played in Azadovsky's case. By convincing Azadovsky to write a note to Lepilina, Rozenberg had played an important role in his case. However, even if Azadovsky hadn't written this note, the judgement would undoubtedly have been the same.

7

A prisoner of conscience

Among the public, Azadovsky and Lepilina's arrest and conviction were almost universally viewed as part of the ongoing suppression and intimidation of the Soviet intelligentsia. Unsurprisingly, the 'Azadovsky Affair' also caused quite a stir in the West.

The exact date of Azadovsky's arrest probably wasn't chosen in advance. However, it happened to fall on the eve of Chekists' Day, the professional holiday celebrating Soviet intelligence workers; it also came right before Christmas in many Western countries. As soon as the holidays were over, a wave of information began appearing in the West. On 1 January 1981, the Parisian paper *La Pensée Russe* published an item on Azadovsky's arrest; the Associated Press distributed a story on the subject to its subscriber agencies around that same time. In early January, the incident was reported in Europe's major newspapers, including *Die Welt, Die Neue Zürcher Zeitung, Le Monde* and *La Repubblica*.

As soon as he was arrested, Azadovsky became a prisoner of conscience. For several years, the image of Konstantin Azadovsky, persecuted scholar, would take on a life of its own, quite separate from the grim realities of his day-to-day existence. Even the authorities were powerless to change things now: the machinery that had been set in motion couldn't be stopped. And the more stubborn the Soviet carceral system proved itself to be, the more deeply entrenched the public perception of Azadovsky as a prisoner of conscience became.

7.1 Censorship

The clearest indication that the criminal proceedings against Azadovsky were political in nature was the fact that his scholarly work could no longer be printed in the USSR. This was the case for most victims of political arrest.

The most painful blow to Azadovsky's career came when his works were excluded from *Literary Heritage*, the Soviet Union's premier historical-literary publication. This series was conceived in the late 1920s by art scholar and Russian cultural historian Ilya Zilbershtein (1905–88); its first volume appeared in 1931. Among Soviet humanities scholars, writing for *Literary Heritage* was considered an honour. The Azadovskys' connection with Zilbershtein went way back: Mark Azadovsky had been actively involved with *Literary Heritage* starting in the 1930s. Konstantin Azadovsky was one of the young scholars invited to contribute to the series in the early 1970s. His long article

'Dostoevsky in Germany (1846–1921)', co-authored with Germanist Viktor Dudkin, appeared in the Dostoevsky volume (1973), while his innovative article 'Bryusov and Libra', co-authored with Dmitry Maksimov, was published in the volume dedicated to Russian Symbolist poet Valery Bryusov (1976).

Zilbershtein also invited Azadovsky to contribute to the volumes dedicated to Russian Symbolist poet Alexander Blok. Azadovsky produced two pieces for this project: an analysis of the German diary of translator Friedrich Fiedler (1859–1917) and an edited version of the correspondence between Blok and early twentieth-century poet Nikolay Klyuev. This second, lengthy article had already been typeset when the news of Azadovsky's arrest came to light. Upon hearing the news, Zilbershtein decided to give himself some extra insurance: he asked permission 'from above' to publish Klyuev's letters to Blok. Alexander Lavrov, Azadovsky's friend and fellow contributor, describes the situation as follows:

> I was at Zilbershtein's shortly after the arrest had taken place, but before the trial. The question at hand was, how could we manage to publish Klyuev's letters to Blok, which appeared in the page proofs for *Literary Heritage*'s second Blok volume? I was there when Zilbershtein called Albert Belyaev, an ideological apparatchik from the Central Committee, and got permission for the correspondence to remain in the book. Ten minutes later, however, Belyaev called Zilbershtein back and demanded that the correspondence be withdrawn (doubtless, this was after consultation with the penal authorities).

On 21 January 1981, a noticeably pared-down version of the volume was approved for publication. When the book came out, *La Pensée Russe* published a response titled '*Literary Heritage* and the Trial of K. Azadovsky'. In it, Serge Deduline asks:

> What could have induced the editors of *Literary Heritage*, one of the most authoritative humanities publications (which, like every other publication in our motherland, is of course entirely 'independent' from the influence of any outside authorities), to turn against their brother and, in doing so, to turn against their beloved field? [What could have induced them] to butcher works that were previously ready for publication?

This question was a rhetorical one. The Soviet censorship's punitive powers were common knowledge at this time.

Nina Katerli went to Zilbershtein to ask the same question. She recalls:

> He received me courteously and heard me out attentively, but then the conversation turned to how we needed to intervene, to step in. . . . At this point, Ilya Samoilovich's expression changed. His hands began to shake and, lowering his voice, he said that, unfortunately, it would be impossible to help. This case wasn't about drugs at all; he had heard from very well-placed sources that this was a political matter, that it was very, very serious and that it would be useless to try to intervene. . .

7.2 The Azadovsky Defence Committee

We have already touched on the effect Azadovsky's arrest, trial and sentencing produced on the Moscow and Leningrad intelligentsia. However, the case sparked an even greater furore in the West. This was in part due to the so-called third wave of emigration, which took place in the 1970s: this mass exodus from the Soviet Union included major Russian cultural figures, many of whom knew Azadovsky personally.

A group calling itself 'the Azadovsky Defence Committee' was formed; its activities were spearheaded by Joseph Brodsky, Sergey Dovlatov, Vladimir Maramzin, Serge Deduline and several other Leningraders living abroad.

La Pensée Russe reported the search of Azadovsky's flat as early as 1 January 1981. After that, people began coming to his defence even without the shield of anonymity; Joseph Brodsky in particular used his clout to raise awareness of Azadovsky's case. Brodsky's biographer, the poet Lev Losev, writes:

> For all his professed contempt for politics, for all the complexity of his poetic thought. . . . Brodsky found himself unwillingly thrust into acting as the representative of thinking Russia in the West. He was community-minded, whether or not he would admit it, and he found himself drawn into political events time and time again.

Knowing the value of his own voice, Brodsky didn't hesitate to use it to intervene on his friend's behalf. On 15 January 1981, *La Pensée Russe* published a phone interview with Brodsky, which was later reprinted in the New York-based Russian-language newspaper *The New American*.

On January 9, *La Pensée Russe* also published an article by Vladimir Maramzin, which is excerpted in the following text:

> [Azadovsky's] arrest signifies a new phase in the war on the intelligentsia; this war has always been waged in the USSR, but over the past decade it has become especially intense. In Moscow, the centre of the human rights movement, its main targets are those who intervene on behalf of the persecuted. In Ukraine, Estonia, Lithuania and Armenia, it targets those who wish to preserve their national independence. In Leningrad, a city of cultural traditions, the authorities' primary concern is to annihilate the cultural element and to sever cultural ties.
>
> Why has Azadovsky in particular been targeted on this occasion? We can only guess. . . . The fact that he has not been charged with a political crime (were they unable to gather the necessary evidence?) is an ominous sign. The investigation is being led by the police at 4 Krylov Alley. The KGB has honed its tactics: the packet of heroin 'found' on the professor's bookshelf is a sign of the times. Some people have foreign currency planted on them, others are beaten up in the street and then taken to court for brawling. But now, more and more often, [the KGB] resorts to drugs, believing that the West won't intervene in such cases. But by now the West understands a great deal. The French newspaper *Le Monde* wrote about Azadovsky's arrest (6 January 1981), and the Italian paper *La Repubblica*

devoted a long article to it (8 January 1981); Deutsche Welle reported on it, and the American papers wrote about it, too. The Leningrad KGB has once again proved its incompetence. Azadovsky the 'drug-using' professor can now join Joseph Brodsky the poet-'parasite' on the agency's list of notable achievements.

Finally, drawing on the releases prepared by Azadovsky's friends in Leningrad, *La Pensée Russe* ran a lengthy think piece titled 'The Case of Konstantin Azadovsky' on 26 February 1981. This article outlined the details of the case and proposed some possible motivations for it.

Foreign support for Azadovsky wasn't limited to France; spouses Lev Kopelev and Raisa Orlova made a statement from West Germany in late January. The couple had arrived in West Germany on a research trip in November 1980; then, on 22 January 1981, they learned that they had been stripped of their Soviet citizenship for committing 'actions unworthy of Soviet citizens', and that they would not be allowed to return to the USSR. Some would have seen it as a blessing to be stripped of their Soviet citizenship and granted the right to live in the West; for Kopelev and Orlova, though, it was a tragedy. At the time, they thought that they would never see their children, grandchildren or friends again.

Kopelev was a human rights advocate who had served time in a labour camp with Solzhenitsyn; he was also an expert on German culture and a close friend of Heinrich Böll, who was awarded the Nobel Prize for Literature in 1972. Azadovsky first met Kopelev in the early 1960s. After Kopelev was expelled from the Writers' Union in the 1970s, the KGB kept him under close surveillance; he was openly persecuted for his criticism of power and his publications abroad. Nevertheless, Azadovsky continued to visit him in Moscow. Both Kopelev and Azadovsky would go on to win the prestigious Friedrich Gundolf Prize, which is awarded by the German Academy for Language and Literature for significant contributions to the popularization of German culture abroad. It is important to note that Kopelev, like Azadovsky, never called himself a dissident; in fact, he objected whenever anyone tried to present him in that light.

And so, Lev Kopelev took the first opportunity he had to spread the word about Azadovsky's arrest. His declaration was broadcast on Deutsche Welle and other radio stations; it was then published in *La Pensée Russe* on 19 February. A translation of his statement appeared in a number of German newspapers, including the influential *Süddeutsche Zeitung*, on 24 January. On 18 October 1981, Kopelev was presented with the Friedrich Gundolf Prize during the Frankfurt Book Fair. He used his acceptance speech, titled 'Don't Lay Down the Weapon of Your Word', as yet another opportunity to remind the world of Azadovsky's plight.

Another important landmark for the case was when a notice ran in *La Repubblica*, one of Italy's biggest newspapers. It appeared in the very centre of the page, marked in bold. It was published through the efforts of Italian Slavonicist Silvana de Vidovich, who had known Azadovsky since the 1960s.

However, Azadovsky's greatest support came from New York, from Brodsky and Dovlatov. The Eighth Avenue offices of *The New American*, Dovlatov's weekly Russian-language newspaper, became the Azadovsky Defence Committee's headquarters.

The issue of *The New American* dated 14/20 January 1981 was mainly dedicated to the Azadovsky trial. It contains this statement from the editor-in-chief:

THE ASSAULT ON THE INTELLIGENTSIA CONTINUES

I have known Konstantin Azadovsky for around twenty years. It is difficult to imagine someone further removed from politics.

[He is] a brilliant young scholar, a man of erudition, a connoisseur of belles-lettres, a philologist absorbed in his academic pursuits. Needless to say, Azadovsky, like all true members of the intelligentsia, has been an advocate for spiritual freedom. But he has not engaged in any human rights activism. And, to be honest, such a role wouldn't have suited him. He has never had that steely character, that selfless courage, those reserves of asceticism and self-sacrifice.

I repeat, [Azadovsky] was a typical member of the intelligentsia: charming, somewhat careless, honest and kind.

And then we heard that Kostya had been arrested by the state security apparatus. This news shocked everyone who knew him. How had he managed to run foul of the KGB's functionaries? Why had they deemed it necessary to arrest someone who was undoubtedly innocent (even from their perspective), someone who enjoyed universal respect?

To answer these questions, it is important to understand how the Leningrad KGB works. The local ideological agencies defy basic logic; they make up for their incompetence with threefold cruelty. In their provincial zeal, they overreach Moscow's general policies time and again.

It is well known that the Moscow state security services operate differently. They force undesirable members of the intelligentsia, those of 'doubtful provenance', into exile abroad. Only those who actively defy the regime are subjected to cruel repression.

We don't know how events will unfold. One would like to think that this ominous mistake on the part of the Leningrad authorities will be set right.

What else can we take comfort in?

Sergey DOVLATOV

But comfort was not on the cards. Soon after this, Dovlatov assigned Natalya Sharymova to write an in-depth article on the recently completed Azadovsky trial. This article, published under the pseudonym N. Kononova, concludes:

Konstantin Azadovsky declared that he has never used drugs, though rumours have begun surfacing in Leningrad that he has 'dabbled'. It would be interesting to ask the people spreading these rumours where they heard them from in the first place. After all, this gossip might be coming from the Big House.

The KGB has probably put an end to Konstantin Azadovsky's academic career, or, at any rate, it has put it on hold for the next ten years or so. Azadovsky hasn't admitted any guilt; he has declared that he has never used drugs, and he has sent an appeal to the city court.

Unfortunately, no one knows what goes on in the bowels of the KGB, not even the American intelligence services . . .

Perhaps Kostya Azadovsky was betrayed precisely by his vibrancy, by his heterodox behaviour.

But, to avoid causing a scandal abroad, someone decided to prosecute K. Azadovsky for a criminal offence. A narcotics charge. As a result, there is not a single senator, a single member of congress who will raise their voice in his defence, no matter how much the university professors who know Azadovsky personally might beg them to. And the average person – whether immigrant or native-born citizen – only shakes their head: 'Where there's smoke, there's fire.'

Though Sharymova couldn't know for certain whether the assertions she was making were accurate, they were definitely logical. And the circumstances she described caused significant difficulties not just for Azadovsky himself, but for those advocating for his freedom abroad.

The rumours that had begun spreading through Leningrad were deliberately disseminated by the security services themselves. For example, before Azadovsky's trial, Investigator Kamenko went to speak at a special meeting at the Mukhina Higher School. During this meeting, which will be discussed in greater detail later in this book, Kamenko mentioned Azadovsky's alleged drug addiction, which had been 'known to the agency since 1969'.

The fact that Azadovsky was facing criminal rather than political charges made it difficult to attract international attention to his case, especially outside of the émigré community. At the time, fabrication of evidence was still a new strategy for the KGB: it was only later that this simple and foolproof means of 'evidence-gathering' would be embraced by the MVD and other security services. For the moment, though, the idea of evidence-planting was dismissed as nonsense, especially since there was usually plenty of real dirt that could be dug up about people who were considered thorns in the authorities' sides. There was Joseph Brodsky's parasitism, Arseny Roginsky's forgeries, Lev Klein's homosexuality, Mikhail Meilakh's samizdat – the list goes on. For the most part, the authorities managed to find some trifle that would allow them to press charges. But, generally speaking, there was an expectation that the investigation would unearth some actual evidence: in Azadovsky's case, the charges were completely fabricated.

Another major article published by the Azadovsky Defence Committee was 'The Azadovsky Affair' by Joseph Brodsky. This article was published in English on 8 October 1981 in *The New York Review of Books*. By the time it appeared, the details of Azadovsky's sentencing, failed appeal and incarceration were already known in the West. Brodsky was clearly agitated when he wrote his 'Letter to the Editor'; the text practically oozes with sarcastic vitriol:

The Azadovsky Affair

To the Editors:

Eight months ago, on December 19, 1980, the Chairman of the Department of Foreign Languages at the Mukhina College of Applied Arts in Leningrad, Professor

Konstantin Azadovsky, was seized on the street. Three months later he was tried on trumped-up charges of possessing drugs, and as you read these lines he is doing time – two years – in a labor camp near Magadan.

To simplify your search of this place on the map of the USSR, you may be advised to find first the Kolyma River that flows into the Arctic Ocean at approximately 62°NL. This name makes every Russian shudder, and not so much because of the temperatures peculiar to this region as because the permafrost basin of this river is the burial ground for millions of Soviet citizens who perished during Stalin's reign.

Even if the charges against Professor Azadovsky were real, he'd never end up in the said parts as a result of them, if only because the main principle of the Soviet penal policy in regard to petty criminals is that they should serve their terms within the administrative confines of their actual habitation. Destinations like Kolyma are traditionally preserved for political prisoners. Professor Azadovsky, however, hardly qualifies for that status either.

Professor Konstantin Azadovsky is one of the best Russian scholars of comparative literature today. . . . Because of the nature of his professional interests, he also maintained scholarly ties with a number of Western specialists in corresponding fields.

The latter activity is in Russia an open invitation for harassment, unless, of course, such contacts are initiated or encouraged by the State itself. However, there is very little for any State in someone's study of folklore motifs in the works of Grillparzer. And throughout twenty years of his academic career Professor Azadovsky has been several times banned from publishing, transferred to teach in the North, interrogated, threatened with reprisals: the State has its own routine. So does a scholar who, if he is any good, doesn't allow anyone's routine to interfere with his own.

It's this typically academic negligence that helped bring Professor Azadovsky to his arrest and subsequent deportation to the Kolyma region. . . . Professor Azadovsky was arrested on drug charges, severely beaten on his head by his guards with the metal door of his cell, and, while feeling ill, was taken to the courtroom. He stood trial, denied the charges, and was transported to the place you may have a hard time finding on the map. As for the drug charges, they make sense only as a spinoff of the Marxist dictum that 'religion is the opium of the people'; in this sense, culture is drugs.

All this may seem odd to you, but it should be remembered that the whole thing took place in Leningrad, which enjoys the reputation of 'the cradle of revolution' and therefore the local KGB apparatus is given an absolutely free hand. It's not that places with a lesser claim to fame lag very much behind Leningrad in the degree of exercised lawlessness – quite the contrary. Still, the authorities there may be mindful of occasional federal scrutiny. In Leningrad they are not, nor are they afraid of foreign journalists, as is often the case in Moscow.

. . . Like everywhere else, in a Socialist state the vigilance and efficiency of its police is measured by statistics. However, the reduction in crime rate isn't necessarily the KGB's idea of a good showing. Hence the character of so many cases and hence often their timing. Professor Azadovsky was arrested on December

19, 1980, not so much because the authorities had a case against him as because the year was drawing to a close and the KGB needed an extra case for its annual report. Furthermore, he was sent so far up North not so much because he had to be isolated as because of the KGB's desire to remind both the intellectual community and itself that the old track still may be put to use. Finally, in those remote parts it is easier to charge a man with whatever offence and extend his sentence. A polar bear would do for a witness.

This KGB decision to resort to its old paraphernalia is the most alarming aspect of Professor Azadovsky's case, and we urge everyone who reads this letter to use every available avenue to convince the Soviet authorities to reverse the verdict and to release the man. Apart from anything else, Professor Azadovsky is the sole source of support to his old and gravely ill mother, the widow of the famous Russian folklorist Mark Azadovsky, who in his own time became a victim during the campaign against 'rootless cosmopolitans' in 1949. The chances for success in this case – as in so many others – are obviously quite slim, but your appeal still may prevent yet another metal pipe plunging into Professor Azadovsky's skull.

Joseph Brodsky
The Azadovsky Defense Committee

7.3 Allies in the north

It is not particularly surprising that the Russian émigré community worked so hard to spread the word about their arrested friend and countryman. What *is* surprising is that news of Azadovsky's arrest was broadcast on mainstream Western radio stations, thus reaching listeners of 'enemy voices'[1] in the Soviet Union.

It was clear from the very beginning that Azadovsky's compatriots abroad would be unable to improve his situation. To sway the Soviet authorities, he would need more distinguished defenders. But his cause was already being championed by high-profile writers like Brodsky, Dovlatov and Kopelev: How much more distinguished could they get? Today, these names are known the world over, but to the Soviet authorities in 1981, they were merely unrecognized authors who had been consigned to the dust heap of history.

This is why it was so important that Azadovsky received such massive support not just from former Soviet citizens but also from his academic colleagues abroad: it was far more difficult to accuse them of ideological bias.

On 27 January 1981, the Committee for the Defence of Democratic Rights and Freedoms, based at Ruhr University in Bochum (West Germany), issued a special appeal to V.S. Semyonov, the Soviet Ambassador Extraordinary and Plenipotentiary to the Federal Republic of Germany. They asked that he consider Azadovsky's case and, what's more, that German lawyers be allowed to attend the proceedings as observers: 'It is only in this way that the Soviet justice system can dispel the suspicion that it is nothing more than the KGB's criminal accessory'.

Scandinavian philologists took a particularly active role in Azadovsky's defence. The first to take up the banner was the Danish Russianist Peter Alberg Jensen, who later became a professor of Slavic Languages at Stockholm University. Not only did he initiate a letter-writing campaign within the academic community, he also united Azadovsky's defenders in Northern Europe into a single group. It was Jensen who prepared a statement on Azadovsky's arrest for Ritzau, Denmark's leading news agency, and who wrote to the prisoner's colleagues and friends. He appealed to Yefim Etkind and Yefim Slavinsky for details about Azadovsky's life and corresponded with Scandinavian newspaper editors to arrange the publication of various materials.

We have included some excerpts from Jensen's letters in the following text. His first missive to London was sent almost at random: he must have decided to contact Slavinsky after seeing his name in the stories about Azadovsky that were circulating in the media. However, finding someone's contact information could pose a real challenge in the days before the internet. Knowing that Slavinsky had worked for a long time at the BBC Russian Service, Jensen sent a letter to BBC headquarters in Portland Place, London (though the Russian Service was based at Bush House in Kingsway). Despite the fact that Jensen bungled both the address and the name of his addressee, the letter eventually reached its intended recipient. This letter, composed in less-than-perfect Russian, would come to play a crucial role in Azadovsky's life:

25/01/1981
Dear Lev Slavinsky!

A week ago, I was asked to write to you and send clippings of what had appeared in the Danish press about the arrest of Kostya Azadovsky. But this letter was delayed because, unfortunately, the publication of our declaration was delayed as well. Generally speaking, it [appeared] in the provinces; in Copenhagen it was difficult to squeeze it in. We, four of Kostya's colleagues and friends, are novices in this sort of thing, and we sent copies of our text to a number of editorial offices. . . . A few words about the newspapers:
Kristeligt Dagblad: small paper based in the capital
Vestkysten: regional, based in Esbjerg, well-established
Politiken: based in Copenhagen, biggest morning [paper] in the country
Aalborg Stiftstidende: regional, based in Aalborg, well-established . . .

We are still waiting for it to come out in two important Copenhagen [papers]; they said that they will be printed any day now.

Tomorrow we will get together to decide on next steps. One of them will be to write in more detail about Kostya and describe his fate. To that end, it would be very good if you could write to me with a brief description of how you viewed Kostya's behaviour during your trial – really, I only know about you from the attached Russian text! Have you written about yourself anywhere? Tell [us where], please. There is an important piece of Kostya's biography that remains unclear to us: how did your trial affect his fate? Our acquaintance with him began in spring 1975, and thus after his return from Petrozavodsk, so we don't know the details.

Who are we? Peter Ulf Møller, Lene Schacke and I are Russianists, philologists and literary scholars, and Nils Bjervig is a Russianist and linguist; all of us are from Copenhagen. I am enclosing the title page of my recent book on Pilnyak as a sort of extended business card.

We are also looking for precise information about the fate of Mark Azadovsky in 1949 – can you tell us where we can read about this?

I am enclosing a copy of the German newspaper *Die Zeit*. And the Russian text about Azadovsky on which we based our first declaration.

Please write to me to say what there has been in England and what you will do. All best, Peter Alberg.

P.S. Keep an eye on the Swedish newspaper *Expressen*: it should appear there. We wrote to Norway, too, but it seems that Kostya doesn't have any friends there. . . . Do you happen to have any snapshots that might come in handy, or perhaps other materials. . .

As the letter states, Jensen was writing on behalf of a group of Scandinavian philologists working to keep Northern Europe apprised of the criminal proceedings against Azadovsky and Lepilina. And, it should be stressed, these were scholars: they were not politicians, human rights advocates or even journalists.

In January 1981, the Scandinavian scholars approached various prominent newspapers in Denmark, some of whose editors agreed to publish the information they were offering. Their articles were based on the materials prepared by Azadovsky's friends in Leningrad, which had been widely disseminated in the West by members of the Russian émigré community. Several versions of this petition were published, including 'Soviet scholar falls victim to a crackdown' (*Kristeligt Dagblad*, 20 January), 'Political arrest' (*Vestkysten*, 21 January) and 'Arrest of a Soviet scholar' (*Aalborg Stiftstidende*, 23 January). An article published on 27 January in Denmark's flagship newspaper, *Berlingske Tidende*, took a similar position: titled 'Danish scholars' friend arrested in Leningrad', it was written by Jens Thomsen.

The scholars also enlisted the help of the fearless journalist Kaj Spangenberg. Spangenberg was a correspondent for Danmarks Radio and the prominent newspaper *Politiken*, where he worked from 1969 up until 1999. He was arrested in the GDR in 1962, in Poland in 1970 and in Argentina in 1974, and had reported from hotspots including Prague in 1968. In 1981, Spangenberg published several articles on Azadovsky's case, starting with one titled 'Harsh punishments for Soviet dissidents', which appeared in *Politiken* on 22 January.

Jensen enclosed these articles in his letter to Slavinsky. Impressed by the group's activism, Slavinsky replied:

6 February

Dear Peter,

Thank you for your letter. It took a long time to reach me because you used the wrong name and address. . . . But the letter did reach me eventually, and I am glad that Kostya has so many friends. . . . Every day I ask myself what can be done for

Kostya, and there is nothing I can think of. Strange as it may seem, in the five years I have spent living in England, I have not made any connections that would be useful in this situation: journalists, for example. We mentioned Kostya in one of our Russian-language radio programmes, just five lines (what was printed in *Le Monde*), and that was it. There has been nothing in the English papers. As soon as anything appears, we will let you know.

About me. I was tried in September 1969 in the Smolninsky District People's Court in Leningrad for smoking marijuana and hashish. About a gram of hashish was discovered during a search. I should say that I did, in fact, enjoy a smoke from time to time, both on my own and with friends (though Kostya never smoked). There were foreigners in my circle of friends; one of them was under surveillance by the KGB, which drew their attention to me. Kostya categorically refused to give testimony against me at the trial. The judge was very unhappy with this, and, along with my sentence, the court issued a ruling saying that Azadovsky's behaviour at the trial had been hostile, that he had refused to give testimony, that he had protected a criminal (which is to say, me) and that, by doing so, he had obstructed the court's work. Of course, this ruling got back to the administration of the place where Azadovsky was working at the time . . . and, as a result, he was sacked and forced to go to Petrozavodsk. . . . In 1972 I returned to Leningrad and we saw each other several times. I remember that, by that time, Kostya's career was back on track. After I emigrated, we didn't correspond (so as not to ruin his career) and news of Azadovsky's success only came to me in bits and pieces: I would hear that he was to defend his PhD thesis soon, that he was teaching, writing a great deal, translating and so on. His arrest took me completely by surprise. Kostya isn't a dissident, he has never made any civic declarations. He is a *kulturträger* by nature, and he didn't wish to emigrate precisely because he considered it his duty to promote culture where it was needed most, which is to say, in Russia.

Jensen had told Slavinsky to keep an eye on *Expressen*, one of Sweden's leading papers, because he already knew that a major article was slated to run there. It was being prepared by Magnus Ljunggren, a friend of Azadovsky's and now one of the leading European scholars on the history of Russian Modernism. On 11 February, his article appeared under the scathing headline 'How words, faces and people disappear within the torture chambers of power'. It concludes by noting how mercilessly Russia had treated Azadovsky, a person who had dedicated his life to the study of his motherland's literature and culture.

Ljunggren wasn't the only Swede to comment on Azadovsky's arrest: he was joined by the Russianist Annika Bäckström, who taught at Uppsala University. Later on, Bäckström would gain fame as the Swedish-language translator of celebrated Russian authors such as Marina Tsvetaeva, Joseph Brodsky, Sasha Sokolov and Gennady Aygi. She had met Azadovsky in Leningrad in the 1960s, when he was a newly minted graduate of the philological faculty. Bäckström was an advocate for liberal ideas and participated in the political movements of her time. The feature story she wrote about Azadovsky was titled 'Russian literature scholar arrested', and it appeared on

11 February in *Uppsala Nya Tidning*. Drawing on the article from *La Pensée Russe*, Bäckström situated the criminal case within the broader context of Soviet political arrests, and she also shared some personal memories of Azadovsky:

> Literature was the air that Kostya breathed, an elixir of life, not something meant to be taken in moderate doses in order to make an impression on others. In Leningrad, where the weather is grey and oppressive for most of the year, Kostya seemed like some exotic creature...
>
> One of our colleagues visited him in November of last year (a month before his arrest). He was in the process of destroying his notes (he must have seen the writing on the wall). His recently completed thesis on the Russian soul lay on his desk. He didn't know when or whether he would be permitted to defend it.... On the same desk stood a small, smirking bust of Voltaire, champion of tolerance and reason.

The two articles that appeared in the Swedish press made a definite stir, and they certainly influenced the course of events moving forward. Another article worth mentioning is 'A few weighty words...', which appeared in the Danish paper *Morgenavisen Jyllands-Posten* under the pseudonym Leander on 28 January 1981.

The Scandinavian campaign on Azadovsky's behalf culminated in a joint letter to the Institute of Slavonic Studies at the University of Copenhagen. In this letter, dated 23 March 1981, a group of Danish Slavonicists asked the institute to invite Azadovsky to lecture in Copenhagen.

7.4 Rilke-Gesellschaft

News of Azadovsky's arrest reached Switzerland on 8 January 1981, when an item titled 'Azadovsky in prison' appeared in the country's leading paper, *Neue Zürcher Zeitung*. Its author was the Swiss Slavonicist, publicist and poet Felix Philipp Ingold (b. 1942), who had shared a lively scholarly correspondence with Azadovsky for years.

After the publication of Ingold's letter, the international Rilke appreciation society joined in the fight. This organization, called Rilke-Gesellschaft, was based in Basel at the time. Its efforts to aid Azadovsky were spearheaded by one of the group's most active members, the prominent Rilke specialist Joachim Wolfgang Storck (1922–2011). Storck composed an official letter on the society's behalf, which was then sent to Vladimir Lavrov, the Soviet ambassador to Switzerland:

> Your Excellency:
>
> On 9 January, the newspaper *Neue Zürcher Zeitung* ran an item reporting that a member of our Society, Konstantin Markovich Azadovsky, had been arrested by the state security services in Leningrad.
>
> We know Konstantin Markovich Azadovsky as a member of our Society and as a distinguished scholar of Slavonic and German literature, which is why the news of his arrest has come to us as such a shock.

With this in mind, permit us to respectfully pose to you the following question: Is the item that appeared in our press based in fact, and is it true that this arrest took place, and that it remains in force? If this is, as we fear, the case, then on behalf of our Society, which is composed of many members, we would like to request that you take steps to allow this world-famous scholar and brilliant representative of Russian scholarship to continue his work under normal conditions.

Storck immediately composed another official letter on Rilke Society letterhead. He signed this one personally before dispatching it on 4 February to Vladimir Semyonov, the Soviet ambassador to the GDR. Storck asks the ambassador 'to convey to the appropriate authorities in your country our common wish: to free the Leningrad scholar and to give him the opportunity to go back to his work'.

Neither embassy issued a reply, and so Storck organized a public crusade. On 5 May 1981, the society sent out a press release titled 'Action in Support of Konstantin M. Azadovsky'. This document outlined the key circumstances of Azadovsky's case: from his arrest and conviction, to the reaction in Europe, to the impact of his academic works. The Rilke Society issued a call for anyone who cared about the scholar's fate to work towards his liberation.

7.5 An island of freedom

Thanks to Jensen's efforts, news of the 'Azadovsky Affair' finally reached the UK. As Slavinsky's letter suggests, the BBC Russian Service was only allowed to broadcast information that had already appeared in the press. No original reporting was allowed.

With this in mind, Jensen wrote to the English writer, translator and journalist Michael Scammell (b. 1935), who was also a Russian literature scholar. Scammell didn't hide his opinion of the Soviet regime: he translated works by the dissidents Vladimir Bukovsky and Anatoly Marchenko and edited an English-language anthology of works originally published in samizdat. Scammell was particularly well known for speaking out in support of incarcerated writers and against censorship. In the early 1980s, he would gain fame for his seminal biography of Solzhenitsyn, which helped him to gain a professorship in the United States, but cost him his personal relationship with the author.

And so, on 3 March 1981, Jensen sent a packet of materials on Azadovsky's trial to Scammell in London. From there, things moved quickly: Scammell replied to Jensen's letter on 13 March, and on 31 March *The Times* published Scammell's long article 'Soviet professor claims drug was planted on him'.

In response, an appeal was issued by a group of British scholars of Russian and German. 'Plea for convicted Soviet scholar' was published as a letter to the editor in *The Times* on 13 July 1981; it had nine signatories. At first, no one had dared to hope that this letter would make it into print: *The Times*, like the rest of the country, was completely absorbed by the wedding of Prince Charles and Lady Diana Spencer, which was to take place on 29 July. Nevertheless, Sir Harold Evans, editor of *The Times*, made this letter a priority:

> Sir, We write as a group of university teachers and translators of Russian and German, and more particularly as admirers of Rilke, to express our dismay at the arrest and imprisonment of the celebrated Leningrad scholar Konstantin Azadovsky. Azadovsky, a profoundly dedicated scholar and critic, who has published numerous studies (e.g. of Grillparzer, Dostoyevsky, Bryusov, Klyuyev, Blok, Pasternak) and is known as the leading Soviet Rilke scholar, was sentenced in March to two years' detention on a charge of possessing five grams of marijuana – a charge which he firmly denies, which consorts ill with all we know of his character and career, and which, from what we have now learnt of his trial, appears to have been quite inadequately substantiated by the prosecution and to have been upheld only through what amounts to a miscarriage of justice.
>
> The interruption and perhaps destruction of Azadovsky's work must mean a severe loss to comparative literature. This is the kind of case, moreover, which is bound to cause damage to cultural relations between the Soviet Union and the West. We wish through your columns to urge the Soviet authorities to reconsider this case and to set Azadovsky free.

This letter was written by Angela Livingstone (b. 1934), who also organized its other eight signatories: Joseph Peter Stern (1920–91), Michael Hamburger (1924–2007), Henry Gifford (1913–2003), Christopher Barnes (b. 1942), Edward Edmund Papst (1922–2002), Donald Rayfield (b. 1942), Irina Frowen (née Minskers, 1915–2007) and Leon Burnett. Nearly all of them knew Azadovsky, either personally, professionally or through his scholarly output. This had been Livingstone's idea: it wasn't enough for the signatories to be sympathetic to Azadovsky's cause; they had to have some kind of connection to him. Livingstone herself, a scholar of Rilke and Pasternak, had met Azadovsky through Yevgeny and Yelena Pasternak; they met on more than one occasion before Azadovsky's arrest, and Azadovsky is thanked in her book *Lou Andreas-Salomé*.

7.6 PEN International

None of these letters had any effect: they didn't receive so much as a reply.

Then, in early March 1981, organizations like Amnesty International began getting involved. The most effective and large-scale campaign on Azadovsky's behalf was organized by PEN International. Founded in London in 1921, PEN International is a worldwide association dedicated to fighting for freedom of expression and defending the rights of writers and journalists. Its Writers in Prison Committee, which works on behalf of arrested authors, was established in 1960.

As soon as Azadovsky's arrest came to light, several national PEN affiliates leapt into action.

In early 1981, while Azadovsky was still in pretrial detention, Danish PEN issued an appeal to the Soviet Writers' Union regarding the persecution of their colleagues. Azadovsky's case features prominently in this document:

> We decry the fact that Konstantin Azadovsky, a literary scholar, translator and candidate for membership in the [Soviet Writers' Union], has been arrested on the back of some dubious allegations. We deem the attempts to destroy the fruits of his academic labour unacceptable, as such acts constitute a form of discrimination against recognized scholarly works.

This document was signed by five individuals: Søren Egerod (1923–95), a general linguist, writer and poet who belonged to the Royal Danish Academy of Sciences and Letters; Erik Vagn Jensen (1930–95), a publisher and secretary of Danish PEN; Uffe Harder (1930–2002), a translator from four languages, chair of Danish PEN and a member of the Royal Danish Academy of Sciences and Letters; Hans Jørgen Lembourn (1923–97), chair of the Danish Writers' Union; and, finally, Eigil Steffensen (1927–2011), chair of the Danish Slavonicists' Association.

In addition to their impressive scholarly achievements, these signatories were known for their political and social activism, which would prove crucial to their work on Azadovsky's behalf. Of the five of them, only Lembourn could be accused of having an anti-Communist bias; the others were, to varying extents, pro-Soviet. Vagn Jensen was a staunch Communist who had earned a reputation for his leftist politics, and he and Steffensen were on the executive committee of the Danish-Soviet Friendship Society. And the Danish PEN Centre itself was by no means ill-disposed towards the USSR: in 1967, it had sent a delegation of Danish writers (consisting of Egerod, Jensen and Steffensen) to visit the Soviet Union.

Their letter was sent not just to Moscow, but to the Danish press as well. Spangenberg summarized this letter in an article titled 'Denmark's protest against the persecution of Soviet writers: a letter to the Soviet Writers' Union', which appeared in *Politiken* on 2 March.

In a stroke of good luck, Copenhagen was scheduled to host PEN International's annual congress in late February 1981. The Swedish delegation moved to add a discussion of Azadovsky's situation to the agenda. On 25 February, conference delegates unanimously approved a resolution demanding Azadovsky's immediate release.

But their efforts were in vain: the court declared Azadovsky guilty on 16 March.

Denmark's leading papers began reporting on the judgement as soon as the trial had ended. *Politiken* published Spangenberg's third article on the subject: 'Soviet dissident convicted on narcotics charges. Danish writers come to his defence.' *Information* ran a feature by Vibeke Sperling titled 'Literary scholar Azadovsky sentenced to two years'. Sperling was a noted political reporter who specialized in Eastern European affairs. She ran the USSR and Eastern European desk at *Information* from 1978 to 1981 and was *Politiken*'s Moscow correspondent from 1981 to 1982. She went on to spend many years working as a political correspondent in the USSR and Russia, where she wrote primarily on human rights issues. In 2003, the Russian Ministry of Foreign Affairs barred her from entering the country as a result of her reporting on the war in Chechnya.

Despite initial setbacks, PEN continued its work on Azadovsky's behalf. In summer 1981, the German and Swiss PEN Centres declared Azadovsky an active member of their affiliates; this was a common practice within PEN at the time.

When Swiss PEN passed the resolution granting Azadovsky membership at their annual meeting on 27 June, they wrote that this decision had been taken 'in the hope that this act will contribute to PEN International's efforts to improve the plight of incarcerated writers'. This resolution was passed in no small part thanks to the efforts of board member and Rilke scholar Magda Kerényi (1914–2004).

On 14 August, the 'high-profile Soviet Germanist and translator' Azadovsky was made a member of the West German PEN Centre during its conference in Darmstadt. At the time, this organization was headed by Martin Gregor-Dellin (1926–88), author of a noted biography of the composer Richard Wagner. The chairman of PEN International was also a German: Heinrich Böll, whose close friend Lev Kopelev had kept him informed about the Azadovsky Affair.

7.7 Gloria Mundi

Azadovsky's political persecution was doing wonders for his reputation as a scholar. It became apparent that, if he was ever released from the GULAG, he would emerge as a 'high-profile Soviet Germanist and translator' whose name was known throughout Europe.

The publicity surrounding Azadovsky's case naturally led to a discussion of his life and works. Brodsky's article refers to Azadovsky as 'one of the best Russian scholars of comparative literature today', while Scammel's feature story in *The New York Review of Books* (dated 15 April 1982) calls him 'a brilliant scholar of comparative literature in the Soviet Union'.

Of course, his newfound academic fame wasn't solely based on the scandal. By this point in his life, Azadovsky had produced a considerable number of serious scholarly works. Unfortunately, most of them had only appeared in Russian and were thus inaccessible to a wider audience. As luck would have it, entirely independent of each other, two people in two different countries took it upon themselves to compile and publish bibliographies of Azadovsky's works: Joachim Storck in Germany and Serge Deduline in France.

Thanks to Storck's efforts, the international Rilke Society dedicated nearly all of the 1982 issue of *Blätter der Rilke-Gesellschaft* to Azadovsky. It opens with a translation of Azadovsky's article 'Rainer Maria Rilke and Gorky', which first appeared in the Leningrad journal *Russian Literature* in 1967; this is followed by a photograph of Azadovsky dug up from the photo archives of *Die Welt*, and then a short item on 'Rilke and Russia', which Azadovsky had published in German in honour of the 100th anniversary of Rilke's birth. The issue ends with Storck's own contributions: a selection of documents related to Azadovsky's political persecution and a bibliography of Azadovsky's works on Rilke.

Azadovsky's second bibliographer was his friend Serge Deduline. Born in Leningrad, Deduline had emigrated in 1981: after a search of his flat, he had been interrogated by the Leningrad KGB and warned to leave the USSR as soon as possible. Once in Paris, he found employment with Radio Free Europe and *La Pensée Russe*. Deduline put together a bibliography and biographical note on Azadovsky and submitted it to *Cahiers du monde russe et soviétique*, the prestigious French journal of twentieth-century Russian history and literature. The bibliography was released in two instalments, the first of which appeared in autumn 1981. The second, which contained supplementary materials, came out in spring 1982. In his introduction, Deduline emphasizes that the publication of this bibliography is 'meant to defend the honour of a young Soviet researcher whose academic productivity has been astonishing (*surprenante*)'.

At Deduline's initiative, Radio Free Europe's Paris Bureau began preparing a story timed to come out around Azadovsky's birthday: 14 September 1982. It aired at the end of that month and ended with the following words, which though dramatic, were certainly sincere:

> Kostya, you're still wringing your hands now, doing hard labour thousands of kilometres away from the places you've called home. But I hope that even when you opened up your veins, driven to desperation by the administration's abuses, you never once doubted in your friends – both at home and far from there. We have always been with you. And though the Leningrad KGB's 'culture specialists' have forced your talents and knowledge into conditions where they're bound to languish, we are certain that you will still leave your mark on [Russian] academia. And that you will do it soon.

Even now, many years later, one cannot help but be struck by the respect Azadovsky's contemporaries had for his work, by the warmth and feeling with which they describe his personal and professional qualities. In the end, Azadovsky achieved a level of global recognition that would, under normal circumstances, be unthinkable for a forty-year-old Soviet humanities scholar. At the time, some expressed their scepticism regarding these 'panegyrics'. However, the truth was that no one knew whether these texts would turn out to be panegyrics or obituaries. In that moment, no one knew if Azadovsky would be freed, or when that might occur, or whether he would be allowed to return to academia if it did.

8

Russian truth

8.1 The mother

Lidia Vladimirovna Brun-Azadovskaya (1904–84) was the daughter of Lidia Nikolaevna Brun (1878–1942) and Vladimir Karlovich Brun (1877–1942), who was descended from Germans who had emigrated to Saint Petersburg in the mid-eighteenth century. In the wake of the 1917 revolutions, her family relocated from Petrograd to Feodosia in Crimea, where Lidia completed grammar school and leveraged her knowledge of English, French and German to find work as a typist. The family returned to Petrograd in 1923, and she qualified as a librarian in 1925. In 1935, she married Mark Azadovsky, and in 1938 she enrolled in the German section of Pedagogical Institute no. 2. She gave birth to Konstantin Azadovsky in 1941, and in March 1942, after surviving the most difficult winter of the Siege of Leningrad, her family was evacuated to Moscow by plane. From there, they took a train to Irkutsk, Mark Azadovsky's hometown, where his mother still lived. After spending three years in Irkutsk, the family returned to Leningrad in spring 1945. There, the Stalinist ideological crackdowns made their lives a living hell.

After Mark Azadovsky's death in 1954, Lidia Vladimirovna devoted herself to the preservation of her late husband's legacy: she was instrumental in the publication of his two-volume masterwork, *A History of Russian Folklore Studies*. She was also a scholar in her own right: her article on forgeries of letters ascribed to Maxim Gorky and memoirs attributed to Lenin was particularly well received. In the 1970s, however, her health began to decline, and by the end of the decade, she almost never left the house. When she marked her seventy-seventh birthday on 15 February 1981, there was very little to celebrate: her son and his partner were incarcerated and money was tight. She was forced to live on the same miserly pension she had been assigned in 1959, which worked out to 39 rubles, 30 kopecks per month after the monetary reform of 1961.

During the months Azadovsky spent in Kresty, Lidia Vladimirovna was only permitted to visit him once – after his trial had already taken place. The meeting lasted only an hour, and she was not allowed to hug or kiss him; they spoke through a glass partition using microphones and headphones. And, of course, they knew that their conversation was being monitored.

Lidia Vladimirovna was moved by the extraordinary generosity and loyalty of her son's friends, who not only worked tirelessly on his behalf but also took over her care in his absence. But she herself was not content to fade into the background: during the investigation, she wrote several passionate and attention-grabbing letters.

On 3 February 1981, Lidia Vladimirovna sent a lengthy appeal to the Presidium of the Twenty-sixth Congress of the Communist Party, then the highest political and social authority in the USSR. She knew her letter might not reach the Congress, and that, if it did, it was unlikely to receive a reply. With this in mind, she wrote another letter on 4 February, this one addressed to one of the most influential literary functionaries of the era: Georgy Markov (1911–91), chairman of the Soviet Writers' Union and a member of the Communist Party. Markov had also known Mark Azadovsky.

Lidia Vladimirovna's pointed letters reveal that she had also been required to give testimony to Investigator Kamenko:

> He explained to me that my son and his wife had been arrested and were being held in Kresty Prison. The investigator took my statement. The interrogation lasted fifty minutes, five minutes of which was spent discussing my son, the rest of which the investigator dedicated to Svetlana's character. He said every dirty, vile thing a person could say about a beautiful young woman. The whole time, I was shaking my head, saying, 'No, no, I don't believe it . . . that can't be . . . .' Then I delivered a speech defending Svetlana, both as a person and as a woman.

They also contain a description of her own situation:

> In one fell swoop, I have been deprived of my children, who are young, healthy and strong. I have been left without anyone to give me my daily bread, in the literal sense: I am seventy-seven years old, I have a heart condition and I am unable to walk. I cannot use public transport, I cannot take a single step down the street without the help of others. I am now in my second month of living on the compassion and magnanimity of kind people.

Her letters may have gone unanswered, but they didn't go unnoticed. On 19 February, during Lepilina's trial, the prosecutor made an indignant reference to the 'letters from Citizen Azadovsky's mother, which radiate hostility towards the Soviet regime'. These letters were presented as an aggravating circumstance when determining Lepilina's sentence.

With the encouragement of Azadovsky's friends, Lidia Vladimirovna continued her letter-writing campaign even after her son's trial had ended. In 1982, she wrote three lengthy complaints to the Central Committee on Azadovsky and Lepilina's behalf: one on 30 May, one on 1 June and one on 29 September. These letters were made public soon afterwards, when they were featured in the 22 July 1983 issue of *Samizdat Materials*, which was dedicated to the Azadovsky Affair.

8.2 Awaiting transfer

On 16 March 1981, Azadovsky was sentenced to two years in a minimum-security corrective labour colony. His appeal was reviewed on 16 April, during a session of the Leningrad City Court's Collegium on Criminal Proceedings presided over by V.G. Ovcharenko. The sentence was declared 'lawful and justified' and put into force.

Despite this major setback, Azadovsky still seemed to hold out hope that he would soon be set free. He imagined that his mother would appeal to Georgy Markov and Ilya Zilbershtein. He also didn't rule out the possibility that his own petition might reach the Central Committee and that the judgement against him would be overturned in light of the glaring procedural violations that had marred his case. This is why his petitions pointedly mention 'violations of socialist legal order' in Leningrad; Azadovsky hoped his words might spark a review that could help in his resentencing.

The fact that Azadovsky wasn't sent to a labour colony as soon as his sentence came into force was suspicious. He remained in the pretrial detention centre, Kresty, though he was transferred to the building for convicted people. The law decreed that 'every convicted person must work', and Azadovsky was no exception: he, too, was given the 'opportunity' to improve himself through daily labour. Kresty housed a factory that supplied the city of Leningrad with cardboard boxes: it was there that the celebrated scholar Konstantin Azadovsky began working off his debt to society.

At first, he thought he might never be sent to a colony, that he might serve his entire sentence in the box factory. However, he only spent a few days glueing boxes together. Then he was pulled from the line and put into a cell along with other convicts awaiting either transfer or the results of their appeals. There, he met Sergey Zilitinkevich, an oceanologist, geophysicist, meteorologist and the son-in-law of Dmitry Likhachyov. Zilitinkevich had been waiting for the results of his appeal since his conviction on trumped-up charges; now, he had managed to arrange for Azadovsky to be transferred to his cell.

In 1994, Azadovsky would write a brief introduction to Zilitinkevich's prison memoirs. In it, he recalls their time together in Kresty:

> It was stuffy in the cell. Stuffy and foul-smelling. Twelve half-naked convicts were packed into a stone cube originally intended for four. People lay on the floor, in front of the door, next to the toilet; they crouched, hunched over, along the wall. Some dozed, others played backgammon using improvised pieces, still others bickered with their neighbours. Time dragged on, drawn-out and dismal. Lights out, wake-up: nothing changed. The unceasing din from outside served to muffle the voices emerging from the windows; unceasing, ponderous cursing sounded in the corridors and cells. And then there was the 'sun': a light on the cell ceiling that shone constantly, all day and all night. So that everyone could always be seen!
>
> One person sat on a top bunk, cross-legged like an Egyptian scribe. Oblivious to the noise and the hubbub, he would write something down on a piece of paper, reread what he had written, cross some things out, then take out a fresh piece of paper and start writing again. The other inmates rarely interrupted him. They'd glance up at him with respect and say, 'The professor is working . . . .' Occasionally, they would ask him questions. He would answer them patiently, kindly – and then go back to his writing.
>
> Such was the exotic setting in which I first laid eyes on Sergey Sergeevich Zilitinkevich, the professor and world-renowned scholar. . . . And so, finding

ourselves in the same place (alas! not for long – only a week or two), Zilitinkevich and I whiled away the dreary prison hours together. It was March 1981.

The status quo was restored two weeks later, as soon as the prison administration realized that Azadovsky had been moved to a different cell without official permission. Once more, his days dragged on in anticipation; it seemed his fate would never be decided. He waited, speculating where he might be sent and when. At the same time, he began receiving letters: from his mother, his friends and even his colleagues in the department.

This extended period of waiting was telling in and of itself: it meant that the authorities hadn't yet decided what to do with him. He couldn't understand what was taking so long. It was only later that he realized that his fate was still under discussion within the halls of the Leningrad KGB, and perhaps even higher.

Meanwhile, Azadovsky's friends and acquaintances continued their efforts on his behalf. His friends in Moscow (the literary historian Alexander Parnis in particular) helped Zigrida Vanag and Genrietta Yanovskaya find him a new lawyer. And Yevgeny Shalman (1929–2008) wasn't just any lawyer, but a famous Moscow defence lawyer who had participated in numerous political cases. He had been slated to defend the noted dissident and human rights activist Alexander Podrabinek in early 1981, but hadn't been granted 'clearance' (the trial, which took place in Yakutsk on 6 January 1981, went ahead without a defence lawyer). Later on, Podrabinek described his first meeting with Shalman in summer 1978:

> Yevgeny Samoilovich was an excellent lawyer. He disliked the Soviet regime and was one of the few Moscow lawyers willing to take on political cases. However, it seemed as if his last case had broken him. While defending Yury Fyodorovich Orlov, he had run up against abuses of power that he couldn't have dreamt of. It wasn't just that his petitions were rejected for no reason, or that the judge, [V.G.] Lubentsova, was openly rude to the defence, or that Orlov received the maximum sentence: seven years in camps and five years of exile. And it wasn't even what went on outside the courthouse: the building was surrounded by a triple cordon of police and KGB, entrance was restricted to those bearing special passes and [officers] incited and then detained [members of the crowd]. A police officer struck Yelena Georgievna Bonner in the head; when she slapped him in response, she was detained, and when Sakharov rushed to her aid, his arms were twisted behind his back. They were both thrown into a police car and taken to the 103rd Police Station. . . . Ira Valitova, Yury Fyodorovich's wife, was allowed into the courtroom, but as soon as she attempted to leave during a recess, she was searched, stripped naked in the presence of three KGB officers. This was all outrageous and illegal, but nevertheless fairly standard. What was unusual was the treatment of the defence lawyer.
>
> 'Can you imagine,' Shalman told me during our meeting, 'I had stayed behind in the courtroom during a recess, and I was dragged out of there and locked up in some other room.' His voice shook, he became agitated at the memory of the humiliation he had suffered two months prior. They had treated this lawyer, a

professional and an equal actor in the trial, like a guilty schoolboy who could be locked up in a dark room. Fortunately, this room happened to have a telephone in it; Shalman called the bar association, which contacted the powers that be, and, finally, Yevgeny Samoilovich was released from the room and permitted to return to the courtroom.

Shalman recognized that Azadovsky's case was an unusual one, and he immediately identified several possible reasons for Azadovsky's sentence to be put under review. He had found enough procedural violations in the investigation and the trial that he believed the RSFSR Prosecutor's Office could be persuaded to lodge a protest (at the time, this agency had the power to overturn any judgement). Shalman held that, regardless of whether or not narcotics had been discovered in Azadovsky's possession, the investigation itself had 'violated the socialist legal order'. Furthermore, the court's examination of the case had been cursory and biased.

However, when Shalman finally arrived in Leningrad in June 1981, Azadovsky had just begun his transfer. Perhaps this was a coincidence, perhaps not.

A few months later, on 12 October 1981, Shalman sent a petition to the Prosecutor's Office, which was, unsurprisingly, rejected. The hopes that Azadovsky's friends had pinned on this 'famous Moscow lawyer' were disappointed, just as Lidia Vladimirovna's hope in Ilya Zilbershtein and Georgy Markov had come to nothing.

Meanwhile, Azadovsky was slowly adjusting to prison life. Terrible as his cell in Kresty might have been, it already seemed like a safe haven compared to the unknown horrors that lay in store. Azadovsky's days began to fall into a rhythm. The shock of the first few weeks gave way to a dull succession of days spent under the unquenchable prison 'sun'. The Soviet national anthem droned out over the radio every morning, the inmates spent an hour in the exercise yard every day and the guards on duty made the same announcement every night before lights out. Soon enough, Azadovsky knew the words to this speech as well as he knew the lyrics of the national anthem:

> Attention, attention! Citizen-prisoners, it is lights out in the pretrial detention centre. The following actions are strictly forbidden: playing board games or any other type of game, talking, moving about the cell and covering the light with paper. The administration warns that offenders will be severely punished.

April came to an end, May passed by and then it was June. Nothing happened. Azadovsky remained in Kresty. He had already worked his way up to the top of his new cell's hierarchy: he commanded a top bunk complete with pillow and blanket.

Because he had already served six months of his two-year sentence, Azadovsky's bunkmates predicted that he would be sent to a colony close to the city. Each day, he expected to be summoned for transfer; the longer he was kept waiting, the more fanciful his theories surrounding the delay became.

In fact, Azadovsky's transfer was delayed for bureaucratic reasons. According to Article 14 of the RSFSR Corrective Labour Code (ITK), people sentenced to incarceration had to be sent to their destination within nine days of their sentence coming into force. Azadovsky's sentence had come into force on 16 April, when the

Leningrad City Court denied his appeal. A copy of the appellate court's ruling ought to have arrived at Kresty on the day it was made. However, according to its incoming stamp, the document didn't appear in the prison office until 5 June 1981. It was only then that arrangements began being made for Azadovsky's transfer.

8.3 Time to go! Gather your things!

Towards evening on 14 June 1981, a shout rang out from the hatch of Azadovsky's cell: 'Azadovsky! Time to go! Gather your things!' Azadovsky realized that he was about to transferred.

He wasn't glad, exactly, but at least it was something new: a sign that life was moving on. In a few hours, he would be deposited at one of the colonies near Leningrad. In two or three weeks' time, he would be able to see his mother again. There would be no glass separating them this time, and they could speak without using headphones; he would even be able to embrace her. He would also be granted the right to send and receive an unlimited number of letters – this was a right he intended to take full advantage of.

After his time in prison, the zone would be a completely different world. Prison is a place of perpetual stillness and oppressive monotony; it is a place of boredom: even the unrelenting drone of the radio feels like torture. The dull, slow passage of time, the interminable days, the streams of people coming in and out . . . But the nightmares that the prisoners witness – the killings, the violence, the particularly brutal beatings – stay with them for a long time. After prison, the zone seems like a relief: it feels like a miracle to be able to look up at the sky. But the zone, too, has its dangers. You might be found hanging by the neck one morning, and no one would bother to investigate: after all, you're surrounded by a barracks full of suspects. Or you might not show up to roll call because you're lying in your bunk, turning blue under your blanket with a shiv stuck in your throat. Anything could happen. A great deal depends on where a prisoner is sent, what crime they've been convicted of and how long a sentence they've been given – to say nothing of their physical strength and psychological resilience. In any event, being transferred to the zone marks the beginning of a new phase in a prisoner's life.

Both in prison and later on, during transfer and in the labour camp, Azadovsky constantly found himself having to explain to his fellow inmates how he, a docent and the head of an academic department, had come to be convicted under Article 224-3. Azadovsky tried to hint at the true motivation behind his case without divulging too many details. For the most part, the other convicts, particularly the *blatnye*,[1] took his words at face value and eventually left him alone. Nevertheless, he faced a constant barrage of questions from curious and persistent cellmates.

Meanwhile, the uproar in the foreign press and on Western Russian-language radio was producing its intended effect: aware that Azadovsky was an object of particular interest to the powers that be, the prison (and, later, camp) administration was more mindful, even cautious, in its treatment of him. This was a sharp contrast to how things were for most prisoners, whose lives were considered worthless. The fact that Azadovsky was being monitored by the KGB kept the prison (and, later, camp) authorities in line. Everyone knew that an accidental 'suicide' or 'death from peritonitis' would cause problems, and so Azadovsky enjoyed a certain degree of protection from the guards' excesses.

However, this level of publicity also had a downside. The case's notoriety abroad left the Soviet authorities with no other choice: Azadovsky had to be sent as far away as possible to prevent him having any contact with the West.

Each day, Lidia Vladimirovna expected to hear that her son had been transferred to a colony somewhere in Leningrad Oblast; in the meantime, uncertainty was taking its toll. On 18 June 1981, she received an unexpected letter from Kresty. Dated 14 June, it was from Sergey Zilitinkevich:

> Today Kostya was taken for transfer. He just now (it is currently evening) managed to come up to my cell and tell me through the peephole that his card says Magadan. Of course, this is unpleasant. The worst part will be the journey itself – it will take about two months. But one of my cellmates insists that the Magadan minimum-security zone (where logging is the main form of labour) is better than the one in Leningrad [Oblast]: there are far fewer rough characters, and it's quieter overall. It's also not out of the realm of possibility that Kostya was mistaken.

That same day, Lidia Vladimirovna wrote a tear-stained telegram addressed to Leningrad's city prosecutor. On 23 June, the prosecutor's senior aide, A.A. Smirnov, issued a reply: he informed her that there were 'no grounds for the prosecutorial authorities to interfere in this matter' and that, moreover, Article 6 of the RSFSR ITK specifically stipulates that 'in exceptional cases, where it is deemed necessary for their successful correction and rehabilitation, convicts may be sent to serve their sentences in suitable corrective labour establishments in other constituent republics.'

The words Azadovsky had uttered at his trial – that whatever sentence he received would be a sentence for his mother, too – had turned out to be true.

8.4 The Grand Tour

Even today, Magadan is fairly remote; the region is only accessible by plane. And of course, there are no direct flights there for prisoners.

Prisoners wouldn't find out where they were being transferred until after they had already left the pretrial detention centre. Their destination was usually indicated in their file, which was kept in a sealed envelope held by an escort guard and written on a corresponding card. The prisoners were treated like human cargo: their final destination would remain a mystery unless an escort guard chose to reveal it to them, or unless they managed to catch a glimpse of this card for themselves.

Azadovsky learned where he was going through above-board channels: he heard it from the guard who was dividing the prisoners up for transfer. He was tormented by the thought of what this information might do to his mother. In fact, he would be transported even farther than he was led to believe: all the way to Susuman, deep in the Kolyma region.

Susuman had been established as a settlement in 1936 by GULAG prisoners on the banks of the Berelyokh River, a tributary of the Kolyma. In 1937, a gold mining operation was launched there. By 1938, Susuman had become a hub for the newly founded Western Metallurgical Directorate of Dalstroy (the Far North Construction Trust of the USSR NKVD), and by 1941 GULAG prisoners had begun construction on the infamous highway joining Susuman and Magadan, known colloquially as the 'Road of Bones'. In 1953, Susuman became the administrative centre of the Susumansky District, which borders the Sakha Republic (also known as Yakutia). The forced labour of the convicts living in Susuman was deemed so essential that Susuman was granted town status in 1964.

Though Susuman (at 62°47'N) lies south of the Arctic Circle (66°33'N), its climate is nevertheless severe; Oymyakon, a rural locality just 350 kilometres away from Susuman, is one of the Northern Poles of Cold. In Susuman, the average temperature in June and July is around +11 degrees Celsius (in July, it can reach +14). In March, the temperature can go down to −40 at night, and the winters are fiercely cold. The average temperature in December and January is less than −50. In the coldest weeks of winter, it drops to −60; the lowest recorded temperature is −67.

Azadovsky spent most of his journey east in a Stolypin carriage, a type of railway carriage named after Pyotr Stolypin, who served as prime minister of Russia under Nicholas II (r. 1894–1917). Such carriages were used to transport settlers to Siberia during the Stolypin agrarian reforms; during the Soviet period, they were repurposed to hold detainees, arrested persons and convicts. To get an idea of what a Stolypin carriage looks like, picture an old-fashioned railway carriage with the following modifications. Instead of walls, each compartment is separated from the corridor by metal lattice; it also has a padlocked metal lattice door. There are usually five regular compartments, along with two more that are divided in half by a wall. Each of the subdivisions, called 'triples', has three bunks: these were used to hold particularly dangerous criminals, escape risks, people with mental illnesses or women. The other parts of the carriage were reserved for guards and provisions. There are no windows in the compartments, just a slit in the corridor at the same height as the upper bunks. This slit, which is also covered with metal lattice, was kept open in warm weather and was usually painted grey. From the outside, Stolypin carriages could be mistaken for the kind used for transporting luggage and post.

Naturally, the hard bunks in these carriages weren't outfitted with mattresses, pillows or blankets. Officially, each compartment was meant to sleep seven, but accounts indicate that they were regularly made to house more than twenty. Prisoners survived on a diet of hot water and dry travel rations consisting of black bread and herring, which were distributed once a day. Prisoner transport carriages didn't follow any schedule: they travelled between the major stations attached to all sorts of trains, not only those meant for passengers. They also spent stretches of time standing idle in sidings, waiting for their next ride to come along. As a result, prisoner transport carriages took a long time to reach their destinations, at least twice as long as the slowest passenger trains. There wasn't any heating or air conditioning. The carriages were cold in winter and unbearably hot in summer, especially when they were forced to wait in a siding. Luckily, by 1981, the bedbugs that had tormented prisoners travelling in Stolypin carriages in earlier decades had died out. Prisoners were to be escorted to the toilets every four hours, but only when the train was in motion; this meant that inmates were unable to relieve themselves during the long hours of waiting between trains. Generally speaking, the escort guards weren't overly concerned with following instructions to the letter: they might not give the prisoners anything to drink or, on the contrary, they might give them plenty to drink, but then not allow them to use the toilets afterwards. In other words, they might 'go rogue', flagrantly abusing their power over the prisoners.

When a Stolypin carriage was attached to a passenger train, the guards would behave more discreetly. They would try to avoid attracting the attention of 'civilian' passengers or provoking the prisoners. They had good reason to be cautious: seasoned inmates had developed an effective method of pressuring the guards. This method, known as 'pitching', was first applied in road vehicles during prisoner transport, but came to be used in trains as well. Everyone in the carriage would lean over in unison, first one way and then the other. Soon, the carriage would begin lifting off the tracks, hitting its wheels against each one in turn. The guards, terrified that the train might go off the rails, would be frightened into doing their jobs.

Inmates were generally taken to the prisoner transport carriage in a prisoner transport vehicle. But if the procedure for putting prisoners into the transport vehicles was fairly routine, the process of loading them onto (or off of) a prisoner transport carriage was something truly dramatic: the barking of German shepherds would mix with the din of guards barking out orders, curses and abuse. After leaving the prisoner transport vehicle, inmates were not allowed to stand: instead, they were required to squat with their hands behind their heads and their eyes trained on the ground. They weren't allowed to look around them. Once the prisoner transport vehicle had been emptied, the inmates were herded towards the prisoner transport carriage at a run, usually across the railway tracks. Urged on by the barking of the dogs and the shouting of the guards, they were not permitted to stop. When they stumbled and fell, they were shouted at or kicked until they got up again. Inmates left the pretrial detention centre wearing their own clothing, including their shoes. However, many of them had had their shoelaces confiscated upon arrest, and so it was difficult for them to walk, let alone run. As a result, by the time they reached the carriage, many of the prisoners were either barefoot or missing a shoe. The reverse process – going from the prisoner transport carriage to a prisoner transport vehicle and then on to a transit prison – was very much the same: the squatting, the dogs, the run from the carriage to the van, the barking, the cursing and the violence. Prisoners considered it an extraordinary stroke of good luck when the rails led directly up to the prison itself.

But that was far from the worst of it. Between their stints in the prisoner transport carriages, the inmates were forced to endure life in transit prisons. However, they weren't admitted to these prisons immediately. First, they would be placed in a 'holding tank'. From there, they would be sent in small groups for body searches and searches of their personal belongings, which they kept with them in a sack. Then, they were made to shower while their sacks were hung on hooks and sent through a high-temperature thermal chamber to eliminate bedbugs and other pests. Finally, they were assigned to a cell. A few days or weeks later, a group of prisoners due to be transported in the same direction would be taken to a Stolypin carriage via prisoner transport vehicle.

The farther away a prison was from Leningrad and Moscow, the more difficulty it had obtaining supplies, and thus the more meagre its rations. The prison 'food' was hardly worthy of the name. At the same time, inspections of the inmates' personal belongings were stricter in the provinces: the guards' zeal could easily deprive a prisoner not only of their woollen socks and mittens but also of their tea, preserves and cigarettes. And, depending on the guards' mood, the search might not end there: they might examine or even read aloud a prisoner's personal letters (which had already undergone censorship) or make obscene comments about the women in their photographs.

Prisoner transfer was a form of Russian roulette. The outrages perpetrated in transit prisons had long since become the stuff of legend. A person could lose everything there: their belongings, their health, their dignity and even their life. Due to a multitude of factors, large and small – the constant moves between transit prisons, frequent searches, unrelenting day-to-day discomforts, bullying, humiliation and abuse – prisoner transport was often the most difficult part of a person's sentence.

For Azadovsky, this period lasted over two months. His journey stretched over 11,225 kilometres: first, thousands of kilometres in a Stolypin carriage to Khabarovsk, then 2,000 more in a civilian aeroplane to Magadan and the remainder in the prisoner transport vehicle that delivered him to Susuman.

To give the reader a better understanding of Azadovsky's 'Grand Tour', which lasted from 14 June to 21 August 1981, its major stops are given here:

Leningrad, Kresty Prison, 14 June 1981
    Prisoner transport carriage: Leningrad–Sverdlovsk, 2,080 kilometres
Sverdlovskaya Prison (about a week)
    Prisoner transport carriage: Sverdlovsk–Novosibirsk, 1,550 kilometres
Novosibirskaya Prison (five days)
    Prisoner transport carriage: Novosibirsk–Irkutsk, 1,840 kilometres
Irkutskaya Prison (five days)
    Prisoner transport carriage: Irkutsk–Khabarovsk, 3,200 kilometres
Khabarovskaya Prison (more than a week)
    Aeroplane: Khabarovsk–Magadan, 1,980 kilometres
Magadanskaya Prison (about four weeks)
    Prisoner transport vehicle: Magadan – Omchak settlement, 375 kilometres
Omchak Maximum-Security Corrective Labour Colony (one night)
    Prisoner transport vehicle: Omchak – Susuman, 200 kilometres
Susuman, Corrective Labour Colony no. 5, 21 August 1981

People under criminal investigation were strictly forbidden from sending or receiving any letters; convicted persons were only allowed to enter into correspondence after they had arrived at the facility where they were to serve out their sentence. During transit, letters could only be sent with the permission of a transit prison warden. In practice, such permission was extremely difficult to obtain: the prisoner would have to submit a written request and then wait for a reply, which was unlikely to arrive before the end of the prisoner's stay.

However, transit gave prisoners the opportunity to avail themselves of another means of communication: the so-called Russian post. They would toss letters written on scraps of paper out of the Stolypin carriages, hoping for passers-by to find them and send them on to their intended addressees. The farther away the prisoners got from the capitals, the more sympathetic the local inhabitants were to their plight; people who spotted letters lying near the railroad tracks were unlikely to pass them by. If the letter included an address, someone might manage to find a stamp and an envelope to send it on. Some compassionate people continued this practice even during the years of the Great Terror, when such good deeds were punishable by incarceration. The letters were left mostly at major stations, where the Stolypin carriages were transferred from one train to another. The authorities knew about this method of communication, of course, but it was difficult to suppress: after all, they couldn't post a guard at every window.

Though prisoners were still careful about what they wrote and how they wrote it, letters sent via 'Russian post' gave them the opportunity to write about topics that would be impossible to broach in prison or camp correspondence, which was subject to censorship.

Azadovsky also sent letters via 'Russian post'. Though the exact number of letters he composed during his two-month-long journey remains unknown, at least a few of them made it back to Lidia Vladimirovna. While he was still in Kresty, he couldn't possibly have imagined that such a lengthy journey lay before him, and so he didn't think to stock up on envelopes. Thus, during transit, he found himself in the difficult position of trying to cadge envelopes from the prisoners he met either in Stolypin carriages or in the bunks of transit prisons.

The first letter Lidia Vladimirovna received was written in Vologda on 15 June – the day after Azadovsky left Leningrad. It was written on a scrap of paper, probably the only thing he could manage to find. The postmark indicates that it was sent from Arkhangelsk on 17 June. How had it ended up there, more than 600 kilometres to the north? In all likelihood, someone had picked up the letter in Vologda before boarding a train to Arkhangelsk and then posted it upon arrival. Again, judging by the postmark, the letter arrived in Leningrad on 24 June, and it reached Lidia Vladimirovna on the 25th.

15 June, Vologda

Mama, I am being taken to Magadan via Sverdlovsk. Transit can take a long time (about a month), so don't worry if you don't hear from me for a while. As you can see, all this is being done consciously, deliberately and methodically.

Don't worry about me, for God's sake. I will write as soon as I get the chance.

I haven't sent a supervisory complaint to the Supreme Court because I don't know if my lawyer (and all of you) would consider it wise. I can't tell what kind of strategy would be most appropriate at this stage. Write to me about all this in your very first letter to me . . .

I also didn't submit a 'legal' complaint while I was in Leningrad, by the way, for the simple reason that it wouldn't have reached its destination.

Sending you warm embraces. I think about you all the time. Stay strong.

The second of Azadovsky's letters to reach Leningrad was tossed out of a window on 4 July during a layover in Baikalsk, a town in Irkutsk Oblast. It was sent on over a week later, on 17 July, and it reached Lidia Vladimirovna on the evening of 22 July:

Mama, my dear,

Today, on 4 July, I arrived in our native Irkutsk, where we will be stopping for several days. It appears that I will not reach my final destination before 1 August.

Transit is going by faster and more smoothly than is typically the case. Of course, there are many day-to-day hardships, but that's nothing. The most important thing now is which colony I end up in and how I establish myself there.

The last time I wrote to you was on 15 June; I don't know if you received that little letter. I feel it necessary to repeat once more that all my hopes now hang on Moscow and on Moscow alone. I didn't send a supervisory complaint to the Supreme Court because I didn't want to do so without consulting my lawyer in Moscow first. I would also like to know if you are familiar with the contents of my supervisory complaint. I think that you all, and my lawyer Shalman first and foremost, must now act without my input.

I think about you every day, about all the problems you are forced to face all on your own, and I suffer greatly from not hearing anything [about you]. How are you feeling this summer? Am I right to think that the weather in Leningrad isn't too oppressive? Are our friends and acquaintances coming to visit you?

Of course, the thought that weighs upon me most heavily is that I won't see you for another year and a half, an entire year and a half. But what's to be done?? My trip to Kolyma will (I hope!) be the final blow dealt to me by the Petersburg authorities, of whom I am a particular favourite. (Is it possible to fight this, to demand to be returned to a local zone? I don't know.)

But perhaps this act is, in some sense, directed against you, too: as revenge against the decisive and purposeful actions you have taken.

How is S[vetlana]? If you go to see her, pass along my most tender words and my certainty that she will remain herself through all of the hardships she faces in the women's minimum-security zone.

Sending you kisses. Be healthy and safe.

P.S. The lawyer R[ozanovsky] is a coward: he did nothing, absolutely nothing for me. The only thing he did was to completely disorientate me on the eve of my trial. Don't pay him anything extra: both Sv[etlana] and I might yet have need of money, especially when we come to the second half of our sentences.

The fourth letter Azadovsky sent from transit was the only one that arrived in an envelope addressed in his own hand. It was addressed to Lidia Vladimirovna, care of

Boris Filanovsky, flat 6, building 6, Zhukovsky Street, Leningrad. The return address was given as: 'Chita Central Post Office, to be left until called for by N.A. Bestuzhev'. This was a reference to the exiled Decembrist Nikolay Bestuzhev, one of the figures Mark Azadovsky had written about.[2]

This letter is not only the longest but also the least inhibited of the ones Azadovsky wrote during his incarceration. Clearly, he wasn't writing with the censorship in mind; on the contrary, he seemed to be revelling in this opportunity to speak freely. The letter was written over several sittings. Either by design or through lack of opportunity, he put off sending it until the last possible moment: he continued writing up until the train had reached the station.

Judging by the postmark, the letter was left in Arkhara, a town in the Amur Oblast, at a station along the Trans-Siberian Railway. The envelope was dropped onto the platform through a window slit and an unknown individual picked it up and put it in a post box. On 12 July, the letter began making its way towards Leningrad, and on 18 July it was delivered to Azadovsky's friends Boris and Tatyana Filanovsky, who passed it on to Lidia Vladimirovna two days later.

10 July 1981

Mama, yesterday we passed through Chita and now we are approaching Khabarovsk. Tomorrow I will be set down (either in Khabarovsk or in Birobidzhan) and, by my calculations, I should arrive in Magadan sometime before the 20th. Don't worry if you don't receive any letters from me. I try to write to you every chance I get (this is, I believe, the fourth letter I have written to you since 14 June), but my opportunities are few and far between, and I don't know whether my letters are reaching you. In any case, in each letter I repeat the most important things pertaining to my case: 1) that I did <u>not</u> send a supervisory complaint to the RSFSR Supreme Court from Kresty, 2) that I tried to send you a copy so that you could make 10 copies of it to use however you see fit. I need to know: Did you get it? 3) that I believe you must now act decisively and without waiting for any guidance from me. Even when I was still in Kresty, the 'guidance' I was able to give you was limited in all sorts of ways, but now . . .

I feel all right, though travelling between transit prisons is exhausting, of course. Please don't worry about me, really: I've more or less learned how to navigate this new and peculiar environment. Things are also fine as far as food is concerned: in short, we're fed. Things will be different in the zone. To survive there in the current conditions, you have to have cash [though this was officially forbidden – P.D]. It doesn't just get you food or ensure a good diet; it can also get you time off from work, early release and much else besides. I'll let you know as soon as (and if) I manage to find a 'channel'. In short, I've become convinced that absolutely everything here runs on money, and there is no doubt in my mind that if I were a typical inmate, I would be heading back to Leningrad as early as December or January. But alas: I have obviously been sent here with all sorts of unspoken instructions and orders. (And so even money can only do so much in my case, but it will still do quite a lot.)

It is precisely such unspoken instructions that will, in all likelihood, make it difficult for me to be transferred to *khimia*[3] or released on parole. And really, what would be the point of working in *khimia* somewhere in Ussuriysk or even Tagil?! The conditions in *khimia* are terrible . . . everyone either makes a run for it or requests to go back to the zone. In Leningrad Oblast, *khimia* is different. If I get transferred to *khimia*, I'll have good grounds to petition to be sent back to Leningrad Oblast, but, again, it would take several months to resolve this matter.

In short, Moscow is now my only hope. If Moscow doesn't challenge the decision made by the Leningrad organs of 'justice', I will have to remain in the zone until December 1982. This conclusion may not be very comforting, but it's realistic!

What weighs on me the most is the thought that I won't be able to see you for another year and a half. And I'm afraid that correspondence won't be easy, either: letters will take at least three weeks in either direction (because of the censorship process). (Things will be different if I can manage to find a 'channel'!) It will be torture for me to go so long without receiving any news of you, of how you are feeling, of how things are going in Leningrad and Moscow! That's why I would like the sentence issued by the Kuibyshevsky People's Court to be changed, if not thrown out entirely.

I don't know what's happening around my case now in Leningrad and beyond. The lawyer R[ozanovsk]y, that two-faced coward, assured me in May that 'things have calmed down, thank God.' If that's true, it's very bad indeed. Because I believe that there are two things that could truly help me. The first is having as much publicity as possible. The second would be unofficial, behind-the-scenes negotiations in Moscow (at various levels, following various leads). The rest is all nonsense and lawyerly scribbling. (By the way, it would be good if both strategies I've mentioned were applied simultaneously and appeared independent from each other.)

By the way, did you know that I wrote a fairly detailed and candid letter to the UN Commission on Human Rights in March? At the same time, I wrote to *The Literary Gazette* and asked that splendid institution to step in and send a representative to my trial. This was all seized from me during a routine search and was never returned. This is just for your information.

* * *

As soon as I arrive in the zone, I will write to you immediately and give you my address. A letter from you would really boost my morale. When you write (and every time you write afterwards), be sure to enclose two blank airmail envelopes. Anyone else who decides to write to me in the zone should do the same. (There aren't enough airmail envelopes to go around!)

* * *

The summer is half gone, and from what I understand, it hasn't been unbearably hot on the banks of the Neva.[4] I hope that you are still living on Vosstaniya Street. What's happening with the building? Could it be that you have moved, or that you will be forced to do so? The thought of it frightens me! What became of my article for *L[iterary] H[eritage]*? (Did anything come of it at all?)

In short, I have a whole slew of questions and problems, and they all press on me, weigh on me; the only thing that brings me comfort is the fact that the remainder of Svetlana's sentence can now be measured in months rather than years. How is she? If you go to see her on 11 August as planned, pass along my most tender greetings. I can imagine how things are for her and how she must suffer. In some ways, the zone is worse for women than for men. Will she be able to remain herself?

* * *

As we were leaving Irkutsk, I managed to catch a glimpse of the Angara River and the Intourist Hotel, which would have provided a far more comfortable stay than the 'hotel' I spent five days in. But then I was met with an unexpected delight. I spent the entire ride to Ulan-Ude on the middle bunk (the only place where you can see out the window on those rare occasions when it's cracked open), and I saw Baikal in all its glory. I haven't been so struck by anything in a long time, though the Baikal landscapes reminded me a bit of Lake Onega in places. And then names I've known since childhood began flashing by: Petrovsky Zavod, Chita, Nerchinsk[5] . . . . Mama, I have traversed almost the entire country, West to East, in a Stolypin carriage. I have seen a lot in the past month, and I have heard a lot. Someday, I will be able to tell you lots and lots of interesting and funny and terrible things. If only that 'someday' would come sooner . . .

* * *

Two authorization letters have been left at Kresty in your name. You can use one of them to collect my watch and ring. The items listed in the other letter (a belt and a scarf) can't be collected, as I took them with me. There are about fifty rubles left in my personal account at Kr[esty]; that money will be transferred to the colony after I arrive. Of course, it won't arrive before December, so I won't be able to rely on it for the time being. (Generally speaking, I repeat, only <u>cash</u> makes any difference in the zone; the money in your personal account is irrelevant.)

Despite your assurances, I still worry about your financial situation. It looks as though I won't be able to transfer money to you before the end of the year. Think about it. In one of my letters from Kresty, I wrote to you that my former life has been destroyed and that it will be impossible to return to it (which is to say, to its former prosperity). When I get out, the only option will be to build a new life. I believe in that new life, and there is no doubt in my mind that I will now be capable of building it. But first we will have to get through ('survive') the remaining year and a half, or even less, since things will get easier once Svetlana is released (the only thing that worries me now is her *propiska*). In short, don't place too much value on objects, paintings and books. The important thing now is that you have some money set aside.

When Tamara Iv[anovna] – Svetlana's sister] goes to see Svetl[ana], have her take ab[out] seventy-five rubles with her (sewn into her hem or hidden in her shoe).

* * *

When I get to the zone, I will be allowed to receive one parcel of up to one kilogram. I will write separately with instructions on what ought to be sent. Think about whether it might make more sense to send these things on from Irkutsk; after all, it's half the distance, so the groceries won't spoil on the way. The only problem is, rumour has it that there's nothing to be found in the city of Irkutsk, and that the locals could do with some fattening up themselves.

Apparently, in addition to these [food] packages, you can also send books and an electric razor. Speaking of books: whatever you send, bear in mind that I will have to leave them in the zone, so don't send anything expensive or rare.

* * *

Well, then, this has turned out to be a long letter. Forgive my handwriting: I'm writing on the train and the carriage is jolting about terribly. Just in case, I am sending this letter (for the first time) to Borya and Tanya's address: you never know, your correspondence might be being monitored.

I will try to write again before I reach M[agada]n.

Stay healthy, mama. Be patient.

K.

The last letter Lidia Vladimirovna received from Azadovsky during transit was sent through official channels: it was authorized by the warden of IZ-47/1 in Magadan, where Azadovsky arrived on 18 July. It was sent at the end of July and arrived in Leningrad on 11 August.

Magadan, 22–25 July 81

Mama, it's me. After spending just a short time in Khabarovsk (where I wrote to you exactly a week ago today), on the 18th I was deposited here, on the shores of the Sea of Okhotsk. In a few days, I will be taken to a colony somewhere in the North (which is to say, north of here), in the settlement, or, rather, the small town of Susuman. It's nearly on the border of Sakha. You see where life can take a person!

Everything I've heard and learned here suggests that incarceration in Kolyma compares favourably to incarceration further inland. Here, for example, they feed [the prisoners] well, provide warm clothing and medical treatment, etc. I'll let you know my final address as soon as I arrive in Susuman.

What exactly awaits me in Susuman, for the time being I cannot say.

I already wrote to tell you that, before I left L[eningrad], when I was still in Kresty, I drafted a detailed supervisory complaint to the RSFSR Supreme Court (which, by the way, I still have yet to send). I don't have any other news to report on my case's progress (or lack thereof). Of course, at this point, if there is any news, it will only come from L[eningrad] or Moscow.

I need your advice on certain matters. For example, I consider the Leningrad Directorate's decision to send me to Magadan unlawful and groundless, and [I would like to] submit a petition to that effect to the Magadan Oblast supervisory prosecutor and perhaps write to Moscow, to the Main Directorate [of Prison Labour Establishments of the USSR MVD] on B[olshaya] Bronnaya Street. But I assume that one of you (either you or the lawyer) must have anticipated me and submitted a complaint on that count. Or perhaps you think such actions are pointless? That's exactly the kind of thing I would like to know (along with many other things besides).

I'm not asking you an endless stream of questions about you, about Svetlana, about home, etc., but of course, that's what preoccupies me most.

I feel all right myself, but to be honest, I'm glad that transit is nearly over.

Sending you hugs and kisses. Take care of yourself. Start writing me a response.

P.S. Morning of the 27th. I'm still here. K.A.

And he would be stuck there for a long time yet. Up until then, his journey across the motherland had moved along at a reasonable pace; however, once he reached Magadan, it was as if someone had slammed on the brakes. Azadovsky spent nearly a month in IZ-47/1. This infamous transit point lay between the 'mainland'[6] and the camps of Magadan and Sakha. It was haunted by the shadow of the GULAG; millions of GULAG prisoners had passed through Kolyma from the 1930s to the 1950s. The colony in Susuman where Azadovsky was headed looked positively pleasant in comparison: it was the only minimum-security zone in Magadan Oblast, where first-time and low-level offenders were sent. The other colonies in the oblast had far worse reputations. There was a medium-security colony in Talaya for first-time offenders convicted of serious crimes; this was where the dissident Andrey Amalrik, author of the famous essay 'Will the Soviet Union Survive until 1984?', had been sent. There were also two maximum-security colonies: one in Novaya Vesyolaya (the evocatively named 'New and Jolly') on the outskirts of Magadan, and one in a settlement called Uptar. Finally, there was a maximum-security prison in the settlement of Omchak that held repeat offenders and people serving life sentences. Azadovsky's convoy spent the night there on its way to Susuman. Inmates bound for all of these establishments stopped in the cramped Magadan Prison on the way to their final destination. Azadovsky was surprised to find that it was a considerable improvement over the other prisons he'd been held in during his two months in transit. Everything was better: the treatment, the conditions, even the food.

There isn't any documentary evidence to explain why Azadovsky spent nearly a month in Magadan, but it was probably for the same reason he had been kept in Kresty for so long. Once more, he was waiting for his fate to be decided. Should he remain in the zone or be exiled to the West? Finally, a decision was taken, and on 20 August a guard shouted those familiar words through the hatch in his cell door: 'Azadovsky! Gather your things!'

The prisoner transport vehicle drove off along the highway, packed to the gills with inmates. Towards evening it arrived in Omchak, where the prisoners were scheduled to spend the night in the local maximum-security prison. Azadovsky might have seen the large banner hanging there, which read:

WORK SPARES US FROM THREE EVILS: BOREDOM, VICE AND NEED.
–Voltaire

On the evening of 21 August 1981, Azadovsky was deposited in Susuman. He wrote to his mother the very next day:

> I hasten to inform you that I arrived at the colony today, and that now, finally, you will be able to write to me freely and as much as you like; you can send letters to the address indicated on this envelope.
> I am very concerned that I haven't heard from you in so long, that I have no news about your health. I would also like to know the status of my case and what you need from me...
> Did you get the letters I sent you from Magadan, Khabarovsk, etc.?
> I am in perfect health (both physically and mentally).
> For the time being, it's hard to say how my situation here in Susuman will play out. In any case, the days pass by, and that in itself gives me hope.

Lidia Vladimirovna received this letter on 5 September, two days after an official notice came from the colony informing her of her son's arrival at the camp. Though this notice had been sent on 26 August, it took a week less than Azadovsky's letter to arrive in Leningrad because it wasn't subject to censorship:

> This notice is to inform you that your son, Konstantin Markovich Azadovsky, arrived at AV-261/5 (address: Susuman, Magadan Oblast), the establishment where he will serve out his sentence, on 21 August 1981.
> According to the law, the convict Azadovsky has the right to receive two parcels, three short visits and two long visits per year, and to send and receive an unlimited number of letters per month.
> After the first half of his sentence has been served, he will also be permitted to receive three packages or deliveries of no more than five kilograms each per year...
> No more than two adults are permitted to visit the convict at a time. The convict Azadovsky will inform you of the arrival time for visits.
> Warden, Penal Establishment AV-261/5
> A.A. Eshchenko
> 21 August 1981

9

Life in *khimia*

9.1 Ulyanovka

Meanwhile, Lepilina was facing troubles of her own. With the help of her lawyer, she had submitted an appeal requesting a mitigated sentence in light of her confession during trial. Apart from anything else, her current sentence meant that she would lose her living space. Lepilina hoped that her sentence might be suspended or reduced. Predictably, though, the Collegium on Criminal Proceedings of the Leningrad City Court upheld the original sentence when it reviewed her appeal on 5 March.

As of 8 March (International Women's Day), Lepilina was still in Kresty; she wouldn't be transferred to US-20/2, the corrective labour establishment to which she'd been assigned, until the end of the month. US-20/2 was a minimum-security women's corrective labour colony in the settlement of Ulyanovka (known as Sablino prior to 1922) in the Tosnensky District of Leningrad Oblast.

Lepilina arrived in the zone in a state of depression, though the fresh air provided a welcome change from her cell. Thankfully, her time in transit had been short. Because she had remained near Leningrad, she would be able to take full advantage of her visitation rights. The ITK granted prisoners of Lepilina's type three short visits (up to four hours) and two long visits (up to three days) per year. However, it is important to bear in mind that visitation – both the length and number of visits a prisoner received – was left entirely to the discretion of the camp authorities. For example, a short visit might be cut off after only half an hour.

Lepilina wouldn't learn of Azadovsky's sentence until late March. It was only in mid-April, when she started receiving letters, that she began to gain a clearer picture of what was going on. Her most frequent correspondent was Lidia Vladimirovna. One of the first letters she received from her was dated 8 April:

My sweet Svetlanochka!

This is the second letter I have written to you. I wrote the first in early March, but it came back to me marked 'Undeliverable'. Of course, now you will receive [this one] . . .

I had a visit with Kostya on 20 March. He seemed better than I expected. He looked exactly the same; his demeanour was cheerful and confident. He is very worried about you. It is unclear when I will be able to visit him again . . .

Svetochka, my life is filled with only one thought: of him and of you. You're all I ever think about, nothing else enters my mind. My dear, write when you can, however much you can. Sending you kisses and hugs.

Lidia Vladimirovna's letters arrived on an almost-weekly basis. They provided Lepilina with much-needed moral support. She had been shocked by the news that her Kostya had been sent to Magadan. She felt depressed and, what's more, racked with guilt. She blamed herself for what had happened, reasoning that, if she hadn't given the authorities an excuse to search Azadovsky's flat, he wouldn't have been put on trial and given this sentence. She was at her wits' end. Strange as it might seem, her arrival in the zone might actually have saved her life: she was distracted from her inner turmoil by the new conditions and new people, the routine of camp life and the constant need to interact with other inmates. Lepilina was also kept under careful observation because of the note in her prison file saying she had suicidal tendencies. She wasn't singled out for particularly harsh treatment: the camp authorities didn't deprive her of visitation rights or keep her in a punishment isolation cell. She soon found her bearings, and, after she realized that her fellow inmates were generally decent people, she managed to assimilate quickly and painlessly.

In Ulyanovka, as in any Soviet zone, the rehabilitation programme consisted of various elements: a restricted diet, daily singing of the Soviet national anthem, roll call on the square, political instruction and, of course, a daily dose of hard labour. If the Soviet regime wouldn't tolerate 'parasitism' among its free citizens, it certainly wouldn't accept it in its prisoners. In the zone, as in the rest of the country, working days were eight hours long, with one day off per week; however, inmates' rights were significantly limited. Prisoners didn't have the right to holiday time, nor did the months or years of labour they performed during their sentences count towards their pensions.

Those who refused to work or who didn't fulfil their work quotas were subject to punishment: they might be stripped of their visitation rights or their right to receive packages. They might be forced to work their full eight-hour shifts during visits from their relatives. The main industry in women's zones was clothing manufacture. Inmates produced a wide variety of items, from work gloves and clothes (items traditionally associated with Soviet – and later Russian – prison labour) to dampers for Red October pianos.

Lepilina wasn't one of the prisoners who refused to work. She didn't cause trouble and she made her quotas in the sewing workshop, so the authorities didn't see any reason to prevent her from seeing her loved ones. Her sister Tamara came to visit her in the zone, as did some friends, who got in by pretending to be relatives. Some details of these meetings appear in Genrietta Yanovskaya's memoirs:

Realizing what was happening with Svetka, I was determined to visit her in Sablino no matter what. . . . In short, I managed to make my way into the zone. I went in as if on official business, I presented my passport. I surrendered it and went in. My case (I had bought the biggest one they had) contained chicken, strawberries and a large amount of tea and cigarettes. It was full to bursting.

Svetka was called into the office; I was standing by the window, wearing the most modest little dark blue dress I could find at home. . . . She came in wearing a kerchief and a blue-and-white [chintz] dress with a number on her chest; she loudly stated her number: 'prisoner number such-and-such has arrived, Citizen Warden.' She didn't recognize me at first. It's terrible to look back on this meeting. I remember giving her something to eat. Later on, my visit caused her some unpleasantness among her comrades. They saw that she had been called in to see the warden, and then she came back with good cigarettes, so they decided she was a 'snitch'.

When Sveta was sent to the zone, she was allowed a one-kilogram parcel. I gathered up everything I could – hand cream, face cream, some slippers, socks – and hurried off to the post office. 'Girls, I'm sending a package to the zone; I can only send one kilogram.' How meticulously they weighed it! And then they said I could fit in another forty grams, so I rushed round the shops looking for some other cream. But by the time I got back, it was too late: they had already sealed the postal sacks. 'But girls, I need to get this to the zone.' And they unsealed the sacks and stuck that little tube inside. And that's how people feel about prisoners in Russia. They could have just sent it the next day, but instead they unsealed the post so that the package would reach its destination sooner. Not because I asked, but because they believed it was the right thing to do . . .

The next time I went to visit Svetka in the Sablino zone, Zigfrida and I went together, posing as Svetka's cousins. This counted as a visit with relatives. One could have died laughing! She was Svetlana Ivanovna Lepilina; meanwhile, her two 'cousins' were called Zigfrida Tsekhnovitser and Genrietta Yanovskaya[1] . . .

When I went to see Svetlana that second time, a letter from Kostya had arrived for her to say he was in transit. But I got them to agree to let me see her first, before they gave her the letter, so I could prepare her for the news. . . . I gave Sveta some valerian drops; at least I was there for her, that made it less terrible.

It is impossible to say whether Lepilina would have made it through this difficult time if it hadn't been for the help and friendship of her fellow inmates. One of the women she grew close to was Natalya Lazareva, a set designer who had been arrested in Leningrad on 26 September 1980 for her role in producing the samizdat feminist journal *Maria*. While her collaborators all emigrated to the West (at the KGB's behest), Lazareva stayed behind; she cherished naïve hopes of joining the Soviet Artists' Union. Around that time, a search of her flat unearthed an appeal, written in her own hand, calling upon the women of the world to speak out against the deployment of Soviet troops to Afghanistan; she was charged under Article 190-1. On 12 January 1981, the Leningrad City Court sentenced her to ten months in a minimum-security colony; she was sent to Ulyanovka, where she would spend the entirety of her sentence.

Another person Lepilina became close to during her time in Ulyanovka was Genya Gutkina (1923–82), an art expert who had been arrested on 3 June 1977. She was charged with several crimes, the most serious of which was antiques trafficking. The investigation against her was led by the KGB's Investigation Department. The case caused quite a stir at the time: Gutkina was accused of exporting Russian artworks to the West, including six pieces by Pavel Filonov. In retrospect, the idea of painting Gutkina as the ringleader of an organized crime syndicate seems rather far-fetched.

Gutkina was taken to Ulyanovka after her trial; later on, she would be transferred to a zone in Gorky Oblast (now Nizhny Novgorod Oblast), and in 1982 she would be released under Article 100 of the ITK, which dealt with cases of serious illness. To put it bluntly, she was sent home to die (which she did, in a matter of weeks).

Gutkina knew Azadovsky from the many years she spent moving in Leningrad's circles of art lovers and collectors. When Lepilina showed up in Ulyanovka, Gesha – as the sixty-year-old Gutkina was known – treated her warmly and helped her to find her feet in this new and perilous world.

9.2 The Gorky Automobile Factory

After Lepilina had been tried and sent to the colony, she was no longer of interest to the powerful forces that had put her and Azadovsky behind bars. This explains why the camp authorities didn't seem to bear her any ill will; after all, if they had wanted to, they could have made up some imaginary offence to punish her for at any time, or created some other obstacle to block her path to *khimia*.

Until the 1990s, '*khimia*' was the term used to refer to 'conditional release from [a convicted person's] place of incarceration with mandatory labour' (as defined in Article 53-2 of the RSFSR Criminal Code). Though Russia has a long history of exploiting prisoner labour, this particular type of forced labour was introduced under Nikita Khrushchev. *Khimia* was a kind of partial imprisonment. Once in *khimia*, a person was technically considered free, but their freedom was severely limited: they were required to live and work wherever they were sent, to check in at the special commandant's office on a regular basis and to sleep in a dormitory.

Khimia's origins can be traced to Soviet policies of the late 1950s and early 1960s. At the May 1958 Plenum of the CPSU Central Committee, Khrushchev gave a speech titled 'On the accelerated development of the chemical industry'. On 7 May, the plenary session unanimously voted to adopt a resolution putting Khrushchev's proposals into action. The scale of the 'Big Chemical' ('*Bolshaya Khimia*') initiative was vast: 100 billion rubles were allocated to the project, to be spent over the course of several years. In order to meet the demands of the burgeoning chemical industry, on 20 March 1964 the Presidium of the Supreme Soviet was forced to issue a decree titled 'On the conditional release of convicted persons on the path to rehabilitation to work on the construction of socially owned enterprises', which resulted in large numbers of prisoners being put on conditional release to spend the rest of their sentences working in the chemical industry. The demand for this kind of industrial labour only increased, and the state adjusted accordingly. But by the late 1970s, this labour source was running dry. In 1980, Yury Churbanov, deputy minister of Internal Affairs and son-in-law of General Secretary Leonid Brezhnev, wrote an article for the in-house journal of the MVD's Corrections Directorate. Titled 'Towards a new life', the article didn't mince words:

It is impossible not to observe the alarming downward trend in the number of individuals on conditional release or serving suspended sentences working in construction and manufacturing. We must not limit the practice of probation and conditional release, but, rather, extend it using every legal means possible, for, as experience shows, this humane practice helps people who have lost their way to straighten out and prove their rehabilitation through labour.

Life in *khimia* was far from cushy. It meant doing the kind of difficult, dangerous industrial labour that free citizens were, for the most part, unwilling to do. One of the conditions of working in *khimia* was that the remainder of a person's sentence would be counted in working days rather than calendar days. Since the Labour Code required that workers be given a certain number of days off, moving to *khimia* also meant that a person's sentence became slightly longer than it would have been if they had remained in a camp.

In those days, the wages in *khimia* were relatively decent: workers there made significantly more than librarians, dishwashers or caretakers, for example. However, not all inmates were willing to work themselves into the ground or sacrifice their health, and so prisoners were more likely to apply for early release on parole instead. To qualify for parole, though, prisoners had to have completed at least half of their sentence (or, in the case of serious crimes, two-thirds). In Lepilina's case, this would mean spending an extra three months in the colony. Besides, she didn't want to risk rejection: the country needed more industrial workers, not more parolees.

People sentenced to less than ten years could only be sent to *khimia* after they had completed a third of their sentence. Thus, Lepilina, who had been sentenced to one and a half years, could only hope to be released to *khimia* after serving six months. She petitioned to be transferred to *khimia* as soon as she was eligible, and, just two weeks later, on 4 August 1981, she was granted conditional release and sent to 'build the national economy' in Gorky (now Nizhny Novgorod) for a period of ten months and fourteen days.

People granted conditional release were sent to their destinations 'in the manner prescribed for persons sentenced to incarceration'. Thus, Lepilina's trip to Gorky resembled the prisoner transit process described in the previous chapter: it featured the same prisoner transport vehicles, the same Stolypin carriages, the same desperate dashes between vehicles, the same escort guards with the same barking dogs threatening to tear the terrified inmates to pieces. Lepilina was released from custody upon arrival in Gorky on 18 August, at which point she was issued a certificate of release (dated 4 August, the day she had been granted conditional release); this was to be her primary form of identification over the coming months.

Lepilina was lucky in her housing assignment: she shared a bright room in a five-story brick dormitory with another woman on conditional release. The warm, clean room, the bathtub with hot running water, the clean linens: all this seemed like heaven on earth after the conditions in the prison barracks, which would haunt her dreams for years to come. Only certain aspects of her life served as reminders that she wasn't free. For example, she had to check in at the RUVD's special commandant's office on a regular basis; she was also required to spend the night in her dormitory and was forbidden to leave the district.

Lepilina was assigned to work in the assembly shop of the Gorky Automobile Factory (GAZ), which manufactured parts for the black Volgas favoured by high-ranking Soviet officials. Thousands of inmates toiled in this factory alone. The assembly shop was filled with enormous, American-made machines, which had been brought over from Oklahoma in the early 1930s. These machines were run by the female workers in *khimia*. They weren't given any health and safety training: upon arrival in Gorky, they were taken to the dormitory and sent straight to the factory floor the next day. Lepilina arrived in a group of thirty people, some of whom lost their fingers in the hydraulic presses shortly afterwards. In a lucky twist of fate, Lepilina managed to avoid working at the machines. Instead, she was assigned to wash machined car parts in a special solution. This work was also not without its dangers: the powerful chemical solution could splash out of the metal basin, burning the workers' arms and legs – to say nothing of the toxic fumes the women had to breathe. In the long term, such conditions amounted to a death sentence. There was only one effective form of protection for the women's arms: a type of thick rubber gloves usually used for working with high-voltage electricity. However, such gloves couldn't be found for love or money in Gorky, so Lepilina's friends in Leningrad went to great lengths to secure her some. She went through endless pairs of thick wool socks, which she had to replace as the acid ate holes in them.

In early September, Lepilina learned that Azadovsky had reached his final destination: the colony in Susuman. This meant that they would finally be able to correspond. Because they weren't officially married, they hadn't been able to write to each other prior to that point. Article 30 of the ITK decreed that 'Correspondence between persons being held in corrective facilities who are not related to each other is prohibited.' Now that Lepilina was in *khimia*, she and Azadovsky could finally communicate.

After her transfer to *khimia*, Lepilina began cherishing hopes of an early release. Parole was to be granted on the condition that a prisoner had 'proved their rehabilitation through exemplary behaviour and an honest attitude towards work'. However, it was precisely Lepilina's exemplary work ethic that made the assembly team so reluctant to let her go.

What would it take to secure Lepilina's early release? Would an early release even be possible? These were the questions that occupied the Azadovskys' friends in that moment. But they were members of the intelligentsia; they didn't have many contacts in the automotive industry. That was where Nina Katerli's husband came in. Mikhail Efros (1933–2000) was a prominent engineer whose contacts among the higher-ups at GAZ allowed him to exert some influence over the factory administration. Soon Lepilina was given to understand that she could count on an early release and that she should start preparing her documents to send to the commission.

Lepilina encountered no further obstacles on her path to early release. Her application was considered in early 1982. In a character reference issued on 11 February, the workshop's head foreman offered a brief assessment of Lepilina's conduct:

> Svetlana Ivanovna Lepilina has worked as a washer in the mechanical processing section of the Assembly Shop at the Gorky Automobile Factory since 19 August

1981. She has made a good impression during her time on the job. She fills her work quotas by 130–140 per cent. She completes all of the tasks assigned to her without complaint. She is respected within the collective.

The process of securing early release was never quick. Lepilina began preparing the necessary documents right after the New Year's holidays, but her review didn't take place until 7 April. Apart from a brief stretch in December (which will be discussed in the following chapter), Lepilina continued her job washing car parts. Finally, the court issued its decision: 'To grant [Lepilina] early release on parole for a period of two months, eleven days'. By that point, she had already served the majority of her sentence: one year, three months and nineteen days.

The next day, Lepilina arrived in Leningrad. She had nowhere to live: having spent over a year in prison, camp and *khimia*, she had lost her right to a Leningrad *propiska*. The three rooms she had occupied prior to her arrest had been placed under the control of the Dzerzhinsky District's Executive Committee, which had promptly signed them over to 'the war veteran Zoya Ivanovna Tkachyova', who had contributed so zealously to the investigation of her former flatmate.

And so, Lepilina moved in with Azadovsky's mother.

Figure 1 Konstantin Azadovsky with a group of East German tourists. Leningrad, July 1961. © Konstantin & Svetlana Azadovsky archive.

Figure 2 Yefim Slavinsky and William Chalsma. Leningrad, 1960s. © Konstantin & Svetlana Azadovsky archive.

Figure 3 Konstantin Azadovsky seeing Yefim Etkind off at Pulkovo Airport. Leningrad, 16 October 1974. © Konstantin & Svetlana Azadovsky archive.

Figure 4 Portrait of Konstantin Azadovsky by Anatoly Belkin. Oil on canvas, 1976. © Anatoly Belkin.

Figure 5 Kama Ginkas, Daniil Ginkas, Genrietta Yanovskaya, Roza Yanovskaya and their dog Jeff (named after Jeffrey Ingram, G. Yanovskaya's favourite character in Sheila Delaney's play *A Taste of Honey*). Moscow, 1980s. © Konstantin & Svetlana Azadovsky archive.

Figure 6 Konstantin Azadovsky in Aida Khmeleva's flat. Moscow, 1973. Photo by Vladimir Sichov. The portrait on the piano is of Yuri Galanskov. © Vladimir Sichov.

Figure 7 Lidia Brun-Azadovskaya. 1970s. © Konstantin & Svetlana Azadovsky archive.

Figure 8 Joseph Brodsky in 44 Morton Street, New York, 1981. © Natasha Sharymova.

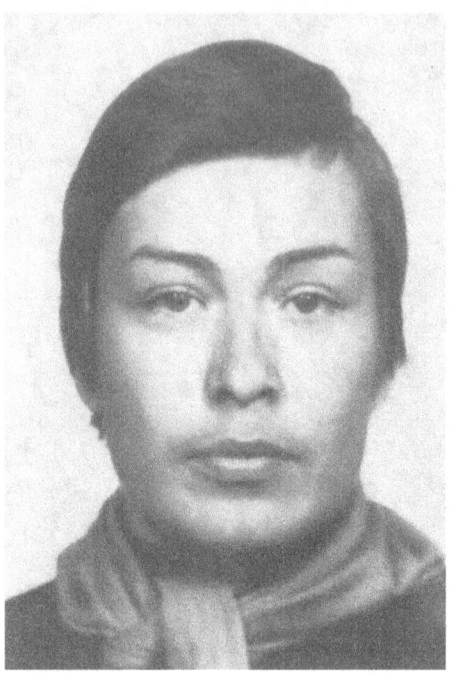

Figure 9 Prison photo of Svetlana Lepilina. Ulyanovka, Leningrad Oblast. Summer 1981. © Konstantin & Svetlana Azadovsky archive.

Figure 10 Svetlana Lepilina's prison badge. 1981. © Konstantin & Svetlana Azadovsky archive.

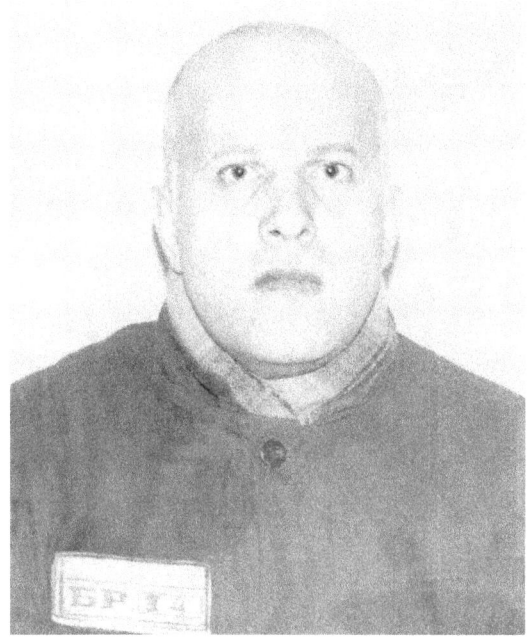

Figure 11 Prison photo of Konstantin Azadovsky. Susuman, Autumn 1981. © Konstantin & Svetlana Azadovsky archive.

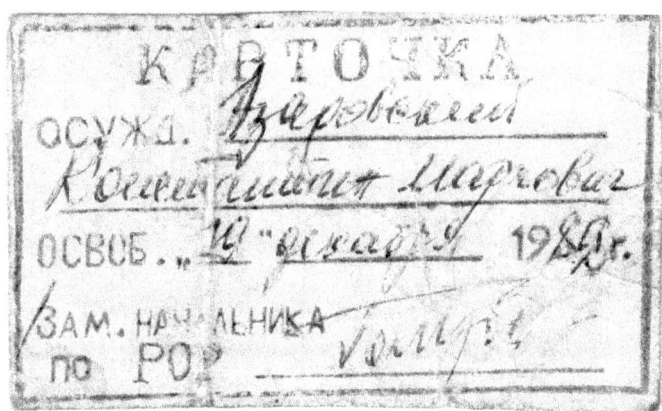

Figure 12 Azadovsky's prison card, issued before his release. 1982. © Konstantin & Svetlana Azadovsky archive.

Figure 13 Soviet prison gate. © Pierre Perrin/Sygma via Getty Images.

Figure 14 Kolyma highway in summer. 1980s. © Konstantin & Svetlana Azadovsky archive.

Figure 15 Susuman city centre, Magadan Oblast. Late 1970s. © Konstantin & Svetlana Azadovsky archive.

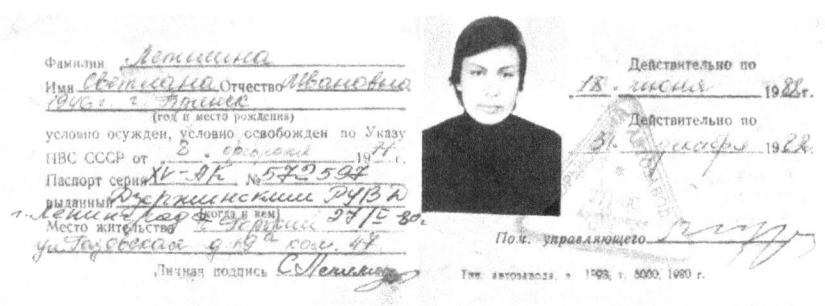

Figure 16 Svetlana Lepilina's Gorky Automobile Plant pass. Autumn 1982. © Konstantin & Svetlana Azadovsky archive.

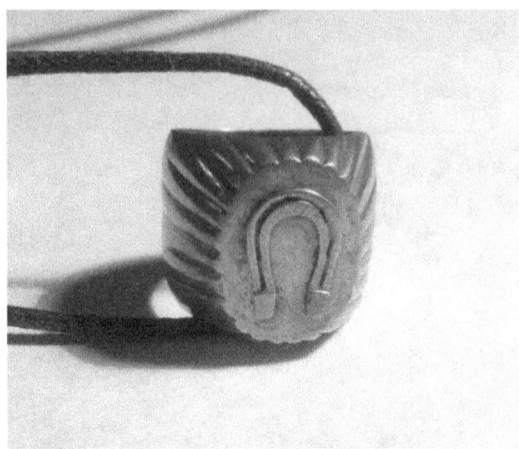

Figure 17 Brass signet ring made by prisoners at the Susuman camp as a wedding gift to Konstantin and Svetlana. December 1981. © Konstantin & Svetlana Azadovsky archive.

Figure 18 Mikhail Feiginzon, doctor at the Susuman prisoners' hospital. Around 1980. © Konstantin & Svetlana Azadovsky archive.

Figure 19 Baptist Anatoly Redin at work in the camp. Susuman, 1980s. © Konstantin & Svetlana Azadovsky archive.

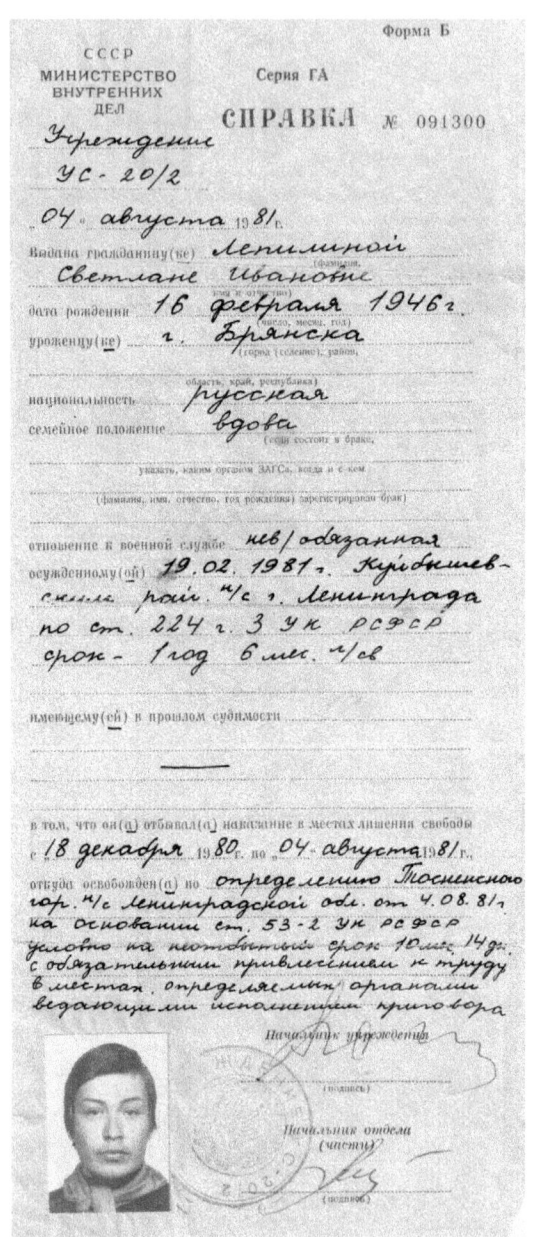

Figure 20 Svetlana Lepilina's certificate of conditional release. August 1981. © Konstantin & Svetlana Azadovsky archive.

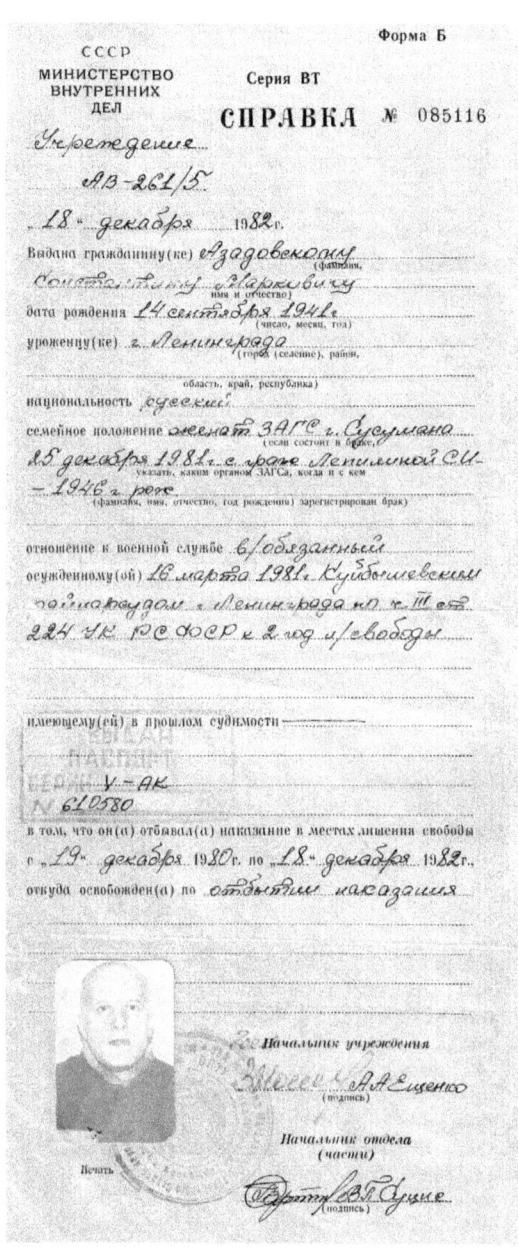

Figure 21 Konstantin Azadovsky's certificate of release. December 1982. © Konstantin & Svetlana Azadovsky archive.

Figure 22 Konstantin Azadovsky after his release. Leningrad, Spring 1983. © Susan Heuman.

Figure 23 Konstantin and Svetlana Azadovsky. Leningrad, Spring 1983. © Susan Heuman.

Figure 24 Kuibyshevsky District Court in Leningrad. 12 August 1988. Back row center: Judge N. Tsvetkov. Foreground: prosecutor A. Yakubovich and defence counsel N. Smirnova. © Konstantin & Svetlana Azadovsky archive.

Figure 25 Azadovsky at his court hearing on 12 August 1988. © Konstantin & Svetlana Azadovsky archive.

Figure 26 Kuibyshevsky District Court in Leningrad. 12 August 1988. Announcing the judgement. © Konstantin & Svetlana Azadovsky archive.

Figure 27 Konstantin Azadovsky and Sergey Zilitinkevich during a court recess on 12 August 1988. © Konstantin & Svetlana Azadovsky archive.

Figure 28 Yury Shchekochikhin and Konstantin Azadovsky during a court recess on 12 August 1988. © Konstantin & Svetlana Azadovsky archive.

Figure 29 Konstantin Azadovsky during a court recess on 12 August 1988. © Konstantin & Svetlana Azadovsky archive.

Figure 30 Konstantin Azadovsky and Galina Starovoitova. Vienna, 1992. Photo by Svetlana Azadovskaya. © Konstantin & Svetlana Azadovsky archive.

Figure 31 Konstantin Azadovsky, Svetlana Azadovskaya and Sergey Dovlatov. New York, 30 November 1989. © Konstantin & Svetlana Azadovsky archive.

Figure 32 Joseph Brodsky, Konstantin Azadovsky and Maria Sozzani with her daughter Anna. New York, October 1993. © Konstantin & Svetlana Azadovsky archive.

10

The Kolyma saga

10.1 Susuman

Azadovsky arrived at Corrective Labour Colony no. 5 (ITK-5) in Susuman on 21 August 1981. He was relieved that his time in transit was finally over, particularly after the month he had spent in Magadan Prison, cheek by jowl with the other prisoners waiting to be transferred to Kolyma's minimum-, medium- and maximum-security camps.

Just because Azadovsky was being sent to a minimum-security facility didn't mean that the conditions awaiting him were any less severe. Of course, minimum-security facilities differed from their medium- and maximum-security counterparts. Medium-security facilities housed first-time offenders sentenced to more than three years for serious crimes, while maximum-security facilities were designated for recidivists or those convicted of particularly dangerous crimes against the state. But the biggest difference lay in the kinds of privileges the inmates were afforded: facility type determined how many packages, deliveries, parcels and letters a person could receive, as well as the rules surrounding visitation with relatives and so on. In his fascinating memoirs, Yury Zolotaryov, who worked at the colony in nearby Uptar, describes the reaction of first-time inmates to their new surroundings:

> The most difficult, most unruly groups of prisoners are found in the minimum-security colonies. When first-time offenders arrive at a colony like this, they go through an extremely painful adjustment period. The fact that they are unable to move freely, the discrepancy between these living conditions and the ones to which they are accustomed – these things are hard enough to take. And then there's the daily routine: everything is done by command, and to top it all off, you're surrounded by people in exactly the same position as you; that doesn't make things seem any brighter.

By the standards of the day, ITK-5 wasn't particularly large: there were several hundred people living there in total. The *blatnye* were less influential in Susuman than they were in the 'mainland' zones, and the colony administration was used to dealing with minimum-security inmates. Most of the colony's population consisted of small-time criminals who had been convicted on charges of disorderly conduct or various other petty crimes: robbery, car theft, falsification of documents, passport violations and so on. A significant proportion of the inmates (most of whom were Ingush) were serving time 'for gold', which is to say, for unlawful prospecting; gold mining was a long-established pillar of the Kolyma economy.

For the most part, Magadan's corrective labour establishments were meant to serve local needs, holding people who had been convicted by courts within the oblast. On the one hand, this made the inmates wary of 'outsiders', but, on the other hand, it made conditions in these camps considerably better. The reason for this was simple: these people all came from the same place, and so when they went home, they were almost certain to come into contact either with former inmates or with their relatives. Thus, there was every incentive for them to treat each other decently.

In short, Susuman was hardly the worst place to be incarcerated in the Soviet Union.

Initially, the news of Azadovsky's transfer to Susuman caused some confusion. His lengthy stay in Kresty, coupled with the two months he spent in transit, made communication mix-ups inevitable. The Munich-based human rights news bulletin *USSR News Brief* reported: 'K. Azadovsky has been granted conditional release with mandatory labour. He is "building the national economy" in the town of Susuman in Magadan Obl[ast].' It was difficult for people to believe that Azadovsky had been sent to a minimum-security colony in Kolyma for such a minor crime; it seemed more plausible that he had been sent there to work in *khimia*.

The situation was patently absurd: a person convicted of a minor crime was shipped all the way across the country, such that, by the time he arrived, he only had a year and four months remaining on his sentence. Why? What was the point?

Ten years before, Andrey Amalrik had made a similar journey. He was arrested in Moscow, brought to Novosibirsk for his trial and then sent to Kolyma to serve his three-year sentence in a medium-security facility. At the time, such a journey was considered shocking. Amalrik was assigned to the medium-security zone in Talaya, halfway between Magadan and Susuman. In his memoirs, he recalls the distrust with which he was viewed, both by his fellow prisoners and by the staff of the transit prisons, convoys and colony. They would speculate as to the real reason he had been sent so far away:

'Are you anti-Soviet or what? To be sent off to Kolyma with that kind of sentence ...!'

'Yes, I am anti-Soviet,' I said, feeling rather proud ...

No one could believe he had been sent all the way to Kolyma to serve such a short sentence – unless politics were involved.

Azadovsky's arrival in Kolyma created a similar stir. When he told people he had been sentenced to two years under Article 224, he was greeted with sceptical smiles. For as long as Azadovsky continued to insist that his offence hadn't been political, most people would nod politely, refusing to believe a word that he said. Some inmates challenged him directly: 'Come off it, brother! No one would send you here, to the edge of the earth, for some fracas at your institute or with a neighbour.'

At first, Azadovsky was treated with caution. When he arrived in the colony, he went through the standard series of conversations with the colony's administrators. He was sent to meet first with the head of the operative unit,[1] then with the deputy head of political education. The administration didn't hide the fact that Azadovsky's presence was unwelcome. As a rule, the staff of corrective labour establishments were not overly fond of 'political' prisoners: they were often a source of written complaints, hunger strikes and other disturbances. Moreover, the local authorities weren't given total control over such prisoners: their superiors on the oblast level and in Moscow were constantly butting in, and other organizations (the Prosecutor's Office, the KGB, the Party, etc.) were constantly enquiring after them. Prisoners with political baggage could make life difficult indeed: they were a headache nobody needed.

The camp administration would have taken Azadovsky's 'baggage' into account when they were determining his job assignment. Contemporary guidance prohibited people considered dissidents from being assigned to 'idiots' work' (in the library, bathhouse, kitchen, etc.). Rather, they were to be treated as harshly as possible.

Once in Susuman, Azadovsky faced a new challenge: How should he act around his fellow inmates, considering his reputation as a political prisoner? What could he do to assimilate as quickly and painlessly as possible? In his seminal book *Punitive Medicine*, Alexander Podrabinek writes:

> It is an inmate's behaviour – 'who they really are' – that determines their place in the prison world. . . . A political prisoner is judged based on how consistent their behaviour is with their beliefs. . . . And the general attitude towards [a political prisoner] is determined not by that person's words, but by their actions. For example, what's the point of harbouring 'anti-Soviet views' if you're just going to tuck your tail between your legs and take whatever the prison guards throw at you? Or, even worse, if you're going to do 'idiots' work': as a foreman, a quota monitor, a cook, an orderly, a warehouse clerk or a librarian.

Azadovsky did his best to remain true to himself and to act in accordance with the principles that had motivated his arrest. The other inmates, who weren't well versed in the nuances of the conflict between the intelligentsia and the state, saw Azadovsky as an 'educated' person first and foremost. He was called 'the professor', just as Sergey Zilitinkevich had been in Kresty. This nickname would follow him throughout his time in Susuman. It is worth noting that attitudes towards educated people varied widely within the carceral system: some inmates regarded them with grudging respect, while others (usually the *blatnye*) treated them with open dislike, taking every possible opportunity to mock them and to demonstrate their physical superiority.

After spending time in nine different prisons, it was hard for Azadovsky to adjust to the Kolyma zone. The issue was not so much the harsh climate as it was the harsh conditions. He felt more vulnerable in the zone, where prisoners were kept in barracks rather than cells. In a cell, there are always witnesses around. In the zone, things are different: no one will be held accountable if you don't wake up one morning.

When Azadovsky arrived in the zone, he learned that Lepilina had been released to *khimia* and was already in Gorky. This news gave his spirits a considerable lift: at least one of them was enjoying relative freedom.

But he was faced with a pressing concern: that his time in Susuman might be only the beginning. This was not an idle fear. Everyone knew it was easy to have time added on to one's sentence in the colonies. A prisoner could be forced to write an 'acknowledgment of guilt' confessing to crimes they had nothing to do with; if they refused, their fellow inmates would be only too happy to testify that that they had heard the prisoner boasting of having committed exactly those crimes. Many inmates were willing to sign anything in the hopes of securing an early release; they could either come up with something themselves or take dictation from the zone's 'godfather' (warden). All it took was a desire on the part of the camp administration to 'solve' a particular crime or punish a particular inmate. This occurrence was particularly common towards the end of someone's sentence.

If the camp administration had already begun building a trumped-up case against a particular prisoner, there was little, if anything, that could be done. All a prisoner could do was try not to provoke such action in the first place. Azadovsky's experience with Fima Rozenberg had taught him to be cautious, and so, from the moment he arrived in the zone, he was guarded in his conversations and his contacts. He viewed anyone who tried to ingratiate themselves with him as a potential provocateur.

Azadovsky was sent to work making gloves in a sewing workshop. This assignment was quite standard for the zone, and it was far from the worst one available. However, the work quotas were so high that prisoners were forced to work more or less constantly. At first, Azadovsky was unable to meet his quotas, and so he did whatever he could to get by, either by striking deals with the shop foreman or by asking his fellow inmates for help. He would pay for these services either in tea or, more frequently, by promising to write a letter, petition or application for pardon on the other inmate's behalf. Azadovsky wrote letters to the Magadan Oblast Prosecutor's Office, the Magadan Corrective Labour Division, the RSFSR Prosecutor's Office, the head of the Main Directorate of Corrective Labour Institutions, the Letters Department of the Central Committee of the CPSU and so on. His lengthy complaints, which would run on for several pages, were a source of annoyance for the administration, but they earned him respect among his fellow inmates.

Once word spread that the 'professor' knew how to write a proper supervisory complaint, his fellow inmates began coming to him asking for help. Not the *blatnye*, of course: their 'thieves' code' forbade them from writing any kind of petition. But other prisoners, those who weren't bound by this 'code of honour', applied to Azadovsky constantly – especially when one of his complaints yielded results, no matter how modest.

Alexander Podrabinek, who was serving a sentence in Bolshaya Markha in the Sakha Republic at the time, played a similar role in his own camp:

> Someone informed the godfather that I was writing supervisory complaints and applications for pardon for the inmates. This didn't violate the law or [the camp's] internal code of conduct, but it did give me some status in the camp, and the administration didn't want that at all. I wasn't keen to write complaints for the inmates, knowing that it wouldn't end well for me. But it was also impossible to refuse them. There was a big commotion each time one of my supervisory complaints was, by some miracle, permitted to proceed. The inmates would be lining up to see me, and so the administration decided to put a stop to it.

The same thing would happen to Azadovsky.

10.2 First meetings

The last thing Azadovsky expected in Susuman was to cross paths with someone he knew. And so it came as a great surprise when, on his very first day in the colony, he learned that a prisoner from Leningrad had only just left Susuman for *khimia*: 'He's from Leningrad, maybe you know him.' Suppressing a grin, Azadovsky replied that there were millions of Leningraders roaming around. But he did, in fact, know the person in question: Georgy Mikhailov (1944–2014), known as Zhora to his friends. In 1979, he had been sentenced to four years in a minimum-security colony with confiscation of property for organizing unlawful exhibitions of Leningrad-based nonconformist artists and for brokering sales of their works. He, like Azadovsky, had been sent to ITK-5; he arrived there in late 1979. Though they had never been close, Azadovsky remembered Mikhailov, and so he began telling stories about Mikhailov's life in Leningrad. Mikhailov had been well liked among the inmates, so this connection served as Azadovsky's way in.

But it wasn't just Leningraders who were sent to Susuman. In late March 1982, there was a new arrival to the colony. He had been sentenced to a year's incarceration for a crime fairly common within this facility: 'resisting a police officer or *druzhennik* as they carry out their duty to maintain public order' (Article 191). However, the fact that he had been sent all the way from Moscow to Magadan made it obvious that he, too, was a political prisoner.

Boris Chernobylsky (1944–98) was a Jew who had been refused permission to emigrate to Israel. He joined a group of Moscow 'refusenik' activists who spoke openly about their right to emigrate and took part in various unsanctioned political actions. During one such action, which took place on 10 May 1981, a police officer shouted '*schnell!*', prompting Chernobylsky to call him a fascist. This earned him a year in a minimum-security colony. The KGB wanted to make sure it was a memorable one, and so they sent him to feast his eyes on the wonders of Kolyma. In early 1982, Chernobylsky found himself in the Susuman zone, where he met Azadovsky. This was an important meeting for both of them: they were glad to find someone they could talk to. They spent all of 1982 together in the zone; Chernobylsky was released just two weeks before Azadovsky.

There was another inmate in Susuman who was bound to attract Azadovsky's attention: Anatoly Redin (1931–88). At the time of his incarceration, Redin was fifty years old and an elder in the Church of Evangelical Baptists in Ryazan. The arm of the Baptist Church to which Redin belonged was known for its extremely negative attitude towards the state; the branch of the KGB responsible for monitoring sectarian movements in the USSR deemed it the 'most extreme and anti-social' of the religious groups. Redin was arrested on 15 April 1981, sentenced to five years and sent to Susuman to put as much distance as possible between him and his flock. The court didn't care that this was Redin's first offence, or that he had four children to feed.

Redin was respected in the zone because of his advanced age and religious faith. Though he was a humble peasant with only a primary school education, he knew how to listen to people, and his opinions carried weight among the inmates. The administration exploited Redin's considerable skill as a carpenter and woodworker, having him install doors, fix furniture and insulate windows. Azadovsky became his assistant in summer 1982, and, for a while, they spent time together every day. Later on, Azadovsky would view this time as a bright spot in his life in the camp.

10.3 Flowers

Incarceration made Azadovsky and Lepilina look at their lives differently: not just their past, but their present, too. They couldn't bring themselves to think about the future.

For the first eight months of their incarceration, they were unable to correspond. When Lepilina first went to work at GAZ, she didn't know where Azadovsky was. It was only in September 1981, when Lidia Vladimirovna received word from Susuman, that Lepilina finally learned Azadovsky's new address. Their letters from this period are too personal to cite, but one can imagine how their shared sufferings brought them together.

That autumn, they decided to make their relationship official. The word 'decided' might seem out of place here: after all, the parties involved were both convicts, one of whom was serving time in the zone, the other of whom was in *khimia*; besides, there were 10,000 kilometres between them. Lepilina didn't want to wait until they were both free, but how could she get permission to go to Azadovsky? It would take a monumental effort. She had to grovel before the administration, beseeching them and bribing them with gifts. But eventually, they let her go.

Genrietta Yanovskaya and Kama Ginkas tell the story of Lepilina's journey in their memoirs:

KAMA: And so the kids decided to get married. . . . It was the funniest thing. So it's against the rules for two people in neighbouring cells to get married, but going all the way across the country, getting married, spending three lawful (and, in this case, prescribed) wedding nights together and then going back again – that's allowed.

GETA: Oh, how we kitted her out! I unpacked their boxes of dishes, got out two little silver spoons, two good plates, cups and napkins, and Sveta lugged all of that out with her. She took an ungodly amount of food; she went dressed in *valenki*,[2] a sheepskin coat and mittens. She ended up having to sit on the floor of the coach, so it was a good thing she dressed warmly.

KAMA: We all had a hand in organizing the journey. First, Sveta came to Moscow; she stayed with me in the basement of the Moscow Art Theatre's dormitory, whence I would take her on to the airport. Sveta was a sturdy woman, but her rucksack looked positively gigantic, even for her. And she had something in either hand as well. It was winter, December, the weather was freezing. First she had to fly to Magadan – with a layover, no less – and then she would be jounced about on a coach and then in an open automobile as well. And everywhere she went, she lugged all that junk with her: her *kutuli*,³ as she called it.

Our basement was abuzz with talk of the wedding. Right before Svetka was scheduled to leave, Katya Vasilyeva [an actress who worked at the Moscow Art Theatre at the time – P.D.] ran down to the market to buy flowers from the frozen Azerbaijanis working there. There was a terrible flower shortage back then, but what's a wedding without flowers? Still, she needed to find flowers that wouldn't die before reaching Magadan. Katya searched for a long time. When she told the Azerbaijanis why she had come and what kind of newlyweds she needed the flowers for, one of the vendors ran round to all his colleagues, telling them the story. Everyone pitched in to find the five best carnations in the entire market. They even packaged them for the journey. And Svetka carried those flowers with her all that way: on the aeroplane, lying on the floor of the coach, in her *kutuli*. And they made it! Believe it or not, those carnations lasted all three days the kids spent together, and died only on the last day. And that's not just a story. It seems incredible. Like a fairy tale. But that's exactly what happened.

GETA: They were married on 25 December, on Christmas day. She spent three days with him.

When word got round that the professor's fiancée, also an inmate, had got permission to leave *khimia* to come and marry him, it caused quite a stir. After all, such grand romantic gestures were practically unheard of in the camps. Azadovsky was approached by Edik Kutserubov, an inmate with whom he was friendly. 'Is it true?' he asked. 'It's true.' 'Well, if it's true, then a wedding present is in order.' And so Edik and his assistants in the woodworking shop turned a delicate brass signet ring with a horseshoe on top, a symbol of the luck and good fortune they wished for the couple.

But a key obstacle remained: How would they get the gift out of the zone? They hatched a plan: on the morning of the day when Lepilina was scheduled to depart, an 'unescorted' prisoner (which is to say, an inmate who worked outside the zone and had permission to move about without an escort) would take a packet containing the ring and the notebook of complaints Azadovsky had written to the RSFSR Supreme Court out of the zone and hide it by the fence in an agreed-upon location.

The Azadovskys' marriage was registered on 25 December in one of the colony's administrative buildings. Lepilina had arrived the night before. When the coach pulled into Susuman at around three in the morning, it stopped in front of the local hotel. It was −60 degrees outside; the room Lepilina stayed in that night was +5. There was no hot water in the room. The bride began her ablutions after her long and strenuous journey. She washed her hair, wrapped it up in a towel and, pulling her coat tightly around herself, went to sleep. She awoke at nine the next morning and hurried off to the Civil Registry Office to meet the registrar. From there, she ordered a taxi, and they set off together for the zone. The frost haze made it impossible to distinguish people or cars. Lepilina thanked the registrar in the taxi, slipping her two smoked sausages she had purchased in Moscow for that purpose. When they arrived at the checkpoint, they went to wait in the building that was indicated to them. An officer brought Azadovsky in soon afterwards. Upon seeing him, Lepilina burst into tears. They registered their marriage through glass: he on one side, she on the other. The officer, First Lieutenant V.V. Zarubin, acted as witness. The woman from the registry office promptly supplied her own signature, and the marriage became official.

Lepilina had to endure one final humiliation before being left alone with her spouse. She was stripped naked by an inspector (Ensign L.I. Davidenko) to check whether she had any contraband – particularly, money – hidden on her person.

The newlyweds spent three days and three nights together: 'three days of happiness', as Lepilina later called it. The visitation room wasn't large, but it was cosy and warm, with a big double bed. It was bitterly cold outside: the temperature dropped down to −65 degrees. Lepilina had brought loads of supplies: they washed down their caviar and buttered bread with lemonade. For the first time since his arrest, Azadovsky was able to eat his fill and get a good night's sleep. Afterwards, Lepilina began telling him the news from the 'mainland'. It was only then that Azadovsky learned what had happened over the previous year. Fearful that their conversation was being monitored, Lepilina told him in a whisper about the letters that had been written in his defence, about Lev Kopelev's declarations in West Germany, about the broadcasts on Western radio stations and, of course, about their friends, who had displayed such astonishing bravery.

After three days, they were forced to part. But Lepilina spent another day in Susuman. That evening, she drove back to the zone and began searching for the packet with the notebook and the ring. She trudged through the deep snow bordering the fence for nearly an hour in −60 degree cold, to no avail. She had nearly given up when she saw it: the packet was lying beside the fence, covered in a dusting of snow. Now she understood why she hadn't noticed it earlier: it was smaller than she had anticipated. The notebook with Azadovsky's complaints was missing. But the precious ring was there.

10.4 Resistance

Azadovsky greeted 1982 with cautious optimism; however, his hopes were soon dashed.

On 14 September 1981, the Presidium of the Supreme Soviet had issued a decree granting amnesty to persons convicted of so-called petty crimes, including those under Article 224-3. The administrative and supervisory committees that had been formed to take such decisions on behalf of individual corrective labour establishments began reviewing prisoner files in November–December 1981. The colony's population gradually started to dwindle. Some inmates were set free, but the majority were released to *khimia*.

Azadovsky doubted that his case would be brought before the commission. According to the decree, a prisoner had to have served at least a third of their sentence before qualifying for early release. Azadovsky met this requirement as soon as he arrived in Susuman. But there was another prerequisite: the camp administration had to issue a written statement saying that the prisoner was 'on the path to rehabilitation', that they hadn't violated any camp rules, that they participated in 'public-spirited' activities, etc. Mindful of this requirement, Azadovsky had taken pains to avoid conflict with the administration from the very moment he arrived in the camp. He followed all the rules, kept his uniform neat, made up his bunk, diligently attended his political education classes and so on. In October 1981, he even joined the camp's educational section, hoping that he might be asked to teach foreign languages there. However, his experience remained untapped.

Azadovsky had dreamt of early release on more than one occasion, and he had certainly considered the possibility that he, like Lepilina, might be released to *khimia*. But because he refused to admit his guilt, he couldn't realistically hope to be set free. Without such an admission, the court wouldn't consider his appeal.

He was also consumed by doubt. During his time in transit and then in the camp, he had heard many stories about what it meant to 'build the national economy': terrible living conditions, widespread drunkenness, outrageous behaviour and difficult, sometimes unbearable, labour. At times, things got so bad that inmates would try to come up with ways to go back to the zone. Azadovsky knew that he wouldn't be sent to a big city like Magadan or Khabarovsk, so he could end up driving logs in the taiga or working on an unfinished section of the Baikal-Amur Railway. Nevertheless, *khimia* had its attractions: there, he would enjoy uncensored correspondence, unlimited telephone calls with his mother and friends and even the chance to negotiate a trip (as Lepilina had done).

On 22 January 1982, Azadovsky learned that the camp administration was prepared to release him to *khimia*. The next day, he wrote to Lepilina:

> Yesterday I was called before the administrative committee, which has finally decided to send me to build the national economy, or, more accurately, to allow me to petition to do so at the next level. As you know, there are two more levels to go. What will come of all this, I don't know . . .
>
> Before my hearing, which I learned about only the day before, I weighed all the pros and cons of *khimia* again, all of its pluses and minuses. As it turned out, there were more pluses. The primary motivating factor was, of course, my mother (which is to say, the prospect of seeing her as soon as possible). I would do anything for that chance.

But just a few days later, his situation changed dramatically. Another inmate, V. Sedletsky, privately told Azadovsky that two people ('obviously not from around here') had come to visit the camp, and that they had spoken to him and to other prisoners. Their questions were all about Azadovsky, his views and inclinations: how he acts, who he associates with, what he says about his friends in Leningrad, what kinds of conversations he has and so on.

This was the start of a chain of events that is reflected in Azadovsky's complaint to the Central Committee dated 15 February 1982:

> On 22 January 1982, I was called before the administrative committee. In the thirteen months since my arrest, I had never violated the rules and had diligently

performed my duties on the shop floor, and so the committee recommended I be sent to build the national economy. However, several days after this decision was taken, two individuals claiming to work for the KGB appeared in the colony (one was from Leningrad, the other was local); they called prisoners in for conversations and exerted pressure on them in an attempt to gather material they could use to discredit me. They also put pressure on the colony administration, which wrote me up for three (!) rule violations in three days (1–3 February) – clearly with an eye towards my upcoming meeting with the supervisory committee. Each of the violations I allegedly committed is fictitious and ungrounded, in violation of the Internal Code of Conduct of the Corrective Labour Division of the USSR MVD and the RSFSR Corrective Labour Code. The goal of the actions undertaken by the administration of ITK-5 is perfectly clear: they want to present me at the next committee meeting as a repeat offender who systematically violates the rules. On 3 February 1982 I submitted petitions concerning the administration's unlawful and unworthy conduct to the Susuman Prosecutor's Office and the Corrective Labour Division of the Magadan Oblast MVD; however, my petitions have remained unanswered.

Clearly, Azadovsky's bid to leave the colony early had been dealt a serious, possibly fatal, blow.

Why had the administration chosen to paint him in such a bad light? To a certain extent, we can recreate what happened using drafts of Azadovsky's protests and complaints.

The first two punishments Azadovsky received were for being visited by prisoners from other crews. Movement between the barracks was prohibited without permission from the guard in charge of a particular crew or the on-duty assistant to the camp warden. Azadovsky appealed the administration's decision, claiming that, in the first instance, the prisoners had come to visit other people in his barrack. As for the second instance, Azadovsky explained that the prisoners had been given permission to visit by Ensign N.A. Klimchuk, 'who, nevertheless, wrote a report on my "violation" several hours later. . . . I saw the statement signed "Klimchuk" with my own eyes. Meanwhile, Klimchuk claims that he didn't write any report.'

On 1 February 1982, Captain Galkin conducted a search of Azadovsky's living area. Azadovsky records: 'Two pieces of paper were seized from me. The first contained a draft of a complaint for the prisoner Skolodchuk (the statement doesn't mention this document at all). The other contained a poem by the seventeenth-century English poet John Bunyan. (Neither paper has been returned to me at this time; I consider this seizure to be groundless.)'

After the search, Galkin wrote Azadovsky up for 'keeping his bedside table in an unsanitary condition'.

Azadovsky continues:

The next evening, in an attempt to bolster Captain Galkin's statement with additional documentation, the administration summoned Korovkin, the on-duty prisoner from crew no. 1 who had acted as search witness. First Lieutenant

Gorshchak and First Lieutenant Chernenko demanded that he confirm the information set forth in Captain Galkin's statement. However, despite the pressure exerted on him, prisoner Korovkin refused to write what was dictated to him and wrote only what happened in reality.

In early February, the situation grew even more dire. We can see this in Azadovsky's letters to Lepilina:

5 February

In the past two days, I have been written up for several rule violations at once; one of them affects you, Svetulik:[4] I've been stripped of my next long visit.

And things only got worse from there.

8 February

I've been written up for yet another rule violation – [I've been given] a reprimand!! And another – I have been stripped of shopping privileges!!

'Shopping privileges' meant the right to go to the colony shop, where, once a month, prisoners could use the money in their personal accounts to buy certain foodstuffs, including that most precious of commodities: tea. According to Article 62 of the RSFSR ITK, prisoners in minimum-security establishments could purchase no more than seven rubles' worth of provisions per month. Being stripped of one's 'shopping privileges' was a punishment administered for minor violations. More serious violations were punished by barring prisoners from receiving their next parcel (of which they were allowed two per year), or even their next five-kilogram package of foodstuffs (prisoners were allowed three such packages or deliveries per year after they had finished half their sentences). The worst punishment of all was to be deprived of one's next visit. All of these measures were taken against Azadovsky. His three appeals to the Susuman Prosecutor's Office went unanswered.

ITK-5's administration had ruined Azadovsky's chance of securing an early release – but why? After all, they had initially been keen to release him to *khimia*. What probably happened is this. When news of the decree issued in September 1981 reached the local MVD, they decided to use it to rid themselves of a troublesome inmate: the political prisoner Azadovsky. But as soon as the KGB caught wind of their plans, the administration was ordered to put a halt to this procedure. In all likelihood, the KGB had simply failed to notice Azadovsky's marriage, and their annoyance with their own oversight made them react more aggressively to this new development. It is also safe to assume that they had never intended to let Azadovsky go after only two years. This assumption is borne out by the events that followed.

Azadovsky felt the noose tightening around his neck. Previously, the colony staff had treated him with indifference, or even with sympathy. But then there was an abrupt change. Even the *blatnye*, who had previously tolerated Azadovsky, began looking at him differently. They struck up strange conversations with him, trying to get him to open up or to agree with politically provocative statements. Azadovsky was no longer thinking about going to *khimia*; rather, his thoughts were consumed by the very real possibility that he might be forced to spend another year or two in the zone.

However, he continued to act using the only weapon he had at his disposal: the pen. On 15 February 1982, he sent the aforementioned complaint to the Special Sector of the Central Committee. He finally understood which force stood behind his misfortunes, and he was ready to declare it to anyone who would listen:

> The decision to 'put me away' was taken by the Leningrad MVD and KGB long before my arrest. Over the course of 1979 and 1980, agents of these organizations systematically monitored me and called various citizens in to be interrogated about me in an attempt to gather material to discredit me . . .
>
> After failing to gather any damaging materials against me, on 19 December 1980, agents of the MVD and KGB (?) conducted a search of my residence, which I consider to be unlawful. . . . The investigation and trial were conducted in an extremely biased manner; in keeping with the KGB's decision to 'punish' me, their goal was to distort the truth rather than uncover it.
>
> There is no doubt in my mind that the false charges brought against me were the result of a KGB initiative. Throughout 1980, a number of people in Leningrad warned me that the KGB was preparing some sort of action against me. . . . The KGB's involvement in my case has been confirmed over the past six months in ITK-5 in Magadan Oblast, where I have been held since 21 August 1981.
>
> . . . As to the ideological accusations levelled against me (mostly behind closed doors), I feel it necessary to clarify that, for a number of years, I really did meet with colleagues from abroad and with official representatives of the West in our country. I trained as a philologist in Western languages, and many of my articles and books have been published and are still being published in the West. All of this was done, and continues to be done, in a completely lawful fashion; I have never hidden my activities or contacts from anyone; I knew that the KGB would show a certain amount of interest in me, but this didn't concern me, as there was nothing scandalous, let alone criminal, in my personal relationships or contacts. I am well acquainted with Soviet law and I have always acted in accordance with it.
>
> Now, regarding my 'views'. I would like to emphasize that – though I do not approve of certain things – I have never permitted myself the liberty of making any public statements or declarations to that effect. In my public appearances, as well as in my private conversations, no matter who I happened to be speaking to, I always tried to defend my country's dignity and culture. I considered myself then and still consider myself to be a Russian Soviet scholar and writer, and that is why the unlawful and unworthy campaign that has been launched against me by certain individuals in the KGB is doubly unjust . . .
>
> I am guilty of nothing and I have been wrongly convicted of a crime I did not commit!
>
> I appeal to the Central Committee of the CPSU with the following urgent requests:

1) That an enquiry be made within the Committee for State Security [KGB] regarding the actual facts of the case against me. That I be made aware of those facts so that I can either confirm or deny them (as I do not rule out the possibility of falsification).
2) That [the Central Committee] assume control of my supervisory complaint to the RSFSR Prosecutor's Office. That the Leningrad KGB be prevented from secretly interfering with the review of that complaint.
3) That the unlawful actions taken against me by the administration of ITK-5 in Magadan Oblast be brought to the attention of the Corrective Labour Division of the RSFSR MVD.
4) That you call for my sentence and the sentence of my wife, S.I. Lepilina, to be overturned as quickly as possible.

I request your help and protection!

Meanwhile, the situation in the camp continued to escalate. From Azadovsky's letters to Lepilina:

2 March

An appalling incident occurred the other day: a lawyer came, and any prisoner who wanted to was allowed to ask him questions. I had submitted a petition in advance stating that I needed to consult him. But they put on some farce, and I wasn't allowed to see him in the end.

4 March

The Susuman prosecutor didn't come, and so, in light of the new circumstances, on 2 March I sent him another petition (this makes three! in a single month) asking him to intercede immediately against the administration's actions. . . .

The second committee (the supervisory one) met yesterday. I was not, of course, approved for *khimia*.

The next day he sent another appeal, this one addressed to the local supervisory prosecutor for the oversight of the MVD and KGB:

My situation in the colony is critical at present. [It has been] since 3 February of this year. My attempts to secure a meeting with the supervisory prosecutor have been in vain (I have written three appeals to the Susuman Prosecutor's Office in the past month). I have been denied the opportunity to consult with a lawyer. . . . The people in charge of the colony refuse to meet me and, at the same time, are preventing me from sending my complaints and petitions from the colony (to the Central Committee and other agencies).

Guided by the Leningrad KGB's misinformation about me, the colony's operative unit has been putting together a 'dossier' on me: they have been calling prisoners in and demanding that they provide information on my conversations and my contacts in the colony. I am being accused based on words I didn't say and things I didn't do. All my correspondence is being monitored, not so much by the colony censor as by KGB operatives: a portion of my letters (both to and from me) are arbitrarily seized.

Over the past few weeks, other prisoners have committed provocative acts against me (there were incidents in the dining hall on 26–27 February, as a result of which I was forced to refuse my food twice).

I have every reason to suspect that the administration – facing outside pressure – is gathering materials to open a new criminal case against me.

This situation raises the question of whether it is prudent to continue holding me in ITK-5. The conflict between myself and the administration grows deeper every day...

I urgently request that you review this matter and take a decision regarding whether it is possible for me to remain in ITK-5.

From Azadovsky's letters to Lepilina:

17 March

The Susuman prosecutor still hasn't come, but I have been promised that he will be here next week. They say it's because he's 'busy', but of course that's not the issue.

24 March

As you already know, Susuman's supervisory prosecutor, comrade [Alexander] Neierdi, came to see me on 18 March. I gave him my complaint from 10–23 February and the petition from March (regarding my current situation in the colony: in it, I raise the issue of whether it is possible for me to remain in ITK-5). I also gave him the text of my complaint to the Central Committee to look at. He promised to come speak to me this week. So far he hasn't come.

This letter also contains details about Azadovsky's life behind bars:

The colony administration is continuing its campaign against me. In March, my shopping privileges were reduced by four rubles for no reason whatsoever (they claimed I wasn't getting up at wake-up time). Now they are preparing to write me up yet again, this time for going into another crew's area to borrow some journals (*Questions of Literature* and *Questions of Philosophy*).

Finally, the letter contains an important aside:

I know that the difficulties I am facing in the colony are blowing in... from the shores of the Neva, not just because it's easy to see, but because I have spoken extensively with the colony's officers, free tradesmen, etc. over the past few weeks.

29 March

On 24 March the supervisory prosecutor from the Magadan Oblast Prosecutor's Office [Neierdi] came to see me. Over the course of two and a half hours I told him about my (i.e., our) case. He did not, however, say anything reassuring. By 2 April, or possibly sooner, there will be an official response to the complaints I submitted to the Susuman Prosecutor's Office and the Corrective Labour Division of the Magadan Oblast MVD. I also expect to receive a response to the petition I submitted to the Prosecutor's Office on 5 March, in which I request a review of the possibility (read: impossibility) of my continued presence in ITK-5. I requested that the prosecutor 'lock me up' in a punishment cell for six months: that's the only way I can manage to avoid contact with the prisoners who are being incited against me and squeezed for 'testimony' by the administration using any means possible.

14 April

There has been no response from the Susuman Prosecutor's Office or from the Corrective Labour Division of the Magadan Oblast MVD. If my complaints are rejected, I'll write . . . to the offices of Soviet Minister of the Interior comrade N.A. Shchyolokov. The excesses employed against me in February, which have also determined the administration's current (aggressive) position against me, are all too blatant, obvious and demonstrable.

Azadovsky's friends in Leningrad were deeply concerned. Clearly, he wasn't exaggerating when he said that the authorities might try to keep him in the zone. Once again, Leningrad's academics and Writers' Union members sprang to his defence. This time, his cause was championed by Boris Bukhshtab, Lidia Ginzburg, Dmitry Maksimov and others.

On 10 April 1982, Lidia Vladimirovna wrote to her son: 'You probably already know that a letter from a group of scholars was sent to the Central Committee on 1 April. It's short, a page and a half, but solid and substantial. It was signed by seven people, all of whom you know.' She was referring to a letter sent to the Special Sector of the Central Committee on 31 March.

Life in the zone was becoming unbearable. Azadovsky was constantly trying to think what he could do to make the administration put him into isolation. After all, any contact he had with other inmates could lead to another conflict or to another written statement being made about his 'views'. The colony's operative unit (led by Major Potaichuk) had begun acting even more brazenly: they called prisoners in for questioning and demanded that they sign documents in exchange for a speedy release. Apparently, the colony administration was under pressure from the KGB to provide concrete evidence that could be used in legal proceedings against Azadovsky.

From Azadovsky's letters to Lepilina:

29 April

My position in the colony remains unchanged. In the coming days, I will once again firmly state that I ought to be 'locked up' for the remainder of my sentence in a punishment isolation cell or punishment cell. It is no longer tenable for me to remain in my crew and lead a normal life (that is, a normal life for the colony).

On the same day this letter was written, Susuman's deputy prosecutor, Alexander Neierdi, made another appearance in the zone. Azadovsky wrote about his visit on the following day, 30 April:

> I saw him, I got back the draft of my complaint to the Central Committee and I asked him a series of questions regarding my position in the colony. He wouldn't be drawn into discussing all the complexities with me . . .
>
> The prosecutor also told me that he thinks it is unlikely that a second set of groundless (which is to say, fabricated) charges will be brought against me. This has reassured me somewhat.

This reassurance didn't last long: each day, Azadovsky was given fresh reason to believe that he would not be left in peace. In early May, he realized that he had to act. Otherwise, the chain of events that had been set in motion back in February would be impossible to stop.

He wrote a letter to Lepilina early in the morning on 5 May, before leaving for work. Its tone was calm, even businesslike. He dated it 6 May, estimating that it would reach Leningrad sometime in the middle of the month. This way, for a while at least, his wife and mother would continue to believe that he was more or less all right.

That same day, Azadovsky slit his wrists in the colony's sewing workshop.

10.5 The punishment isolation cell and the infirmary

Suicide was common in the camps. Prisoners experienced serious hardships: the shock of their arrest, investigation and trial, the reduction of their lives to the four walls of a prison cell, the abuses they suffered during transit, the adversity of everyday life in the camps, the back-breaking physical labour, the struggle to survive and form relationships with the other inmates, and the criminal hierarchy in which not everyone managed to find their place. All too often, these pressures gave rise to suicide attempts. Prisoners would maim themselves, starve themselves, cut themselves, hang themselves or swallow needles or other metal objects. Azadovsky had suffered a great deal since the beginning of the year, and his preferred means of protest – writing complaints – had proved futile. In the end, he may have seen suicide as his only option.

After providing Azadovsky with the necessary medical treatment, the administration wrote him up for his latest rule violation: 'self-injury with the intent to avoid work'. They sent the 'offender' to a punishment isolation cell, where he would spend the next month.

But was Azadovsky trying to end his own life or to save it? By cutting himself, Azadovsky had managed to accomplish what he hadn't been able to achieve in any other way: finally, he was allowed to spend an entire month in isolation. Whether or not his self-harm was part of a premeditated plan, he had put his life in real danger. On 25 August 1982, Azadovsky wrote a complaint to the Prosecutor's Office:

> On 5 May, in a state of emotional distress and severe depression due to the systematic and unjustified harassment I faced from the administration and the management of the sewing workshop where I worked at the time, I cut open the veins of my left arm. The administration interpreted this as an act of intentional self-injury, and I was put in a punishment isolation cell for five days. After the first day, [this] was extended to fifteen days. In the punishment isolation cell, seized by another fit [of depression], I attempted to slit my wrists a second time. The administration used this incident as justification to extend my time in the isolation cell to thirty days.

In other words, Azadovsky tried to take his own life more than once – the second time using shards from a broken light bulb. Even if his first attempt had been a deliberate ploy to get sent to the punishment isolation cell, this second attempt was clearly an act of desperation.

And so, Azadovsky spent a full month in punitive isolation. Although this time provided him with a much-needed psychological break from the harassment he suffered among the general population, the living conditions in punitive isolation were tantamount to torture. Apart from a bowl of broth once a week, he subsisted on nothing but bread and water. He was locked in a concrete cell with no access to fresh air; the walls were covered in hoarfrost. He wasn't allowed to sit down during the day. He was forced to vacate the wooden bench that he slept on at six in the morning, at which point the guard on duty would fix it tightly against the wall. It would be taken down again in the evening and left in place for precisely eight hours. None of this was conducive to good health.

Azadovsky had begun developing health problems during his incarceration, and now they were becoming worse. He was in need of medical attention, and so, as soon as he was released from punitive isolation on 5 June, he was sent straight to the infirmary.

'If there can be such a thing as a little corner of heaven in hell, that is the camp infirmary', Alexander Podrabinek observed. This particular piece of heaven occupied a building within the Central Hospital of the Magadan UVD, which serviced AV-261/5 (the official name for ITK-5) as well as other establishments run by the Corrective Labour Division of Magadan Oblast. It was built on the site of the infirmary where the famous camp writer Varlam Shalamov was treated in 1945.

In the infirmary, inmates enjoyed unimaginable luxuries. They were given work release, the opportunity to sleep as much as they wanted, white sheets and a much-improved diet: there was even butter for the bread.

More important, though, were the relationships Azadovsky formed there. The first was with local construction magnate Erik Raisky (1933–2009), who had been sentenced to ten years' incarceration after a run-in with the Magadan Oblast Committee of the Communist Party (in the late 1980s, he managed to move to Saint Petersburg and establish a major construction firm there). Classed as an invalid, he spent his entire sentence in the infirmary.

One day, Azadovsky, who had seen Raisky around the infirmary and was impressed with the way he expressed his thoughts, sat down on the edge of his cot and introduced himself. This was the beginning of a friendship that would last until Raisky's death.

10.6 And let us not be weary in well doing!

The second person who extended a helping hand to Azadovsky during his time in the infirmary wasn't an inmate. He was a doctor, Captain Mikhail Feiginzon (1937–2008).

Feiginzon had earned a psychiatry degree in Minsk, but, as a Jew, he was unable to practise there. He and his family arrived in Susuman in 1970: not only was he able to work as a doctor, but he was also given a flat and a much larger salary.

Feiginzon was an unusual character for Kolyma, and for the camp especially. He wrote poetry, organized poetic and philosophical gatherings in the Susuman library and for a while went for morning runs (even when the temperature dropped to –50, which made quite an impression in the camp). He occasionally came to the zone to provide health counselling for the prisoners; he was known for his lively, distinctive way of talking (he spoke with a Belorussian Jewish accent). Feiginzon was a confident, calm and reserved psychiatrist, a competent professional who felt genuine sympathy for his patients. This made the inmates wary of him. Daily life in the camp had taught them to see the prison staff as alien and potentially dangerous. Feiginzon seemed like he had come from another planet.

Later on, Azadovsky would often compare Feiginzon to Friedrich Haass (1780–1853), who had once served as head doctor of Moscow's prisons. Haass, a German Catholic, had made it his mission to alleviate prisoner suffering. Extremely idealistic, he took his motto from Galatians 6:9: 'And let us not be weary in well doing!'

For his part, Feiginzon was immediately struck by Azadovsky's story. Not only did the doctor believe Azadovsky, but he did everything in his power to help him.

10.7 A letter to Andropov

After a month in the infirmary, Azadovsky returned to the zone in early July 1982. With the administration's approval, he was transferred from the sewing workshop to a construction crew, where he briefly worked as Redin's assistant in the joinery section.

Meanwhile, Azadovsky continued receiving unwanted attention: other inmates informed him that they were being called in, interrogated and pressured. Convinced that the authorities were planning to charge him under Article 190-1 ('systematic circulation . . . of false statements which defame the Soviet state or social system'), Azadovsky started developing a defence strategy. It was around this time that he decided to appeal to the KGB leadership directly. He began writing a petition.

On 21 August, the anniversary of his arrival in Susuman, Azadovsky received some unexpected news: without any complaints or requests on his part, he was being sent back to the infirmary 'for mental health treatment'. And, sure enough, the on-duty assistant to the camp warden came to take him to the Central Hospital, where he was put under the care of M.S. Feiginzon. He would remain there for the next month.

On 23 August, he wrote to his mother:

This time I am being held in the medical ward under the care of a psychiatrist, a very talented specialist. They say I am in a 'reactive state', which manifests itself in my extreme excitability, my tendency to obsessive thoughts, my inability to get a good night's sleep, etc. None of this is particularly dangerous, but it won't hurt to be treated for it, either. I entered this system a completely healthy person and would like to leave it just as healthy – both physically and mentally.

During his time in the infirmary, Azadovsky wrote a petition addressed to KGB chairman Yury Andropov and gave it to the camp's special unit to be sent. This time, Azadovsky was absolutely certain his complaint would not be 'lost': the KGB's power was too great, and the MVD's fear of it was even greater. Azadovsky wrote:

From my very first weeks in the colony, I have been convinced that the administration has been receiving information about me from Leningrad, from the Committee for State Security [KGB]. Over the past year, I have been called a 'dissident', 'anti-Soviet', a 'student of Sakharov' and even . . . a 'Zionist' on multiple occasions . . .

In early February 1982 (after the administration had put me forward for conditional early release building the national economy), two KGB agents arrived at the colony. Over the course of three days, they held talks with the administration, spreading slanderous reports against me and indulging in what I view as unacceptable allegations. . . . Under such direct pressure, the administration wrote me up for three rule violations in quick succession, all of which were fabricated . . .

My circumstances in the colony remain highly alarming. Guided by the recommendations they have received about me, the administration has become biased against me (I have been artificially recast as a 'repeat offender' against camp rules and there is constant talk of a new conviction, administrative supervision, etc.). The comments that some of the officers, Lieutenant Sukhov in particular, permit themselves to make about me – citing the KGB as their source – (Azadovsky is an 'enemy', Azadovsky 'must be shot', etc.) are remarkable for their extreme ill intent. Since they say these things to the other prisoners as well, their remarks are also provocative in nature (they whip people up against 'free-thinkers').

As I already attempted to explain in my letter to the Central Committee of the CPSU, I have absolutely nothing to do with the activities I have been accused of behind closed doors since December 1980. I am not a dissident, I have never engaged in anti-Soviet activities and I am not personally acquainted with any dissidents. Still less could I be labelled a 'Zionist'.

It is worth noting that, in 1970s official jargon, 'Zionist' was simply a code word for 'Jew'. This term was mainly applied to people who had been denied exit visas to emigrate from the Soviet Union. For example, Boris Chernobylsky, Azadovsky's friend in Susuman, would certainly have been labelled a 'Zionist'. The term was also used more broadly: it was applied to a wide range of free-thinkers, 'dissidents' and educated people who didn't wish to collaborate with the Soviet regime. Officially, though, anti-Semitism wasn't tolerated within the USSR. Thus, instead of referring to people directly as Jews or employing unsavoury ethnic slurs, the authorities resorted to euphemism (much as they had in the 1940s, when the euphemism of choice was 'cosmopolitan').

Azadovsky concluded his lengthy missive as follows:

> I request a reply from the Committee for State Security [KGB] detailing their true objections against me and stating the reasons behind the control they have exercised over me and the criminal case against me for the past several years.

This letter was registered with the colony's special unit on 23 July 1982 and sent to the head of the Susuman KGB, Lieutenant Colonel Vladimir Kobzar, for 'clarification'.

In early September, Azadovsky learned that he wouldn't be allowed to receive his next package of foodstuffs, even though he had received official permission for the package in August. The foodstuffs that arrived from Leningrad were sent straight back again. During the two years, Azadovsky spent in incarceration, he received just one delivery of foodstuffs (in Kresty, just before New Year's 1981), one five-kilogram package and two smaller parcels. Everything else was sent back or went missing.

Meanwhile, in the infirmary, Azadovsky continued suffering humiliations at the hands of the camp authorities. In a complaint dated 14 September, he wrote:

> Today at 11h30, I was stopped at the entrance to the Central Hospital shop by a threatening shout from Ensign Teslyuk: 'Azadovsky, where do you think you're going?' The shop was already open at the time, and there was a large crowd of prisoners standing outside it.
>
> I turned to the ensign and requested (as I normally do in such situations) that, first of all, he address me in a respectful manner[5] (as required by the internal code of conduct of the Corrective Labour Division of the USSR MVD). Then I entered the shop.
>
> Ensign Teslyuk lunged after me (I was already at the counter, chatting with the woman who worked there) and started pulling at the sleeve of my pea coat, shouting, 'All right, then, let's go.' I repeated my request that the ensign address me in a respectful manner.
>
> At that point, Teslyuk changed his tone and requested that I accompany him to the hospital's special ward. I complied with his demand. After shutting the door behind me, the ensign began shouting at me threateningly: 'We'll see who comes out on top!', 'I'll make life sweet for you' and so on. The whole time, he kept using the word 'intelligentsia' as if it were an insult.
>
> An on-duty hospital inspection officer walked in on this conversation, and Teslyuk said, 'Azadovsky's jacket was unfastened. That's a uniform violation. Write him up, will you?' The inspector replied, 'Sure, I'll write him up.'

It is important to note that Ensign Teslyuk was reprimanded as a result of Azadovsky's complaint: this kind of outcome was rare.

In all likelihood, Azadovsky's letter to the KGB didn't make it all the way to Moscow: instead, it was waylaid by the local KGB, which reviewed it and then sent back to the capital for further information.

At this point, Lieutenant Colonel Kobzar felt it necessary to meet Azadovsky face to face. Their meeting took place in the staff room of the Susuman infirmary in the presence of Azadovsky's attending physician, Feiginzon. As it turned out, Kobzar and Feiginzon were well acquainted: they both frequented the local bookstore, where there was a special room for perusing and purchasing new books, which were in short supply back then.

Their conversation was calm and fairly comprehensive. The head of the local KGB proved to be intimately familiar with the details of Azadovsky's life; Azadovsky had never met a stranger who knew so much about him. Kobzar's accusations indicated that Azadovsky was suspected of espionage or even treason. Of course, Investigator Kamenko had let slip as much to Azadovsky back in December 1980. Kobzar rejected Azadovsky's claims that he was innocent before the Soviet state. Using Azadovsky's letter to Andropov as a starting point, he presented two major lines of argumentation.

First, in the 1970s in Leningrad, Azadovsky had visited the consul of a capitalist country on more than one occasion. In Kobzar's view, this constituted a serious offence. The fact that the consul was a colleague, a professional Slavonicist who 'just happened' to be serving as a diplomat, was no excuse.

Second, when Azadovsky chose not to cooperate with the KGB in 1963, he had lost the right to refer to himself as a Soviet citizen (as he had in his letter to Andropov). After all, taking a negative view of the KGB meant taking a negative view of the Soviet state more broadly.

Azadovsky protested, saying that his refusal to cooperate had been for moral rather than political reasons. At this point, Kobzar asked Azadovsky to sign a loyalty oath.

At the end of this conversation, Azadovsky asked, 'Regardless of what you had against me, was planting narcotics really necessary? And why drag my wife into it?' The lieutenant colonel answered sternly: 'Well, I don't know about that. Narcotics were found in a search of your home. And as for your wife – you can sort all that out when you get back to Leningrad.'

Azadovsky understood that the game wasn't over just yet. But at the same time, he could breathe a sigh of relief: now there was some hope that he would be released. Whether it was because of his letter or because there had been changes at the top, he didn't know.

With his mental health somewhat restored, Azadovsky returned to the zone. He was put back in the same sewing workshop where he had begun his career as a camp labourer a year earlier. Though less than three months remained of his sentence, he continued to have run-ins with the administration on an almost-daily basis.

A new conflict had arisen between Azadovsky and the colony administration, and it was far more dangerous than the one that had taken place earlier that year. From August to October 1982, prisoners had been compelled to work ten-, twelve- and even fourteen-hour shifts in the sewing workshop. This change hadn't been sanctioned by the warden. The prisoners weren't paid for their additional labour, nor were they given any extra time off. They were pushed to the brink of exhaustion, given no more than three or four hours to sleep every night. Azadovsky submitted a written complaint to the Prosecutor's Office on behalf of his entire brigade, as a result of which the fourteen-hour shifts were banned. However, from that moment on, the colony authorities began treating Azadovsky as an enemy.

Once again, Feiginzon came to the rescue. He convinced the camp warden that it would be easier for everyone involved if Azadovsky spent the final weeks of his sentence in the infirmary. After all, if Azadovsky had to be carried out of the zone feet first, there would be hell to pay.

Thus, Azadovsky spent the final month and a half of his sentence in the infirmary with Raisky and Feiginzon.

10.8 Release

The end of 1982 was an eventful time in the USSR. On 10 November, the All-Union Radio played classical music for almost the entire day. Then, at 10.00 am on 11 November, it was announced that General Secretary Leonid Brezhnev had passed away. A month and a half later, on 27 December 1982, the Presidium of the Supreme Soviet of the USSR declared a prisoner amnesty. Ostensibly, this act was intended to mark the sixtieth anniversary of the formation of the Soviet Union; in fact, changes in the Soviet head of state were often accompanied by such amnesties.

In retrospect, Brezhnev's death was a watershed moment in the history of the Soviet state, but that wasn't how it appeared at the time. The thought certainly hadn't occurred to Azadovsky, who was preparing for his release. On the morning of 18 December, Azadovsky penned the final petition he would send from Susuman. This was also the only petition he wrote during his time in the camp that he didn't have to send via the special unit: he put it in the post himself later that day.

> On 12 December of this year, the administration of ITK-5 committed yet another violation of my rights: I was unlawfully deprived of a short visit with my wife, Svetlana Ivanovna Azadovskaya, who arrived in Susuman on 15 December of this year.
>
> I had submitted a request for a short visit in October of this year, and it was approved by the administration that same month.
>
> In response to the refusal of Major Masalkov, ITK-5's Deputy Warden in charge of regulations and operational activities, to grant my request for a visit with my wife, I went on a hunger strike. I intended this act first and foremost as a protest against the actions the administration had taken against me through nearly all of 1982; towards the end, these acts took on a blatantly abusive character.
>
> Thus, I refused food from 16 December until the time of my release. I requested that the warden explain why my visit had been cancelled; this request was not fulfilled.

After finishing his petition, Azadovsky packed up his belongings and waited to be called. For the last time, he heard someone shout: 'Azadovsky! Time to go! Gather your things!' He was taken to the security checkpoint, where his passport was returned and he was issued a certificate of release. He embraced his wife, and, together, they left the security checkpoint and stepped into freedom.

They went to the bus stop, and for the first time Azadovsky saw the zone from the outside: it was surrounded by a long, concrete wall topped with barbed wire and punctuated by watchtowers manned by armed guards. The bus arrived and they went back to the hotel. After resting for a while, they went to the post office to send the journals and books Azadovsky planned on taking with him from the zone. They put in an order for two telephone calls; it was daytime in Susuman, but in Leningrad it was late evening. First, Azadovsky called his mother. She had been sleeping, but managed to pick up the phone and hear his voice. She said something to him, but the connection was bad, so he couldn't make it out. Then he called Geta Yanovskaya. 'Geta, it's me.' 'Kostya!' she said, 'We've been expecting you.' That was the entire conversation. The very fact of the phone call was evidence of Azadovsky's release.

Azadovsky and Lepilina spent the night on a coach, on the eighteen-hour journey down the Kolyma Highway to Magadan. They talked for the entire trip, interrupting each other in their haste.

What would the future hold for them? Azadovsky certainly wouldn't be permitted to teach. Could he still be a scholar? He would have a lot of catching up to do, but he tried not to focus on that. The most important thing was that his mother was alive and that he would see her soon.

What was he feeling at that moment, after all that time spent in prison and the zone? There was bitterness and anger, of course, but, more importantly, he felt a sense of certitude and calm. He had withstood a serious ordeal and grown in the process.

The flight from Magadan to Moscow was delayed by four hours. When they finally arrived, they were met by their friends Kama Ginkas and Alexander Parnis.

The next day, after a good night's sleep and another phone call to his mother, Azadovsky went outside. This was the first time he'd been out on the street in two years. He was overwhelmed by the crowds and the city noise; he had grown unaccustomed to freedom. Braving the metro (also a great source of stress), he went to the outskirts of Moscow to visit his friend Boris Chernobylsky.

Azadovsky and Lepilina spent two days and nights in Moscow. They arrived in Leningrad on the morning of 22 December 1982. A crowd of friends came to greet them at Moskovsky Railway Station.

Life began again.

11

The start of a long road

The country changed very little in the years 1983–4; the only difference was that Andropov had replaced Brezhnev as general secretary. The 'bright future' promised by the party and the state was still nowhere in sight.

Azadovsky was determined to clear his name, but he didn't know how best to go about it. He proceeded by trial and error, seeking out cracks in his criminal case that might later be used to exonerate him. Each time one of his complaints was rejected, he submitted one to a higher authority; this process dragged on for several years and took up a tremendous amount of his time. But Azadovsky was determined to do battle with the hydra that had ruined his life.

Most of Azadovsky's friends believed his struggle was in vain, and so they tried to talk him out of it. They presented well-reasoned arguments that all ended with the same advice: that Azadovsky abandon his campaign and move on with his life. He might even consider emigration to the West. But Azadovsky wouldn't listen; he was in no hurry to abandon his country.

While Azadovsky was still in the zone, Lepilina had managed to secure one of the few jobs still available to her. Becoming a caretaker gave her the right to a temporary *propiska*, which meant she could stay in Leningrad. After his return, Azadovsky eked out a living teaching private lessons and selling books from his library and art from his father's collection.

Azadovsky's return to academia would be a slow and difficult process, but, for the time being, he was willing to write for the desk drawer. During that period, translation was the best-paid and least dangerous profession for a humanities scholar. Before his arrest, Azadovsky had been contracted to produce a scholarly translation of *Grimms' Fairy Tales* for the series *Literary Monuments*. With the help of Dmitry Likhachyov, this contract was reconfirmed in 1983. The project provided Azadovsky with some much-needed money while raising his morale.

But he spent most of his time writing complaints. At first, these complaints focused on his unjust sentence. Time and time again, he was given the runaround. He received laconic form rejections, like this one from the chairman of the Leningrad City Court, V.I. Poludyakov, dated 27 April 1983:

> Your guilt in this crime was established by a court based on a body of evidence verified during court proceedings. In particular, there was a note that you yourself wrote to Lepilina with a view towards elaborating a version of events in which you

ostensibly had nothing to do with the hashish found in your flat during a search. The court gave an appropriate evaluation of the evidence and had good grounds to declare you guilty.

So in 1983, Azadovsky changed tactics. He stopped trying to challenge the judgement in its entirety; instead, he concentrated on refuting individual pieces of evidence that had factored in his sentencing.

11.1 Missing property

The Azadovskys rang in 1983 together in the flat on Vosstaniya Street.

During the two years of her son's incarceration, Lidia Vladimirovna had been haunted by the fact that if she died before her son's release, he would lose not just the flat but also his right to a Leningrad *propiska*.

Lepilina had lost hers as soon as she was sentenced. Her rooms had gone to Zinaida Tkachyova, the flatmate who testified against her. This wasn't uncommon in the Soviet Union: people who lived in communal flats would eagerly inform on their neighbours for the chance to move into their rooms.

Lepilina didn't stand a chance of recovering her living space; however, she did have the right to reclaim the things that had been there prior to her arrest. Tkachyova had made sure to dump most of her former flatmate's belongings in the basement of the Office of Housing Operations before Lepilina's release, but some things were missing.

An official prosecutorial enquiry undertaken at the Azadovskys' request revealed that rings and earrings belonging to Lepilina had been taken by Tkachyova, who had participated in the search of Lepilina's rooms; meanwhile, the bag confiscated from Lepilina during her detention and the photographs of Russian poets seized from Azadovsky's flat had disappeared from Investigator Kamenko's safe 'due to a defective lock'. This gave the Azadovskys grounds to make legal claims against Kamenko. And so they submitted a document demanding that, for causing them material losses and emotional distress, Kamenko be charged for negligence under Article 172 of the RSFSR Criminal Code. This crime was punishable by dismissal, up to one year's community service or even up to three years' incarceration.

Of course, realistically speaking, no one was going to bring charges against Investigator Kamenko, but Azadovsky couldn't forgive him for the role he had played in fabricating the charges against him and his wife. Also, in Russia it was difficult to predict which courses of action might bear fruit.

The Azadovskys' loss was deemed insignificant, and so the enquiry didn't find anything criminal in Kamenko's actions. Besides, as it turned out, Kamenko had already been 'terminated from the MVD for being unfit for his position' (this termination did not, however, prevent him from finishing his studies at Leningrad State University's law faculty, where he was studying part-time).

Under pressure from the police, Tkachyova 'voluntarily surrendered' the jewellery she had seized during the search. Meanwhile, the loss of the property under Kamenko's care gave grounds for the Azadovskys to demand restitution. The correspondence surrounding this process dragged on for several years; finally, the Azadovskys took the issue to court. On 12 May 1988, the Kuibyshevsky People's Court in Leningrad handed down a decision awarding them compensatory damages for the photographs and books that had been lost.

They were awarded 315 rubles, 50 kopecks, roughly equivalent to a professor's monthly salary. But that wasn't all. The most important thing Azadovsky gained from this lawsuit was access to information he never would have had otherwise.

11.2 Burned books

From the very beginning, the Azadovskys had objected to the destruction of the books that had been seized from both their flats. Only Azadovsky's criminal case contained any mention of 'dubious' (which is to say 'anti-Soviet') literature; it included a report from the censorship (Gorlit). Lepilina's case contained nothing of the sort. However, after her release, her case took on fresh political overtones.

Lepilina wrote a petition to the Leningrad branch of Gorlit on 1 April 1983:

I am writing to request an explanation for the following situation.

On 19 February 1981 the Kuibyshevsky District Court in Leningrad sentenced me to one year, six months under Article 224, paragraph 3. On 7 April 1982, I was granted early release by the Avtozavodsky District Court in Gorky and returned to Leningrad.

On 28 March 1983, when the personal belongings seized during the search of my flat on 20 December 1980 were returned to me, I was surprised to learn from the investigator, Lieutenant E.E. Kamenko of the Investigation Department of the Kuibyshevsky RUVD, that my books could not be returned to me because they were all anti-Soviet volumes unfit for distribution in the USSR.

I then appealed to Captain S.M. Goroshchen, assistant director of the Investigation Department of the Kuibyshevsky RUVD, who informed me that your organization issued a report on the books that had been seized from my flat, on the basis of which these books were declared anti-Soviet and were 'destroyed'. However, he did not present me with this document.

The entire situation seems suspicious to me. First of all, no such document appears in the criminal case against me, and in 1981, during my investigation and trial, no one accused me of possessing anti-Soviet literature. Besides, the books that were seized from me could in no way be construed as 'anti-Soviet'. . . [the list of seized works has been omitted.]

I am writing to you for answers in connection with the circumstances laid out above: Were the aforementioned volumes really submitted to Lenoblgorlit, and was any report ever issued on them? If such a report actually exists and all of the volumes seized from me were declared 'anti-Soviet' and 'unfit for distribution in the USSR', then I urgently request to be presented with the expert findings.

Soon afterwards, Lepilina was contacted by the Leningrad censorship, who invited her to a meeting on 19 April. She was greeted by the organization's head, who explained that they had not received any materials connected with the search of her flat and that no findings had been issued on the books mentioned in her letter. Lepilina asked that he provide an official statement to that effect, which she received on 21 April.

In October, after filing a complaint with the Prosecutor's Office about the missing books, Lepilina was invited in to see the prosecutor, V.K. Muravyov, at which point he presented her with the results of their enquiry. First, he returned four of the nine books she had mentioned. Then, he showed her a report from Lenoblgorlit dated 7 January 1983 and signed by Markov, the city's head of censorship. The report indicated that four other books had been deemed 'unfit for import and distribution in the USSR'. The final book, a French copy of Albert Camus's *The Stranger*, had been declared lost.

At that point, Lepilina revealed the ace up her sleeve: the document from Lenoblgorlit certifying that no works related to her case had been submitted for evaluation. In response, the prosecutor speculated that the head of the directorate might have been pressured into issuing a backdated report.

When Lepilina asked what agency could be powerful enough to sway the city's head of censorship, the prosecutor smiled wryly. And on 15 November, she received an official response signed by the deputy prosecutor confirming everything they had discussed during their meeting.

If the question of Lepilina's missing books remained shrouded in mystery, the circumstances around Azadovsky's seemed relatively clear: the censorship report with the scratched-out reference to the KGB had given him plenty to go on.

Azadovsky's main goal was not to recover his books, which had been destroyed by court order in 1981; he had received official confirmation of that fact on 30 November 1983. However, he wanted to dispute Gorlit's findings or, at the very least, to call them into question. Why did he feel this was necessary? Azadovsky was probably considering the possibility of a retrial, and so he was attempting to 'compromise' the documents that had influenced his earlier sentencing.

And so, on 20 December 1983, Azadovsky submitted a complaint to the Main Directorate for the Protection of State Secrets in Print Media (Glavlit USSR) in which he disputed Gorlit's findings point by point. In conclusion, he wrote:

> In accordance with the expert evaluation issued by Lenoblgorlit, Investigator Lieutenant E.E. Kamenko of the Kuibyshevsky RUVD in Leningrad issued a resolution stating that 'various foreign publications of an anti-Soviet nature were discovered and seized during a search of citizen Azadovsky's flat. . . . These malicious tracts against the Soviet State contained libellous inventions against the Soviet state . . .' (p. 55 of the case [against me]). I emphatically protest such formulations: I have never possessed such volumes. I have only dealt with texts that are necessary to my scholarly work as a specialist in twentieth-century Russian literature. The books that were seized from me cannot possibly be construed as 'anti-Soviet'. The investigator's resolution contains illegitimate generalizations and, for all intents and purposes, constitutes a fabrication.

The censorship didn't issue a response to this petition, or to any of the ones that followed. However, in 1986, Azadovsky managed to see the original statement attesting that his books had been burned in 1981 because they were 'unfit for import and distribution in the USSR and [did] not possess any scholarly or historical value'. Later on, Azadovsky would publicize this document widely.

11.3 The character reference

One of the most egregious documents that played a role in Azadovsky's sentencing was his workplace character reference. He only learned the story behind this document after his release.

On 13 February 1981, soon after his arrest, there had been an extended meeting of the Soviet and active party members of the Vera Mukhina Higher School. Investigator Kamenko spoke to the assembled crowd about Azadovsky's character, and elections were held to determine who would act as his civic accuser.

Later on, falsified minutes from this meeting were included in the case against Azadovsky. Only his accusers' speeches were recorded accurately; his defenders' arguments were twisted beyond recognition.

So now, Azadovsky was attempting to contest this false character reference, or, in other words, to restore his honour through the Soviet court system (the 'fairest in the world'). He persuaded several of his former colleagues to act as witnesses if necessary. On 25 November 1983, Azadovsky filed a claim with the court challenging the contents of his character reference. He wrote: 'This document is libellous from beginning to end: it contains a whole series of allegations made without any documentary evidence that tarnish my reputation as an individual and as a Soviet citizen.' He then proceeded to refute each section of the reference point by point. In conclusion, he demanded that the rector, Shistko, and the party organizer, Bobov, be charged under Article 130 of the Criminal Code for 'the fabrication and dissemination of libellous inventions'.

However, the court of first instance, the Collegium on Criminal Proceedings of the Leningrad City Court and the Presidium of the Leningrad City Court all refused to bring charges (on 5 December 1983, 15 December 1983 and 4 April 1984, respectively).

Despite Azadovsky's initial optimism and the witnesses he had managed to secure, his attempts to dispute the character reference and bring his libellers to justice turned out to be in vain. At each level, the courts declared that the character reference represented the 'voice of the collective' and that the document's signatories could not be held responsible for what the people had decided.

11.4 Identifying the missing officers

One of the questions that haunted Azadovsky over the years was: Who had really searched his flat on 19 December 1980? This question should have been easy to answer: after all, Article 141 of the UPK decreed that everyone present at a search must be named in the search report.

But in this case there was a hitch. The search had been conducted by five police officers, four of whom were there from the beginning and one of whom arrived later on. All five were in civilian dress. There were also two search witnesses, Konstantinov and Makarov. However, the search report only lists the witnesses and two police officers: Artsibushev and Khlyupin. At Azadovsky's insistence, a third officer's name was also recorded: 'Bystrov', who pushed Azadovsky when he made to answer the phone. No mention is made of the fourth officer who arrived along with the rest or of the fifth officer, the 'specialist' who joined them later. Their names do not appear anywhere in the criminal case against Azadovsky.

Even on the day of the search, Azadovsky had understood the importance of noting the participants' names: he recorded all of their surnames on a sheet of paper. However, at the end of the search, he found that it had gone missing from his desk. He never laid eyes on it again.

Azadovsky emphasized this fact in each of his complaints. He pointed to the breach of procedure and demanded to know the names of the other people present at the search. However, this request was never satisfied. The first reply Azadovsky received was in response to his complaint to the RSFSR prosecutor; it was issued by the Leningrad City Prosecutor's Office on 27 January 1984:

> The presence of the five police officers you mention was an operative necessity. No unauthorized persons were present. Thus, the actions taken by the police do not represent any violation of the socialist legal order.

11.5 'There will be no place in the motherland for you . . .'

The Azadovskys' proactive approach was genuinely puzzling, both to the Leningrad authorities and to some of the couple's friends. They were reminded on more than one occasion that they had 'only' been sentenced to a year and a half and two years, respectively. Their sentences paled in comparison with those that had been issued in similar cases.

The Azadovskys were slowly returning to their former lives, but the law enforcement agencies still treated them as ex-convicts. As such, they were periodically summoned for 'preventative conversations', which doubled as an opportunity to encourage them to stop filing complaints. It made no difference that the Azadovskys' convictions were set to 'expire' relatively soon (three years after their releases). The couple would be treated as ex-convicts for the rest of their lives.

And so, Azadovskys decided to leave the country forever. Why? Yefim Etkind, who was forced to emigrate from the USSR, encapsulates this experience nicely:

> These are people who have, for the most part, decided of their own accord to leave their country for another one, to cross a tightly controlled border without any hope of return. Some of them are opportunists and Philistines. . . . There is also an in-between category: these people have left because in the West things are better

and freer and living is easier; you can travel to different countries, read different parties' newspapers, not be afraid of snitches, spooks, microphones in the ceilings and the sound of the doorbell at night . . .

There are other people who leave, too: people who believe in their own spiritual strength and know that they will be unable to develop that strength in the motherland. Personnel departments won't hire them. They are unable to enrol in postgraduate studies, even though it's painfully clear that they were made to do scholarly research. They are not admitted to conferences. They have trouble getting their books published. . . . This is hard and terrifying. Russian cultural figures are departing for different Western countries; our culture is collapsing. Poets create using language, and when they are surrounded by an alien tongue, they gradually grow mute, their sense of language dulls, their words die away. Scholars are formed within their schools, they have their enemies and allies. When they find themselves in an alien world, all alone, more often than not they waste away . . .

When a thread is pulled out of a piece of fabric, not only does the thread lose its sense of purpose, but the fabric itself is disfigured: it unravels. You have to emigrate when the noose is slipped around your neck, when staying would be both fatal and futile – when the thread has been pulled out of the fabric anyway and it can't be woven in again.

The Azadovskys had their pick of potential destinations. Finally, Azadovsky accepted an invitation from the University of Caen Normandy, one of the oldest universities in France, where he was offered a place in the Slavonic department and the title of *professeur associé*. He wanted to return to teaching, which he had greatly missed. He was also tempted by the opportunity to immerse himself in Western European culture.

In those years, leaving the USSR didn't just mean moving to another country. It required a series of painful and humiliating formalities. You were forced to relinquish your living space to the state and pay a 500-ruble fee for each individual leaving the USSR. At the same time, you were stripped of your Soviet citizenship, as well as any pension contributions you had made in the USSR. You were barely allowed to bring anything with you when you left. There was, however, one bullet that Azadovsky managed to dodge. On 3 August 1972, the Presidium of the Supreme Soviet of the USSR had issued a decree titled 'On the compensation of state expenses related to the education of Soviet citizens leaving to take up permanent residence abroad'. According to this decree, a graduate of Leningrad State University would be required to pay the government 6,000 rubles, while LSU doctorate and higher doctorate holders would owe an additional 5,400 and 7,200 rubles, respectively. According to this system, Azadovsky would have owed the Soviet government 11,400 rubles, the price of two Zhiguli-brand automobiles. This was an astronomical sum. Fortunately, by the end of the decade, this decree was no longer enforced; the Jackson–Vanik amendment to the Trade Act of 1974 had served to temper Moscow's excesses.[1]

The MVD's Visa and Registration Department (OVIR) wouldn't accept an invitation from a university as grounds for issuing an exit visa, and so the Azadovskys had to secure a notarized invitation from 'relatives' in Israel, which they obtained in early spring 1984. However, Lidia Vladimirovna passed away on 24 April, which meant that her son and daughter-in-law were occupied for some time making the necessary arrangements. Finally, in winter 1985, the Azadovskys submitted their petitions to emigrate at their local OVIR.

Unfortunately, right around that time, the procedure surrounding exit visas had become considerably more complicated, and success was far from guaranteed. After the Twenty-sixth Congress of the CPSU in 1981, the official attitude towards potential emigrants changed dramatically; the international community's protestations no longer had any effect on the state's repressive policies against 'traitors'. The number of rejected exit visa applications rose sharply in the early 1980s, peaking at 80 per cent. The situation didn't improve when Gorbachev came to power in March 1985 – in fact, things only grew worse: the rules for leaving the country became stricter, while the number of approvals decreased. Many citizens, especially those with postgraduate degrees, didn't stand a chance: their applications wouldn't even be reviewed.

Azadovsky's friends in the West were aware of the situation and did their best to help. First, they organized the official invitation from the Azadovskys' 'relatives' in Israel. Though the connection was fictitious (the Azadovskys didn't have family living in Israel), the Soviet authorities weren't usually too picky on this count: they knew perfectly well that many emigrants 'to Israel' would attempt to stay in Europe or go on to the United States. Lev Kopelev, who enjoyed a certain degree of celebrity in the German-speaking world, also reached out to help. In summer 1984, he and Heinrich Böll went to visit former Austrian chancellor Bruno Kreisky, who still played a prominent role in European politics. Immediately afterwards, representatives of the Austrian embassy in Moscow contacted Azadovsky to offer their assistance.

However, these efforts didn't help the Azadovskys' visa applications. Several months later, they were called down to the OVIR and told that their applications had been denied. When they asked why, they were informed that their departure had been deemed 'inadvisable'. And so they joined the ranks of the so-called refuseniks. Back then, people labelled refuseniks couldn't be employed in certain professions, which meant that they were often left without any means of supporting themselves and their families. People who worked in the arts were unable to publish, exhibit their works, give concerts and so on. They were branded as pariahs, traitors to the motherland.

But when an exit visa was granted, it was only valid for a specific period of time, usually no longer than a month. This presented its own challenges. It was impossible to dispense with all the required formalities within such a short period of time: the prospective emigrant needed to complete the necessary paperwork, surrender their flat to the state, liquidate their remaining assets (if there was no one to pass their belongings on to) and so on. And so, visa applicants had to start all of these processes before they found out whether their applications would be successful. Thus, from late 1985 to early 1986, the Azadovskys liquidated practically all of their belongings.

It was only in late 1986 that the state gradually began to relax its repressive policies against potential emigrants. In 1987, it loosened its grip enough to allow a new mass exodus from the Soviet Union. Emigration became particularly accessible to those who had never been privy to state secrets.

The euphoria occasioned by these democratic advances was so great that certain liberal-minded citizens, overcome by a feeling of hope for the future of their country, decided not to leave it after all. This was what happened in the Azadovskys' case.

11.6 Bingo!

Azadovsky had managed to sue the state for 315 rubles, 50 kopecks. However, after decades of using its law enforcement agencies to deprive citizens of their money, their property and even their lives, the state wasn't prepared to part with a single kopeck. The ruling in Azadovsky's favour created no end of trouble for the people responsible for this unthinkable loss.

As it turned out, while Azadovsky had been busy wading through judicial sophistry, the MVD and the Prosecutor's Office had also been hard at work. Azadovsky had sent complaints to Moscow to all sorts of organizations (from the MVD to the Central Committee), and though most of them were dismissed with a simple form letter, some of them actually triggered internal reviews. We can't know for certain how many such reviews took place, but in the years 1983–6 there were definitely several.

One review was launched in response to a resolution issued by the Prosecutor's Office on 16 September 1986; it was signed by the Kuibyshevsky District prosecutor's assistant. Naturally, the complaint was rejected on all counts. At that point, Azadovsky appealed to the Prosecutor's Office for permission to look at the review materials. This request was fully in line with the legislation of the time. However, when he was given the materials related to his civil suit, he realized that the findings from the official review had also been included in the file. Azadovsky couldn't believe his eyes. He copied out extracts and asked permission to return.

He wasn't shown anything on his next visit, or on any of his visits after that. Luckily, he had already managed to copy out a great deal. There, among the materials for prosecutorial review no. 225, Azadovsky had finally found the answers to the questions that had been gnawing at him since 1980.

So, what did he find?

First of all, he found information on the 'police officers' who participated in the search of his flat on 19 December 1980. According to the review, 'present at the search were KGB operatives Arkhipov, Shlemin, et al.'. This 'et al.' implied that the last missing name also belonged to a KGB officer. Because the KGB operatives who came to search Azadovsky's flat had introduced themselves as police officers, it was safe to assume that they had presented falsified police credentials, which was prohibited during investigative actions.

Second, he learned that all the materials seized from his flat – books, manuscripts, photographs and so on – had been handed over to the KGB that very day, and that it was the KGB that had ordered the expert evaluation from Gorlit. He also learned that 'KGB operatives delivered the appropriate evaluations, after which the photographs were returned to Investigator Kamenko. The rest was destroyed, as confirmed by a statement written by KGB operatives.'

Thus, Azadovsky received confirmation that his books had, in fact, been destroyed, as well as documentary evidence that at least three KGB agents had been involved in his case. The review included a copy of a statement documenting the 'total destruction by burning of materials unfit for import and distribution in the USSR that do not have any scholarly or historical value'. This statement was signed by three KGB officials: Deputy Department Chief E.V. Volodin and Azadovsky's 'old friends' Deputy Department Chief Yu.A. Bezverkhov and Criminal Intelligence Investigator A.V. Kuznetsov.

Azadovsky also gained vital information on Lepilina's criminal case.

The review contained a statement dated 28 November 1983 from Captain Artsibushev, who had detained Lepilina and led the search of Azadovsky's flat the following morning. He claimed that '[Lepilina's] bag was seized with the intent of strengthening the link between Lepilina and Azadovsky'. He also admitted to delivering the items seized from Lepilina to the head of the RUVD in the presence of KGB operatives. This document was followed by a receipt dated 22 December 1980: 'I, V.I. Arkhipov, an agent of the Leningrad City and Oblast KGB, have received the items seized from Lepilina indicated in the search report.' In other words, not only had the KGB been involved in the case against Lepilina, but it had been the very same agents who had taken part in the case against Azadovsky.

The fact that the items seized from Lepilina's flat hadn't figured in the case against her was explained by the findings issued by the RUVD's Investigation Department:

> Because the items and documents seized from Lepilina were unconnected to her criminal activities, when the investigation came to an end and the indictment was drawn up, Investigator Kamenko sent the case to court without asking the KGB to return the items and documents that had been seized from Lepilina or requesting documents regarding the fate of those items.

In other words, the blame for the missing items was being laid at Kamenko's door.

It is also worth citing Kamenko's explanation dated 24 November 1983:

> I didn't see the items seized from Lepilina's flat during the search; they were immediately taken by KGB operatives. . . . In 1983, Lepilina came to me and demanded that I return the items seized during the search. I made a call to the KGB and was brought a sack of items that Lepilina identified as belonging to her, and I returned those things to her against a receipt. Apart from the items indicated in the receipt, the KGB did not return any other items to me.

Thus, Azadovsky had discovered documentary evidence confirming the KGB's involvement in the criminal cases against him and his wife. He was even able to determine the real names of the agents involved. This was a striking turn of events. Though citizens had the legal right to see materials from reviews that had been conducted at their request, Azadovsky should not, strictly speaking, have been given access to these documents. Because they were related to KGB operations, the Prosecutor's Office ought to have 'closed' them, which is to say, labelled them as highly sensitive. However, this course of action would have been difficult to justify: a narcotics case and a civil suit for property loss shouldn't have warranted that kind of secrecy.

The system might have lured the Azadovskys into its trap, but now it was being held hostage by its own rules and regulations.

12

The journalist

The next stage in Azadovsky's case was made possible by Yury Shchekochikhin (1950–2003), a brave and talented Moscow-based investigative journalist who launched his own investigation into the Azadovsky Affair. Known for his remarkable personal and professional integrity, Shchekochikhin would later gain fame as a writer, television presenter and politician. Even now, twenty years after his tragic and mysterious demise, he symbolizes an era of freedom in modern Russian history.

Shchekochikhin began his journalistic career at the age of seventeen. He worked for *Komsomolskaya Pravda* for several years, and then in 1980 he joined the staff of *The Literary Gazette*, one of the most widely read papers of the day. It was there that he discovered his vocation as an investigative journalist. In 1988, he became the first person to explicitly liken the Soviet state to the mafia in print.

It might seem odd that a paper called *The Literary Gazette* would concern itself with questions of law and order. In fact, this paper had surprisingly wide latitude in terms of what it was able to print. This was partly because it was run by Alexander Chakovsky, an influential writer and a member of the Central Committee. It was generally believed that Chakovsky had an unspoken agreement with the party leadership, which allowed *The Literary Gazette* to publish articles on hot-button issues of the day, provide coverage of dubious, messy criminal cases and so on.

In the early 1980s, it would have been unthinkable for the paper to have picked up a story that bore clear signs of KGB involvement. However, by 1987, times had changed: despite economic hardship, the Gorbachev thaw was gathering steam.

Later on, Shchekochikhin would recall hearing about the Azadovsky Affair from a mutual friend, the historian Natan Eidelman (1930–89): 'Natan came to my home and asked whether the paper might try to untangle this snarl the KGB had made.'

Shchekochikhin wanted to meet Azadovsky in person. Azadovsky didn't have a regular job at the time, so he often travelled to Moscow to conduct research in the city's libraries and archives. During one of these trips, he went to see Shchekochikhin.

After they had drunk the requisite glass of vodka, Azadovsky began telling his story, trying to keep his account as dispassionate as possible. Shchekochikhin listened attentively, smoking one cigarette after another. He had heard a great deal during his years as a journalist, but Azadovsky's story touched a nerve. When Azadovsky finished, Shchekochikhin sat quietly for a long time. Finally, exhaling a cloud of tobacco smoke, he broke the silence, exclaiming: 'The bastards!'

And so, Shchekochikhin agreed to take on the case. He quickly developed a plan of attack. Azadovsky's experience as a writer and a scholar was about to come in handy: this mission was going to involve a lot of writing.

12.1 Letter to the editor

The Literary Gazette needed formal grounds to launch its investigation, so Shchekochikhin asked Azadovsky to write a letter to the editor. He promptly complied, and the letter was sent on 14 September 1987 (Azadovsky's birthday). He ended it by declaring: 'I demand justice for myself and my wife, [whose rights] have been and continue to be trampled on in Leningrad. I request that *The Literary Gazette* assist me in securing our rehabilitation.'

But this letter wouldn't be enough on its own. First, there was some concern that the sharpness of its tone would raise red flags within the paper. In any case, Azadovsky would need to enlist some serious outside support. Shchekochikhin suggested that Azadovsky might bolster his heartfelt plea with a joint letter to the editor signed by a group of Moscow and Leningrad writers.

Initially, it was hard for Azadovsky to work out which writers might be convinced to join him in this undertaking. When he returned to Leningrad, he explained the situation to his close friends Nina Katerli and Mikhail Efros. They drafted a letter to the editor outlining Azadovsky's scholarly merits, as well as the circumstances surrounding his criminal case: 'There is every reason to believe', it read, 'that flagrant violations of the law have taken place.'

The next step was collecting signatures. Azadovsky made the rounds of everyone who had said they would support him. In the beginning, these were Leningraders: Yakov Gordin, Daniil Granin, Nina Katerli, Alexander Kushner, Dmitry Likhachyov and Boris Strugatsky. Then he set off for Moscow, where his first order of business was to see Veniamin Kaverin, author of the extremely popular novel *The Two Captains*. Over the course of an evening spent at Kaverin's dacha in the famous Soviet writers' colony in Peredelkino, Azadovsky told his story and described his current situation. Kaverin, who had known Azadovsky's father, was moved. Not only did he sign the letter himself, but he also called other writers he thought might be amenable to the cause. As a result, the letter gained six signatories: Grigory Baklanov, Vyacheslav Kondratyev, Bulat Okudzhava, Anatoly Pristavkin, Anatoly Rybakov and Arkady Strugatsky. Perestroika had begun, and the names of writers like Rybakov and Pristavkin carried some weight: their works were considered vivid symbols of the era. There would be thirteen signatories in all. This might not seem like very many, but gathering them cost a tremendous amount of effort. Despite all the signs that a new era was dawning, the same regime remained in power and the KGB and the Central Committee were still working at full force. It took a great deal of courage for a writer (even a famous one) to attach their signature to a letter claiming that a criminal case had been fabricated by the KGB – especially since the case had happened only recently.

12.2 The waiting game

With the approval of the editor-in-chief, *The Literary Gazette* began its investigation. This process also began with an official letter, this time addressed to Oleg Soroka, the Soviet deputy prosecutor general. The letter was accompanied by a number of supporting documents and contained a request for a thorough review of Azadovsky's complaint.

That winter, the paper sent a representative to Leningrad. For this assignment, Shchekochikhin chose the greatest asset he had at his disposal: former head of the Moscow Police, Major General Ivan Minaev, who was then employed by *The Literary Gazette*. His press credentials, and, more importantly, his status as a general, would be crucial to opening the necessary doors. However, as it turned out, Minaev was unable to review the Azadovskys' case files, as they had already been sent to Moscow at the request of the Prosecutor General's Office. This fact was not, in itself, disappointing. It meant that the cases were no longer under the control of the Leningrad authorities. A faint glimmer of hope appeared that they might be given a fair review.

Following in Azadovsky's footsteps, Minaev asked to see the materials from the prosecutorial review of Azadovsky's civil suit against the Kuibyshevsky RUVD – the documents that proved KGB involvement in Azadovsky's case. It had taken Azadovsky years to gain access to these materials; Minaev received them within several days. This was a genuine, if modest, victory: now *The Literary Gazette* was able to write to the deputy prosecutor general with an argument supported by extracts from the prosecutorial review. However, the Prosecutor's Office was none too eager to initiate a conflict with the KGB.

A month passed, then two, then three and then it was 1988. Still, *The Literary Gazette* received no answer. Meanwhile, on 26 February 1988, the Presidium of the Supreme Soviet of the USSR appointed a new first deputy prosecutor general: former Russian minister of justice Alexander Sukharev. In March, the paper issued a new letter, this time addressed to Sukharev, complaining that, under Soroka, the Prosecutor General's Office hadn't responded to them in five months. *The Literary Gazette* expressed its hope that the new first deputy prosecutor general would be more attentive to its citizens' appeals – as befitted a country on a course towards democratization and glasnost.

Shchekochikhin tried to turn the shake-up in the Prosecutor General's Office to his advantage. However, he knew that it was no use counting on Sukharev, who took an infamously dim view of the intelligentsia and of human rights issues more broadly. For example, in the abstract for his 1978 PhD thesis (titled 'The Legal Education of Workers in Developed Socialist Society'), Sukharev writes:

> The latest political farce consists, in particular, of the wild speculation surrounding the bogus issue of 'human rights violations' in socialist countries, which is aimed at hoodwinking the international public and justifying the repressive treatment of workers in capitalist states.

Given his track record, Sukharev could hardly be relied upon for support. The Azadovskys needed a miracle.

12.3 Sukharev's protest

And a miracle occurred. On 30 March 1988, First Deputy Prosecutor General Alexander Sukharev exercised the power granted to him under Article 371 of the UPK to challenge judgements, rulings and resolutions issued by any Russian court: he sent a document to the Presidium of the Leningrad City Court asking them to overturn its 1981 ruling on Azadovsky's case. According to the UPK, the Presidium was required to promptly review this protest and either accept it (by overturning the initial as well as all subsequent rulings) or reject it. However, rejection was out of the question: it would have been unthinkable for the Leningrad City Court to publicly lock horns with the prosecutor general.

Sukharev was confirmed as Soviet Prosecutor General on 26 May 1988. To Sukharev's credit, his actions reflected the spirit of change that was sweeping over the country, the spirit of perestroika. In a speech delivered on 9 June 1989 at the Congress of People's Deputies of the USSR, Sukharev declared that in 1988

> [w]e were forced to release 2182 people from punitive isolation or from courtrooms because they had been wrongly arrested, because they had been wrongly repressed. That is a disgrace! And, all told, six and a half thousand people have suffered in this way. I am only referring to the people who were already in custody, as it were. This is a matter of principle. (Applause)

The Presidium's next meeting took place on 29 April 1987. Sukharev's protest was accepted and the following resolution was issued:

> The judgement handed down by the Kuibyshevsky District People's Court in Leningrad on 16 March 1981 and the ruling issued by the Collegium on Criminal Proceedings of the Leningrad City Court on 16 April 1981 against Konstantin Markovich Azadovsky are to be overturned and the case is to undergo new judicial proceedings in the same court with a different judge from the trial stage.

This was what Azadovsky had been waiting for, and it was all thanks to Shchekochikhin and *The Literary Gazette*. Azadovsky would be given the chance to prove his innocence – though of course, it was only a chance; success was far from guaranteed.

13

The retrial

And so, litigation was to start all over again. It might seem illogical to retry a case eight years after a crime allegedly took place, but that was what the law dictated. Still, this situation had its advantages. Namely, if Azadovsky was given a public trial (as required by law), he would be able to demonstrate the flimsiness of the evidence against him and publicly point the finger at the people who had framed him. He was still hoping to force the KGB operatives to appear before the court. There was no doubt in Azadovsky's mind that he would finally be acquitted and that his exoneration would, in turn, pave the way for a review of Lepilina's sentence.

No one knew what to expect from this kind of trial, which was as new and unusual as the changes sweeping the country at the time. The very fact that the prosecutor general had lodged a protest in such a high-profile case was seen as a sign of perestroika. Many hoped that this test case would represent a break with the Soviet past, when it had been possible for the KGB to initiate false judicial proceedings against an innocent person.

Azadovsky, who by this point had been elected to the Soviet Writers' Union, was also hopeful that justice would prevail. He hired Natalya Smirnova to represent him in the retrial. Though Smirnova had only recently begun practising law, she had nearly twenty years' experience working in judicial bodies.

In early summer 1988, the Presidium of the Leningrad City Court sent Azadovsky and Lepilina's criminal case files down to the district court. At that point, Azadovsky was once again given the opportunity to view the case against him, which would be reviewed by N.A. Tsvetkov, a judge in the Kuibyshevsky District Court. To present the government's charges against Azadovsky, the city prosecutor chose a relatively young but experienced lawyer by the name of A.E. Yakubovich. During the trial, Yakubovich seemed far more confident than the judge, to say nothing of the two nondescript assessors.

The preliminary proceedings took place on 21 June. Azadovsky had submitted an extensive petition to the court office ten days prior, requesting a whole slew of documents: the criminal case against Lepilina, the materials from the prosecutorial review, documents from the Mukhina Higher School and so on. In the same petition, he had asked that certain individuals be called in to the proceedings: Investigator Kamenko, Officers Artsibushev and Khlyupin, KGB operatives Arkhipov and Shlemin, and Shistko and Bobov, who had signed his workplace character reference. He also demanded verification of the expert analysis ostensibly issued by Gorlit, as well as a subpoena of *Leningrad Pravda* regarding its 1969 article on the Slavinsky trial. Finally, he petitioned for the identification of the mysterious police officer who appeared in the search report only as 'Bystrov'.

In short, Azadovsky had decided to present every scrap of evidence he had that the 1981 investigation and trial had been biased, and that the evidence against him had been fabricated. He used the word 'fabrication' frequently during this period. The judicial establishment found it scathing and even slightly outrageous, but, in Azadovsky's view, it was the most accurate way to describe what had happened.

13.1 The proceedings of 19 July 1988

It was a public trial in the true sense of the word. In 1981, it had been a miracle that even a few members of the public managed to penetrate the courtroom. In 1988, the courtroom was packed with sympathetic people who had been following the twists and turns of the Azadovskys' cases for years: their friends, acquaintances and colleagues, as well as like-minded individuals and members of the press.

The atmosphere in the courtroom was also dramatically different than it had been in 1981. There was a sense of spectacle: it was as if the audience had come to see a play, not a trial.

In the beginning, it seemed as if Judge Tsvetkov was trying to act in accordance with the spirit of perestroika. The first thing he did was to grant Azadovsky's petition that video and audio recordings be made of the proceedings. As soon as the microphone was turned on and the camera started rolling, the court began reviewing Azadovsky's other petitions.

However, the appearance of justice quickly melted away, and the audience forgot the oppressive summer heat. It felt like a trial from eighty years prior, in the days when the prosecution and the court worked hand in hand against the accused. This time, the defendants' bench stood empty behind the metal latticework, while Azadovsky sat in the front row of the courtroom. However, just as before, he sensed that the organs of justice were working against him.

Azadovsky had requested that KGB agents Arkhipov and Shlemin be examined as witnesses and that he be given access to the materials from the prosecutorial review that proved their involvement in his case. The judge immediately sided with the prosecution, declaring that these requests had 'no direct bearing on the formulation of the charges brought against Azadovsky', and so his petitions were denied. It was clear that the court intended to manipulate the case so as to eliminate any whiff of KGB involvement.

The judge read out the 1981 indictment. Azadovsky confirmed that he denied any guilt. He repeated his assertion that the case against him had been fabricated and that the artificial separation of his and Lepilina's cases spoke to the fact that the narcotics had been planted. He also provided an explanation for the note he sent her in Kresty, which had served as the main piece of evidence against him the first time around.

Then Azadovsky declared that one of the search witnesses, Konstantinov, had aided the police and KGB during the search of his flat and should thus be called in to give testimony.

At that point, Azadovsky's lawyer took over. Smirnova confidently and methodically enumerated the UPK violations that had occurred during the investigation and presented evidence of bias during the investigation and trial. She was trying to force the court to call in additional witnesses, the KGB operatives first and foremost. She also drew the court's attention to the fact that none of the witnesses who had given testimony in the first case had actually seen Khlyupin discover the narcotics.

Next, Yakubovich interrogated Azadovsky about the Slavinsky Affair. He declared that the materials from Slavinsky's trial ought to be taken as proof of Azadovsky's character. After all, in the descriptive part of the court's ruling, Azadovsky's name appears on the list of people to whom Slavinsky had 'dealt' 0.25 grams of hashish each. 'This is a legal document; why didn't you lodge a complaint about it in 1969?' Azadovsky was at a loss. In 1969, he had been kicked out of his postgraduate studies and forced to move to Petrozavodsk; he hadn't had the time or inclination to dispute the inclusion of his name in the descriptive part of the ruling, especially since it didn't appear anywhere in the operative part. Besides, who would have thought that this moment would come back to haunt him?

Yakubovich went on to ask Azadovsky whether he was aware that they had considered charging him under three different articles of the Criminal Code in 1969: 224, 228 and 70.

Article 224 was the one Azadovsky was charged under in 1981: in 1969, there had been no evidence supporting such charges. Article 228 ('the production, dissemination or promotion of pornographic compositions, printed matter, images or other objects of a pornographic character') had been considered after the search of Azadovsky's flat yielded foreign magazines, including an issue of *Playboy*. However, only the sale and dissemination of such materials was punishable by law; possession wasn't a crime. Charges under Article 70 ('Agitation or propaganda carried out with the aim of subverting or weakening Soviet power . . . the dissemination of slanderous inventions against the Soviet political and social system with that same aim; as well as the dissemination, production or possession of such literature with that same aim') would have been considered in light of some of the books that had been seized from Azadovsky's flat. These books, which included works by Anna Akhmatova and Osip Mandelshtam, had been published abroad and were 'banned from import to the USSR'. However, such charges weren't brought against Azadovsky at the time, possibly because there wasn't any proof that Azadovsky had used Akhmatova and Mandelshtam's poetry in the service of 'anti-Soviet agitation and propaganda'.

Yakubovich's question made it clear that there was documentary evidence attesting to the fact that the investigative team had considered trying Azadovsky for a political crime back in 1969. However, there hadn't been sufficient evidence to press charges at the time. But the prosecutor's goal was to cast aspersions on the defendant's character. According to Yakubovich's logic, the fact that the investigative team had attempted to bring charges against Azadovsky under three different articles in 1969 was conclusive proof of Azadovsky's amoral, antisocial ways.

The proceedings continued.

13.2 The voice of conscience

The highlight of 19 July was the witness examinations. In the end, none of the KGB operatives were called in to testify, but officers Artsibushev and Khlyupin, search witnesses Konstantinov and Makarov, and Investigator Kamenko were all present. They each took the stand in turn. The most substantive, even sensational testimony came from Oleg Artsibushev, who had been a senior inspector in the Anti-Narcotics Department of the Leningrad UVD in 1980.

In 1983, as part of the prosecutorial review initiated at Azadovsky's request, Artsibushev had been required to explain the KGB's involvement in the search of Azadovsky's flat. Azadovsky had seen this testimony when he went to review the documents related to the civil suit concerning his lost property. Though Artsibushev didn't dare to explicitly name the KGB in court, he did reveal a number of other details. Some key excerpts from the audio recording of Artsibushev's wide-ranging testimony have been reproduced below.

First, Artsibushev made some clarifying remarks on Lepilina's detention. The fact that the stop had been premeditated had been unequivocally confirmed by the two witnesses (who were, in fact, *druzhinniks*):

> Petrov: We were asked to detain citizen Lepilina; Lepilina was described to us and we detained her based on that description. We didn't see her exit the café; we were standing in the courtyard.

> Mikhailova: I participated in the raid. We were asked to detain a citizen fitting a certain description. We detained her when she entered the courtyard.

Azadovsky's lawyer pointed out that it was Lepilina's detention that led to the emergency search of Azadovsky's flat. Instead of tracking down the person who had given her the narcotics or searching Lepilina's own flat, the investigators had immediately gone to look for drugs in Azadovsky's. Artsibushev revealed that this strategy came from the very top of the Leningrad police. He had been ordered to go to the prosecutor's home at two in the morning to get his signature on the search warrant.

Judge Tsvetkov questioned Artsibushev about the people who participated in the search. The captain was perfectly aware of the KGB's role in the case and was terrified he might let something slip. He tried to stick to the official version of events: 'I looked at their identification; they had police identification.' This was the correct answer, but it also provided clear confirmation of something Azadovsky had learned from his civil suit in 1988: that the KGB agents had entered Azadovsky's home using false documents.

During the questioning, particular emphasis was placed on the circumstances surrounding the discovery of drugs in Azadovsky's flat. On this point, Artsibushev seemed to take the side of the accused. This came as a complete shock.

> Artsibushev: Well, I said almost immediately that we, the officers, got the impression that someone had planted the drugs on him.

Lawyer: You mean, you got the impression that someone had planted the drugs on him?

Artsibushev: Someone had an interest in him being arrested.

Lawyer: Who specifically? You had no impression of that?

Artsibushev: His enemies, I think; everyone has enemies.

The courtroom was also captivated by the testimony of search witness Konstantinov. Konstantinov claimed that he had just happened to be standing near the entrance to Vosstaniya Square metro station at 8.00 am on 19 December 1980: the fact that he was head of his workplace Komsomol operative detachment was merely a coincidence. His questioning included the following exchange, which was later published in one of Shchekochikhin's articles:

> Question to Konstantinov: How did you come to be a search witness?
> Answer: A police officer approached me by the exit of Vosstaniya Square metro station and asked for my help.
>
> Question: Where do you live?
> Answer: On Vasilyevsky Island.
>
> Question: How did you come to be on Vosstaniya Square, which is to say, in a different part of the city, so early in the morning?
> Answer: (Pause) I wanted to take a walk...
>
> Question: What kind of community service did you do in 1980?
> Answer: I was the head of the Komsomol detachment where I worked.
>
> Question: Do you still maintain that you came to be a search witness by coincidence?
> Answer: (Pause) Yes...
>
> Question to police officer Artsibushev: Was it a coincidence that you approached Konstantinov?
> Answer: The evening beforehand it had been agreed that some guys from the Komsomol operative detachment would come along with us to act as search witnesses. We agreed to meet next to the Vosstaniya Square metro station.
>
> Question to Konstantinov: When you arrived at Azadovsky's flat, you weren't surprised as to the reason for the search?
> Answer: I noticed that he had a whole lot of books in foreign languages in his flat...

Next came the testimony of officer Nikolay Khlyupin. First, he warned that his memory of the situation wasn't perfect, which may well have been true: after all, the events in question had taken place seven and a half years prior. Then, he went on to describe how he had come to find the packet with narcotics in it. At that point, however, the court had already heard Artsibushev's testimony, which supported Azadovsky's claim that the drugs had been planted, and so Khlyupin found himself with his back against the wall.

As Azadovsky's questions grew increasingly pointed, Khlyupin made an extraordinary statement, which was recorded in the court report: 'The bookshelves where I found the packet of narcotics were examined by KGB operatives before I got there, so you have just as much reason to suspect them as me!'

Though these revelations may not have decided the outcome of the case, they certainly suggested what it would be. The fact that Artsibushev, the search's leader and an expert in anti-drug operations, had declared that the evidence was probably planted put the case in a very different light. Meanwhile, Khlyupin's outburst confirmed that the search participants who hadn't been officially identified or recorded in the search report were, in fact, KGB operatives.

Azadovsky had known for a long time that Artsibushev was ashamed of his role in the search. After all, on the day of Azadovsky's arrest, Artsibushev had let slip that he '[didn't] like all this.' Nevertheless, the candour he displayed on the witness stand came as a shock to both sides.

Of course, he didn't tell the whole truth, but what he had said was more than enough. And though he didn't give up the names of the KGB agents themselves, he did say that the operation had been overseen by the upper echelons of the city police, mentioning two generals by name: General Georgy Zigalenko, chief of the Directorate for Criminal Investigation, and General Vladimir Kokushkin, chief of the GUVD.

13.3 The proceedings of 20 July 1988

On the second day of proceedings, things went back to normal: there were no more unforeseen outbursts. Artsibushev, who had seemed willing to talk the day before, appeared completely changed. He had clearly received a 'talking-to' the previous evening. He didn't recant his earlier testimony, but he stopped giving direct answers.

Meanwhile, Yakubovich's strategy remained unchanged: he methodically, pedantically opposed any petitions related to the KGB agents or the prosecutorial review. The prosecutor justified his unwillingness to call Arkhipov and Shlemin to the stand by stating that 'the court is only examining the charges brought against Azadovsky under Article 224.'

When Kamenko, the officer in charge of both Azadovsky and Lepilina's investigations, took the stand, he aimed to say as little as possible. For example, when Azadovsky observed, 'In your explanatory report from 1983, you wrote that KGB agents were involved', Kamenko laconically replied, 'If I wrote it, then it must be true.'

When Yakubovich returned to the question of how the drugs had ended up in Azadovsky's flat, he didn't consider Artsibushev's theory (which placed the blame on Azadovsky's 'enemies'), and, of course, he didn't bring up Khlyupin's mention of the KGB. Rather, the prosecutor built his strategy around 'Citizen Lepilina, who was convicted of drug possession and confessed her guilt'. This approach only added to the tense atmosphere of the proceedings.

Lepilina took the stand. She gave a detailed account of what happened on the day she was detained and the humiliations she was subjected to. Her testimony was the highlight of the second day's proceedings:

> When Breiman [Lepilina's lawyer] came to the closing of the case against me, I seized onto him like a drowning man clutches at straws. I trusted in him completely, and while he was preparing me for the trial, he said: 'There's nothing for it, you'll have to confess your guilt. There's nothing you can do to help Azadovsky anyway; his case is being handled by the KGB, so his number is up.' Breiman told me that if I confessed my guilt, then maybe 'I would get six months and I could keep my flat,' and so I confessed my guilt in court. The testimony I gave in court was a false confession; incidentally, given the condition I was in at the time, I would have confessed to anything, signed anything. In that moment, I began to feel profound indifference towards everything that was going on.
>
> I have never used narcotics, I've never had anything to do with them. I took the packet from Hassan thinking it was medicine. I was convicted of a crime of which I was totally innocent. There is not one piece of evidence in the case against me that demonstrates my relationship with narcotics.

Azadovsky submitted petition after petition requesting the materials from the prosecutorial review and asking that the KGB operatives be brought in to testify. Finally, the judge found an out. He unexpectedly agreed with Azadovsky: 'There isn't any doubt that state security agents participated in the search. Yes, they participated, I do not doubt your words.' This statement baffled the defence. Under the circumstances, however, it was easier for Tsvetkov to admit that Azadovsky was right than it was for him to continue reviewing the same petitions over and over again, especially since each one served as a reminder of the KGB's involvement in the case. As for Azadovsky's request that the KGB agents be called in to testify, the judge replied, 'There's simply no need.' He advised Azadovsky to address his grievances to the City Prosecutor's Office.

It became obvious that Azadovsky wouldn't be acquitted immediately, even if the court didn't find him guilty. The judge and prosecutor began taking the case in a different direction, emphasizing the question of 'how the narcotics had come to be in Azadovsky's flat'.

Back in 1981, Azadovsky had allowed for the possibility that the drugs might have been 'brought in [to the flat] without his knowledge by acquaintances' (this was recorded in the descriptive part of the ruling). But when he heard Artsibushev and Khlyupin's testimony during the 1988 retrial, Azadovsky began to think that the narcotics had appeared on his bookshelf as part of a larger set-up. 'I can hypothetically allow', he said, 'that this might have been done by one of my acquaintances; not of their own volition, of course, but as part of this whole chain.' His statement was rather vague, and even in that moment, he probably would have been hard-pressed to explain what 'chain' he was referring to.

Finally, the judge announced his decision to postpone the rest of the proceedings until 11 August.

13.4 The proceedings of 11 August 1988

On 21 June, convinced that neither the judge nor the prosecutor was willing to hear the three magic letters 'KGB', Azadovsky had decided to fall back on his old standby: petition-writing. On 14 July, he submitted a document to the Leningrad City Prosecutor's Office addressed to the 'supervisory prosecutor responsible for the KGB', requesting that she 'immediately intervene, determine the location of the KGB agents in question and take steps to secure their appearance at the Kuibyshevsky People's Court on 19 July'.

This petition landed on the desk of Inessa Katukova, head of the Department of Investigative Oversight for the State Security Services. Katukova was infamous among the 'free-thinking' factions of the Leningrad intelligentsia. In the 1970s, she had acted as prosecutor in a number of high-profile political cases; she had written a series of guidelines for dealing with 'ideological sabotage' and was a welcome guest in any office of the Big House. And yet, shockingly, it was Katukova who set the wheels in motion for Azadovsky's retrial. On 1 August 1988, she sent a letter to Court President Raisa Klishina requesting that the KGB agents involved in Azadovsky's case be summoned to court to be examined as witnesses.

What motivated Katukova's actions? Was it her confidence that this attempt to summon the agents to court would be in vain? Or was it somehow connected with the democratic transformations taking place within society? The winds of change might not have reached the district courts, but it was altogether possible that they were making themselves felt on the municipal level.

Prompted by the prosecutor's letter, on 1 August 1988 Judge Tsvetkov wrote to Major General Vitaly Prilukov, head of the Leningrad KGB. His letter contained a strongly worded request for information on 'why KGB operatives Arkhipov and Shlemin were present in Azadovsky's flat on 19.12.80 and where they are located at the present time'. Tsvetkov ordered Prilukov to 'ensure their appearance in court as witnesses on 11.08.88 for 11 am'.

The proceedings of 11 August began with Judge Tsvetkov reading out the letter he had received on 8 August from the Big House's personnel department:

> On 19.12.80, Leningrad Oblast KGB operatives V.I. Arkhipov and V.V. Shlemin were present in Azadovsky's flat during a search related to a criminal case being conducted by operatives of the Leningrad Oblast and City GUVD.
>
> The KGB was contacted about the search of Azadovsky's flat by head of the Fifteenth Department of the UUR GUVD comrade Yu.M. Badaev, who, based on a petition in his possession, asked that operatives be sent to evaluate materials falling under the jurisdiction of the KGB in the event that such materials should be found during the search.

Comrades V.I. Arkhipov and V.V. Shlemin are currently on routine leave outside of Leningrad, and it is therefore not possible to ensure their appearance as trial witnesses on 11.08.88.

Another document was also read out: the GUVD's response regarding the conduct of officer Bystrov, who had pushed Azadovsky during the search and whose name had been included in the search report at Azadovsky's insistence:

Further to your enquiry, we inform you that the personnel department of the Leningrad Oblast and City Executive Committee GUVD has no record of a Viktor Ivanovich Bystrov serving on 19 December, nor is he in service at this time.

On this intriguing note, a recess was called until the following morning.

13.5 The proceedings of 12 August 1988

The last day of witness examination was 12 August. After Khlyupin was questioned, Artsibushev took the stand. He reiterated his main thesis:

I agree with Khlyupin's assessment that the narcotics were found in an unusual place; a drug user wouldn't keep [drugs] where these were found. Thus, we may conclude that [Azadovsky] has enemies, or that one of his acquaintances had been there, and that they were the one who planted the drugs.

Then the closing speeches began, given by the prosecutor, the defence lawyer and the accused. The prosecutor's speech was brief, but shocking: he petitioned to have the case sent back for reinvestigation. Up until then, there had been hope that he might recommend Azadovsky be acquitted: after all, the evidence was clearly insufficient to convict him. But he didn't. Moreover, he repeated the argument that, because the investigation had shown that Lepilina was living in Azadovsky's flat at the time, they would need to ascertain that the drugs had not, in fact, belonged to her.

Smirnova expressed her 'sorrowful amazement' at the prosecutor's actions and at the court's decision. She appealed to the idea that Soviet society was on the threshold of major democratic transformations:

[A]ll the conditions of glasnost and democracy come to an end today with a petition made in keeping with the best traditions of the Era of Stagnation. . . . More often than not, when there wasn't enough evidence in a case to convict and a defendant ought to have been declared not guilty, the case would be sent for reinvestigation so that it could be discontinued, not under the conditions of glasnost, not under the conditions of open court proceedings, but under the conditions of obscurity, the opposite of glasnost . . .

Finally, Azadovsky made his closing speech:

Over the course of these proceedings, I have spoken constantly about the fraud and fabrications involved in the crime perpetrated against myself and my wife. From the very beginning, everything I have said has been fully confirmed by these hearings. All of the primary documents related to this case – the search warrant, the search report, the expert evaluation, the workplace character reference and others – have been fabricated.

It is now entirely clear that the court that declared me guilty in 1981 had absolutely no interest in uncovering the objective truth. However, the bias and incompleteness of the 1981 judicial enquiry, as brought to light by the Soviet Prosecutor's Office, was not the result of personal mistakes or court errors. Judge Lukovnikov fulfilled the task that the Leningrad authorities had set for him: to sentence me to two years at any cost, despite the obvious facts. To knowingly sentence an innocent person!

There is one more fabrication in this case, which, unfortunately, the current court has also chosen to ignore. This is the fabrication that makes this entire case unprecedented. I am referring to the criminal case against Lepilina. The case against me and the case against Lepilina are, without a doubt, a single case. And, of course, the case began as a joint one. However, in late January 1981, the cases were deliberately separated with the aim of separating materials whose contents were inextricably intertwined, to distort, to occlude the essence of the case, as well as to somewhat reduce the scale of the planned provocation. You would have to be blind not to see it!

. . . This bias has manifested itself, first and foremost, in [the court's] determination to write the KGB operatives out of the case. First, the court resolved to call Arkhipov and Shlemin into court as witnesses, then it rejected my petitions on the subject, justifying its actions by saying that the KGB operatives had 'no bearing on the formulation of the charges brought against me'. Meanwhile, it is clear from the case materials that, in all likelihood, it was KGB operatives who planted the drugs in my flat. Khlyupin's testimony points to this directly. And so I cannot believe that the judicial enquiry has been sufficiently comprehensive. The true perpetrators of everything that has happened have been deliberately erased from the case.

. . . The Leningrad KGB operatives were perfectly aware that their actions constituted provocations. Otherwise, why would they have used false names during the search of my flat? Why would they erase their organization's name from the expert analysis? Why would they invoke an imaginary report that the KGB ostensibly received from the head of the Fifteenth Department of the GUVD?

In their efforts to 'put me away', the organizers of the criminal case against me mercilessly sacrificed another, totally innocent person: S.I. Lepilina. She was used like a thing, an inanimate object: she was used for the sole purpose of providing an excuse to search my flat.

I do not know the extent to which the KGB and MVD operatives were working independently and the extent to which they were fulfilling orders from the

Leningrad Party leadership. One thing is clear: the case against myself and my wife was fabricated by the Leningrad authorities in advance. It is the duty of higher-level authorities to discover the truth and hold the guilty parties responsible.

In light of the above, I ask the court:

1) To issue me a judgement of not guilty, as I have not committed any crime.
2) To send a recommendation to the higher judicial instances regarding the case against Lepilina, as the materials of both criminal cases, when considered together, attest to her total innocence.
3) To issue a special ruling on the legal violations committed by the police officers of the UUR GUVD and the Kuibyshevsky RUVD in the course of their investigative activities. Because it has come to light during court proceedings that senior members of the Leningrad police were involved in this case, a copy [of the ruling] should be sent to the Soviet Ministry of Internal Affairs.
4) To issue a special ruling on the legal violations committed by the Leningrad Oblast KGB operatives. To send it directly to the USSR KGB for a review of those circumstances that were not reviewed by the Kuibyshevsky District Court.

The court retired for deliberation. Yury Shchekochikhin describes the scene in the courtroom:

And so the agonizing hours of anticipation stretched on and on. The courthouse had emptied out long ago, the doors had been locked, a custodian had come through carrying an empty bucket (there's a superstition about that, it's bad luck, I think) and we were the only ones still there, filling the corridor, the stairwells and the courtroom, which remained frozen in anticipation. And then – [there was the sound of] telephone calls coming from the deliberation room . . .

. . . finally, through the stairwell, through the corridor: 'They're coming, they're coming . . .' The judge was coming . . .

The prosecutor, Yakubovich, was walking down the corridor, shifting his weight from side to side, his gaze fixed straight ahead . . .

It took around two minutes to read out the court's ruling, no more: 'Without reviewing the possibility that the appearance of narcotic substances in Azadovsky's flat might have been facilitated by other individuals, it is impossible to come to a conclusion regarding Azadovsky's guilt or innocence of the charges brought against him . . .'

The case was sent for additional investigation so it could be closed later on (quietly, without any noise, in the silence of offices). No one present had any doubts about that.

A murmur ran through the courtroom. . . . The judge quickly disappeared into his chambers . . .

What went through my head at that moment? I'll tell you what. What kind of time scale is that – eight years! The people who initiated the fabrication of the case against Azadovsky were still in the pink of health and at the height of their powers, and even the signs on the doors of many offices remained the same. Even those who had retired were unlikely to have changed their ways . . .

So what happened next, after the court proceedings?

I remember, after the trial, I stayed at Konstantin and Svetlana's flat until late in the evening, waiting until it was time for me to set off for the airport. Svetlana cried. I comforted her as best I could . . .

13.6 The aftertaste

The Azadovskys and their friends were extremely disappointed. These months had taken a serious toll, both physically and emotionally. However, the tribulations they had endured in recent years had prepared them for anything – and at least this time the couple wouldn't be incarcerated.

Of course, Azadovsky didn't back down. On 15 August, three days after the trial had ended, he sent a telegram addressed to General Secretary Mikhail Gorbachev, asking him to intervene immediately and 'put a stop to this lawlessness'. Then, on 22 August, he submitted a complaint to the Presidium of the Leningrad City Court, which concluded:

> Unwilling to see that all the case materials point to my total innocence, the court has cravenly wriggled out of issuing a not-guilty judgement. The court has refused to acknowledge the patently illegal acts of KGB operatives, thus placing them above the Law. I consider the court's position to be anticonstitutional.

But the document that would have the most far-reaching consequences was the complaint Azadovsky sent on 15 August to Politburo member and KGB chairman Viktor Chebrikov. He wrote:

> Despite the obvious nature of all the evidence obtained by the court, the court cravenly wriggled out of issuing a judgement. Instead of acquitting me, it has sent the case for additional investigation and charged the investigatory bodies with exposing the so-called enemies who might have planted narcotics in my flat. Why is this attempt to find the 'alleged culprits' being undertaken now, eight years after the fact? To remove the truly guilty parties from the case: your underlings, who unlawfully came to search my flat.

In all likelihood, it was this letter that finally spurred the KGB's Moscow leadership into action and triggered an internal review. It was also at this point that the KGB leadership took the monumental decision to admit a mistake – a small mistake, but nevertheless, this admission allowed Azadovsky to throw the procedural side of the case against him into question.

On 29 September, Azadovsky received a message from the KGB's Investigation Department signed by Major Vladimir Popov, a senior investigator for Especially Important Cases:

It has been established that two operatives of the Leningrad Oblast USSR KGB unlawfully took part in a search of your flat conducted by the police on 19 December 1980. In light of the facts set forth in your complaint, an internal investigation of this event is underway; you will be notified of the outcome at a later date.

In response, Azadovsky sent the KGB an even more detailed petition, enumerating the misdeeds that hadn't made it into the first letter:

During the preliminary investigation, Bezverkhov and Kuznetsov were 'running' Investigator Kamenko of the Kuibyshevsky RUVD, who was only nominally in charge of both criminal cases. In fact, all of the investigative actions were orchestrated by Kuznetsov and Bezverkhov. In July of this year (1988), while being examined during judicial proceedings, Kamenko publicly admitted that he was in constant contact with KGB operatives regarding this case. On 24 November 1983 Kamenko gave written testimony to Petrov, head of the Investigation Department of the Leningrad Oblast GUVD, saying that, during the investigation, one of the KGB operatives had brought in photographs that had been seized from my flat, asserting that 'Azadovsky obtained these photographs illegally, with the anti-Soviet intent of sending them abroad'... etc.

Azadovsky wasn't the only one filing complaints against the Kuibyshevsky Court's decision. Many of the people who had been present in the courtroom submitted their own letters of protest: there is a whole stack of such documents addressed to various institutions, from the Leningrad Oblast Committee to the Central Committee of the CPSU.

13.7 Closing the case

As the proceedings drew to a close, Azadovsky wrote several complaints and petitions. He could only guess what might happen next. He assumed that there would be a pointless investigation to determine who had planted the drugs, and that his friends and acquaintances would be subjected to meaningless interrogations. But nothing happened. None of his acquaintances received so much as a telephone call.

In fact, all the action was taking place under cover of secrecy. Officially, the investigation was being run by the Investigation Directorate of the GUVD, overseen by the City Prosecutor's Office. However, the KGB's Investigation Department was conducting its own review, far away from prying eyes.

The brief respite after the trial gave Azadovsky the opportunity to turn his attention to other matters. That autumn, he finished writing a book about the Russian poet Nikolay Klyuev for Soviet Writer Publishing House. Then, in mid-October, Azadovsky was granted permission to leave the USSR for the first time in his life: he spent a month and a half in West Germany.

Azadovsky had become something of a celebrity in Western Europe by this time. The public had eagerly followed his trial in the early 1980s, and they knew he was a scholar, too. Germany welcomed him with open arms, inviting him to lecture at universities in Tübingen, Karlsruhe and Cologne.

Azadovsky returned home from his first trip abroad on 4 December 1988. While he had been off addressing the lecture halls of Europe, a number of momentous decisions had been taken in his case. First, on 14 November, a ruling had been issued discontinuing the criminal case against Azadovsky in accordance with Article 208, paragraph 2 of the UPK, which applied to situations in which there was 'insufficient evidence of the accused's participation in the execution of the crime after all possibilities for the collection of additional evidence have been exhausted'.

This ruling came as yet another disappointment: Azadovsky had expected that he would either be found not guilty or the case against him would be dismissed 'in the absence of a crime'. Azadovsky didn't want to be acquitted just because there was 'insufficient evidence' to convict him, and so he immediately appealed to the RSFSR Prosecutor's Office: 'The case against me gives every reason to conclude that nothing in my actions did or could possibly constitute a crime; the actions of our public officials, on the other hand, have been criminal indeed.'[1]

It seemed as if this process would never end.

There was a silver lining, though. As he read over the court's resolution, Azadovsky realized that he had, in fact, managed to get to the KGB operatives:

> Leningrad Oblast KGB operatives V.I. Arkhipov and V.V. Shlemin, who were present during the search of Azadovsky's flat on 19.12.1980, were questioned during the additional investigation. They confirmed that a narcotic substance had been seized from Azadovsky's flat: five grams of hashish.

Though the resolution failed to mention that the operatives had unlawfully participated in the search using false names, the fact that they had been called in to give testimony in the first place signalled a turning point in the case.

On 25 January 1989, the Leningrad City Prosecutor's Office overturned the decision of the GUVD's Investigation Directorate and sent the case back for a new investigation. And so the cycle continued. On 10 February 1989, in accordance with procedure, Lieutenant Colonel Kramarev (who in the 1990s would go on to lead the Leningrad police) called Azadovsky in for yet another round of questioning. On 13 February, the case was dismissed yet again, on the same grounds: insufficient evidence.

However, a great deal had changed in Russia over the past few months. The Soviet system was starting to collapse, though not many people were in a position to realize it at the time. In any case, the Prosecutor's Office proved more foresighted (or better informed) than the police. Literally the next day, 14 February, the City Prosecutor's Office stepped in to change the formulation of the ruling, dismissing the case against Azadovsky 'in the absence of a crime'.

And so, more than eight years after his ordeal began, Konstantin Markovich Azadovsky was finally exonerated.

13.8 Lepilina

Azadovsky had managed to clear his name. However, because Lepilina had confessed her guilt during her 1981 trial, the case against her was considered ironclad.

On 10 February 1989, Azadovsky was questioned by the GUVD's Investigation Directorate in connection with his protest against the application of the term 'insufficient evidence' to his case. During his interrogation, Azadovsky submitted another petition: he wanted his wife's sentence overturned, her case joined with his and a joint investigation following the line of enquiry that both he and his wife had been framed. On 13 February, Lieutenant Colonel Arkady Kramarev dismissed this petition on the grounds that it was not within the investigation's power to overturn a sentence, 'and therefore it would also be impossible to resolve the issue of joining the criminal cases'.

All of Azadovsky's subsequent appeals to the prosecutorial authorities received the same reply: the court's decision had been sound, Lepilina had confessed her guilt during the investigation and the trial, and so on.

Yury Shchekochikhin continued his efforts on the Azadovskys' behalf. In 1992, after being elected to the Congress of People's Deputies, he sent a 'deputy request for information' to the Soviet Prosecutor's Office regarding Lepilina's case. The file was sent back to Moscow, where it was reviewed, and on 27 April 1992 the Azadovskys received the usual reply.

It seemed as if all hope of exoneration had been lost.

14

The aftermath

Though the courtroom had been packed with journalists, writers and human rights advocates for Azadovsky's retrial, there was no guarantee that the case would receive any news coverage. The Soviet press was still extremely limited in 1988: the era of glasnost had only just begun. If an article so much as mentioned the KGB by name, the entire story would be subject to the agency's approval (this explains the abundance of euphemisms employed during this time: even articles that contained no criticism of the KGB would refer to the agency as the 'authorities', the 'relevant authorities', etc.). None of the Leningrad papers dared to write about Azadovsky's retrial. Nevertheless, the Azadovskys put their faith in Yury Shchekochikhin, who arrived from Moscow in the final days of the proceedings.

14.1 *The Literary Gazette*'s investigation

Shchekochikhin had served as the catalyst for the latest round of judicial proceedings: it was his intervention that had prompted the Soviet deputy prosecutor general to lodge a protest. Now, he set about writing an investigative feature piece.

This long article, titled 'A Leningrad Affair, 80s-style', was written in late August 1988. The title is a reference to the infamous 'Leningrad Affair' (1948–50), a series of fabricated criminal cases used by Stalin as an excuse to execute a number of prominent Leningrad officials and imprison members of their families. But days passed, then weeks, and the story still didn't appear in the paper. Shchekochikhin later described the circumstances surrounding the article's publication:

> The made-up page was already hanging up in the editorial office; I had already called Kostya and Svetlana in Leningrad: 'It's finally done!'; I was already imagining the reaction the day after the article came out in the paper.
>
> Suddenly, one evening, literally two days before the issue went to press, the article disappeared from the paper's mock-up and landed instead on the desk of KGB Chairman V.A. Kryuchkov.

In other words, the article hadn't been sent for standard approval; it had gone straight to the top of the KGB. The ensuing review lasted almost a year, which meant that, for almost a year, the article couldn't be printed in any form.

Finally, in late May or early June 1989, the KGB issued a notice outlining the agency's objections:

1) A certain bias in the [article's] approach to its material. The author primes his reader to see the Azadovsky case in a political light, as if it had been incited by the KGB. He attempts to draw parallels with the mass trials of 1937. There are no grounds for doing so (in that instance, there were extrajudicial actions, torture, etc.). In this instance, there was a violation of the UPK: the names of KGB operatives were not recorded in the search report, and they were punished as a result (this is not mentioned).
2) Insufficient neutrality in presentation. The issue of political crimes was not raised during the investigation or the trial; the only issue was narcotics. The author does not question Azadovsky's assertion that KGB operatives were involved in the discovery of the narcotics, though the Prosecutor's Office did not confirm this speculation.
3) The author references the letter sent to Azadovsky by the Leningrad City Prosecutor, but fails to mention the agency's refusal to bring criminal charges against MVD and KGB operatives in the absence of a crime (i.e. the court did not recognize that any fabrication had taken place in connection with the narcotics, and so it would not be possible to operate on that assumption).

Shchekochikhin continues:

And then I did something I had never done before: . . . I wrote a letter to Kryuchkov and sent a copy to Gorbachev. It ended up being a long letter: five and a half pages. I ended it like this:

'I do not want to go any further into the details of this case. Something else is bothering me – disturbing me, quite frankly. Your operatives could have issued a response to the paper after [the article] appeared (for it, against it, that doesn't matter). They could have contradicted me. They could have taken me to court, accused me of libel. That's how it's done in states governed by the rule of law, the kind of state we aspire to create! No – [you employed] the same old, tried-and-tested methods: interdictions, phone calls, whispers! Exploiting the entrenched privileges of the USSR KGB . . .'

That letter . . . reflected our mood at the time, those halcyon days of hope when you could still utter the word 'perestroika' and give your Western friends t-shirts with 'Glasnost' and 'Gorbachev' written on them with a sense of pride in your own country. And not just your Western friends . . .

. . . I wrote letters to some other people and waited for their response; I called Kostya and Svetlana from time to time, not knowing how to console them . . .

And then out of the blue, one evening, the telephone rang. It was Galina Starovoitova (she was one of the people I had written to): 'We backed Kryuchkov into a corner! He said that publishing articles was the editors' business, not the KGB's' . . .

This article was published ... in August 1989. On Wednesday the 9th.

This is how Shchekochikhin's article came to be published a year after its writing. In the end, the title was changed to 'A Trial, 80s-style'.

It was no accident that People's Deputy Galina Starovoitova (1946–98) decided to step in: she was a long-time friend of Azadovsky's. She did everything in her power to make sure that the article was published – and she wasn't alone. A number of scholars and cultural figures rallied round the Azadovskys, insisting that the article be published. Dmitry Likhachyov, whose name carried a great deal of weight during the period of perestroika, sent a separate letter to the editor-in-chief of *The Literary Gazette*.

This article caused a sensation in Russia. Shchekochikhin didn't mince words: he declared that the Great Terror of the 1930s had never ended, and that even now, anyone the state considered undesirable could be mercilessly destroyed by the security services, with the Soviet justice system acting as their accomplice.

14.2 The breakthrough

The fact that the case against Azadovsky had now been dismissed in the absence of a crime opened up new possibilities. As early as 16 November 1988, Azadovsky received a notice from the GUVD referencing the 'Statute on the procedure for receiving restitution for damages inflicted on a citizen through the unlawful actions of pretrial investigation authorities, the Prosecutor's Office or the court'. According to this statute, Azadovsky had the right to seek to be 'reinstated to his former employment, or, where that is impossible, to be given an equivalent position' and to receive 'compensation for lost earnings, fines paid, court fees, fees paid for legal assistance, etc.'. Here is what Azadovsky managed to achieve:

First, on 14 February 1989, the GUVD's Investigation Directorate awarded Azadovsky compensatory damages to the sum of 6,795 rubles, 89 kopecks. This was an astronomical sum, even with skyrocketing inflation.

Second, Azadovsky was able to initiate another round of proceedings in connection with the fabricated workplace character reference. This lengthy lawsuit finally came to an end on 25 September 1989, when Judge T.I. Sapotkina ruled to fully uphold the plaintiff's claim regarding the protection of his honour and dignity against the Leningrad V.I. Mukhina Higher School of Art and Industry and the people who had signed the character reference.

Third, in accordance with this ruling, Azadovsky was to be reinstated at the Higher School, either to his former position or to an equivalent one. After everything that had happened, though, Azadovsky didn't seriously consider going back to teach there. Instead, the ruling served as a powerful symbol that things had 'gone back to normal'. On 13 July 1989, Azadovsky was once again made a docent in the department of foreign languages. He submitted his resignation soon afterwards and, in October of that year, he bid farewell to the School and to Soviet higher education in general.

14.3 The mysterious fifth person

As we have seen, nearly all the most important evidence of KGB involvement in Azadovsky's case was gathered by Azadovsky himself: he was the one who discovered Shlemin and Arkhipov's names, who identified their colleagues Bezverkhov and Kuznetsov, and so on.

However, one person present at the search had yet to be identified: the 'specialist' who was called in by Captain Artsibushev after the search turned up foreign books and photographs of Russian poets.

Though Artsibushev claimed that he couldn't remember any of the 'police' officers' names, he did let slip that 'all of them had common surnames.' He seems to have been telling the truth, as far as he knew: for example, Arkhipov's cover ID was under the far more common name of 'Bystrov'. But none of the petitions Azadovsky filed or the questions he posed in court had got him any closer to tracking down the mysterious fifth person.

In summer 1989, he finally got his hands on the information he needed. In the spirit of perestroika, Azadovsky had been admitted to the Soviet Writers' Union in 1988. And, lo and behold, one evening at a gathering at the Leningrad House of Writers, Azadovsky caught sight of a familiar face. This person seemed at home there; many of the writers went up to greet him. 'Who's that person with the moustache?' 'Why, it's Pavel Krenyov! Don't you know him?'

Krenyov, who wrote stories for children and young adults, was another member of the Writers' Union. However, Krenyov was a pseudonym: his real name was Pavel Pozdeev. Pozdeev had been born in 1950 in a village in Arkhangelsk Oblast; after completing his military service, he had enrolled as a distance learning student in the journalism faculty of Leningrad State University, where he graduated in 1976. He appeared on the KGB's books as an operational officer starting on 1 December 1975. He was part of the Fifth Directorate, which dealt with counter-intelligence and the fight against ideological sabotage. Pozdeev was a familiar figure in the House of Writers in the 1980s, but he was known less in his capacity as an author and more as the KGB agent in charge of overseeing the Union's operations. He became a union member in 1987.

Azadovsky recognized Pozdeev as the fifth 'police officer' who had participated in the search of his flat, the 'specialist' who had examined his photographs and personal papers. Naturally, Azadovsky's next complaint to the Prosecutor's Office (in August 1989) included Pozdeev's name along with the rest.

Krenyov's prose clearly draws on his experience working for the KGB. Published in an anthology titled *Skirmish: Stories about KGB Agents* (1987), his 'Guests from across the Ocean' is told partly from the perspective of a young KGB agent whose knowledge of English allows him to pose as a translator for foreign spies. This story includes characters lifted directly from Azadovsky's case. For example, the opening scene takes place during a border check of foreign citizens (read: smugglers and spies) on a Moscow–Berlin train:

> People in military and official uniforms began moving through the carriages. A standard customs check began, of the type that would take place several times

per shift. Three people entered carriage sixteen: the border guards – Lieutenant Arkhipov and Staff Sergeant Shlemin – and an inspector from the Brest customs office.

Though it is difficult to say how much of his work was inspired by real-life events, this particular passage was clearly meant as a gift to Pozdeev's closest colleagues in the Fifth Directorate: Viktor Arkhipov and Vladimir Shlemin, who were with him at the search of Azadovsky's flat. And in 1987, they were immortalized as characters in a spy story with a print run of 200,000 copies!

It is unclear whether Azadovsky had any personal contact with Krenyov/Pozdeev in the late 1980s to early 1990s. However, an interview with Azadovsky ran in the Arkhangelsk paper *Northern Pravda* on 3 December 1996, when Pozdeev was standing for governor.

This interview appeared as part of an article titled 'Colonel Pozdeev's Military Secret', written by the famous Arkhangelsk journalist Aleksey Peshkov. Peshkov questioned Pozdeev about his involvement in the Azadovsky Affair, but the candidate 'brushed it aside, declaring, first, that he respected Azadovsky very much and would be willing to meet him; second, that he had not been in Petersburg during the time in question; and third, that this fact would be easy to verify'. The tenacious reporter called Azadovsky for comment, and his response was also printed in the paper:

> Yes, Pavel Grigoryevich was intimately involved in my case. . . . He is the same Pozdeev who used to oversee our writers' association. Generally speaking, I can understand why he is trying to distance himself from his participation [in the case]. The entire procedure [surrounding] the search and arrest was completely unlawful. Naturally, he doesn't want to admit taking part in it. And as for meeting him? I don't see the point. If a person is going to look me in the eye and insist, 'No, Konstantin Markovich, you are mistaken,' how am I supposed to prove to them that the earth is round?

Pozdeev lost his election.

14.4 A futile mission

The reversal of the legal system's position towards Azadovsky raises an important question: When the judgement against him was overturned and Azadovsky was acquitted, what happened to the people who had worked so hard to put him behind bars in the first place?

Azadovsky had his own notion of what ought to happen to them:

> I will endeavour to ensure that those individuals who had a hand in the development and implementation of the case against me (the searches, arrests and interrogations) are found guilty of violating the laws that were in force in

> 1980–1981, and that they are declared criminals. [Taken from a 1994 interview with Alexander Altunyan]

And that is precisely what he attempted to do, appealing to Article 176 of the Russian Criminal Code, which dealt with the 'criminal prosecution of a person known to be innocent'. Of course, such a feat was beyond Azadovsky's power. His fight to bring the persons responsible for framing him to justice took place within the same legal framework that had given rise to the Azadovsky Affair in the first place: within the context of a closed society, of socialism with an inhuman face, in a country where the security services still held all the power.

All of Azadovsky's attempts to hold Judge Lukovnikov, Investigator Kamenko, and the police officers and KGB operatives involved in his case accountable proved to be in vain. This was, perhaps, inevitable as, in the intervening years, many of them had risen through the ranks to positions of power in the Big House and elsewhere.

Azadovsky spent a tremendous amount of time and energy chasing the spectre of justice. Were his actions laudable? Laughable? Absurd? Even today, it is not uncommon in Russia to see some poor, unfortunate soul at the post office, sending off stacks of paper addressed to the president himself. . .

But Azadovsky had plenty of other things to do. He had invitations to speak at universities, opportunities to travel the world, his academic work, his family, his friends. How did he manage to maintain this double life? And, more importantly, why did he bother?

There seemed to be several motivating factors. The first was the sense of dignity and self-respect that had been ingrained in him since childhood, the 'old-fashioned' conception of honour that the intelligentsia still cherished. The second was his naïve, idealistic (and, in Russia, completely unfounded) faith in laws and justice. Surprisingly, Azadovsky had been able to maintain this faith throughout the years, despite everything he had experienced. Third, Azadovsky thought, and rightly so, that if he sat back and allowed his case to gather dust, he would lose all hope of discovering what had actually happened, of finding and punishing those responsible and of getting the judgement against Lepilina overturned. It was this third impetus that manifested itself most strongly. And, as events would later show, the game wasn't over yet.

15

Rehabilitation

15.1 A new Russia

In the early hours of 19 August 1991, a group of high-ranking Soviet officials formed the State Committee on the State of Emergency (GKChP) and attempted to wrest control of the country from Soviet president Mikhail Gorbachev. Later that day, Russian president Boris Yeltsin issued a statement decrying their actions as a coup d'état. On Tuesday 20 August, the front page of *The Neva Times*, Leningrad's largest independent newspaper, featured several items: the GKChP's declaration, Yeltsin's statement and an appeal titled 'To the citizens of Russia' signed by the country's leaders: President Yeltsin, chairman of the Council of Ministers of the RSFSR Ivan Silaev, and acting chairman of the Presidium of the Supreme Soviet of the RSFSR Ruslan Khasbulatov. An excerpt from a speech given by Anatoly Sobchak at an emergency session of the Leningrad Soviet was printed at the bottom of the page: 'Those who have stood in the way of justice ought to be put on trial.'

Another item appeared in the centre of the page: an appeal from Leningrad's progressive intelligentsia. It was signed by just six people, one of whom was Konstantin Azadovsky:

> Fellow citizens!
>
> Can it be that it was only a mirage, the idea that our lives have meaning, the idea that our great motherland has a future? Can it be that a half a dozen traitors will deprive our children of their last hope to see their native country free, civilized and happy? Can it be that we will hand them over to the Party, police and military bosses – who are so well-fed, without talent or honour?
>
> The conspirators have plotted to bring this country to ruin. If we let them, then we deserve our fate.
>
> We won't let them!
> There are 300 million of us.
> We are not slaves!

The events of that year – the suppression of the putsch, Yeltsin's rise to power and the dawn of a new Russia – gave Azadovsky fresh hope. But the status of his case remained unchanged. Moreover, the new mayor of Leningrad, Anatoly Sobchak, turned out to have close ties with the Big House, whence he received considerable support.

During this period of democratization, a retired KGB general by the name of Oleg Kalugin began gaining in prominence. A protégé of Yury Andropov, Kalugin was a former intelligence officer who had been 'exiled' to Leningrad, where he served as deputy chief of the Leningrad KGB from 1980–7; he was released from active duty in 1989 and forced into retirement in February 1990.

Kalugin, who had written to Gorbachev about the need for reform within the KGB as early as 1987, had no interest in becoming a pensioner at the age of fifty-five, and so he joined the pro-democracy movement. He was elected a Soviet People's Deputy in 1990 and served as an advisor to KGB chairman Vadim Bakatin for several months following the August Coup. He emigrated to the United States in 1995 and eventually became a US citizen. His outspokenness did not go unnoticed in his native land: in 2002, he was tried in absentia for divulgence of state secrets and sentenced to fifteen years' incarceration.

In 1990, journalists both at home and abroad asked Kalugin on numerous occasions whether he was familiar with the details of Azadovsky's case: after all, he had been in charge of the Leningrad KGB during that time. Kalugin invariably replied that the case had been cooked up in the Big House; according to him, the mastermind behind the whole affair was First Deputy Chief of the Leningrad Oblast KGB General Vladilen Bleer.

Finally, it seemed as if Azadovsky might have his answer. However, there were reasons not to accept Kalugin's version of events at face value. Kalugin and Bleer had run the Leningrad KGB together, and so it was impossible to rule out Kalugin's own involvement.

Later on, the KGB would advance the rather more dubious theory that Kalugin himself had been the driving force behind the Azadovsky Affair. But, though Kalugin had an extensive network of contacts within the Fifth Directorate, it was General Bleer who oversaw the section's work with so-called dissidents.

15.2 Old habits

On 18 October 1991, President Yeltsin signed a new law titled 'On the rehabilitation of victims of political repression'; the Presidium of the Supreme Soviet of the RSFSR resolved to form a commission on the matter on 16 December of the same year. The commission's powers were fairly broad, but one in particular is worth noting: it was given full access to the records of courts, military tribunals, prosecutorial bodies, state security agencies, the MVD and so on. It also had the right to 'request from government bodies . . . documentation and other information necessary to the Commission's activities'.

The commission was empowered to consider instances of political repression dating back to 7 November 1917 (25 October Old Style),[1] the official date of the October Revolution. New legislation had charged it with examining cases of 'individuals who have been rehabilitated according to standard procedure when there are grounds to consider the fact of their prosecution and conviction a form of political repression'. Thus, Azadovsky's case came under the commission's purview.

Shortly before this crucial bill was signed into law on 3 September 1991, Azadovsky had written to the chair of the Russian Supreme Soviet's Security Commission, Sergey Stepashin. A copy of this letter was sent to KGB chairman Vadim Bakatin. At the end of his appeal, Azadovsky writes:

> I can well imagine that KGB operatives were governed by completely different directives in 1980 than they were in, say, the mid-to-late eighties. Nevertheless, the measures taken against myself and my wife cannot be justified by appealing to 'the times'. I am a philologist, translator and literary scholar; I never engaged in so-called 'dissident' activities, I did not disseminate 'anti-Soviet' literature and my contacts with foreign citizens were always of a strictly professional nature. The same is true of my wife. So why, on what grounds, did KGB operatives so cruelly (and, moreover, unlawfully!) ruin our lives?!

Azadovsky's request that Stepashin's commission 'investigate the circumstances of the case, establish the true motivations behind it and punish the guilty parties' was redirected to the Russian Prosecutor General's Office, which had reviewed Azadovsky's appeals many times before. On 27 February 1992, it issued a familiar response:

> The law enforcement officials who took part in the investigation are not subject to disciplinary action because the statute of limitations has passed. Your suggestion that narcotic substances may have been planted in your flat by police officers or the KGB has been reviewed, but no objective confirmation has been found. . . . The complaint's allegation that Lepilina is innocent of the crime with which she was charged is unfounded. Lepilina's conviction . . . has been declared lawful. The protestation against the decisions taken by the court in that case has been rejected by the leadership of the Russian Prosecutor's Office.

As soon as the Commission for the Rehabilitation of Victims of Political Repression started its work, Azadovsky made yet another appeal to the justice system. On 10 September 1992, he sent a lengthy petition to Moscow, which included the following statement:

> What can be rectified now, twelve years later? By insisting that all possible avenues for establishing the truth have been 'exhausted', the Prosecutor's Office is attempting to achieve a single goal: to hush up this case and avoid any analysis of it. Meanwhile, any unbiased lawyer familiar with the details of the case would immediately recognize that the actions of the investigator, prosecutor and judge were deliberate and knowingly unlawful from the very start (Lepilina's arrest, the search, etc.). If appropriate investigative action were to be taken, it would be easy to establish which of the search participants had planted the narcotics on me. But this is precisely what the Prosecutor's Office is trying to prevent at all costs!

> ... I request that the Russian Supreme Soviet's Commission for the Rehabilitation of Victims of Political Repression examine the attached materials (54 pp.) and declare me a victim of political violence perpetrated by the KGB. I also request the opportunity to petition the Russian Prosecutor General's Office regarding the rehabilitation of my wife, S.I. Lepilina (Azadovskaya).

But Azadovsky was in for a nasty surprise. In a letter from the Prosecutor General's Office dated 31 December 1992, Deputy Prosecutor General Yevgeny Lisov informed Azadovsky that his petition to the Supreme Soviet's Commission for the Rehabilitation of Victims of Political Repression had been reviewed by the Prosecutor General's Office. Azadovsky had no idea how this diversion had occurred, but he was once more overcome by a feeling of dread.

The prosecutor's reply was essentially a remix of the phrases Azadovsky had heard so many times before: 'The allegations that [evidence] was fabricated by state security agencies was not confirmed.' 'During the preliminary investigation and court hearing, Lepilina confessed her guilt. . . . There are no grounds to lodge a protest against the judgement in Lepilina's case.' 'It has proved impossible to establish the specific reasons for your transportation to Magadan Oblast to serve out your court-appointed sentence because [your] personal file and the documents related to your transportation were destroyed after reaching the end of their retention period.' And so on and so forth.

Of course, by this point, Azadovsky was used to this sort of response, and so he didn't take it too much to heart. He was, however, tormented by another thought: if he wasn't able to clear his name under the new regime, perhaps the new regime was only an illusion; perhaps his living nightmare would never end.

15.3 The commission's decision

Alexander Kopylov was one of the few deputies who managed to remain uncorrupted despite holding a high-ranking administrative post during the Soviet years. He entered politics during the early days of perestroika and democratization; he became a People's Deputy, and, together with his colleague Vladimir Ryzhkov, organized demonstrations against the GKChP on behalf of the Democratic Russia movement during the August Coup. In 1991, he became chair of the Commission for the Rehabilitation of Victims of Political Repression.

The commission had a hard time finding its feet. One of the greatest challenges it faced was how to navigate its relationship with the state security services. On 18 September 1992, *The Russian Gazette* (the flagship newspaper of the new Russia) published an interview with Kopylov titled 'Brought low by lawlessness – and now by the law?' In it, Kopylov describes how difficult it was to gain access to documents marked 'secret' or 'top secret':

> Why does the process of rehabilitating victims of political repression and restoring their rights drag on for such a painfully long time? The fact is, from the late twenties

up until recently, classified regulations establishing criminal and other forms of legal liability were widely applied in this country. The aim [of this legislation] was clear: to conceal the repressive nature of the legal system, its non-conformance with the principles of international law and morality. At the recommendation of the Supreme Soviet's Commission for the Rehabilitation of Victims of Political Repression, the President of Russia has issued a decree titled 'On the removal of restrictive designations from legislative and other acts justifying mass repression and encroachments on human rights'.

Now the challenge is for the governmental bodies that hold these types of documents (the Security Ministry, the Ministry of the Interior, the Prosecutor General's Office, etc.) to bring their practices into compliance with the President's decree in a timely manner.

Kopylov is referring President Yeltsin's decree no. 658, dated 23 June 1993. The second point of this decree was particularly relevant to Azadovsky's case. It specified that the decree applied not just to laws and regulations but to more private documents as well: for example, 'minutes of meetings of quasi-judicial bodies, internal correspondence and other materials directly related to political repression'.

Therefore, despite the fact that the Prosecutor's Office had only just rejected Azadovsky's petition, Kopylov's commission was fully justified in reviewing it again – this time, in an independent and unbiased fashion.

The Supreme Soviet of the RSFSR issued the results of its review on 17 June 1993:

Dear Konstantin Markovich,

... In its decision of 24 May 1993, the Commission determined that you were subjected to politically motivated repression in 1981, which means that articles 12–16 of the RSFSR law 'On the rehabilitation of victims of political repression' apply to your case. A certificate to this effect issued by the Commission is enclosed herewith.

We hereby inform you that the Commission has sent a letter to the Russian Prosecutor General, V.G. Stepankov, requesting that he conduct a supplemental review of the case against your wife, S.I. Lepilina (Azadovskaya) and consider the possibility of her rehabilitation. You will be informed of the outcome by the Russian Prosecutor General's Office.

With deep sympathy for the groundless political repression you have suffered at the hands of the totalitarian regime, I wish you, Konstantin Markovich, good health and prosperity in life.

Respectfully yours,
Committee Chair
People's Deputy of the Russian Federation
A.T. Kopylov

The Russian Gazette reported Azadovsky's successful rehabilitation on 6 August 1993, in an article written by Kopylov titled 'Names Restored':

K. Azadovsky, known in Saint Petersburg as a human rights advocate,[2] was sentenced in 1981 to two years' incarceration for acquiring narcotics from an unknown individual and for unlawful possession of narcotics, according to his sentence. It wasn't until 1989 that the Leningrad Prosecutor's Office dropped the criminal charges against Azadovsky in the absence of a crime. This was after he had already served his entire sentence – in Magadan Oblast, no less.

The Commission has established that Azadovsky's arrest was the result of a clear and direct provocation on the part of the security services, which had been secretly monitoring him since 1976 for making anti-Soviet statements.

Azadovsky never met Kopylov face to face, nor did he ever appear before the Supreme Soviet, and so he never learned what evidence the commission had received regarding his case. But for Kopylov to declare in the country's leading paper that Azadovsky's case had been motivated by a KGB provocation and that he had been under surveillance since 1976, there must have been credible documentary evidence to that effect.

In 1992, a parliamentary delegation had been sent from Moscow to Saint Petersburg. It consisted of two high-profile members of the Supreme Soviet and an equally well-known human rights advocate: Sergey Kovalyov, chair of the RSFSR Supreme Soviet's Commission on Human Rights, Viktor Sheinis, secretary-general of the RSFSR Supreme Soviet's Constitutional Commission, and Arseny Roginsky (1946–2017), an expert serving on the Commission on Human Rights. They were also there in their capacity as representatives of the Commission on the Transfer and Reception of the Archives of the CPSU and the KGB into State Storage and Their Subsequent Use, which had been formed by the Russian Supreme Soviet on 14 October 1991.

One of the commission's tasks was to 'determine the scope and types of archival documents held by the KGB (including those held by its acting subdivisions) that are subject to being transferred into state storage'. With this goal in mind, the parliamentary delegation headed to the Big House, where they were greeted by Sergey Stepashin and sent on to the KGB archive.

As their first order of business, Arseny Roginsky, a former political prisoner himself, wanted to see his own operational development file (DOR).[3] As it turned out, all files of that type had been burned.

On 6 September 1990, KGB chairman Vladimir Kryuchkov had signed Order no. 00111: 'On the development of a system for the inventory and storage of documents related to agents of the state security services'. This order called for the destruction of thousands of files in the KGB's central and territorial archives by the end of the year. These were files documenting the KGB's domestic intelligence work: personal and working files on agents, suspended agents, safe house keepers and resident spies, as well as operational collection files[4] and card indices of operational materials. Then, on 24 November 1990, Kryuchkov signed Order no. 00150, which stated that all DORs and operational surveillance files (DONs)[5] categorized under 'anti-Soviet propaganda and agitation' were to be destroyed as well. This effectively did away with all Fifth Directorate files dealing with the Era of Stagnation. The KGB was attempting to burn the bridges to its dark past so it could concentrate on building its 'bright future'.

Upon learning that these files had, in fact, been destroyed, Roginsky asked to see the archival record of files related to the Fifth Directorate. This inventory, unlike the files themselves, had been preserved. It contained brief chronological entries for each DOR opened by the Leningrad KGB starting in 1967, the year of the Fifth Directorate's formation. Each entry included the operative's real name, their birth year, their code name, the dates on which the file was opened and shut and the number of volumes the file comprised. Each bore a stamp indicating that the file in question had been destroyed. However, the inventory itself provided some valuable information. Along with his own name, Roginsky found the names of practically all of his Leningrad acquaintances.

He noticed an interesting pattern: the pseudonym the KGB chose for a particular individual would begin with the same letter as their actual surname, and was often somewhat derogatory. For example, Roginsky, a historian, was given the code name 'Reviewer', while the historian and writer Yakov Gordin was dubbed 'Gnome' and the poet Yulia Voznesenskaya was referred to as 'Roach Fish' (in Russian, *vobla*). The list also included someone with the code name of 'Azef':[6] this was Konstantin Azadovsky.

Without the actual file, there wasn't much that could be done with this information. However, the very fact that Azadovsky's name appeared on this list meant that he had been under 'cultivation'[7] by the Fifth Directorate; this, in turn, testified to the political character of the criminal case against him. The Fifth Directorate's reports regarding the 'exploitation'[8] of Azef and Reviewer's DORs offered even more compelling evidence for this connection.

Though the information Roginsky copied out in the archives answered the question of *who* had organized the provocation against Azadovsky, it didn't offer any insight as to how the operation had been executed. As it later turned out, the Commission for the Rehabilitation of Victims of Political Repression had far more significant documentation on that count.

And so, Azadovsky was finally recognized as a victim of political repression. After years of fighting to clear his name, he had been vindicated by the Supreme Soviet itself.

Now he found himself facing a new puzzle. He knew that there was documentary evidence proving the KGB's involvement in his and Lepilina's cases. But what was it?

Though Azadovsky had received an official letter and certificate of rehabilitation from Kopylov's commission, this victory was purely symbolic; the Leningrad authorities dragged their feet in acknowledging the commission's decision. It wasn't until 2001 that the Saint Petersburg Prosecutor's Office finally issued Azadovsky a document confirming that he had, indeed, been subjected to political persecution. This was not just a symbolic victory: it gave Azadovsky the right to various monetary and social benefits.

15.4 The review of Lepilina's sentence

Azadovsky's rehabilitation paved the way for a review of Lepilina's case. On 10 August 1993, at the behest of the Prosecutor General's Office, the Saint Petersburg Prosecutor's Office finally issued a resolution on the revival of proceedings in Lepilina's case 'in light of newly discovered circumstances'. The document reported that '[i]nformation has been brought to light indicating that Lepilina may have been the victim of a provocation.'

However, on 31 December 1993, the prosecutor, Alexander Borodin, discontinued the investigation due to 'lack of grounds for revival of proceedings'. The justification he used was a familiar one: 'Lepilina confessed her guilt during both the investigation and judicial proceedings.'

The files were sent back to Moscow, but they weren't left to languish in the archives, as they would have been in the not-so-distant past. Instead, they landed on the desk of Nikolay Dedov, a senior prosecutor in the Prosecutor General's Office, who didn't agree with his Petersburg colleague:

> Examination of the materials by the Russian Federation's Prosecutor General's Office has revealed that this resolution was not based on the supporting evidence. The case materials make it clear that Lepilina did not confess her guilt at any point during the preliminary investigation . . .

Dedov demanded that the Saint Petersburg Prosecutor's Office take additional explanatory statements from Lepilina.

The Azadovskys were unaware that any of this was going on. They hadn't received an update on Lepilina's case since June 1993, presumably because the Prosecutor General's Office hadn't yet issued its final decision. Frankly, they had long since given up hope that the case would be fairly reviewed.

Then, in early March 1994, the Azadovskys' telephone rang: it was the City Prosecutor's Office, summoning Lepilina to an urgent meeting. Once there, she was questioned about some details of her criminal case and then asked to put some things in writing.

> In an explanation given to the Saint Petersburg Prosecutor's Office on 4 March 1994, S.I. Azadovskaya (Lepilina) stated that she changed the testimony she gave in court on the recommendation of her lawyer, the late Breiman, in an attempt to reduce the criminal punishment she was facing. To the same end, she did not contest her guilt in the cassational appeal she wrote with the help of her lawyer, though she had not actually suspected that what Hassan had given her under the guise of 'mountain herbs' was, in fact, hashish; rather, she believed that it was a smokeable headache remedy.

This statement was sent to the Prosecutor General's Office, where Dedov arrived at the following, long-awaited conclusion:

> Under the circumstances, it is impossible to conclude that S.I. Azadovskaya's (Lepilina's) intent to acquire and possess a narcotic substance has been proved. In accordance with the principle of presumption of innocence, all ambiguities must be interpreted in her favour, which means that her conviction and cassational ruling are subject to reversal and that the criminal case against her is to be dismissed.

And so, on 5 April 1994, Senior Prosecutor Dedov issued a ruling overturning all previous judicial and prosecutorial enquiries and reviews, including those carried out by the Prosecutor General's Office. The case was referred to the Prosecutor General's Office's Supervisory Directorate for the Legality of Criminal Court Rulings for review, and the assistant prosecutor general signed off on the ruling as early as 18 April. On 1 June 1994, the Saint Petersburg City Court Presidium had no choice but to uphold the prosecutor general's opinion, overturn Lepilina's conviction and discontinue the criminal proceedings against her in the absence of a crime.

Lepilina was notified of this ruling via post in late June 1994. She was shocked, to say the least, and so was Azadovsky. The document read:

> During the investigation launched in light of newly discovered circumstances, archival documents from the former USSR KGB and Leningrad Oblast KGB were added to the case materials. These documents make it clear that Lepilina came to the USSR KGB's attention as the cohabiting partner of K.M. Azadovsky, who had been on its operational register since 1978 for suspected anti-Soviet agitation and propaganda.
>
> It proved impossible to secure legally admissible materials proving Azadovsky's involvement in such activities through Lepilina, and so, in October 1980, the KGB decided to prosecute Azadovsky and Lepilina for criminal offences. At the same time, the Kuibyshevsky RUVD in Leningrad was informed that Azadovsky and Lepilina were involved in the acquisition, possession and consumption of narcotic substances. In fact, there was no such information in the KGB files. On 18.12.80, RUVD operatives detained Lepilina after she received jeans and a packet of hashish from a foreigner – a KGB agent.
>
> A KGB report dated 21.09.88 indicates that the criminal prosecution of Azadovsky and Lepilina occurred as a result of the work of an agent-provocateur (Hassan), who gave Lepilina jeans provided by another KGB operative, as well as hashish, which he obtained himself (pp. 137–8).
>
> Findings issued by the Leningrad Oblast KGB on 22.12.88 state that the decision to proceed with the exploitation of Azadovsky's DOR by subjecting him to prosecution was made by the leadership of a KGB section without sufficient grounds, in the absence of any concrete information. When he gave Lepilina the jeans and the packet of hashish, the foreign agent was engaging in a provocation, as the two had not agreed on this transaction beforehand (pp. 162–8).
>
> It was not possible to question Hassan, as he is currently located outside of Russia.
>
> Under the circumstances, it is impossible to conclude that S.I. Azadovskaya's (Lepilina's) intent to acquire and possess a narcotic substance has been proved. Thus, in light of the fact that there were circumstances of which the court was unaware testifying to the fact that that Lepilina did not commit a crime under Article 224, paragraph 3 of the RSFSR Criminal Code, her conviction and the cassational ruling against her are subject to reversal in light of the newly discovered circumstances.

After nearly fourteen years, it finally seemed as if the Azadovskys had emerged victorious. But, alas, their story wasn't over . . .

16

The heart of the matter

It is important to bear in mind that Russian society had changed dramatically in the years since Azadovsky's conviction was overturned in 1988. By 1994, the Azadovskys were living in an entirely different historical era. Moreover, thanks to the income Azadovsky made from his international scholarly projects, the couple enjoyed a comfortable lifestyle. By this time, Lepilina's exoneration would have no effect on their material circumstances. It was strictly a moral victory.

Nevertheless, this event gave rise to new and important questions. The first thing the Azadovskys attempted to do was gain access to the criminal case against Lepilina. After all, the Court Presidium's ruling had indicated that the file contained some intriguing documents: a 'KGB report' and 'findings issued by the Leningrad Oblast KGB'. They were referenced by page number, and the fact that these references were to pages 137–8 and 162–8 meant that there were other documents in between.

However, when the Azadovskys asked to view their files, they were informed that this wouldn't be possible: the documents had disappeared from both court and prosecutorial archives.

16.1 The general

How did the KGB react to the Azadovsky Affair throughout the 1980s and early 1990s? It certainly didn't keep silent. On the contrary: it issued replies to all of Azadovsky's complaints and allegations. Of course, the 'soldiers on the invisible front' preferred to give their answers orally rather than written form (take, for example, Azadovsky's conversation with Lieutenant Colonel Kobzar in Susuman in late 1982). In the late 1980s, Azadovsky was called in for yet another salutary conversation. It was full of implicit threats: Azadovsky was accused of 'tarnishing the KGB's honour'. Subsequently, though, his appeals began to be taken more seriously, especially as he made a habit of addressing them to the very top: to Yury Andropov (1982), Viktor Chebrikov (1988), Vladimir Kryuchkov (1989) and so on. These complaints invariably garnered a written response.

On the morning of 30 March 1989, Azadovsky received a letter from the Leningrad KGB. It was dated 27 March and signed by the organization's deputy chief, State Security Lieutenant General Vladilen Bleer. Bleer's name held no fond associations for Azadovsky: he had first heard it during a court recess in July 1988, when Artsibushev alluded to the people in the Big House who had organized the case against him. And now the general himself was writing Azadovsky a letter – what could this mean?

The letter bore no resemblance to an official response: it was written on ordinary paper rather than letterhead, and it didn't include a reference number, stamp or seal. All there was was a handwritten signature and a date at the bottom of the second page. Bleer wrote:

> Acting under orders from the Soviet Committee for State Security [KGB], the Leningrad Oblast KGB has conducted an internal investigation into the circumstances described in your complaints of 15 August, 12 October and 8 December 1988, which were addressed to the Chairman of the USSR KGB and the Investigation Directorate of the USSR KGB.
>
> During this investigation, it was confirmed that the KGB had nothing to do with the prosecution of yourself and Citizen Lepilina in December 1980 for crimes under Article 224 of the RSFSR Criminal Code. No information was uncovered indicating KGB interference in the investigation of those cases.
>
> While reviewing a number of foreign citizens with ties to foreign security services who arrived in the USSR during that time, the LO KGB received information indicating that some of them were in contact with you; this contact included giving you foreign publications with libellous contents. With the police's permission, KGB operatives participated in a search of your residence with the aim of verifying this information.
>
> Literature seized during the search of your flat was declared by Lenoblgorlit to be (by the standards of the time) libellous and unfit for import and distribution in the USSR. These materials were destroyed in accordance with standard procedure.
>
> The version of events you set forth – in which the LO KGB operatives involved in the search of your flat were responsible for the narcotics discovered there – was not confirmed either by the investigation undertaken by the City Prosecutor's Office in response to your petition or by our own review.
>
> It was also established that the decision for KGB operatives to participate in the police search was taken without sufficient grounds. During the search, there was a violation of the requirements set forth in Article 141 of the RSFSR UPK: the names of the KGB operatives were not recorded in the search report. The parties responsible for these violations have been subjected to disciplinary action.
>
> The KGB operatives were, in fact, acting to verify a report submitted to law enforcement officials by Citizen Z.I. Tkachyova testifying to your and S.I. Lepilina's suspicious contact with foreigners.
>
> In connection with this report, [the LO KGB] conducted conversations with a number of individuals. However, as has been established, no misconduct took place [during these conversations] and no confirmation of [Tkachyova's] suspicions was received. Similarly, no confirmation was received regarding the dissemination of slanderous statements about you or S.I. Lepilina by KGB operatives.
>
> The LO KGB did not conduct any kind of review in connection with you after 1981; no restrictive measures were taken against you at any time before or after

that year. No one from the agency was sent to Magadan Oblast to the facility where you were serving out your sentence.

We were unable to issue a response to your petition before the Prosecutor's Office had arrived at its decisions regarding the investigative actions carried out [by that office] in relation to your criminal case and the investigation of the GUVD and KGB operatives who participated in it.

We apologize for the violation of UPK norms that was committed by KGB operatives.

Needless to say, Azadovsky interpreted this 'apology' as yet another insult, and on 5 May 1989, he sent a long letter to KGB chairman Vladimir Kryuchkov systematically debunking the falsehoods in Bleer's letter using materials from his criminal case and retrial. At the same time, Azadovsky introduced what was, to his mind, a compelling new argument:

In summer 1988, in the Kuibyshevsky District Courthouse, Artsibushev assured me (in the presence of witnesses) that, long before Lepilina's detention and the search of my flat, he had discussed a 'plan of attack' (involving narcotics) against Lepilina and myself with the heads of the LO KGB. According to Artsibushev, the same exact 'plan' had been deployed against the Leningrad writer L.S. Druskin, whose flat had been searched, ostensibly for narcotics, by Artsibushev in spring 1980 at the KGB's behest.

This correspondence continued, but without any result. The only wrongdoing that the KGB was willing to acknowledge was its failure to comply with the UPK by omitting its operatives' names from the search report. Azadovsky received replies to this effect from Chief of the Inspection Directorate Lieutenant General Sergey Tolkunov (2 June 1989), Senior Inspector Major General Alexander Oleinikov (21 October 1990) and Chief of the Leningrad KGB Lieutenant General Anatoly Kurkov (27 December 1990).

16.2 Proof

These responses were clearly disingenuous. At this point, the Azadovskys knew for a fact that there was documentary evidence supporting their theory that the KGB had been involved in the criminal cases against them: namely, a KGB report from 1988 indicating that 'the criminal prosecution of Azadovsky and Lepilina occurred as a result of the work of an agent-provocateur.'

These gaps and omissions gnawed at Azadovsky. For such a long time, he had been trying to prove that the KGB was at the root of all his sufferings. Now he finally knew that there was evidence, but he wasn't able to access it.

How could they get their hands on the criminal case against Lepilina? Once again, Shchekochikhin came to the rescue. By this time, he had become a deputy in the State Duma. As soon as he heard about the Presidium's ruling, he immediately started thinking of ways to gain access to the documents referenced in it. In the end, Lepilina was allowed to view the criminal case against her, which was held in the archives of the Kuibyshevsky District Court. In theory, she ought to have been granted this access as soon as she requested it; in practice, it took significant effort.

For the first time, Lepilina engaged in the sort of work that had occupied her husband for years: wading through piles of papers. She was painfully aware that everything depended on her. Each day, as she was handed her criminal case, she feared that it would be the last time she saw it. Over the course of a week, she carefully copied out page after page of the file by hand.

On 28 September 1994, excerpts from these documents were published in *The Literary Gazette* as part of an article by Shchekochikhin titled 'In Disguise'. It was a triumph of investigative journalism: finally, the KGB's involvement in the Azadovskys' cases had been proved using documentary evidence. And that evidence was irrefutable.

17

Proof

17.1 The 1988 investigation

The KGB conducted its own investigations into the Azadovsky Affair in the late 1980s. The first serious review of the case took place in August and September 1988 in response to a complaint addressed to KGB chairman Viktor Chebrikov, who was also a Politburo member and former head of the KGB's Fifth Directorate. The completed report was presented to Chebrikov on 28 September 1988, just two days before he was named to the Secretariat of the CPSU. Excerpts of this report appear in the following text:

> On the instruction of the USSR KGB leadership, representatives of the USSR KGB's Inspection Directorate and Investigation Department were sent to Leningrad to review Azadovsky's complaint. During this review, [the representatives] examined all of the KGB's operational materials from 1961–1986 related to Azadovsky, as well as the archival records of the criminal cases against Azadovsky and Lepilina.
>
> It was established that, during the years 1961–1963, Azadovsky, then a student in Leningrad State University's philological faculty, was a KGB agent utilized for studying foreigners who had come to the USSR as part of the youth tourist initiative; however, he was suspended from the agent network for refusing to report information about persons of interest to the KGB.
>
> In 1967, Azadovsky came to the KGB's attention as someone who maintained contact with foreigners suspected of belonging to hostile security services; that same year, he was put under cultivation as part of a group operational cultivation file (DGOR)[1] code named 'Passage', which was categorized under 'anti-Soviet agitation and propaganda'. During work on the DGOR, it was established that, for a number of years, Azadovsky and his close associate Slavinsky supplied foreigners with the works of 'unrecognized' Leningrad poets and made slanderous statements about current events in the USSR. In return, the foreigners gave them ideologically harmful literature, which they disseminated within their circle. Additionally, on more than one occasion, Azadovsky attended illicit gatherings hosted by Slavinsky at which narcotics were consumed . . .
>
> On the basis of legally admissible materials gathered during Azadovsky's cultivation and the Slavinsky investigation, social prophylactic measures were

taken against Azadovsky, and he was expelled from Herzen Sate Pedagogical Institute in Leningrad ...

In September 1978, a DOR was opened on Azadovsky under the code name 'Azef'; it was categorized under 'anti-Soviet agitation and propaganda, statements of a revisionist nature'. This file contains information stating that Azadovsky authored a number of ideologically harmful literary texts; that he verbally disseminated slanderous falsehoods within his circle regarding the founders and leaders of the Soviet state; that he maintained ties with foreigners; that, in conversation with them, he compromised the reputation of domestic political activities carried out by the Soviet government; and that he actively used [his foreign contacts] to communicate with individuals who had emigrated from the USSR and to receive ideologically harmful literature from abroad. Azadovsky used his wife, Lepilina, as an intermediary for meeting with foreigners; at his instruction, she would travel to Moscow to make contact with diplomatic representatives of capitalist states.

During work on the DOR, it proved impossible to obtain legally admissible materials related to Azadovsky's hostile and other unlawful activities. Nevertheless, in October 1980, the leadership of the KGB's Fifth Directorate took the decision to exploit this file by bringing criminal charges against the subject. At the same time, the KGB informed the Kuibyshevsky RUVD in Leningrad that Azadovsky and Lepilina were involved in the acquisition, possession and consumption of narcotic substances, although such information did not appear in the DOR ...

In December 1981, the Susuman branch of the Magadan Oblast KGB (where Azadovsky was serving out his sentence) opened an operational surveillance file [DON] on him. During work on this file, [the KGB] received information indicating that, while incarcerated, Azadovsky had been making attempts to establish contact with persons in the West to inform them of his conviction. There was no intelligence indicating that he was engaged in hostile work in any corrective facility. However, in December 1982, the following preventative measures were taken in Azadovsky's case: an operational officer had a conversation with him, after which he was registered with the Tenth Group of the Magadan Oblast KGB.

After completing his sentence in late 1982, Azadovsky returned to Leningrad and established contact with a number of foreigners, with whose help he planned to emigrate. In 1980, he received an official invitation from Austria. That same year, Azadovsky applied for permission to emigrate to Israel. This request was refused because he did not have any relatives abroad. In May 1986, Azadovsky's DON was closed because no evidence of hostile activities had been found ...

During the present review, it has emerged that the criminal charges against Azadovsky and Lepilina were preceded by provocations committed by 'Baryte', a foreign agent in the employ of the KGB's Fifth Directorate who had been dangled[2] in front of Lepilina by the KGB in November and December 1980.

Acting in accordance with an assignment given to him by agency operatives comrades I.V. Yatkolenko and A.M. Fyodorovich, 'Baryte' arranged to meet Lepilina on the evening of 18 December 1980 in a café near Azadovsky's building. There, in order to carry out the exploitation of [her file], he gave her jeans and a packet of narcotics that were chemically identical to the narcotics later found in

Azadovsky's flat. A report from Baryte dated 20 December 1980 notes that Lepilina expressed interest in the narcotics and promised to sell them. During the present enquiry, comrade Fyodorovich explained that the aforementioned jeans had been acquired with the operational aim of having Baryte give them to Lepilina, while comrade Yatkolenko explained that the indicated narcotics belonged to Baryte, an agent with whom he was in contact. During the aforementioned meeting between the agent and Lepilina, Fifth Directorate operatives comrades A.L. Kuznetov and I.V. Yatkolenko recorded that the jeans and narcotics had been handed off and informed the surveillance service of that fact.

... The fact that Lepilina was detained with narcotics on her person was used as grounds to conduct a search of Azadovsky's residence on 19 December 1980.

With the approval of the leadership of the KGB's Fifth Directorate, operational officers comrades V.I. Arkhipov and V.V. Shlemin participated in the search together with Artsibushev and Khlyupin of the GUVD's [Directorate for] Criminal Investigation. [Arkhipov and Shlemin] introduced themselves as police officers and presented cover documents confirming their story. Later on, Artsibushev officially invited KGB operative comrade P.G. Pozdeev to the search to evaluate the literature in Azadovsky's flat; however, in violation of the requirements set forth in Article 141 of the RSFSR UPK, the aforementioned KGB operatives were not included in the search report as having participated in this investigative activity. When questioned about Azadovsky's assertions, the KGB operatives explained that none of the individuals involved in the search had planted narcotics and that they viewed Azadovsky's assertions to that effect as an attempt to compromise the investigation and escape criminal liability for narcotics possession.

The log of 'S' measures[3] included in his DOR shows that Azadovsky had been visited by 'Rachmaninoff', an agent of the KGB's Fifth Directorate, on the evening prior to the search of his flat (after Lepilina's detention). However, the DOR does not contain any documentation regarding the aim or outcome of this visit. During a conversation, comrade A.V. Kuznetsov, the Fifth Directorate operative who was in contact with this source, explained that Rachmaninoff had been instructed to go to Azadovsky's home with the aim of ascertaining the flat's layout, though this was not critical to the operation's success, as a 'D' measure[4] had been undertaken in his domicile in August 1980.

The aforementioned unlawful activities carried out against Azadovsky and Lepilina by KGB operatives were able to occur for the following reasons. The Fifth Directorate's leadership took the decision to exploit Azadovsky's operational development file without approval from the appropriate section, in violation of KGB Chairman's Instruction no. 5/S-79. Moreover, the operational materials connected with Azadovsky were not submitted to the KGB's Investigation Department for examination and legal recommendation, even during the preparation and execution of the file's exploitation. No exploitation plan was developed. Due to the amateurish and ill-considered actions of certain KGB operational officers during this exploitation, Azadovsky became aware of the measures taken against him in connection with his criminal prosecution, which laid the groundwork for his complaints. They were facilitated by the gross tactical miscalculations and violations of criminal procedural legislation committed by Investigator Kamenko of the Kuibyshevsky RUVD, who led the criminal investigations against Azadovsky and Lepilina. Notably, during the search of Azadovsky's flat, a police officer amateurishly seized a packet of narcotics in the presence of only one search witness; additionally, as indicated earlier, the KGB operatives were not named in the search report. These issues, along with others, later gave grounds for protest and a reversal of the judgement in Azadovsky's case.

It should be noted that Leningrad Oblast KGB operatives Arkhipov and Shlemin were called in as witnesses during the judicial proceedings of July and August 1988. However, in accordance with a decision taken by the agency leadership, [they] did not appear in court, which only heightened Azadovsky's suspicion that the KGB had been involved in his criminal prosecution. This impression was encouraged by the search witnesses' inconsistent court testimony, as well as police officer Khlyupin's comment that he had found the narcotics in a place in Azadovsky's flat that had already been examined by KGB operatives. While being questioned as a witness, former police investigator Kamenko declared that he had taken all of the decisions in Azadovsky's case on his own, and that he had not been under any pressure from the KGB. He also explained that he had been in contact with operational officers from the Leningrad Oblast KGB during the investigation, and that he had given them literature seized from Azadovsky's flat for evaluation. This literature was found to be ideologically harmful and unfit for distribution within the territory of the USSR, as a result of which it was destroyed by KGB operatives comrades E.V. Volodin, Yu.A. Bezverkhov and A.V. Kuznetsov; a signed document to this effect was attached to Azadovsky's criminal case file.

Thus, a review of Azadovsky's allegations regarding the participation of Leningrad Oblast KGB operatives in his and Lepilina's conviction for the acquisition of narcotic substances has found them to be justified. The complainant's assertions that evidence of his guilt was fabricated by planting narcotics in his domicile are currently under investigation by the Prosecutor's Office as part of a criminal case in connection with Azadovsky's prosecution.

In light of the circumstances set forth above, we find it prudent to instruct the Leningrad Oblast KGB to conduct an internal investigation into its operatives' unlawful actions after a final decision has been reached in Azadovsky's criminal case and to report back to the USSR KGB with results and actions taken.

As for Azadovsky's present complaint, he is to be informed that the unlawful participation of Leningrad Oblast KGB operatives in the search of his flat has been established; it should be made clear to the petitioner that [these operatives] will be subject to disciplinary action.

Senior Inspector
Inspection of the [LO] Directorate of the USSR KGB
Colonel V.I. Vasilyev
22 September 1988

Approved by:
Chief of the USSR KGB Inspection Directorate
Lieutenant General S.V. Tolkunov
22 September 1988

Senior Inspector
Department of Internal Affairs, USSR KGB Investigation Department
Major V.P. Popov
21 September 1988

Approved by:
Chief of the USSR KGB Investigation Department
Major General L.K. Borisov

This document sheds new light on the Azadovsky Affair; it also requires certain caveats and commentary.

First, the caveat: the USSR KGB's Inspection Directorate can only be trusted up to a point. Much of this report was based on the statements of Leningrad KGB operatives, who were naturally inclined to shift as much of the blame as possible onto the Azadovskys, as well as the MVD's investigative bodies.

Now, on to the commentary. For the most part, this will consist of bringing the sequence of events presented in the document into line with what actually happened.

Previous chapters of this book have described the KGB's attempts to recruit Azadovsky at the age of nineteen, as well as his refusal to cooperate with the agency. In this context, the language used in the document (which characterizes Azadovsky as a 'KGB agent' who was 'utilized for studying foreigners', etc.) appears deliberately skewed. The assertion that 'Azadovsky authored a number of ideologically harmful literary texts' is also untrue: his scholarly and literary output couldn't be considered 'ideologically damaging' even by Soviet standards. Additionally, the claim that 'at [Azadovsky's] instruction, [Lepilina] would travel to Moscow to make contact with diplomatic representatives of capitalist states' is completely made up: the fact that 'it proved impossible to obtain legally admissible materials related to Azadovsky's hostile and other unlawful activities' suggests there was no evidence to support it.

One of the most outrageous statements contained in this document is the declaration that 'in October 1980, the leadership of the KGB's Fifth Directorate took the decision to exploit this file by bringing criminal charges against the subject.' In other words, after failing to establish that Azadovsky was guilty of any political crime, KGB operatives had decided not to let all their hard work go to waste: the least they could do was make sure that Azadovsky ended up behind bars.

After this decision had been taken, the KGB's next step was to seek out a suitable article under which to bring charges against him. Conveniently, they found the solution in Azadovsky's own DOR: He had been involved in a narcotics case in 1969, so why not use narcotics again in 1980? This logic explains the deliberate misinformation the KGB fed to the Kuibyshevsky RUVD regarding Azadovsky and Lepilina's drug use. To its credit, the Inspection Directorate openly admitted that 'such information did not appear in the DOR. This fact explains why the investigative team flatly refused to perform drug testing on Azadovsky and Lepilina in the years 1980–1: a negative result would have seriously damaged the prosecution's case.

This report also confirms Azadovsky's suspicion that the KGB had continued monitoring him throughout his time in Susuman. The assertion that 'while incarcerated, Azadovsky had been making attempts to establish contact with persons in the West to inform them of his conviction' seems particularly absurd: Susuman was too isolated to support any such attempts.

The report goes on to describe the inner workings of the campaign of provocations that was mounted against the Azadovskys. By comparing this document with others, including the Azadovskys' own testimony, we can reconstruct the exploitation of Azadovsky's DOR almost step by step.

'Hassan' was an agent recruited by the KGB's Fifth Directorate; his code name was Baryte. Though the report claims that Baryte was 'dangled' in front of Lepilina, in KGB parlance, he was actually 'introduced' to her. In the process of 'agent introduction', it is the agent (not the person under cultivation) who attempts to initiate a relationship with the target. That is precisely what happened in this case. Hassan met Lepilina through an intermediary at a banquet. He introduced himself as a Spanish student studying at Leningrad State University, got Lepilina's telephone number and came to visit her at work on several occasions.

What follows is a timeline of the events that took place on 18 December 1980.

In Lepilina's testimony, she states: 'That morning I had spoken with Azadovsky on the telephone and said that I might drop by to see his mother.'

It wouldn't take a professional spy to guess that the Azadovskys' phone had been tapped (this suspicion would later be confirmed by documentary evidence). As soon as the KGB heard that Lepilina was planning a visit to the Azadovskys', they signalled for Hassan to put their plan into action.

Hassan telephoned Lepilina at work to tell her he was leaving the country, possibly for good, and that he wanted to say goodbye. He suggested a meeting place close to the Azadovskys' building, with the assumption that she would go there directly afterwards.

The groundwork for this mission had already been laid. One operational officer had secured the jeans that Baryte was to pass on to Lepilina; another had furnished the drugs. An interesting detail appears several times in the materials related to the investigation: not only were the drugs seized from Azadovsky and Lepilina chemically identical, but they were also wrapped the same way, using the same kind of foil. The fact that the two sets of drugs were identical suggests that they came from the same source, and the KGB admits that the drugs seized from Lepilina came from its own agent, Baryte. If, back in the early 1980s, the two samples had been tested not just for their chemical composition, but for physical similarity, the experts would have concluded that the two samples came from the same source, which would have meant that Azadovsky and Lepilina's cases would have had to have been tried jointly.

So, what happened next? Once KGB operatives 'recorded that the jeans and narcotics had been handed off and informed the surveillance service of that fact', Lepilina was 'escorted' to the courtyard of No. 10 Vosstaniya Street, at which point she was 'handed off' to the RUVD.

The report's description of the search of Azadovsky's flat also yielded a wealth of new information. For one thing, it provided official confirmation that Pozdeev had participated in the search.

It is hardly surprising that the KGB operatives involved tried to distance themselves from the narcotics planting. However, a question arises: If the two packets came from the same, KGB-controlled source, how had the second one come to be in Azadovsky's flat?

The report states that Azadovsky's flat had been visited by a Fifth Directorate agent code named Rachmaninoff; '[h]owever, the DOR does not contain any documentation regarding the aim or outcome of this visit.' So why had the agent gone there on the eve of the search?

On 18 December 1980, at around seven in the evening, Azadovsky received a call from Mikhail Orekhov, a musician employed at Lenconcert. Azadovsky had met Orekhov on several occasions; he moved in the same circles as Lepilina. Orekhov asked if he could stop by, claiming that he wanted to get Azadovsky's opinion on two antique drawings. He came over around eight, and Azadovsky invited him into his study. But Orekhov hadn't brought the drawings; he said that he had 'just come by to apologize'. After they had chatted for a while, Orekhov asked his host to bring him a glass of water from the kitchen. When Azadovsky returned, Orekhov gulped down the water and left.

This odd behaviour, combined with Kuznetsov's statement (that 'Rachmaninoff had been instructed to go to Azadovsky's home with the aim of ascertaining the flat's layout, though this was not critical to the operation's success'), makes it fairly obvious where the narcotics on Azadovsky's bookshelf came from.

The report also mentions that an 'S' measure (wiretapping) occurred in Azadovsky's flat on 18 December, while a 'D' measure (search) had taken place in August. Such actions were part of the KGB's system of 'lettered measures', in which each letter referred to a different type of technical–operational activity.

The fact that this report mentions 'S' measures supports the idea that the operation was launched on the morning of 18 December, after the KGB had recorded Lepilina's call. It is also worth noting that Azadovsky's DOR contains a 'log of "S" measures', which is to say, a stenographic record of *more than one* telephone conversation.

In August 1980, while Azadovsky was on a trip to Lithuania and his mother was on holiday in Leningrad Oblast, the KGB took advantage of their absence to perform a covert search. However, Azadovsky had brought home Baltsvinik's collection of photographs that autumn, while his mother was confined to their flat. The photographs, which hadn't been there in the summer, would have come as a shock to the KGB operatives searching the flat in December. This turn of events was what necessitated Pozdeev's last-minute involvement in the search.

Finally, this report allows us to answer a fundamental question: After catching Lepilina red-handed, why did the KGB wait until the next morning to perform a search of Azadovsky's flat? It wasn't because they had to wait for permission: according to Article 168 of the UPK, 'in cases where time is of the essence, a search may be conducted without a prosecutor's warrant, but the Prosecutor's Office must be informed of the search within twenty-four hours.' The explanation is simple: the hashish wasn't yet on Azadovsky's bookshelf. An agent had to go and put it there.

This document provides important insight into the disciplinary measures the 'guilty parties' in the KGB were facing. But what exactly were they 'guilty' of? Point 12 of the Rules and Regulations of the USSR KGB states:

> The state security services must strictly observe the socialist legal order in all of their activities. They are required to utilize all of the rights granted to them under the law to make sure that not a single enemy of the Soviet state escapes the punishment they deserve and that not a single citizen is subjected to unfounded prosecution. Violations of the socialist legal order and abuses of power must be strictly curbed, as these are activities that impinge upon socialist legality and the rights of Soviet citizens.

The report to Chebrikov demonstrates that the KGB couldn't care less about the rights of Soviet citizens. The agency was far more concerned with the fact that its 'sterling reputation' had been tarnished, that 'Azadovsky became aware of the measures taken against him in connection with his criminal prosecution, which laid the groundwork for his complaints.' This unthinkable situation was compounded by the fact that, during the 1988 trial, Arkhipov and Shlemin 'did not appear in court, which only heightened Azadovsky's suspicion that the KGB had been involved in his criminal prosecution'.

The report's authors blame Investigator Kamenko of the Kuibyshevsky RUVD for the worst blunders in the case, citing his 'gross tactical miscalculations and violations of criminal procedural legislation'. Even Officer Khlyupin is taken to task for 'amateurishly seiz[ing] a packet of narcotics in the presence of only one search witness'.

This grievance speaks volumes. It seems that Khlyupin, who had been informed of the packet's location in advance, was supposed to lead the search witness over to the bookcase and put on a show: if he had discovered the hashish in front of a witness, Khlyupin couldn't have been accused of producing the packet from his own pocket, and Arkhipov and Shlemin couldn't have been accused of planting it in the flat.

17.2 The KGB investigation

Technically, Azadovsky was still under investigation while this report was being written. Thus, its authors suggest that it would be 'prudent' to wait until 'a final decision has been reached in Azadovsky's criminal case' 'to conduct an internal investigation into [the KGB] operatives' unlawful actions'. The KGB chairman signed off on this proposed course of action.

After the GUVD's Investigation Directorate discontinued the case against Azadovsky on 14 November 1988, the KGB launched its own internal investigation, personally overseen by Leningrad Oblast KGB Chief Major General Prilukov. The investigation's aim wasn't to unearth new information – that had been the Moscow commission's job – but to compile a concrete list of culprits to be punished. It was important to demonstrate to the KGB leadership that appropriate measures were being taken.

In December 1988, nearly all of the agents who had been involved in the 1980 operation were obliged to write explanatory reports addressed to the KGB chief;

they were also interrogated verbally. Reading over these documents, which also appear in Lepilina's file, one cannot help feeling that their responses were coordinated. Each operative's testimony follows the same pattern: first, the operative denies any personal responsibility; then, in an attempt to justify Lepilina's entrapment, they shamelessly smear her character. This strategy is reminiscent of what happened during the interrogation of Azadovsky's mother: Investigator Kamenko spent most of the time dragging Lepilina's name through the mud.

Major General Prilukov approved the commission's findings on 22 December 1988. Since this document reprises many of the points that appear in the report to Chebrikov referenced earlier, it is presented here in an abridged form:

> The decision of V.P. Aleinikov, Chief of the First Department of the Fifth Directorate, to exploit Azadovsky's operational development file (categorized under anti-Soviet agitation and propaganda, statements of a revisionist nature) by prosecuting [Azadovsky] for a criminal offence was taken without sufficient grounds. The DOR contained no information confirming that the subject had engaged in the indicated activities during the period of exploitation. Neither criminal intelligence investigator A.V. Kuznetsov, who was responsible for the DOR, nor Division Chief Yu.A. Nikolaev developed an exploitation plan. The decision to exploit the operational record file was taken without approval from the appropriate section or the Investigation Department of the USSR KGB, in violation of KGB Chairman's Instruction no. 5/S-79. Additionally, the materials in the DOR were not presented to the Leningrad Oblast KGB's Investigation Department for evaluation.
>
> In his explanation regarding this exploitation, comrade V.P. Aleinikov points out that 'in addition to a review of the primary version of the file, the action plan for "Azef" approved by the LO KGB leadership made provisions for the documentation and possible exploitation of the file under criminal statutes.' . . . Meanwhile, the DOR action plan that comrade V.P. Aleinikov signed off on a month and a half before the DOR's exploitation made no provisions for any measures related to the documentation of the acquisition, possession or consumption of narcotics on the subject's part.
>
> According to the plan of agent-operational measures developed for Azef's DOR (October 1980), the foreign source Baryte was to be introduced into the cultivation in accordance with a separate report. The main goal of introducing the foreign source into Azadovsky's cultivation was to intercept communications between the subject and any foreign contacts; additionally, provisions were made for identifying potential future criminal activities on the subject's part.
>
> According to Division Chief comrade Yu.A. Nikolaev, the decision to introduce a foreign agent into this operation was taken by the Department leadership, comrades V.P. Aleinikov and E.V. Volodin. They were also the ones who chose the foreign source Baryte, who was in contact with that department.
>
> In violation of the plan for the foreign agent's utilization approved by the Fifth Directorate, Chief of the First Department of the Fifth Directorate comrade A.M. Fyodorovich, in the presence of a senior criminal intelligence investigator in that same department, comrade I.V. Yatkolenko (who was that agent's point of

contact), developed a mission to pass jeans and a packet of narcotics to Azadovsky's cohabiting partner Lepilina for subsequent exploitation. Baryte's execution of these actions constituted a provocation, as he and Lepilina had not agreed to such a course of action during their previous encounters. Yu.A. Nikolaev's explanation states that he developed Baryte's mission to give Lepilina narcotics together with Department Chief V.P. Aleinikov. Conversely, V.P. Aleinikov does not include this fact in his account; however, in a private conversation, he stated that he was not a party to the 'set of measures involving the foreign agent Baryte'.

The present investigation has established that, after Lepilina's detention with narcotics, [KGB] operatives comrades V.I. Arkhipov and V.V. Shlemin were engaged by the Kuibyshevsky RUVD to participate in a search of Azadovsky's flat in the guise of police officers. This occurred on the instruction of Division Chief comrade Yu.A. Nikolaev and Department Chief comrade V.P. Aleinikov. This event took place in violation of KGB Chairman's Instruction no. 5/S-79, which stipulates that 'in exceptional cases, KGB operational and investigative officers may take part in investigative actions (searches, inspections, interrogations, etc.) <u>at the request of the Prosecutor's Office and with the approval of the appropriate operational sections of the Investigation Department of the USSR KGB.</u>' [Emphasis in original]

Comrade Yu.A. Nikolaev indicates in his explanation that the decision to include [KGB] operatives V.I. Arkhipov and V.V. Shlemin in the police operational investigation group responsible for the search was taken together with Division Chief comrade V.P. Aleinikov. [Aleinikov], in turn, explains that this decision was taken with the approval of the Directorate leadership; however, he cannot say precisely who granted the approval at this time.

The explanations of comrades V.P. Aleinikov, Yu.A. Nikolaev, V.I. Arkhipov and V.V. Shlemin indicate that the latter two were briefed and given one task: to evaluate and cull anti-Soviet and ideologically harmful documents (literature, etc.) that would be of interest to the KGB and of use in the exploitation of the DOR. As for Azadovsky's assertions, the aforementioned operatives insist that none of the search participants planted narcotics; they view Azadovsky's assertions to that effect as an attempt to compromise the investigation and escape criminal liability for narcotics possession.

Comrades V.P. Aleinikov, Yu.V. [sic] Nikolaev, V.I. Arkhipov and V.V. Shlemin committed gross violations of the norms of criminal procedural legislation. In violation of the requirements set forth in Article 141 of the RSFSR UPK, comrades V.I. Arkhipov and V.V. Shlemin were not recorded in the search report as participants in this investigative action, which naturally struck Azadovsky as suspicious. Moreover, the event in question was fundamentally doomed to failure and exposure, as Shlemin did not have any cover documents.

These issues, along with others, later gave grounds for protest and a reversal of the judgement in Azadovsky's case.

Gross tactical miscalculations were committed, in particular, by comrades Yu.A. Bezverkhov and A.V. Kuznetsov, who were responsible for Azadovsky's DOR. In an attempt to obtain materials confirming Azadovsky's unlawful activities, they orchestrated conversations with the subject's contacts, as well as Lepilina's, without performing preliminary reviews or checks, without accounting for the nature of these contacts' relationships with Azadovsky and Lepilina. . . . Comrades Yu.A. Bezverkhov and A.V. Kuznetsov did not write reports on their conversations with these individuals. Comrades Yu.A. Bezverkhov and A.V. Kuznetsov categorically deny having had conversations with the other contacts Azadovsky names in his complaint and petition.

The present investigation has established that no one from the KGB visited the facility in Magadan Oblast where Azadovsky was serving out his sentence; as far as we are concerned, no restrictive measures were taken against him.

Thus, the present internal investigation has confirmed the information regarding the involvement of Leningrad Oblast KGB operatives in Azadovsky and Lepilina's convictions. The complainant's suspicion that narcotics were planted in his domicile by KGB operatives was not confirmed. [Emphasis in original]

. . . In light of the above, the commission believes that the serious violations and unlawful activities carried out by comrades V.P. Aleinikov, Yu.A. Nikolaev, V.I. Arkhipov, V.V. Shlemin, A.V. Kuznetsov and I.V. Yatkolenko warrant disciplinary action.

At the same time, the commission notes that, as former Chief of the Fifth Directorate Colonel V.I. Polozyuk and criminal intelligence investigator Captain A.M. Fyodorovich have been dismissed from the KGB, no disciplinary action is to be taken against them. Former Deputy Chief of the First Department of the Fifth Directorate Colonel E.V. Volodin died in 1988. In determining the culpability of comrades V.P. Aleinikov, Yu.A. Nikolaev, V.I. Arkhipov, V.V. Shlemin, A.V. Kuznetsov and I.V. Yatkolenko and assigning them their punishment, the commission deems it necessary to take into account the fact that, for the past 8 years, they have, by and large, received favourable reports and have not committed any violations in their official operational activities. Moreover, comrade A.V. Kuznetsov undertook the exploitation of Azadovsky's operational record file while he was still a junior criminal intelligence investigator.

Deputy Chief Technical Operations Directorate LO KGB Colonel	V.D. Yermakov
Deputy Chief of the Personnel Department LO KGB Major	V.K. Kuznetsov
Senior Inspector LO KGB Inspection Colonel	O.K. Shumov

This document was clearly composed by someone with a good understanding of what ought and ought not to be said. As a result, this carefully edited document is less revealing than the reports cited within it. For example, the explanatory report given on 6 December 1988 by Major A.V. Kuznetsov, chief of the Seventh Direction of the Fifth Directorate, provides a wealth of new information:

In mid-October 1980, on the instruction of the division and department leadership, former Deputy Division Chief comrade Yu.A. Bezverkhov made me responsible for Azef's investigational development file, which had been opened in November 1978...

... I frequently utilized agents Cabin Boy and Rachmaninoff in Azef's case; practically speaking, these agents did not have a close connection with Azef, but they maintained friendly relations with his cohabiting partner, Lepilina...

The plan of agent-operational measures for this case, which was designed to determine the nature of Azef's contacts with foreigners, involved dangling a foreign agent (who was in contact with Comrade I.V. Yatkolenko) via Lepilina. Division operative comrade A.M. Fyodorovich was assigned to organize activities involving the foreign agent. For the dangling, I was tasked with introducing [Baryte] to Lepilina through the agent Cabin Boy in the restaurant of Hotel Leningrad, which I did...

After 10.12.80, I went on scheduled leave.... During this leave, I went into work on 18 and 20.12.80, as I was needed to participate in operational measures for this case. On 18.12.80, during a short briefing session with Divison Chief comrade Yu.A. Nikolaev, I was tasked with seeing Lepilina over to the Seventh Directorate's surveillance after her meeting with Baryte in the café by Vosstaniya Square metro station, where I was sent along with comrade I.V. Yatkolenko. After documenting Lepilina's meeting with Baryte and recording the fact that she had received various items from the foreigner, I gave the agreed-upon signal to the surveillance service upon leaving the café, at which point I returned to the office...

I learned that narcotics had been found during a search of Azadovsky's flat during a telephone conversation I had in my home on 19.12.80. At the same time, it became necessary for me to come into work on 20.12.80 to participate in a search of Lepilina's flat. The search of Lepilina's flat was conducted by police operatives; they also invited search witnesses and representatives of the Housing and Utilities Directorate [to be present at the search]. I received instructions regarding the participation of myself and comrade P.G. Pozdeev in the search from comrade Yu.A. Nikolaev. We were tasked with evaluating any manuscripts and printed materials belonging to Azef that might be found in Lepilina's flat...

After I returned from leave in January 1981, comrade V.I. Arkhipov and I were jointly tasked with organizing Azef's in-cell cultivation. In January and February 1981, comrade V.I. Arkhipov and I, along with an agent of [Kresty's] operative unit, conducted several meetings with the in-cell agent; I conducted two or three meetings with the agent on my own, i.e., with only the [prison officer] present. All materials received during the process of in-cell cultivation were reported to Department Chief comrade V.P. Aleinikov and Division Chief comrade Yu.A. Nikolaev; they were also included in [Azef's] DOR.

... Once or twice, I was sent to Kamenko to pass along or receive up-to-date materials. To the best of my knowledge, the evaluation of the literature was delivered by comrade P.G. Pozdeev via Gorlit on the instruction of comrade V.P. Aleinikov. Later on, I signed a document composed by comrade E.V. Volodin regarding the destruction of a number of volumes seized from Azef that, according to Gorlit's findings, were unfit for import and distribution in the USSR.

... Azef learned my surname from the document regarding the destruction of his literature, which, for reasons unknown to me, he was permitted to view.

Kuznetsov appears to have been involved in all aspects of the exploitation of Azadovsky's DOR. He orchestrated Rachmaninoff's role in the operation and was even called in from leave to take care of this important case, one of the first in his illustrious career. This document also confirms that Lepilina's circle was infiltrated by not one but two agents: Lepilina was introduced to Baryte by another agent, code named Cabin Boy. Thus, the story that Hassan had simply been 'dangled' in front of Lepilina doesn't hold water.

Additionally, this report reveals that a briefing took place in the Big House on 18 December during which the KGB operatives planned their next moves: in all likelihood, this meeting took place immediately after the agency received the operational report on Lepilina and Azadovsky's phone conversation. Everyone present must have realized that the trap was to be sprung that very evening.

The document also provides new details regarding the search of Lepilina's flat: as it turns out, KGB agents P.G. Pozdeev and A.V. Kuznetsov had been present there, too. Needless to say, their names did not appear in the search report.

And that's not all. The document also confirms that Vadim (Fima) Rozenberg, the informer from Azadovsky's cell in Kresty, had been planted there by the Fifth Directorate itself. After his successful work in Azadovsky's case, it is little wonder that the KGB chose to utilize him again in its operation against the Solzhenitsyn Fund.

At the end of his report, Kuznetsov emphasizes that Azadovsky was able to 'unmask' him as a KGB operative because he had been shown a document regarding the destruction of his literature. In fact, Azadovsky didn't see that document until later: he learned Kuznetsov and Bezverkhov's surnames from the photocopies of their 'calling cards'.

Yu.A. Bezverkhov, then a lieutenant colonel in the state security services, presented his own explanatory report to V.M. Prilukov on 13 December:

> K.M. Azadovsky's operational development file was opened in October 1978; it was categorized under 'treason against the Motherland in the form of providing aid to a foreign government in the execution of hostile activities against the USSR'.
>
> During work on this case, which had been put under my charge, information was received indicating that the subject was disseminating within his circle slanderous inventions regarding our social system and that he maintained extensive contact with foreigners, a number of whom were emissaries of anti-Soviet organizations, most of whom harboured hostile or negative attitudes towards our social system and the leaders of our country.
>
> K.M. Azadovsky's meetings with foreigners generally took place in the flat of Azadovsky's cohabiting partner, S.I. Lepilina, in the evening or at night.
>
> In 1980, the Dzerzhinsky District Department of the LO KGB received a petition from S.I. Lepilina's flatmate Tkachyova. In it, she reported that S.I. Lepilina, K.M. Azadovsky and their contacts (including both Soviet and foreign citizens) were organizing orgies in the flat and asked to be protected from this [behaviour].

With the approval of the department leadership, comrade E.V. Volodin took the decision to have a conversation with one of S.I. Lepilina's contacts with the goal of potentially gaining documentary evidence of the activities reported by Tkachyova.

During a preliminary study of S.I. Lepilina's social circle, her contact M.G. Tsakadze was singled out for this purpose; Tsakadze worked as an actress at Lenconcert at the time, and her character reference was favourable. K.P. Sadovnik, the director of Lenconcert, introduced me to M. Tsakadze as a 'handler'. M. Tsakadze was not informed that the KGB's interest in her was based on her connection with K.M. Azadovsky and S.I. Lepilina. Based on M. Tsakadze's positive character reference and my impression of her at our meeting, I gave her my surname and telephone number on a piece of paper. Tsakadze, in turn, gave me her address (she was renting a room at the time). We agreed that she would call me if she received any information regarding unlawful activity on the part of her acquaintances. Subsequently, meetings with her were run by A.V. Kuznetsov, who was charged with handling this case from this point on. Based on his accounts of conversations with her, I know he did not ask her any questions of a provocative nature.

I conducted two meetings with Tsakadze, during which she talked about her acquaintances who maintained contact with foreigners, including S.I. Lepilina. I did not ask M.G. Tsakadze any questions of a provocative nature, nor was the KGB's interest in S.I. Lepilina and K.M. Azadovsky emphasized. I did not meet or hold conversations with Isametdinova, Petrova, or Baltsvinik's wife.

In late November 1980, I went to Kislovodsk on regular leave, and I returned in late December. The case's exploitation was carried out in my absence.

When I returned from leave, I was charged with helping to destroy the literature that Glavlit had determined to be ideologically harmful and unfit for distribution in the USSR. The destruction order, which was signed by E.V. Volodin, myself and Kuznetsov, was given to the Investigation Department of the Kuibyshevsky RUVD.

I did not go to Susuman, Magadan Oblast, where K.M. Azadovsky was serving out his sentence. I was not involved in the measures connected with the recruitment of agent Baryte.

Our old friends Shlemin and Arkhipov also wrote explanatory reports to the KGB chief. By 1988, Vladimir Vladimirovich Shlemin had become a lieutenant colonel in the state security services and was running the Kingiseppsky City Department of the LO KGB. He reported the following:

Sometime around December 1980, on the instruction of comrade Yu.A. Nikolaev, then a division chief in the First Department of the Fifth Directorate of the LO KGB, senior criminal intelligence investigator comrade V.I. Arkhipov and I were sent to a search of K.M. Azadovsky's flat that was being conducted by operatives of the Fifteenth Division of the Directorate for Criminal Investigation of the Leningrad Oblast City Executive Committees' GUVD. Before we left for the search, comrade V.I. Arkhipov and I were briefed by comrade Yu.A. Nikolaev, who guided us to search for anti-Soviet or otherwise politically harmful literature in Azadovsky's flat.

Because I was concerned with the literature, I spent the whole search from beginning to end examining all the books and manuscripts on the bookshelf. Azadovsky sat behind me against the opposite wall, constantly 'advising' me to lay aside one or another 'anti-Soviet book'. I culled several books that had been published abroad, both in Russian and in foreign languages. . . . After a while, a police officer drew everyone's attention to the fact that he had discovered a small packet with some kind of substance in it on the bookcase. The search witness who had witnessed the fact of the aforementioned packet's discovery came over.

Because this was so long ago, I can't [say] what claims Azadovsky made in that moment. Afterwards, Azadovsky attempted to make a telephone call, but was stopped by comrade V.I. Arkhipov. Azadovsky demanded that a note be included in the [search] report saying that he had been manhandled and [also demanded] that comrade V.I. Arkhipov present his documents, which he did. The search report was written up by a police officer. I know that I was not recorded in the report as a participant in this investigative activity. I am not at liberty to explain why this happened, but I acknowledge my guilt in not insisting that my information be recorded in the search report. While I was at the search, I only had my LO KGB identification documents with me. . .

Major V.I. Arkhipov was still working at the central office in 1988; he was a senior criminal intelligence investigator in the First Direction of the Fifth Directorate:

On the instruction of comrade Yu.A. Nikolaev and comrade V.P. Aleinikov, I became involved in Yu.M. Badaev's police operational group with the goal of participating in the search of K.M. Azadovsky's flat in the guise of police officer comrade Viktor Ivanovich Bystrov. At K.M. Azadovsky's insistence, during the search on 19 December 1980, I presented him with official documents identifying me as a GUVD officer. In accordance with instructions given to me by comrade Yu.A. Nikolaev and comrade V.P. Aleinikov, I did not participate in the search for narcotics during the search of K.M. Azadovsky's flat; rather, I was employed in the examination of literature that had been printed abroad and [Azadovsky's] notes, with the goal of uncovering documents with politically harmful contents. Some of the documents and literature found in K.M. Azadovsky's flat were seized and recorded in the search report.

I did not sign the aforementioned report because I was only there to carry out my own tasks; practically speaking, I wasn't employed by the GUVD, I wasn't a part of the police operational investigation group and I wasn't an anti-narcotics specialist. I categorically deny K.M. Azadovsky's speculation that I was involved in the alleged planting of narcotic substances in his flat during the search on 19.12.80, especially as I never went near the spot where the narcotics were found. In the presence of two search witnesses, GUVD operative Khlyupin discovered what later turned out to be narcotics on one of the bookshelves; this [detail] was also recorded in the search report by police officer Artsibushev . . .

After the search, I believe this was on 20.12.80, on the instruction of Department Chief comrade V.P. Aleinikov, I went and signed out a portion of the physical evidence seized during the search from Investigator comrade Kamenko of the Leningrad Kuibyshevsky RUVD. This evidence from the criminal case against K.M. Azadovsky was relevant to the work on 'Azef's' DOR: specifically, the books published abroad, K.M. Azadovsky's notes and other typewritten and handwritten documents belonging to the accused. This physical evidence was packed into a bag along with an inventory list in my presence; a copy of the list remained with the investigator, comrade Kamenko. I gave the aforementioned bag, still sealed, to the chief of the First Division of the First Department of the Fifth Directorate, comrade Yu.A. Nikolaev.

After reviewing these explanatory reports, on 2 February 1989, Prilukov signed off on order no. 023: 'On the development of an additional internal investigation into the unlawful actions committed by KGB operatives against K.M. Azadovsky'. This document offers some long-awaited insight into the consequences faced by the operatives responsible for the violations that occurred in Azadovsky's case:

1) For violating acts of law during the exploitation of Azadovsky's operational development file, Colonel Vladimir Petrovich Aleinikov is to be severely reprimanded.
2) For committing unlawful acts during the execution of operational measures during the exploitation of Azadovsky's file, Lieutenant Colonel Yury Alekseevich Nikolaev is to be severely reprimanded.
3) Taking into account the fact that former chief of the Fifth Directorate Colonel V.N. Polozyuk has retired due to his age and that criminal intelligence investigator Captain A.M. Fyodorovich was dismissed without pension benefits for health reasons (for shortcomings in his work and behaviour), disciplinary action is not to be taken against them.
4) For committing serious tactical errors during the development and exploitation of Azadovsky's file, which subsequently led to the exposure of the state security apparatus's interest in the subject, Lieutenant Yury Alekseevich Bezverkhov and Major Alexander Valentinovich Kuznetsov are to be admonished.
5) For violating the norms of criminal procedural legislation by participating in the search of Azadovsky's flat without being recorded in the search report, Major Viktor Ivanovich Arkhipov and Lieutenant Colonel Vladimir Vladimirovich Shlemin are to be admonished.
6) For inadequate oversight and omissions in the guidance given to subordinates engaged in operational measures related to Azadovsky's DOR, Major General Valery Stefanovich Novikov, former deputy chief of the Fifth Directorate, is to be reprimanded.

17.3 The Prosecutor's Office's investigation

We also have materials from the review of Lepilina's case conducted by the Prosecutor General's Office, which was launched in reaction to the many petitions the office received protesting Lepilina's innocence. At the prompting of the Moscow authorities, this review was officially initiated by a resolution issued on 10 August 1993 by N.A. Vinnichenko, chief of the Department of Supervision of Compliance with Federal Laws in the Saint Petersburg Prosecutor's Office. It was carried out by A.M. Borodin, a high-profile lawyer who served as a prosecutor for the Moskovsky District of Saint Petersburg.

This investigation didn't run smoothly. When the City Prosecutor's Office asked for an update on 18 October, they were told that the review had been delayed 'for reasons beyond our control'. On 1 December 1993, the deadline was pushed back again, this time until 31 December, because 'Security Ministry employees Yu.A. Nikolaev, V.P. Aleinikov and A.M. Fyodorovich had not appeared for questioning.' The City Prosecutor's Office had to intervene to secure their statements. However, it seems that the prosecutor privately informed the former KGB operatives why he was obliged to disturb them. During questioning, each of them eagerly 'recalled' new details confirming Lepilina's guilt.

I.V. Yatkolenko, who now served as deputy chief of a division, gave his statement on 26 November 1993. He reaffirmed his previous testimony, but with caveats:

> Because a great deal of time has passed since 1980, I can't remember all the details of my participation in the aforementioned operational activities. During questioning, I was presented with an explanatory note made in my name to the Chief of the Leningrad Oblast KGB dated 7 December 1988; after looking over this note, I would like to state that the note was written by me, I completely affirm what is written in it. At the same time, I would like to add that I did not see the actual moment when Baryte handed something over to Lepilina . . .
>
> After a day or two, I met Baryte and asked him about his meeting with Lepilina. I don't remember our whole conversation verbatim now, but, according to Baryte, he didn't force Lepilina to take the narcotics. Baryte gave me a written account of the circumstances surrounding his meeting with Lepilina. Perhaps this document is in his personal file, if it hasn't been destroyed upon reaching the end of its retention period, but it certainly doesn't appear in Azadovsky's file, because one of the people conducting the review found it in Baryte's file.

This document introduces some important nuances to Yatkolenko's account. For example, in 1988, he had stated that he was present in the café during the handoff; in 1993, he clarified that he had not witnessed the handoff itself. It isn't entirely clear why he chose to emphasize this particular detail; perhaps he feared what the others might say in their testimony. In any case, the main theme of Yatkolenko's testimony is *intent*; he makes a concerted effort to prove that Lepilina took the drugs from Baryte willingly.

Later on, Yatkolenko introduces a new piece of 'evidence': an account written by Baryte outlining the details of the operation. He even gives the document's former location: Baryte's personal file. This detail is worth noting, first of all because Yatkolenko would have known perfectly well that Baryte's file had already been destroyed. Second, he deliberately uses the term 'personal file' despite knowing that Baryte didn't have one: what Baryte had was an 'operational collection file' (OP), the kind of file kept on foreigners visiting the USSR. Baryte wasn't an agent, exactly: he didn't have an agent file, just an OP that never developed into anything more. The KGB might have caught him committing narcotics crimes or participating in black marketeering and decided to take advantage of the situation by introducing him to Lepilina.

Yatkolenko might have forgotten that Baryte's operational collection file had been examined during the prosecutorial review in 1988. In any case, the materials from that review do not support Yatkolenko's claim that there was agent testimony from Baryte confirming that Lepilina had knowingly accepted narcotics. This suggests that such testimony never existed. In 1993, however, Yatkolenko felt confident that his claim would not be verified because the KGB's agent files had already been destroyed.

The prosecutor, Borodin, wrote a letter to Deputy City Prosecutor Yevgeny Sharygin asking for his 'assistance calling [former KGB operatives] in for questioning', and, as a result, Aleinikov and Nikolaev appeared in his office on 15 December 1993.

Vladimir Aleinikov, who was employed at the time as a consultant for the Saint Petersburg Council for Tourism and Sightseeing, confirmed the official version of events, but unexpectedly revealed a new name:

> as far as I know, Lepilina accepted the narcotics of her own volition; she understood that what she was taking was narcotics, and no one forced her to take them. The individual who gave Lepilina the narcotics was a foreign source. I can note that what happened with Lepilina could not have taken place without the approval of the Leningrad Oblast KGB leadership. As I recall, Azadovsky's operational file (which Lepilina's check had been part of), or, more accurately, the plan that had been worked out in relation to that file, was approved by Oleg Danilovich Kalugin.

Why would one KGB officer so blatantly give up another? The reason is simple, and it is one that was touched upon earlier. Kalugin was – and still is – considered a traitor due to his public criticism of the KGB. He could be used as a scapegoat for practically anything.

In 1993, former division chief in the First Department of the Fifth Directorate Yury Nikolaev was serving as deputy chairman of the board for Rossiya Bank. He, too, confirmed Lepilina's interest in acquiring drugs:

> On the day Lepilina was detained, the foreign source was equipped with a recording device, which recorded Lepilina asking him whether he had brought narcotics for her, i.e., the initiative in receiving the narcotics came from Lepilina, no one forced her to take the narcotics, she understood that what she was acquiring was narcotics.

Finally, it would seem, here was the unassailable proof they needed to show that Lepilina had knowingly accepted narcotics: an audio recording! However, Nikolaev was the only person ever to reference this important piece of 'evidence', and he didn't do so until 1993. There was no audio recording, just as there was no written account from Baryte. If such evidence had ever existed, it would have been referenced in earlier prosecutorial reviews. However, by 1993, all operational files had been destroyed, and so the former operatives felt free to let their imaginations run wild.

A.M. Fyodorovich, formerly of the Fifth Directorate, wasn't questioned due to his serious mental health issues.

17.4 The Supreme Soviet Commission

The final set of documents pertaining to this case was released in summer 1994. It comprised copies of correspondence received by the chair of the RSFSR Supreme Soviet's Commission for the Rehabilitation of Victims of Political Repression; copies were also attached to Azadovsky and Lepilina's criminal case files. It was thanks to these letters that Azadovsky was declared a victim of political repression, and that Lepilina was able to secure a new, unbiased investigation.

The official response Kopylov received from the Security Ministry's Saint Petersburg Directorate to his enquiry of 12 April 1993 offers a summary of Azadovsky's case, and in conclusion states:

> In accordance with the findings of a subsequent internal investigation into the unlawful activities committed against K.M. Azadovsky by operatives of the Leningrad Oblast KGB, a number of operational officers and people in positions of power in the LO KGB were subjected to appropriate disciplinary measures by an order from the directorate's chief issued on 02.02.1989.
>
> K.M. Azadovsky was removed from the operational register of the Saint Petersburg City and Oblast Directorate of the Security Ministry of the Russian Federation on 17.07.1986, when his period of operational surveillance expired. The materials contained in K.M. Azadovsky's operational record file were destroyed in 1990 in conformance with standard USSR KGB regulations regarding retention periods for operational materials at that time.

The fact that we still have the text of this document is significant; when the House of Government was shelled in autumn 1993, many documents related to the 'Kopylov Commission' went up in flames.

This concludes the list of available documents related to the reviews of the Azadovskys' cases conducted by the KGB and Prosecutor's Office. In all likelihood, these materials remain in the archives to this day, along with the materials from other reviews. But what became of the operational files? The ones on Azef, Baryte, Rachmaninoff and Cabin Boy? They were destroyed long ago, in 1990...

18

The aftermath

And so, the archives revealed their secrets. Even now, this seems like an incredible stroke of good luck; in 1994, it felt like a miracle.

Former KGB chairman Vladimir Kryuchkov had seen to it that a significant portion of the KGB archives was destroyed, thus dealing a serious blow to the study of twentieth-century Russian history. In the wake of 1991's August Coup, the KGB began lifting the veil of secrecy surrounding the documents that hadn't been burned, but this moment of transparency was brief. Kryuchkov explains why in his memoirs, which he drafted from a cell in Matrosskaya Tishina Prison, where he was being held for his role in the coup:

> It is no accident that security services around the world keep the operational side of their work a closely guarded secret. Public disclosure of operational secrets could provoke a whole host of questions, raise eyebrows among the uninitiated and lead to serious consequences.

Kryuchkov was absolutely right, and the furore surrounding the publication of the documents surrounding Azadovsky's case proved it.

But these documents were only made public in 1994, which is to say, after the state security archives were closed again. So, how did documents detailing the KGB's operational activities make their way into the papers? This, too, can be attributed to the changes taking place within the country. The former KGB had given copies of these documents to the Prosecutor General's Office; however, by the time the office had completed its review, it didn't know who to return them to. By 1994, the KGB had undergone major structural changes: it had been split into several different agencies. The Prosecutor's Office ought to have returned these documents, but the classified document management system had yet to be restructured, and they couldn't risk returning them to the wrong place. As a result of this confusion, the report from the prosecutorial review was attached to Azadovsky's criminal file, which he had the legal right to read.

In the end, it was these documents that allowed Azadovsky to exonerate himself and to uncover the secret mechanisms that lay behind his case. Such outcomes were incredibly rare.

18.1 'In disguise'

As soon as Yury Shchekochikhin got his hands on the documents related to Lepilina's case, he set about writing another article. On 24 September 1994, *The Literary Gazette* published a long story titled 'In Disguise: Chronicle of a Provocation, 1980–1994'. By this point, Shchekochikhin was a national celebrity: he was particularly well known for his conversations with Gorbachev in 1991.

This article became an important symbol of the individual's victory over the security services. In it, Shchekochikhin describes the KGB's operation and the highhanded behaviour of the courts and prosecution; he appeals to his readers, attempting to convey the senselessness and inhumanity of the Azadovskys' sufferings at the hands of the totalitarian machine. The article closes with a poetic meditation on the case's broader meaning:

> I wanted to end this story with a single demand: that everyone involved in this provocation be charged under the articles of the Criminal Code dealing with offences against public justice (and I request that the Russian Prosecutor General's Office consider this publication grounds for doing so).
>
> But then I realized that this story is not just about how the regime runs roughshod over the individual. No, it is also about the courage this true member of the intelligentsia has displayed through his resistance . . .
>
> But then I thought and I thought, and I decided, 'That's not it!' This story is about something else. It's about love . . . yes, love!
>
> Once upon a time, there was a MAN and a WOMAN. To arrest HIM, they had to arrest HER. During the investigation, SHE incriminated herself by saying that it was HER packet of five grams of hashish that had been found on HIS bookshelf; the poor thing thought that SHE could save HIM that way, not suspecting that HE was the one they were after.
>
> 'My infinitely dear, my good and unhappy [one]. I think of you every day and every hour. No matter how many years they give us, no matter where we are – I will always be with you. If I am released, I will find you right away. Hold on, my darling.'
>
> Konstantin wrote this note in his cell to send to Svetlana in hers. It was intercepted in Leningrad's Kresty [Prison]. And so this note from HIM to HER was left to languish in his criminal file. SHE did not receive it at the time.

18.2 Attempts to bring the guilty parties to justice

The use of fabricated evidence in the Azadovskys' prosecution was a criminal offence, and so Azadovsky, along with several Petersburg-based social agencies, demanded that the government launch an investigation into the circumstances surrounding the cases. Azadovsky already had copies of the KGB's secret documents in his possession when he sent a petition to the Russian Presidential Commission for Human Rights on 26 August 1994.

Azadovsky didn't receive a response right away. First, the petition was redirected to the Prosecutor General's Office, whence it was referred to the Saint Petersburg City Prosecutor's Office; from there, the documents were sent on to the Military Prosecutor's Office, which dealt with cases brought against KGB operatives. Finally, on 20 June 1995, Prosecutor Nikolay Vinnichenko declared that charges would not be brought against the former KGB operatives on the grounds that no crime had been committed.

By the 1990s, criminal investigations into the planting of narcotics, ammunition and other types of evidence were no longer rare; these methods had become common practice within the state security services. But the Prosecutor's Office didn't want to set a precedent. Moreover, some of the Leningrad KGB's former operatives, including those involved in the Azadovsky Affair, had come up in the world: many of them had been promoted, transferred to Moscow and so on.

18.3 Frankfurt International Airport

In response to Shchekochikhin's article, the authorities set in motion a series of events that the journalist Olga Kuchkina described in an article for *The New Daily Gazette*:

> On 16 October 1994, the Petersburg writer and academic Konstantin Azadovsky was approached in Frankfurt International Airport by a man who addressed him in unaccented German, asking him to take a small bundle of medicine to pass along to his sick wife, who lived in Petersburg...
>
> 'Excuse me, as you can see, my hands are full, I can't take your bundle,' he said to the 'German'. His interlocutor insisted: 'Check one of your bags.' 'Then I'll get held up for a long time at the airport; my wife will worry.' And Azadovsky apologized again.
>
> The airport employees rushed him through his document check. As it turned out, he was the last passenger to arrive: they had only been waiting for him. He also found it strange that the man had ignored all the other people getting on the flight, that he had waited for the very last passenger to make his request. Out of the corner of his eye, he saw the 'German' approach two men and say something to them. The aeroplane didn't take off for about a half hour. An impatient passenger asked a flight attendant to find out from the captain what the trouble was. The flight attendant made an announcement: 'It's a technical issue. We're waiting for two passengers; there's been some kind of hold-up with their documents.' But Azadovsky had been the last passenger! A few minutes later, the two men from earlier boarded the aeroplane and walked past Azadovsky without looking at him. They didn't have any luggage. Now there was no doubt in Azadovsky's mind as to what had happened.

In his 19 October 1994 complaint to Acting Prosecutor General Aleksey Ilyushenko and Chief of the Federal Counterintelligence Service (FSK) Sergey Stepashin, Azadovsky wrote,

It is my belief that this action was orchestrated by operatives of the Petersburg FSK or former operatives of the LO KGB who are now employed in different institutions. . . . As the incident in Frankfurt Airport clearly demonstrates, operatives of the former KGB will go to any lengths to physically annihilate, or, at the very least, to compromise me.

At this point, our story begins to veer uncomfortably close to the plot of a spy novel: the insistent stranger, the bundle of 'medicine', the delayed flight, the excruciating wait. . . It was just like something out of a film.

In all likelihood, the bundle contained narcotics in some form, and whether it was powder, pills or marijuana, the result would be the same. A border agent in Frankfurt or Saint Petersburg would politely enquire, 'What have you got in that bundle?' and ask him to open it, whereupon Azadovsky would recount the story of the German and his medicine (so reminiscent of the Spaniard and his headache remedy). Then it would turn out that the two gentlemen who had been having 'trouble with their documents' were prepared to act as witnesses: they hadn't seen any German, but they clearly remembered seeing Azadovsky arrive at the terminal with the bundle in hand ('he was late, he was glancing around nervously. . .'). They could also have arranged an 'anonymous phone call' to the German border agents, tipping them off about a suspicious man carrying a bundle. This would have been a master stroke: a member of the Deutsche Akademie für Sprache und Dichtung with a prior narcotics charge caught red-handed with drugs at Frankfurt International Airport. . .

However, none of this happened. Azadovsky reacted swiftly and sensibly. He had developed street smarts. He had made the long journey from Kresty to Susuman once before, and he had no desire to do so again. And he had particular reason to be vigilant during this time: the anti-terrorism section of the Saint Petersburg FSK was headed by one of his former tormentors, A.V. Kuznetsov.

The response Azadovsky received to his complaint was familiar to the point of tears: it 'had been reviewed and no confirmation was found'. The reply also emphasized that the agency 'strictly abides by the Laws of the Russian Federation'.

On 12 November, while in Munich, Azadovsky appealed to the German Federal Foreign Office, outlining his theory as to why this latest incident had taken place. Then, on 22 November, Lev Kopelev submitted a petition of his own:

> What happened to Azadovsky in Frankfurt Airport was undoubtedly an attempt to pass him narcotics and thus lend credibility to his 1981 conviction, which has since been overturned – to give it fresh momentum, as it were. Back then, it turned out to be a chance acquaintance who had hidden a packet of narcotics on his bookshelf, which was subsequently 'discovered' during a search the next day. It seems that the Frankfurt incident was intended to play out in the same way.

Neither Azadovsky nor Kopelev received an official response. The German intelligence services could have made quick work of such an investigation, but, in all likelihood, they were wary of damaging their relationship with their Russian counterparts.

One thing is relatively certain: this was the final act of the security services' campaign against Azadovsky. Perhaps they received orders to leave him in peace. Or perhaps, as far as Azadovsky was concerned, they finally had decided to 'strictly abide by the Laws of the Russian Federation'.

18.4 Time to stop

Azadovsky had always been a maximalist, and his difficult path – through prison, camp and the battle to restore his good name – had left no room for any indecision or weakness. It was incarceration that taught him to grit his teeth and bear the unbearable; his natural impetuosity gave way to patience. And though, practically speaking, none of the people who ruined the Azadovskys' lives had been called to answer for their actions, Azadovsky couldn't bring himself to give up his life's work.

And life itself wouldn't allow him to let go: it was full of reminders of the past. For example, in the early 2000s, he was informed that his rehabilitation documents were invalid without a duplicate decision issued by the Prosecutor's Office. Once again, Azadovsky was forced to write to the powers that be in an attempt to set things right.

On 15 September 1993, Azadovsky met Boris Yeltsin as part of a delegation of writers. During the dinner that followed, Azadovsky attempted to draw Yeltsin's attention to his case and to the need for lustration[1] more broadly. Marietta Chudakova, who was also present at the meeting, wrote: 'Unmoved by the festivities, K. Azadovsky began speaking emphatically about one of the most outrageous disgraces in Russian life today: [the fact that the KGB operatives] who had put him in a camp still occupied their posts.'

Azadovsky eventually realized the futility of his attempts to bring the former police and KGB operatives to justice. From time to time, though, when new people came to power, he would grit his teeth and start writing again.

His last appeal, dated 1 November 1999, was addressed to Prime Minister Vladimir Putin himself. In it, he recounts his personal saga and requests that his petition be sent to the Prosecutor General's Office, that criminal charges be brought against the former state security operatives who participated in his case, that his petition be personally reviewed and so on and so forth.

It is hard to say what Azadovsky hoped this letter would achieve. It is unlikely that it reached its intended recipient, but it did make its way to the Prosecutor General's Office, whence it was sent to the Saint Petersburg City Prosecutor's Office. There, of course, it was established that Azadovsky's requests to bring these individuals to justice had already been denied on more than one occasion and there was no reason for the Prosecutor's Office to change its position on the matter now.

Azadovsky received this final reply on New Year's Eve: 31 December 1999. The last year of the twentieth century was drawing to a close. It had been a bloody century in Russian history, marked by revolution and by war, by physical and spiritual repression. It had been a century full of human pain and suffering. It was time for Azadovsky to bid it farewell.

It was time for him to enjoy life as a free man. To be a scholar. To spend time with his family, who had endured so many hardships.

But never forget.

And never forgive.

Conclusion

Azadovsky wrote his first academic article at the age of eighteen, on Schiller's early poem 'Rousseau'. This was the first step on his path to becoming a distinguished Germanist, and he regarded it with no small pride, especially when the work was published several years later in the journal *Questions of Literature*. He couldn't help mentioning it when he first met famed literary scholar Boris Eikhenbaum. Eikhenbaum looked at Azadovsky and then said, rather gloomily, 'Well, look, I started with Schiller, too. And no good has come of it.'

What did he mean by this? Was it an example of Eikhenbaum's signature irony, or was it a comment about the danger of studying comparative literature in the USSR during this time? Comparative literature is concerned with finding points of cross-cultural connection; its practitioners must read great works of global literature, study different languages and interact with the people who speak them. In the USSR, such activities were inherently risky. In the second half of the 1940s, during the anti-cosmopolitan campaign, Azadovsky's father and his colleagues had suffered for their refusal to praise all things Russian at the expense of all things foreign. But Konstantin Azadovsky belonged to a generation raised during a period of thaw, and thus saw comparative literature in a completely different light.

The historical changes that began in 1991 affected every area of life, including the humanities: they affected freedom of speech, freedom of assembly, freedom of expression, freedom of movement and freedom of scholarship. In today's Russia, where these freedoms are once again under attack, it is hard to imagine what a fruitful time the 1990s were for humanities scholars.

After making his first trip abroad in 1991, Azadovsky received frequent invitations to visit foreign universities. His contemporaries thought, and not without reason, that he would leave his motherland behind for a cushy professorship in the West; he could have done so on numerous occasions. In the end, though, he decided to remain in Russia. Like many others intoxicated by the new freedoms of the Yeltsin era, Azadovsky was convinced that his country had a bright future ahead. He felt that his own fate was somehow intertwined with that of his country, and so he couldn't bring himself to leave. Today, Azadovsky is known as a prominent literary scholar; few recall that he was once a political prisoner as well.

In the 1990s, Azadovsky became a member of the Deutsche Akademie für Sprache und Dichtung; in the 2000s, he was awarded the Order of Merit of the Federal Republic of Germany, the country's highest honour. He has received numerous European prizes, including the prestigious Friedrich Gundolf Prize for the popularization of German culture abroad. The fact that his work is valued more highly abroad than it is in his native land is fully in keeping with the themes of this book: Azadovsky has always needed Russia, but Russia has never needed him.

* * *

In closing, I would like to say a few words about the time during which the events of this book took place. In his memoir *A Prison Requiem*, music scholar Alfred Mirek (1922–2009) describes the year he spent in Kresty in connection with fabricated criminal charges:

> Folk wisdom holds that, 'sooner or later, the truth will prevail.' And so it does. Folk wisdom is firm in its convictions. But neat phrases usually call for some clarification.
>
> Most people interpret 'sooner' as sometime during the insulted and injured party's lifetime, when they can use what's left of their strength to rehabilitate their reputation and their good name, shaking themselves off and cleansing themselves of all the nastiness and filth they have been ducked in so zealously for so long. That's the ideal 'sooner'. 'Later' is once the person is already gone, and their relatives have washed them clean (literally speaking) for their burial. Their name is 'rehabilitated' timidly, self-consciously, for the most part *en passant*, with declarations of 'it just turned out that way' or, better still, 'that's just the way things were back then.'
>
> It's very convenient to chalk everything up to the times. Especially for those who ought to be given their due for the moral and physical crimes they have committed. But for some reason, all too often, these people continue to enjoy the same respect, profits and happiness as they did before. And their greatest happiness derives from the fact that they are alive and unharmed, while the people they have driven to their graves are unable to come back to haunt them.

These days, it is becoming increasingly difficult to talk about what life in the Soviet Union was actually like. The unquestioned narrative set forth in the 1990s – that the Soviet Union was a totalitarian state throughout its whole existence – has been reduced to an alternative interpretation of events, one that clashes with the views held by today's pro-government historians. The outrageous distortion of Russian history at the hands of Russian historians can only lead to a repetition of past mistakes. After all, the 1980s were also preceded by an era of relative freedom during which the country repudiated the inhumane practices of its Soviet past. In 1956, during the Twentieth Congress of the Communist Party of the Soviet Union, Nikita Khrushchev called for the country to 'completely restore the Leninist principles of Soviet socialist democracy expressed in the Constitution of the Soviet Union, and to do battle against the excesses of those who abuse their power'. At the time, many hoped that the totalitarian era was gone for good.

However, as it turns out, sound bites aren't enough to heal a society's moral rifts, and backsliding is an inevitable feature of any period of change. The Era of Stagnation saw the return of attitudes that had been in vogue a generation earlier: the disregard for individual rights that had run rampant in the 1930s re-emerged in the 1970s and

1980s. The persecutions resumed. The KGB, which was in dire need of reform, if not total abolition, underwent a dramatic expansion instead. At the same time, former KGB chairman Yury Andropov was elected general secretary of the CPSU, giving the agency reason to believe that it was both utterly essential and entirely untouchable. As a result, to quote a 1991 report issued by a parliamentary commission led by Sergey Stepashin, 'the USSR KGB became an independent political force with its own interests and objectively transformed into an institution that was above the government.'

In Azadovsky's case, the KGB acted not so much *above* the government as *outside* it. It was able to send people to prison for political reasons without formally getting involved: it had other government agencies to do its dirty work for it. When discussions took place within the KGB about the need to plant evidence to facilitate the Azadovskys' arrests, these despicable actions were likely cloaked in high-flown language about 'national security', the 'intrigues of Western intelligence services', the 'need to act' and so on. Such conversations resulted in a series of unchecked, unlawful acts against Azadovsky, as well as others like him. Each time this happened, Russian democratic institutions (including the pseudo-democratic institutions of the Soviet era) sustained a serious blow.

This raises an important question: If the KGB was acting outside the law, then why didn't the agencies responsible for the protection of citizens' rights (the courts, the Prosecutor's Office, etc.) attempt to intervene? The answer is obvious: these agencies were all part of a single, merciless organism. The fact that Azadovsky managed to clear his name at all was a happy accident of timing. Had the Soviet regime remained in power, the Azadovskys would still be considered criminals to this day.

It is interesting to consider whether the violations of 'Soviet legal order' that occurred in the Azadovskys' cases were an isolated incident, or whether they were part of something more. The evidence suggests that they were part of an elaborate and officially sanctioned KGB counter-intelligence programme. There was a wave of high-profile arrests among the Leningrad intelligentsia in the early 1980s: Lev Klein, Arseny Roginsky, Mikhail Meilakh and so on. It is extremely hard to believe that the Leningrad KGB would have been able to implement such a complex operation without the knowledge of the national KGB leadership.

The Azadovskys' arrests proved that there was another viable way of getting rid of the USSR's ideological enemies. Charging the intelligentsia with political crimes was a messy and unreliable undertaking; it was much safer and easier to charge them with other offences. This approach came with an added bonus: people who were not officially considered political prisoners often had difficulty rallying support behind their cause. International organizations were hesitant to defend Russian citizens facing criminal (rather than political) charges.

Soon, this tried-and-tested method spread throughout the KGB. In the 1990s, the planting of drugs and ammunition became commonplace. Unfortunately, this method of neutralization remains in use in Russia to this day.

The fact that the Azadovskys were falsely charged with criminal offences is not that unusual. What makes their case so unique is that they eventually managed to expose the conspiracy against them. As Yury Shchekochikhin observes, behind this story 'lie thousands, millions more'. Those stories will not end in consolation or exoneration; they will be buried along with the people who lived them.

But this was not the only chapter in the Azadovskys' story. They have since moved on with their lives.

And yet some things from that period remain with them to this day – not only the bad things, but the good as well. Were it not for this tragedy, would they still be together today? The way they see it, they received their reward long before their official rehabilitation, on that Christmas day in 1981, in frozen Susuman. . .

Notes

Introduction

1 Boris Grebenshchikov (b. 1953) was one of the founding fathers of Russian-language rock music.
2 'Developed socialism', also known as 'real socialism', was a term often used during the Brezhnev era to indicate that the Soviet Union had passed into a more advanced stage of socio-economic development.
3 Comrades' courts were peer-elected, non-professional tribunals that functioned within entities like collective farms, universities and individual blocks of flats. They had the power to try minor offences and mete out punishments including small fines and 'measures of social pressure' (including warnings, reprimands and demanding public apologies).
4 'Era of Stagnation' was a term coined by Mikhail Gorbachev to describe the period spanning roughly from Leonid Brezhnev's rise to power in 1964 to the mid-1980s; the 'stagnation' in question was economic, political and social.
5 The Red Terror (1918–23) was a bloody campaign of political repression waged by the Bolsheviks during the Russian Civil War, targeting those who had been branded as 'class enemies' and 'counterrevolutionaries'.

Chapter 1

1 The Siege of Leningrad (8 September 1941–27 January 1944) was a military blockade of the city by German, Finnish and Spanish troops during the Second World War. Lasting 872 days, the siege resulted in widespread death from starvation and bombardment and has become a powerful symbol of the resilience and bravery of the people of Leningrad.
2 The Great Terror (1936–8), also known as the Great Purge, was a brutal campaign of political oppression under Joseph Stalin.
3 The anti-cosmopolitan campaign (1948–53) targeted Jews in the Soviet Union, persecuting them for their status as 'rootless cosmopolitans'.
4 See note on unofficial culture from the introduction.
5 'Samizdat' (a portmanteau from the Russian *sam*, 'self', and *izdatel'stvo*, 'publishing') is a term used to describe dissident literature clandestinely written, copied and disseminated in the former Soviet Union.
6 See note on comrades' courts from the introduction.
7 Slavinsky had a difficult road ahead of him. He was convicted by the Smolninsky District Court in Leningrad under three articles of the Criminal Code: acquisition

and possession of narcotic substances with intent to sell (224-1), attempts to do the same (5-224-1) and maintenance of a den of debauchery for the use of narcotics (226). He was sentenced to four years in a minimum-security colony, most, but not all, of which he spent in a labour camp. Shortly after his release, he emigrated from the USSR. He spent many years working for the BBC Russian Service in London, where he gained a reputation as one of the station's most colourful correspondents. – P.D.

8   The Moscow Helsinki Group, also known as the Moscow Helsinki Watch Group, was established in 1976 to monitor Soviet compliance with the Helsinki Accords and report Soviet human rights abuses. *A Chronicle of Current Events* was a samizdat periodical in circulation from the late 1960s to the early 1980s; it focused on judicial and human rights violations committed within the Soviet Union. 'Refusenik' was a term used to describe people who were refused permission to emigrate from the Soviet Union, particularly Soviet Jews seeking to emigrate to Israel.

9   In the Soviet Union (as in Russia today), two levels of doctorate degrees were awarded: *kandidat nauk* and *doktor nauk*. The lower of the two degrees is roughly equivalent to a doctorate in many other countries.

Chapter 2

1   'Kostya' is a common Russian nickname derived from the name Konstantin.
2   'Sveta' is a common Russian nickname derived from the name Svetlana.
3   The *druzhina*, or Voluntary People's Guard, was made up of volunteer detachments whose stated aim was to help law enforcement agencies maintain public order. Though formally independent from the police, they often worked alongside them.

Chapter 3

1   Alexander Solzhenitsyn (1918–2008) was a Russian dissident writer best known internationally for *The Gulag Archipelago*, a non-fiction work about Soviet forced labour camps. He was awarded the Nobel Prize in Literature in 1970. Andrey Sakharov (1921–89) was a Russian nuclear physicist and dissident known for his activism for human rights and nuclear disarmament. He won the Nobel Peace Prize in 1975.

2   In autumn 1980, following widespread industrial action, Polish workers formed the independent national trade union Solidarity, with Lech Wałęsa at its head. Soon afterwards, the organization began making political demands. Tensions rose throughout 1981, and in December Prime Minister Wojciech Jaruzelski declared martial law, interning several thousand activists. Opposition to the regime continued to increase; the whole world was watching. In all likelihood, it was the situation in Poland (or, more accurately, the fear that this situation generated) that triggered a wave of repression in the USSR, particularly in 1981–2. – P.D.

3   'The zone' is a term widely used to refer to the Soviet system of corrective labour camps and colonies.

Chapter 4

1. For more information on this topic, see the work of Russian censorship historian Arlen Blyum. – P.D.

Chapter 6

1. In Soviet jurisprudence, a civic accuser was a representative elected by a particular workers' collective to participate in a criminal trial on behalf of the prosecution.

Chapter 7

1. 'Enemy voices' was a term used to refer to foreign radio broadcasts that could be received in the Soviet Union, including stations like Voice of America and Radio Liberty.

Chapter 8

1. *Blatnye* (singular: *blatnoi*) is a slang term used to refer to a subset of inmates who lived by a code of conduct known as the 'thieves' code'. These hardened professional criminals would often prey on petty and political prisoners.
2. The Decembrists were a group of pro-reform noblemen who were either executed or exiled to Siberia for their role in the failed Decembrist Uprising of 1825.
3. *Khimia* (literally, 'chemistry' or 'chemicals') is the unofficial term used to refer to conditional release with mandatory labour. It is discussed in greater detail in Chapter 9.
4. The Neva is the main river that runs through Saint Petersburg.
5. These cities are all associated with the exiled Decembrists.
6. The 'mainland' is a term used in isolated regions like Kolyma to refer to the rest of the country.

Chapter 9

1. 'Svetlana Ivanovna Lepilina' sounds like the name of an ethnically Russian person, while the names 'Zigfrida Tsekhnovitser' and 'Genrietta Yanovskaya' sound markedly Jewish.

Chapter 10

1. The operative unit was in charge of discipline and investigation within corrective facilities.

2 *Valenki* are traditional Russian boots made of felt.
3 *Kutuli* is a Northern Russian dialect word used to refer to a bag packed to the gills.
4 'Svetulik' is an affectionate nickname derived from the name Svetlana.
5 Like Spanish or French, Russian distinguishes between a formal and informal 'you' (*ty* and *vy*, respectively). In this passage, Ensign Teslyuk addresses Azadovsky using the informal *ty* throughout.

Chapter 11

1 The Jackson–Vanik Amendment to the Trade Act of 1974 was a US federal provision designed to exert economic pressure on countries with non-market economies that restricted freedom of emigration.

Chapter 13

1 When a case is dismissed 'in the absence of a crime', the court declares that no crime has been committed. When it is dismissed due to 'insufficient evidence', a crime may have been committed, but there isn't enough evidence to convict someone of it. Azadovsky wants to be found not guilty in the absence of a crime because he wants there to be no question about his innocence.

Chapter 15

1 Russia officially transitioned from the Julian calendar to the Gregorian calendar in early 1918. Thus, dates for historical events that occurred prior to this calendar reform are often given with both 'Old Style' and 'New Style' dates.
2 Though Azadovsky never considered himself a dissident, his efforts to clear his own name earned him a reputation as a human rights advocate.
3 According to the top-secret *Counterintelligence Dictionary* published by the KGB Academy in 1972, an 'operational development file' (DOR) would be 'opened with the goal of exposing, preventing and suppressing hostile activity among individual Soviet citizens when reliable information had been received regarding their criminal acts'.
4 According to the top-secret *Counterintelligence Dictionary* published by the KGB Academy in 1972, an 'operational collection file' was a 'file in which information is collected on foreigners who have come to the USSR from capitalist and developing countries for a period of time (regardless of the length and purpose of their visit) who are of operational interest; this includes individuals who are currently undergoing ideological indoctrination, are being groomed for recruitment, etc.
5 According to the top-secret *Counterintelligence Dictionary* published by the KGB Academy in 1972, an 'operational surveillance file' (DON) would be kept on 'particularly dangerous perpetrators of crimes against the state who have served their sentences and who might, in view of their potential, be of interest to enemies, as well as

on individuals whose history of hostile activity means that they could pose a threat to the Soviet state'.
6   Yevno Azef (1869–1918) was a Russian socialist revolutionary and double agent. He worked for the Okhrana, the Russian Empire's secret police, while simultaneously serving as head of the Socialist Revolutionary Party's terrorist wing.
7   Cultivation (*razrabotka*) was the process whereby the security services would take measures to study a particular subject and achieve specific aims in relation to them. This could include recruiting the subject, compromising them, disrupting hostile activities on their part and so on.
8   Exploitation (*realizatsiia*) was the process whereby the security services acted on information contained within a subject's file in order to bring about an intended effect upon the subject. In Azadovsky's case, this meant putting the pieces into place for his criminal prosecution.

Chapter 17

1   According to the top-secret *Counterintelligence Dictionary* published by the KGB Academy in 1972, a 'group operational cultivation file' (DGOR) would be 'opened with the goal of exposing, preventing and suppressing hostile activity among groups including Soviet citizens as well as foreigners permanently residing in the USSR and stateless persons, when the collective intelligence or other hostile work of such a group has been confirmed by reliable information'.
2   According to the top-secret *Counterintelligence Dictionary* published by the KGB Academy in 1972, 'dangling' was a 'form of agent infiltration into the agent network of a foreign intelligence agency, an anti-Soviet organization at home or abroad, etc., wherein the initiative for making contact with the agent comes from the enemy. The KGB uses available information regarding the enemy's desire to make contact with a particular individual, who, from their point of view, is well positioned to carry out subversive activities (if not now, then in the future).'
3   'S' measures comprised the 'audio monitoring of telephone conversations' – or, in layman's terms, wiretapping. According to the guidance of that time, such measures required approval from the KGB leadership.
4   'D' measures were covert searches.

Chapter 18

1   'Lustration' refers to policies designed to prevent perpetrators of crimes under previous regimes from holding positions of power.

Bibliography

Printed sources in Russian

Abramova, S. P. 'Korotkie vstrechi'. *Mishpokha: istoriko-publitsisticheskii zhurnal* 32 (2013): 128–9.
Alekseeva, V., and E. Vul'fovich. '"Pora bit" trevogu!'. *Novyi amerikanets*, 27 January–2 February 1981, 4.
Amal'rik, A. A. *Zapiski dissidenta*. Moscow: Slovo, 1991.
Ametistov, E. M. 'Neobkhodimo podvesti chertu: Chlen Konstitutsionnogo suda o probleme, podniatoi "LG"'. *Literaturnaia gazeta*, 12 October, 2.
Anisin, N. M. 'Pogrom na Liteinom: "Perestroika" KGB v gorode na Neve'. *Den*, 18–24 October 1992, 4.
Arkhangel'skii, A. N. 'Evgenii Pasternak'. *Radio Ekho Moskvy*, 31 July 2012. Available online: http://echo.msk.ru/blog/archangelsky.
Azadovskii, K. M. 'Homo soveticus'. *Novoe literaturnoe obozrenie* 109 (2011): 343–50.
Azadovskii, K. M. 'Iz "Susumanskikh pesen"'. In *Tret'e zazerkal'e: Al'manakh k semidesiatipiatiletiiu El'gi L'vovny Linetskoi*, 48–51 (unpublished manuscript, 1984), typescript.
Azadovskii, K. M. 'Kak szhigali Serebrianyi vek'. *Literaturnaia gazeta*, 3 November 1993, 6.
Azadovskii, K. M. 'Mezhdu tiur'moi i volei'. *Zvezda* 1 (1994): 36–7.
Azadovskii, K. M. '"Ne obmanites" / Svoi vzgliad'. *Nevskoe vremia*, 3 September 1991, 3.
Azadovskii, K. M., and A. V. Lavrov. 'Pamiati D. E. Maksimova (1904–1987)'. In *Valerii Briusov i ego korrespondenty*, 583–91. Literaturnoe nasledstvo, vol. 98, no. 2. Moscow: Nauka, 1994.
Bakatin, V. V. *Izbavlenie ot KGB*. Moscow: Novosti, 1992.
Baltsvinik, M. A. *Zdes' khorosho, khotia s pogodoi mne ne povezlo . . . : Stikhi, pis'ma, fotografii. Vospominaniia sovremennikov*. Edited by B.Ia. Frezinskii. Saint Petersburg: Bel'veder, 2006.
Belinskii, A. N. 'Vspominaia Valentina Pikulia'. *Topos: Literaturno-filosofskii internet-zhurnal*, 29 February 2009. Available online: https://www.topos.ru/article/6143.
Belov, V. A. '"Perm'-36. Pravda i lozh", ch. 11'. *Sut' vremeni*, 18 April 2013. Available online: http://eotperm.ru/?p=1297.
Bezrodnyi, M. '"Delo" Konstantina Azadovskogo'. In *Mucheniki terror*, edited by Z. Dicharov, 15–20. Raspiatye: Pisateli – zhertvy politicheskikh repressii, vol. 5. Saint Petersburg: Izdatel'stvo "Russko-Baltiiskii informatsionnyi tsentr BLITs", 2000.
Blium, A. V. *Kak eto delalos' v Leningrade: Tsenzura v gody ottepeli, zastoia i perestroiki, 1953–1991*. Saint Petersburg: Akademicheskii proekt, 2005.
Bobkov, F. D. *Poslednie dvadtsat' let: Zapiski nachal'nika politicheskoi kontrrazvedki*. Moscow: Russkoe slovo, 2006.
Brodskii, I. 'Arest Konstantina Azadovskogo'. *Russkaia Mysl*, 15 January 1981, 3.
Brodskii, I. 'Zaiavlenie Iosifa Brodskogo'. *Novyi amerikanets*, 26 July–1 August 1981, 10.
Brodskii, I. and S. Dovlatov, et al. 'Pisateliam, liudiam iskusstva, uchenym!'. *Novyi amerikanets*, 14–20 January 1981, 4.

Bukovskii, V. K. *I vozvrashchaetsia veter* . . . Moscow: Novoe izdatel'stvo, 2007.
Chaika, E., and T. Bespokoeva. 'V gostiakh u skazki, ili Otkrytoe pis'mo kandidatu v gubernatory Arkhangel'skoi oblasti Pavlu Pozdeevu'. *Severnyi komsomolets* 24 (1996): 7.
Chakovskaia, A. E. 'Liberal'nye tendentsii v pechati v epokhu zastoia, 1980–1985 gg. (na materialakh "Literaturnoi gazety")'. PhD diss., MGU, Moscow, 2008.
Churbanov, Iu. M. 'Ekzamen na professional'nuiu zrelost'. *K novoi zhizni: Ezhemesiachnyi zhurnal MVD SSSR dlia rabotnikov ITU* 1 (1980): 2–6.
Dediulin, S. V. [D.D.] '"Delo Konstantina Azadovskogo": Vecher v Dome pisatelia'. *Russkaia mysl*, 20 October 1989, 10.
Dediulin, S. V. [S.D.] 'Glavnym delom ego zhizni byli poiski i sokhranenie materialov po istorii kul'tury Rossii'. *Russkaia mysl*, 29 January 1981, 5.
Dediulin, S. V. '"Literaturnoe nasledstvo" i delo K. Azadovskogo / "My zhivem v vek iubileev"'. *Russkaia Mysl*, 4 June 1981, 6.
'Delo Konstantina Azadovskogo'. *Russkaia Mysl*, 26 February 1981, 6.
Demidov, E. 'Esli vy nachal'nik . . .'. *K novoi zhizni: Ezhemesiachnyi zhurnal MVD SSSR dlia rabotnikov ITU* 1 (1978): 8–11.
Dovlatov, S. 'Nastuplenie na intelligentsiiu prodolzhaetsia'. *Novyi amerikanets*, 14–20 January 1981, 4.
Dovlatov, S. *Rech' bez povoda . . . ili Kolonki redaktora*. Moscow: Makhaon, 2006.
Druskin, L. S. 'U nikh rabota takaia'. In *Spasennaia kniga: Vospominaniia leningradskogo poeta*, 367–74. London: Overseas Publications Interchange, Ltd., 1984.
Druian, B. G. 'Tom agatovyi'. *Voprosy literatury* 6 (2012): 387–426.
'Ekho odnogo protsessa'. *Sovershenno sekretno* 7 (December 1989): 10–11, 23.
El'zon, M. D. 'Avtobibliografiia (s primechaniiami) (1964–2000)'. Edited by N. Tarasova and A. Reitblat. *Novoe literaturnoe obozrenie* 2, no. 90: 173–206.
Etkind, E. G. *Zapiski nezagovorshchika. Barselonskaia proza*. Saint Petersburg: Akademicheskii proekt, 2001.
Feiginzon, M. S. '"Piat" stikhotvorenii ottsa'. Edited by Ol'ga Arkad'eva. *Mishpokha: istoriko-publitsisticheskii zhurnal* 32 (2013): 125–7.
Galushkina, A.Iu., ed. '"Literaturnoe nasledstvo": Stranitsy istorii. Iz arkhiva S.A. Makashina (K 80-letiiu osnovaniia izdaniia)'. *Russkaia literatura* 2 (2011): 63–98.
Gamper, G. S. 'Na ochnoi stavke s proshlym . . .' *Koshachii iashchik*, 6 December 2001. Available online: http://www.pereplet.ru/kot/39.html.
Gasparov, B. M. 'Poteriannoe pokolenie uchenykh'. *Novoe russkoe slovo*, 3 September 1981. (Reprinted in *Russkaia mysl*, 15 October 1981, 7.)
'Georgii Mikhailov v ssylke'. *Russkaia mysl*, 30 July 1981, 6.
Ginkas, K. M., and G. N. Ianovskaia. 'Istoriia Kosti Azadovskogo'. In *Chto eto bylo? Razgovory s Natal'ei Kaz'minoi i bez nee*, 197–215. Moscow: ART, 2014.
Gordin, Ia. A. *Pushkin. Brodskii. Imperiia i sud'ba*. Moscow: Vremia, 2016.
Gordin, Ia. A. *Rytsar' i smert', ili Zhizn' kak zamysel: O sud'be Iosifa Brodskogo*. Moscow: Vremia, 2010.
Goricheva, T. M. '"Ia ne mogu chernoe nazvat' belym!"': K protsessu nad Natal'ei Lazarevoi'. *Russkaia mysl*, 5 February 1981, 6.
Grazhdanskii kodeks RSFSR. Ofitsial'nyi tekst s prilozheniem postateino-sistematizirovannykh materialov. S izmeneniiami i dopolneniiami na 1 dekabria 1975 g. Moscow: Iuridicheskaia literatura, 1976.
Iasnov, M., ed. *El'ga L'vovna Linetskaia: Materialy k biografii. Iz literaturnogo naslediia. Vospominaniia. Bibliografiia. Fotodokumenty*. Saint Petersburg: Simpozium, 1999.
Iliukhin, V. I. *Vozhdi i oborotni*. Moscow: Paleia, 1994.

Internal KGB Circular. 'Instruktsiia po uchetu v organakh Komiteta gosudarstvennoi bezopasnosti pri Sovete Ministrov SSSR ugolovnykh del i lits, privlechennykh po nim k ugolovnoi otvetstvennosti. Sekretno; prilozhenie k prikazu Predsedatelia KGB pri SM SSSR'. Issued by Iu. V. Andropov. no. 0454, 9 August 1977.

Ivanov, B. I., and B. M. Varfolomeev, eds. *Skhvatka: Povesti o chekistakh*. Leningrad: Lenizdat, 1987.

Ivanov, V. A., and E. V. Dolgopolova. 'Leningradskii gorodskoi sud vo vtoroi polovine 1940-kh – nachale 1990-kh godov'. In *Rossiia v XX veke: chelovek i vlast': Sbornik statei*, edited by M. V. Khodiakov, 224–59. Saint Petersburg: Izdatel'stvo SPbGU, 2013.

'K takoi registratsii Sovet tserkvei ne prizyval'. *Bratskii listok* 4/5 (1979): 1–2.

Kaminskaia, D. I. *Zapiski advokata*. Moscow: Novoe izdatel'stvo, 2009.

Katerli, N. I. 'Vtoraia zhizn'. *Zvezda* 9 (2005): 11–79.

Katerli, N. I. 'KGB rukami militsii. (Delo Azadovskogo)'. In *KGB: vchera, segodnia, zavtra / V Mezhdunarodnaia konferentsiia, 11–13 fevralia 1995*, edited by L. Isakova, E. Oznobkina and A. Banketov, 142–7. Moscow: Obshchestvennyi fond "Glasnost'", 1996.

Katerli, N. I. 'Kto takie "druz'ia naroda"'. *Moskovskie novosti*, 13 December 1992, 3.

Katerli, N. I. 'Rasprava'. *Vechernii Peterburg*, 27 Octover 1994, 3.

'"Khartiia Penklubov soderzhit nepremlemye dlia sovetskikh literatorov polozheniia"/ Dokumenty svidetel'stvuiut: Iz fondov Tsentra Khraneniia Sovremennoi Dokumentatsii'. *Voprosy literatury* 1 (1996): 224–39.

Kheifets, M. R. 'Mesto i vremia'. In vol. 1 of *Kheifets M.R. Izbrannoe. V 3-kh tt*. Kharkiv: Folio, 2000.

Klein, L. S. *Perevernutyi mir*. 2nd edn. Donetsk: Farn, 2010.

Klein, L. S. *Trudno byt' Kleinom: Avtobiografiia v datakh i monologakh*. Saint Petersburg: Nestor-Istoriia, 2010.

'Kniga – istochnik znanii'. *Gorniak Severa*, 26 Maia 1981, 4.

Kononova, N. [Sharymova, N.Ia.]. 'Delo Konstantina Azadovskogo / Press-agentstvo "Zashchita"', *Novyi amerikanets*, 26 July–1 August 1981, 10–11.

Kopelev, L. '"Ne pokladat' oruzhiia slova . . .": Rech' na tseremonii vrucheniia Premii Mira Nemetskogo obshchestva knigotorgovli vo Frankfurte 18 oktiabria 1981'. *Russkaia mysl*, 5 November 1981, 8–9.

Kopelev, L., and R. Orlova. 'Zaiavleniia L'va Kopeleva i Raisy Orlovoi'. *Russkaia Mysl*, 19 February 1981, 12.

Kopylov, A. T. 'Vozvrashchennye imena / V komissiiakh Verkhovnogo Soveta'. *Rossiiskaia gazeta*, 6 August 1993, 2.

Kopylov, A. T., and E. A. Zaitsev. 'Unizhali bezzakoniem. A teper' – zakonom?'. *Rossiiskaia gazeta*, 18 September 1992, 2.

Krakhmal'nik, L. G., and N. A. Struchkov, eds. *Sovetskoe ispravitel'no-trudovoe zakonodatel'stvo: Sistematizirovannyi tekst Osnov ispravitel'no-trudovogo zakonodatel'stva Soiuza SSR i soiuznykh respublik . . .* Moscow: VNII MVD SSSR, 1979.

Krasavchenko, T. N. 'Vospriiatie Rossii i russkikh v angliiskoi literature na rubezhe XX–XXI vekov'. *Novye rossiiskie gumanitarnye issledovaniia* 3 (2008). Available online: http://www.nrgumis.ru/articles/134/

Kriuchkov, V. A. *Lichnoe delo*. Moscow: Eksmo, 2003.

Kublanovskii, Iu. M. 'K arestu Mikhaila Meilakha (12 iiulia, Parizh)'. *Russkaia mysl*, 14 July 1983.

Kuchkina, O. A. 'Voz'mite professora v operativnuiu razrabotku: Konstantin Azadovskii obrashchaetsia k meru Sobchaku s trebovaniem ogradit' ego ot bespredela FSB / Spetssluzhby'. *Novaia ezhednevnaia gazeta* 28 September–4 October 1995, 4.

Kudrova, I. V. *Proshchanie s morokoi*. Saint Petersburg: Kriga, 2013.
Kupchenko, V. P. *Dvadtsat' let v dome M.A. Voloshina, 1964-1983: Vospominaniia, dnevniki, pis'ma*, edited by R. P. Khruleva. Kyiv: Bolero, 2013.
Kuz'minskii, K. K., and G. Kovalev. 'Tezka Azadovskii'. In vol. 4-1 of *U Goluboi Laguny: Antologiia noveishei russkoi literatury*, 521. Newtonville, MA: Oriental Research Partners, 1983.
Lavrov, A. V. 'O Dmitrii Sergeeviche Likhacheve'. In *Dmitrii Likhachev i ego epokha: Vospominaniia, esse, dokumenty, fotografii*, edited by E. Vodolazkin, 111-13. Saint Petersburg: Logos, 2002.
Lebedev, V. 'Zhizn' vo slavu universiteta'. *Pedagogicheskie vesti* 11 (November 2001): 2.
'Leningradskaia militsiia obviniaet KGB'. *Russkaia Mysl*, 18 November 1988, 6.
Losev, L. V. *Iosif Brodskii: Opyt literaturnoi biografii*. Moscow: Molodaia gvardiia, 2008.
Lur'e, L.Ia. 'Andropovskii zazhim'. *Zvezda* 4 (2000): 230-3.
Maramzin, V. '23 dekabria v Leningrade arestovan Konstantin Azadovskii (9 ianvaria, Parizh)'. *Russkaia Mysl*, 15 January 1981, 3.
Materialy Samizdata / Arkhiv Samizdata. Radio Svoboda. B.m., vyp. no. 30/83, 22 July 1983, [po delu Azadovskogo:] AS 5000-5010.
Meilakh, M. B. 'O Sofii Viktorovne Poliakovoi'. In *Trudy VI Mezhdunarodnoi letnei shkoly na Karel'skom pereshejke po russkoi literature*, edited by A. Balakin et al., 173-85. Poselok Poliany (Uusikirko) Leningradskoi oblasti: Institut russkoi literatury RAN, 2010.
'Mikhail: Nadezhda Grigor'eva beret interv'iu u Mikhaila Meilakha'. *Zvezda* 8 (2002): 236-8.
Mikhel'son, S. V. 'Ogovor'. *Leningradskii rabochii*, 10 November 1989, 12-13.
Mikhel'son, S. V. 'Sindrom donositel'stva / Vozvrashchaias' k napechatannomu'. *Leningradskii rabochii*, 13 April 1990, 6.
Mirek, A. M. *Turemnyi rekviem: Zapiski zakliuchennogo*. Moscow: Prava Cheloveka, 1997.
Morozova, N. A. *Anatomiia otkaza*. Moscow: RGGU, 2011.
Mosiakin, A. G. *Strasti po Filonovu: Sokrovishcha, spasennye dlia Rossii*. Saint Petersburg: Amfora, 2014.
Murin, Iu. G. 'Dvadtsat' tsentov za gostainu: Arkhiv generala Volkogonova okazalsia v SSHA...'. 14. *Sovershenno sekretno* 1 (2008): 14.
'Nagrady - zhurnalistam. / Soobshchenie LenTASS'. *Leningradskaia pravda*, 5 May 1990, 3.
Naiman, A. G. *Rasskazy o Anne Akhmatovoi*. Moscow: Khudozhestvennaia literatura, 1989.
Nikitchenko, V. F., ed. *Kontrrazvedyvatel'nyi slovar'*. Moscow: Naucho-izdatel'skii otdel Vysshei krasnoznamennoi shkoly KGB ot SM SSSR im. F. E. Dzerzhinskogo, 1972.
'O sovershenstvovanii izdatel'skoi deiatel'nosti Akademii'. *Vestnik Akademii nauk SSSR* 2 (1982): 16-25.
'"Oni radi imeni Ego poshli, ne vziavshi nichego"'. *Bratskii listok* 5 (1981): 2.
Orlov, I. B. 'Biuro mezhdunarodnogo molodezhnogo turizma "Sputnik": mezhdu "Stsilloi ideologii" i "Kharibdoi pribyli"'. *Problemy rossiiskoi istorii* 10 (2010): 142-54.
Peshkov, A. P. 'Voennaia taina polkovnika Pozdeeva'. *Pravda Severa*, 3 December 1996, 3.
Podrabinek, A. P. *Dissidenty*. Moscow: AST, 2014.
Podrazhaite vere ikh: 40 let probuzhdennomu bratstvu, 1961-2001. Moscow: Izdanie Soveta tserkvei EKHB, 2001.
Radi bezopasnosti strany: Sbornik khudozhestvennykh proizvedenii o deiatel'nosti sovremennykh chekistov. Leningrad: Lenizdat, 1985.
'Rasplata neminuema / Proisshestviia'. *Vechernii Leningrad*, 5 June 1969, 4.

'Rasstreliannoe pokolenie prosit poshchady: Interv'iu Ol'gi Karlovoi s A. T. Kopylovym'. *Rossiiskaia gazeta*, 26 February 1993, 1–2.
'Razgovor o poezii'. *Gorniak Severa*, 25 April 1981, 2.
'Rezoliutsiia'. In *KGB: vchera, segodnia, zavtra / V Mezhdunarodnaia konferentsiia, 11–13 fevralia 1995*, 142–7. Moscow: Obshchestvennyi fond "Glasnost'". 1996.
Rezunkov, V. '"Memorial": pis'mo k El'tsinu ushlo, no rano poluchat' pozdravleniia'. *Chas pik*, 7 December 1992, 3.
Ronkin, V. E. *Na smenu dekabriam prikhodiat ianvari . . .: Vospominaniia byvshego brigadmil'tsa i podpol'shchika, a pozzhe politzakliuchennogo i dissidenta*. Moscow: Zven'ia, 2003.
Sakharov, A. D. *Vospominaniia*. Vol. 1. Edited by E. S. Kholmogorova and Iu. A. Shikhanovich. Moscow: Prava cheloveka, 1996.
Seliverstov, K. L. 'Rozhdestvo pod shkonkoi'. In *V "Krestakh": K 100-letiiu Peterburgskoi odinochnoi tiur'my*. Special issue, *Peterburgskii literator* 10–11 (1993): 12.
Severiukhin, D.Ia. 'Samizdat Leningrada 1950-e –1980-e: Opyt literaturnoi entsiklopedii'. In *Pravo na imia: Biografika KHKH veka. Chtenie pamiati Veniamina Iofe. Izbrannoe, 2003–2012*, 572–9. Saint Petersburg: Nauchno-informatsionnii tsentr 'Memorial', 2013.
Shchekochikhin, Iu. P. 'Delo obraztsa vos'midesiatykh / Rassledovanie "LG"'. *Literaturnaia gazeta*, 9 August 1989, 13.
Shchekochikhin, Iu. P. and G. B. Raby. 'Riazhenye: Khronika odnoi provokatsii: 1980 – 1994 / Rassledovanie "LG"'. *Literaturnaia gazeta*, 28 September 1994, 13.
Shchekochikhin, Iu. P. and G. B. Raby. *XX vek. Religiia predatel'stva*. Samara: Federov, 1999.
Shchelokov, N. A. 'Sveriaia s vremenem dela svoi'. *Vospitanie i pravoporiadok* 1 (1982): 2–6.
Sheinis, V. L. 'Poezdka v gorod Chekhov. Potaennye arkhivy'. In *Vzlet i padenie Parlamenta: Perelomnye gody v rossiiskoi politike (1985–1993)*, 619–30. Moscow: Izdatel'stvo R. Elinina, 2005.
Shmidt, Iu. M. 'Kommentarii iurista'. *Vechernii Peterburg*, 27 October 1994, 3.
Shneerson, M. A. 'Chelovek i bezzakonie'. *Novyi amerikanets*, 26 July–1 August 1981, 11.
Shul'ts, V. '"Nemetskoe delo" v Estonii'. *Heimat – Rodina: Novaia ezhemesiachnaia gazeta* 47 (2006). Available online: https://berkovich-zametki.com/Nomer35/Slosman1.htm.
Slosman, Il'ia. 'Leningradskoe "samoletnoe" delo. Versii Butmana i Chernoglaza'. *Zametki po evreiskoi istorii: Setevoi zhurnal evreiskoi istorii, traditsii, kul'tury* 1 (2015). Available online: https://www.berkovich-zametki.com/2015/Zametki/Nomer1/Slosman1.php.
Sokolov, A. A. *Anatomiia predatel'stva: "Superkrot" TSRU v KGB: 35 let shpionazha generala Olega Kalugina*. 2nd edn. Moscow: Proekt Liubianka, 2005.
'Soobshchaiut'. *Russkaia Mysl*, 1 January 1981, 5.
Stepankov, V. K., and E. K. Lisov. *Kremlevskii zagovor*. Moscow: Ogonek, 1992.
Sukharev, A.Ia. 'Garantirovano zakonom: Pervyi zamestitel' ministra iustitsii SSSR A.Ia. Sukharev otvechaet na voprosy spetsial'nogo korrespondenta "Literaturnoi gazety" V. Aleksandrova'. *Literaturnaia gazeta*, 27 October 1976, 10.
Sukharev, A.Ia. 'Otvety na voprosy po povodu vydvizheniia ego kandidatury na post General'nogo prokurora SSSR, 8 iiunia 1989'. In vol. 3 of *Pervyi s"ezd narodnykh deputatov SSSR, 25 maia – 9 iiunia 1989 g.: Stenograficheskii otchet*, 175–204. Moscow: Verkhovnyi sovet, 1989.
Sukharev, A.Ia. 'Pravovoe vospitanie trudiashchikhsia v razvitom sotsialisticheskom obshchestve'. PhD diss., Akademiia obshchestvennykh nauk pri TSK KPSS, Moscow, 1978.

Tonkov, E. N. 'Porcha chelovecheskaia'. *Leningradskii universitet*, 6 October 1989, 8–9.
Toporov, V. 'Delo Azadovskogo'. In *Dvoinoe dno: Priznaniia skandalista*, 293–324. Moscow: AST, 1999.
Vasil'ev, G., and R. German. '"Uzniki sovesti"? Net, liudi bez chesti!'. *K novoi zhizni: Ezhemesiachnyi zhurnal MVD SSSR dlia rabotnikov ITU* 1 (1979): 67–9.
Vasil'eva, I. 'Zasedenie kluba'. *Gorniak Severa* 90 (1982): 2.
'Vesti iz SSSR: Po materialam biulletenia K. Liubarskogo (no. 9 – 12)'. *Russkaia Mysl*, 23 July 1981.
Vin'kovetskaia, D. *Ekho vyklikaet imena. Iakov. Iosif. Boris. Sergei. Igor'*... Saint Petersburg: Fond russkoi poezii, 2015.
Zhmaev, A. M. *Tuda i obratno: Retrospektivnyi dnevnik*. Edited by T.Ia. Zhmaeva. Saint Petersburg: ADIA-M + DEAN, 1995.
Zhogin, N. V., ed. *Rukovodstvo dlia sledovatelei / Prokuratura SSSR. Vsesoiuznyi institut po izucheniiu prichin i razrabotki mer preduprezhdeniia prestupnosti*. Moscow: Iuridicheskaia literatura, 1971.
Zil'bershtein, I. S., and L. M. Rozenblium. 'Novoe o Bloke / 100 let so dnia rozhdeniia A. Bloka'. *Literaturnaia gazeta*, 26 November 1980, 5.
Zil'bershtein, I. S., and L. M. Rozenblium 'Ot redaktsii'. In *Aleksandr Blok: Novye materialy i issledovaniia*, 5–7. Literaturnoe nasledstvo, vol. 92, no. 2. Moscow: Nauka, 1980.
Zolotarev, Iu. T. 'Uptar posle GULAGa'. In *Na Severe Dal'nem*, 83–140. Magadan: MAOBTI, 2003.
Zubarev, D. I.., and G. V. Kuzovkin, eds. *Dokumenty Moskovskoi Khel'sinkskoi gruppy, 1976–1982*. Moscow: Moskovskaia Hel'sinkskaia Gruppa, 2006.
Zviagintsev, A. G. *Rudenko: General'nyi prokuror SSSR*. Moscow: Olma Media Grupp, 2012.

Printed sources in other languages

Andersen, H. [Leander]. 'Et par borgerlige ord...'. *Morgenavisen Jyllands-Posten*, 28 January 1981, 3.
'Arrestation d'un universitaire à Leningrad'. *Le Monde*, 7 January 1981, 3.
'Azadovskij arrestato a Leningrado'. *La Repubblica*, 8 January 1981, 10.
Bäckström, A. 'Rysk litteraturforskare arresterad'. *Uppsala Nya Tidningen*, 11 February 1981, 10.
Bjervig, N., P. A. Jensen, P. U. Møller, and L. T. Schacke. 'Politick fængsling'. *Vestkysten*, 21 January 1981, 5.
Bjervig, N., P. A. Jensen, P. U. Møller, and L. T. Schacke 'Sovjetforsker fængsling'. *Aalborg Stiftstidende*, 23 January 1981, 6.
Bjervig, N., P. A. Jensen, P. U. Møller, and L. T. Schacke 'Sovjetforsker offer for kampagne'. *Kristeligt Dagblad*, 20 January 1981, 5.
Brodsky, J. 'The Azadovsky Affair'. *The New York Review of Books* 28, no. 15 (1981): 49.
Deduline, S. 'Bibliographie des travaux de K. M. Azadovskij'. *Cahiers du monde russe et soviétique* 22, no. 2–3 (1981): 339–42.
Deduline, S. 'Complément là bibliographie des travaux de K. M. Azadovskij'. *Cahiers du monde russe et soviétique* 22, no. 1 (1982): 117–18.
'Der sowjetische Rilkeforscher Konstanin M. Azadovskij (Eine Dokumentation.) / Zusammengestellt von Joachim W. Storck'. *Blätter der Rilke-Gesellschaft* 9 (1982): 79–92.

'"Die Polen sind ein grossartiges Volk": Der ausgebürgerte Sowjet-Schriftsteller Lew Kopelew über Dissidenten, die Sowjet-Union und Polen'. *Spiegel Gespräch*, 26 January 1981, 112–14.
Elliott, G., and H. Shukman. *Secret Classrooms: An Untold Story of the Cold War*. London: St Ermin's Press, 2002.
Galeotti, Mark. 'A Glossary of Russian Police & Security Service Acronyms and Abbreviations'. Available online: http://web.archive.org/web/20050827052500/http://www.keele.ac.uk/depts/hi/resources/modern%20resources/PoliceGlossary-v3.pdf.
Ingold, F.Ph. 'If. K. M. Asadowski in Haft'. *Neue Züricher Zeitung*, 8 January 1981, 33.
Kopelew, L. 'Hinterlist der Gewalt / Lew Kopelew fordert "Helft Arsenij Roginskij!"'. *Die Welt*, 23 October 1981, 19.
'Kopelew: Wir glauben an Russlands Zukunft'. *Süddeutsche Zeitung*, 24–25 January 1981, 49.
'Leningrader Germanist verhaftet'. *Die Zeit*, 16 January 1981, 2.
Livingstone, A., et al. 'Plea for convicted Soviet scholar / Letters to the editor'. *The Times*, July 13 1981, 11.
Ljunggren, M. 'Am arresteringen av litteraturvetaren Asadovskij: Så försvinner orden, bilderna, människan i maktens gömmor'. *Expressen*, 11 February 1981, 4.
Mitrokhin, Vasili. *KGB Lexicon: The Soviet Intelligence Officer's Handbook*. London: Routledge, 2002.
'P.E.N. Soviet Center: Mr. Morgan's warning of "Infiltration"'. *The Times*, 15 June 1955, 7.
'Rilke-Forscher verhaftet wegen Auslandskontakten?'. *Der General-Anzeiger*, 12 January 1981, 9.
Scammell, M. 'Soviet Professor Says Drug Was Planted on Him'. *The Times*, 31 March 1981, 7.
Scammell, M. 'The Azadovsky Case'. *The New York Review of Books* 29, no. 6 (1982): 35–6.
'Sowjetischer Germanist in Leningrad verhaftet'. *Die Welt*, 9 January 1981, 15.
'Sowjetischer Germanist verhaftet'. *Der Tagesspiegel*, 9 January 1981, 15.
Spangenberg, K. 'Dansk protest mod forfølgelse af Sovjet-forfattere: Brev til den sovjetiske forfatterforening'. *Politiken*, 2 March 1981, 4.
Spangenberg, K. 'Sovjet-afviger i fængsel efter hash-dom . . .'. *Politiken*, 21 March 1981, 3.
Spangenberg, K. 'Strenge straffe til Sovjet-afvigere'. *Politiken*, 22 January 1981, 2.
Sperling, V. 'Litteraturforskeren Azadovskij idømt to år. Hans indsats i sovjetisk pragtværk om Blok fjernet i korrekturen'. *Information*, 20 March 1981, 6.
Thomsen, J. 'Danske forskeres ven i Leningrad anholdt'. *Berlingske Tidende*, 27 January 1981, 5.
'Verzeichnis der Arbeiten über Rainer Maria Rilke von Konstantin Markovic Azadovskij / Zusammengestellt von Joachim W. Storck'. *Blätter der Rilke-Gesellschaft* 9 (1982): 93–4.

Index

NOTE: Page references in *italics* refer to illustrations; page numbers followed by n. indicates notes.

Admoni, Vladimir 56
Akhmatova, Anna 7, 10, 25, 175
Aleinikov, V.P. 217–20, 223–6
Alekseev, Mikhail 39
Amalrik, Andrey 105, 136
Andropov, Yuri 54, 153–4, 205, 237
anti-cosmopolitan campaign 7, 27, 78, 154, 235, 239 n.3
anti-Soviet literature 161–3, 206, 212, 213, 223
Ardis (publishing house) 46
Arkhipov, Viktor Ivanovich 167, 168, 193, 211, 216, 218–20, 222–4
 and Azadovsky's retrial 173–4, 178, 180–2, 186, 192, 212
 explanatory report of 222–4
Artsibushev, Oleg Nikolaevich
 and Azadovsky's retrial 173–4, 176–9, 181, 186, 192, 206–7
 participation in Azadovsky's house search 18–23, 164, 207, 211, 223
 participation in Lepilina's detention 16, 44
 statement during prosecutorial review 168
Austria 166, 210
Azadovsky, Konstantin Markovich
 (newfound) academic fame 86–7
 access to legal counsel 31–3
 arrest of 21–3
 awards, prizes and memberships 74, 235–6
 bibliography 86–7
 career of 12–13, 58–61, 71–2, 86–7, 165, 185–6, 235–6
 certificate of release *127*, 157
 closing speech at retrial 182–3
 during court recess *130–1*

 and East German tourists 114
 education of 8–9, 11
 emigration 164–5
 family history of 7–8, 89
 friends and associates of (*see* friends and associates)
 interpersonal conflicts of 27, 35
 memories of Kresty Prison 30
 'non-conformity' of 13
 portraits of *116*, *118*, *128–9*
 prison photo of *121*
 rehabilitation 199–201
 return to academia 159, 191
 works of 8, 12, 71–2, 84, 86–7, 185
Azadovsky, Mark Konstantinovich
 (father) 7–8, 55, 71, 78, 80, 89, 90, 101, 235
Azadovsky Defence Committee 73–8
Azadovsky retrial 41, 173–4
 July 19 1988 proceedings 174–8
 July 20 1988 proceedings 178–80
 Aug 11 1988 proceedings 180–1
 Aug 12 1988 proceedings 181–4
 judgement 183–4
 possibility of 162
Azadovsky trial
 appeal 90–4
 Kheifets's refusal to represent Azadovsky 38–9
 proceedings of 64–9
 separation of Lepilina and Azadovsky cases 28, 31, 37, 66, 174, 182

Babushkina, L.N. 50
Bäckström, Annika 81–2
Baklanov, Grigory 170
Baltsvinik, Mikhail, photograph collection of 25–6, 56, 215
Barnes, Christopher 84

'Baryte'. See 'Hassan'/'Baryte'
Belkin, Anatoly 116
Belyaev, Albert 72
Berkovsky, Naum 8–9
Bezverkhov, Yury Alekseevich 56, 167, 185, 212, 218–20, 224
  explanatory report of 221–2
blatnye 94, 135, 137, 138, 145–6, 241 n.1
Bleer, Vladilen 196, 205–7
Blok, Alexander 12, 25, 72, 84
Bobkov, Filipp 54
Boborykin, Alexander 10–12
Bobov, V.Ia. 50, 163, 173–4
Böll, Heinrich 74, 86, 166
books and photograph collection
  KGB's interest in and destruction of 56, 166, 167, 212, 215, 222
  loss of/missing 160–3, 168, 176
  seizure of 19–20, 25–6, 45–7, 185, 192, 206, 223, 224
Borisov, L.K. 213
Borodin, Alexander M. 202, 225, 226
Breiman, Ilya Mikhailovich 40–2, 44, 179, 202
Brodsky, Joseph 4, 8, 33, 46, *119*, *133*
  support for Azadovsky 73–8, 86
Brun, Lidia Vladimirovna (Azadovsky's mother) 7, 89, 95, 99–101, 104, 106–8, *119*, 140, 149, 157, 160
  appeals of 90
  death of 165–6
Bukhshtab, Boris 27, 149
Bukovsky, Vladimir 31–2, 40–1, 51, 83
Burikhin, Igor 46
Burnett, Leon 84
Bystrov, V.I. 20, 164, 174, 181, 192, 223. *See also* Arkhipov, Viktor Ivanovich

'Cabin Boy' 220, 221, 227
Cahiers du monde russe et soviétique 87
censorship 45–7, 54, 71–2, 98–9, 101, 102, 106, 161–2, 241 n.1.
  See also Leningrad Oblast Directorate for the Protection of State Secrets in the Press (Lenoblgorlit or Gorlit)
Chakovsky, Alexander 169

Chalsma, William 47, *115*
character reference 12
  for Azadovsky
    Boborykin's 10–11
    workplace 45, 50–1, 66, 68, 163, 182, 191
  for Lepilina 39–40, 42–3
  issued by khimia workshop's head foreman 112–13
  for Tsakadze 222
Chebrikov, Viktor 184, 205, 209, 216
Chernobylsky, Boris 139, 154, 157
Chudakova, Marietta 233
Churbanov, Yury 110–11
classified documents/information 5–6, 32, 53, 198–9, 229
'clearance' of lawyers 31–3, 40, 92
Commission on the Transfer and Reception of the Archives of the CPSU and the KGB into State Storage and Their Subsequent Use 200
Communist Party of the Soviet Union (CPSU) 5, 13, 55, 66, 110, 166, 200, 209, 237
Communist Party of the Soviet Union (CPSU) Central Committee 5, 7, 19, 34, 72, 90, 91, 110, 138, 143, 146–50, 153, 167, 169, 170, 185
compensatory damages 160–1, 167, 191
comrades' courts 2, 39, 239 n.3
Conspiracy Against the Soviet State (documentary) 69–70
Corrective Labour Code/Corrective Labour Colony (ITK) 107
  Article 6 95
  Article 14 93
  Article 30 112
  Article 62 145
  Article 100 110
cosmopolitanism. *See* anti-cosmopolitan campaign
CPSU. *See* Communist Party of the Soviet Union
criminal charges 3, 25
  against Azadovsky 22, 76, 211–12, 217
  against Lepilina 15–17, 210–11

Criminal Procedural Code (UPK)   22, 32
    Article 26   28
    Article 51   39
    Article 141   163, 206, 211, 218
    Article 168   215
    Article 184   46–7
    Article 208-2   186
    Article(s) 300–303   43
    Article 371   172
    violations of   22, 40–2, 46, 175, 190, 206, 207, 211, 212, 216, 218

Decembrists   101, 241 n.2
Dedov, Nikolay   202–3
Deduline, Serge   72, 73, 86–7
Demin, V.I.   10
Denmark   79, 80, 82, 85
developed socialism   239 n.2
de Vidovich, Silvana   74
DGOR (group operation cultivation file)   209, 243 n.1
dissident movement   2, 13, 31, 45, 65, 83, 92, 105, 137, 154, 196, 239 n.5, 240 n.1
    support for Azadovsky   26–9
DON (operational surveillance file)   200, 210, 242 n.5
DOR (operational development file)   49, 200, 201, 203, 210, 211, 213–15, 217–18, 220–1, 224, 242 n.3
Dovlatov, Sergey   73–5, 78, *132*
drugs, possession of
    charges against Azadovsky   3, 22, 28, 65, 69, 73–4, 200
    charges against Lepilina   3, 15–18, 40–2, 66–7, 178, 214, 225–6
    circumstances of discovery of (*see* house search)
drug use
    alleged of Azadovsky   10, 49, 74, 76, 181, 213–14
    alleged of Lepilina   41, 67, 213–14, 226
    Lepilina's denial of   179
    Slavinsky case   9–10, 48–9, 68
druzhina (Voluntary People's Guard)   16, 43, 240 n.3
Dudkin, Viktor   72

Efros, Mikhail   112, 170
Egerod, Søren   85
Eidelman, Natan   169
Eikhenbaum, Boris   235
Etkind, Yefim   8, 79, *115*, 164–5
Evans, Sir Harold   84
evidence, Azadovsky's note (16 February) to Lepilina as   69–70
evidence of bias   93, 146, 174–5, 182, 197–8
evidence-planting   19–21, 23, 30–1, 34, 68–9, 73, 76, 155, 174, 197–8, 215–16, 218–19, 221, 223, 231, 237
    dismissal of   76, 197, 219
    proof for   210–11
    Prosecutor's Office's investigation of   212
    witness testimony at Azadovsky's retrial   176–8, 181–2, 184, 185
exit visa   153, 164–6
exoneration
    Azadovsky's   186
    Azadovsky's bid for   159–60
    Lepilina's   203, 205
    Lepilina's appeal for   187

Federal Counterintelligence Service (FSK)   231–2
Feiginzon, Mikhail   *124*, 152, 153, 155, 156
Fiedler, Friedrich   72
foreigners, contact with   13, 222
    Azadovsky's   10, 15, 25, 48–50, 57–61, 206, 209–10, 213, 220, 221
    Lepilina's   15–16, 203, 206, 222
    Slavinsky's   9, 27, 81
Frankfurt International Airport   231–3
friends and associates   3–4, 12, 13, 25, 34, 44, 55, 60, 72, 86–7, 89–90, 92, 93, 100, 101, 112, *115*, *117*, *119*, *125*, *130–3*, 139, 141, 142, 151–2, 154, 157, 159, 164, 169, 174, 184, 185, 191. *See also* PEN International
    at Azadovsky trial first hearing   64–5
    campaigns on behalf of Azadovsky

Azadovsky Defence
    Committee   73–8
  British   83–4
  German   78, 86
  immediate circle of friends   26–9
  Scandinavian philologists   79–82
  Swiss   82–3, 86
  help to secure exit visa   166
  hiring of lawyer for Azadovsky's
    appeal   92–3
  hiring of lawyer for Azadovsky's
    defence   31, 39
  hiring of lawyer for Lepilina's
    defence   40
  Leningrad   8–9, 15, 18, 23, 49, 143,
    149, 170
  Lepilina's visitors during labour colony
    time   108–9
Frowen, Irina   84
FSK. *See* Federal Counterintelligence
    Service
Fyodorovich, A.M.   210–11, 217–20, 224,
    225, 227

Galkin, Captain   144–5
Germany
  Azadovsky's trip to   185–6
  support for Azadovsky   74, 78, 86, 142
Gibian, George   47–8
Gifford, Henry   84
Ginkas, Kama   15–16, 65, *117*, 140–1,
    157
Ginzburg, Lidia   27, 149
Gippius, Zinaida   46
Gorbachev, Mikhail   166, 184, 190, 195,
    196, 230, 239 n.4
Gordin, Yakov   64, 65, 170, 201
Gorky Automobile Factory   110–13, 123
Gorlit. *See* Leningrad Oblast Directorate
    for the Protection of State
    Secrets in the Press
Granin, Daniil   170
Grechishkin, Sergey   27
Gregor-Dellin, Martin   86
guilt, Lepilina's admission of   31, 35–7,
    40–4, 67, 107, 178–9, 187, 198,
    202
Gutkina, Genya   109–10

GUVD. *See* Leningrad Oblast Main
    Internal Affairs Directorate

Haas, Friedrich   152
Hamburger, Michael   84
Harder, Uffe   85
'Hassan'/'Baryte'   15–17, 179, 202, 203,
    210–11, 214, 217–18, 221, 222,
    225–7
house search
  on 1 June 1969   10–11, 13, 175
  on 19 December 1980   18–21,
    25–6, 28, 47, 66–7, 73, 146, 155,
    159–60, 162, 184–6, 190, 193–4,
    197–8, 206–7, 232
  Arkhipov's explanatory report
    on   223–4
  identity of officers involved in   163–
    4, 167, 174
  identity of the 'specialist' involved
    in   192–3
  KGB's 1988 review on   211–12,
    215–16
  KGB's internal investigation
    report   218
  Kuznetsov's explanatory report
    on   220–1
  of Lepilina's flat, 20 December 1980
    18, 39–40, 42, 160–2, 168
  Shlemin's explanatory report
    on   222–4
  witness testimony at Azadovsky's
    retrial   176–9, 180–2

Ilyushenko, Aleksey   231–2
Ingold, Felix Philipp   82
insufficient evidence   186, 187, 242 n.1
intelligentsia   48, 54, 195, 230. *See also
    individual names*
  adversarial relations between the
    Russian State and   1–2, 7, 11,
    27, 71, 73, 75, 171, 180
  carceral system's attitudes
    towards   137, 154
  high-profile arrests   237
  views of   12, 194
Intourist   58–61
Isametdinova, Natalya   55, 222

ITK. *See* Corrective Labour Code/
  Corrective Labour Colony
Ivanov, I., '"Intellectual Adventures"
  ...over the Abyss' 47–9

Jensen, Erik Vagn 85
Jensen, Peter Alberg 79–81, 83

Kalugin, Oleg 196, 226
Kamenko, Yevgeny Emilyevich
  arrests of Lepilina and
    Azadovsky 18, 22, 23, 28, 155
  on Azadovsky's collection of foreign
    publications 47
  Azadovsky's legal charges
    against 160–2, 194
  and Azadovsky's missing books 167–8
  and Azadovsky's retrial 173–4, 176, 178, 212
  Brun's testimony to 90, 217
  charges against Azadovsky 38
  charges against Lepilina 40
  contact with KGB 185, 220, 224
  decision not to instigate criminal
    proceedings against
    Azadovsky 47, 53
  KGB 1988 review on 212, 216
  obtainment of negative character
    references 39, 50
  special meeting at Vera Mukhina
    Higher School 76, 163
Kaminskaya, Dina 31–2
Karelian State Pedagogical Institute 12
Karp, Poel 65–9
Katerli, Nina 64, 72, 112, 170
Katukova, Inessa 180
Kaverin, Veniamin 170
Kazakina, Alla 31
Kerényi, Magda 86
KGB Fifth Directorate 2, 54, 192–3, 196, 200–1, 209–11, 213–15, 217, 219, 221–7
KGB Inspection Directorate 5, 207, 209, 213–14
KGB Investigation Department 54, 109, 184–6, 209, 211, 213, 217, 218
KGB/Leningrad KGB

  in 1970s and 1980s 2, 45, 53, 86–7, 109, 137, 139, 189, 192–3, 215, 226, 236–7
  1988 report to Chebrikov 209–16, 225
  archives and documents of 4–6, 200–1, 203, 205, 229–31
  attempt to recruit Lepilina for
    intelligence work 56–7
  Azadovsky's 1981 petition to 56
  Azadovsky's charges about
    involvement of 153–4
  Azadovsky's refusal to cooperate
    with 59–60, 81, 155, 209, 213
  and Azadovsky's retrial 173–6, 179–80, 182–5
  at Azadovsky's trial 92
  clearance of lawyers 32–3, 41
  consequences faced by operatives
    involved 224
  and Gorlit's report 45, 54
  identity of officers involved
    in Azadovsky's house
    search 167–8
  interest in Azadovsky 12–13, 15, 27, 57–61, 94–5
  internal investigation by 206–7, 216–24, 227
  involvement of 3, 25–7, 39, 41, 48–9, 53–6, 144–9, 152–5, 178, 179, 182–3, 197, 231–3
    Brodsky on 77–8
    evidence for 52, 162, 167–8, 176, 178, 182, 186, 192, 196, 207–8, 219
  reaction to Azadovsky Affair 205–7
  response regarding Azadovsky's house
    search 180–1
  and Shchekochikhin article 169–71, 189–90
  violations committed by 183, 190, 206–7, 211, 218
  Western media on 73–8, 87
Kheifets, Mikhail Ruvimovich 32–3
Kheifets, Semyon Aleksandrovich 31–3, 38–9
khimia 102, 110–13, 136, 137, 139–43, 145–7, 241 n.3

Khlyupin, Nikolay Nikolaevich 22, 31, 164, 173, 175, 176, 179, 211, 216
  discovery of drugs by 19–20, 223
  testimony of 21, 177–8, 181, 182, 212
Khrushchev, Nikita 110, 236
Klein, Lev 34, 76, 237
Klimchuk, N.A. 144
Klyuev, Nikolay 12, 25, 72, 185
Kobzar, Lieutenant Colonel 154, 155, 205
Kokushkin, Vladimir 178
Kondratyev, Vyacheslav 170
Kononova, N. *See* Sharymova, Natalya
Konstantinov, D.A. 20–1, 164, 175–7
Kopelev, Lev 74, 78, 86, 142, 166, 232
Kopylov, Alexander 198–200, 227
Korovkin 144–5
Kovalyov, Sergey 200
Kramarev, Lieutenant Colonel 186, 187
Krenyov, Pavel. *See* Pozdeev, Pavel Grigoryevich
Kresty Prison 48
  Azadovsky's post-conviction time in 89, 91–5, 98, 99, 101, 103–5, 136–7
  Azadovsky's pre-trial detention in 23, 29–39, 45, 63, 90, 154, 174, 221, 230
  Lepilina's pre-trial detention in 18, 23, 29–35, 107
  Mirek's experience 63–4, 236
Kryuchkov, Vladimir A. 189, 190, 200, 205, 207, 229
Kuchkina, Olga 231
Kuibyshevsky District Directorate of Internal Affairs (RUVD) 17, 183, 185, 203, 210, 212–14, 216, 218, 222, 224
  Azadovsky's civil suit against 160–2, 176
  prosecutorial review of Azadovsky's civil suit against 167–8, 171
Kuibyshevsky District People's Court 29, 64, 102, *129–30*, 160–1, 169, 172, 173, 180, 183, 207–8
Kushner, Alexander 170
Kutserubov, Edik 141

Kuznetsov, Alexander Valentinovich 56, 167, 185, 211, 212, 215, 217–19, 222, 224, 232
  explanatory report of 219–21
Kuznetsov, V.K. 219
Kuznetsova, Marianna 8

labour colony. *See* Susuman labour colony (ITK-5); Ulyanovka (US-20/2) labour colony
Lavrov, Alexander 26, 27, 72
Lavrov, Vladimir 82–3
Lazareva, Natalya 109
Lembourn, Hans Jørgen 85
Leningrad City Court 44, 63, 75, 90–1, 93–4, 107, 109, 159–60, 163, 172, 173, 184, 203
Leningrad KGB. *See* KGB/Leningrad KGB
Leningrad Oblast Directorate for the Protection of State Secrets in the Press (Lenoblgorlit or Gorlit) 167, 206, 220
  Azadovskys' complaint to 162–3
  censorship report of 45–7, 54
  censorship report of, verification of 174
  Lepilina's petition on seized books to 161–2
Leningrad Oblast Main Internal Affairs Directorate (GUVD) 4–5, 43–4, 178, 180–3, 185, 191, 207, 211, 222–4
  house search conducted by 18–22
  Information Centre of 4–5
Leningrad Oblast Main Internal Affairs Directorate (GUVD) Investigation Directorate 10, 11, 20, 55, 185–7, 191, 216
Leningrad State Pedagogical Institute. Foreign Languages Department 8, 12, 27, 209–10
Lepilina, Svetlana Ivanovna (Azadovsky's wife)
  access to Kuibyshevsky District Court archives 207–8
  appeal for exoneration of 187
  arrest of 3, 15–18, 28, 176, 210–11, 214

Azadovsky's note (16 February)
   to   37–8, 67–70, 159–60, 174, 230
Brun's defence of   90
certificate of conditional release   111, *126*
denial of guilt   178–9
early release of   112–13
exoneration of   203, 205
Gorky Automobile Plant Pass of   *123*
journey to her marriage   140–2
KGB's attempt to recruit   56–7
lack of news about   31, 35–7
prison photo of   *120*
prosecutorial review on detainment of   168, 224–7
seized books of   161–2, 168
transfer to *khimia*   110–13
at Ulyanovka labour colony   107–10
Lepilina trial   31
   admission of guilt   40–4, 67, 187, 202
   charges   39–40, 66, 210–11
   judgement   42–4
   review of judgement   201–3
letters, personal
   of Azadovsky to Lepilina   145, 147–50
   of Azadovsky to mother   153
   of Azadovsky to mother, during transfer to labour colony   99–106
   of Brun to Lepilina   107–8
Likhachyov, Dmitry   56, 159, 170, 191
Linetskaya, Elga   8
Livingstone, Angela   84
Ljunggren, Magnus   81
Lokhov, V.V.   42, 44
Losev, Lev   73
Lukovnikov, Alexander   64, 65, 68, 182, 194

Magadan   77, 95, 96, 99, 101, 104–6, 108, *123*, 136, 138, 139, 141, 143, 157, 198, 200, 207, 219, 222
Makarov, G.S.   20–2, 164, 176
Maksimov, Dmitry   27, 72, 149
Manuilov, Viktor   27
Maramzin, Vladimir   33, 73–4
Markov, Boris   45, 162

Markov, Georgy   90
marriage   140–2
   wedding ring gift   *124*
Matnyak, Vladimir   16, 43–4
media
   Associated Press   71
   A Chronicle of Current Events   13, 26, 240 n.8
   Danish newspapers   79, 80, 82, 85
   Deutsche Welle   26, 74
   'enemy voices'   78, 241 n.1
   Expressen   80, 81
   La Pensée Russe   33, 71, 73, 74, 82, 87
      'The Case of Konstantin Azadovsky'   74
      '*Literary Heritage* and the Trial of K. Azadovsky'   72
      Maramzin's article   73–4
   La Repubblica   71, 73–4
   Le Monde   71, 73, 81
   Leningrad Pravda
      Ivanov's unpublished article on Slavinsky trial   45, 47–9, 174
   The Literary Gazette   102
      'In Disguise'   207–8, 230
      investigation by   169–72, 189–91
      'A Leningrad Affair, 80s-style'/A Trial, 80s-style'   189–91
   Literary Heritage   71–2
   Neue Zürcher Zeitung   71, 82
   The Neva Times   195
   The New American   73
      14/20 Jan 1981 statement from editor-in-chief   74–5
   The New Daily Gazette   231
   The New York Review of Books
      Brodsky's 'Letter to the Editor'   76–8
   Northern Pravda   193
   Politiken   79, 80
      'Denmark's protest against the persecution of Soviet writers: a letter to the Soviet Writers' Union'   85
   Radio Free Europe   26
      Paris Bureau   87
   Ritzau (news agency)   79
   The Russian Gazette   198–200
   Samizdat Materials   26–7, 29, 90

Süddeutsche Zeitung 74
The Times
   'Plea for Convicted Soviet Scholar' 83–4
   'Soviet professor claims drug was planted on him' 83
Meilakh, Mikhail 33, 76, 237
Memorial (society) 4, 6
Mikhailov, Georgy (Zhora) 139
Mikhailova, L.V. 42, 43, 176
Minaev, Ivan 171
Ministry of Internal Affairs (MVD) 3, 5, 20, 76, 105, 110, 144–7, 149, 154, 167, 196, 213
   'Towards a new life' 110–11
   Visa and Registration Department (OVIR) 165–6
Mirek, Alfred 63–4, 236
Møller, Peter Ulf 80
Moscow Helsinki Group 13, 240 n.8
MVD. *See* Ministry of Internal Affairs

Neierdi, Alexander 148–50
Nikolaev, Yu.A. 217–20, 222–6
'Nikolay Mikhailovich' 59, 60
Novikov, Valery Stefanovich 224

Okudzhava, Bulat 170
OP (operational collection file) 225–6, 242 n.4
Orekhov, Mikhail 215
Orlov, Yury Fyodorovich 92–3
Orlova, Raisa 74

packing the courtroom 65
Papst, Edward Edmund 84
Parnis, Alexander 92, 157
PEN International 84–6
Peshkov, Aleksey 193
petitions, appeals and complaints 4, 19, 28, 31, 35–8, 56, 63, 64, 66, 69, 78, 85, 90–3, 99–101, 105, 111, 141–4, 147, 150, 152, 154–5, 157, 159–60, 164, 167, 173–4, 178–82, 184–5, 187, 192, 197, 205, 206, 209, 212, 216, 219, 224–5
   1982 Feb 15, to Special Sector of the CPSU Central Committee 34, 146–7, 153
   1982 Mar, to local supervisory prosecutor 147–9
   1982 Aug 15, to Chebrikov 184
   1982 Dec 18 156–7
   1983 Apr 1, to Main Directorate for the Protection of State Secrets in Print Media 161
   1983 Dec 20, to Main Directorate for the Protection of State Secrets in Print Media 162
   1989 May 5, to KGB chairman 207
   1992 Sept 10 197–9
   1994 Aug 26, to Russian Presidential Commission for Human Rights 230–1
   1994 Oct 19, to Acting Prosecutor General and FSK Chief 231–2
   1994 Nov 12, to German Federal Foreign Office 232
   1999 Nov 1, to Prime Minister Putin 233
   to Andropov 152–4
   challenging the judgement 159–60
   to chief of Kuibyshevsky District Investigation Directorate 36
   to Prosecutor's Office 138, 145, 149, 151, 156, 162, 164, 171, 180, 186, 187, 192, 197
   role of petitioner in labour colony 138, 156
Petrov, O.A. 42, 43, 176
Petrova, Lyudmila 25, 26, 56, 222
Phillips, Anthony 10, 47–9
photograph collection. *See* books and photograph collection
Pilnyak, Boris 46, 80
Podrabinek, Alexander 92–3, 138, 151
Poland 27, 80, 240 n.2
political crime 2, 25–6, 32–4, 47, 51, 53–5, 71–3, 76, 109, 136–7, 139, 152, 175, 213, 237
political repression 3, 6, 53, 75, 196–201, 227, 239 n.5, 240 n.2
Polozyuk, V. 219, 224
Poludyakov, V.I. 159–60
Popov, Vladimir P. 184–5, 213
Pozdeev, Pavel Grigoryevich (Pavel Krenyov) 192–3, 211, 215, 220–1

Pozen, V.A.   42, 65
pretrial detention   40
　of Azadovsky   23, 29–35
　of Lepilina   18
　time between trial and   63–4
Prilukov, Vitaly   180, 216–17, 221, 224
prison cellmates/inmates
　at Kresty Prison   29–30, 33–7, 69–70, 91–2, 94–5
　at Susuman labour colony   69–70, 94, 137–41, 143–6, 151–2
　at Ulyanovka labour colony   109–10
prisoner labour. *See khimia*
prisoner transport   96–106
Pristavkin, Anatoly   170
Prosecutor's Office   137, 190, 191, 200, 201, 207, 212, 215, 218, 231, 233, 237
　1981 Feb 11, letter of support for Azadovsky to   27–9
　1981 Oct 12, Shalman's petition to   93
　1986 prosecutorial review   167–8, 171, 179, 182, 185
　1992 response to Azadovsky's petition to Stepashin's commission   197–9
　Azadovsky's complaints and petitions to   138, 144–5, 147, 149, 151, 156, 164, 167, 180, 186, 187, 192
　and KGB's operational activities documents   168, 229
　and *The Literary Gazette* investigation   171–2
　missing books issue and   162
　permission to search Azadovsky's flat   18
　review of Lepilina's case   224–7
　review of Lepilina's sentence   201–3
Pushkin, Alexander   7
Putin, Vladimir   233

'Rachmaninoff'   211, 215, 220, 221, 227
Raisky, Erik   151–2, 156
Rait-Kovalyova, Rita   56
Ravich, M.   27, 35
Rayfield, Donald   84
Redin, Anatoly   *125*, 139–40, 152
Red Terror   239 n.5

refuseniks   166, 240 n.8
release
　Azadovsky's   156–7
　Lepilina's   112–13
Rilke, Rainer Maria   8, 12, 84
Rilke-Gesellschaft (Basel)   82–3, 86
Roginsky, Arseny   200–1, 237
Romm, Anna Sergeevna   9
Rozenberg, Vadim (Fima)   33–7, 69–70, 221
Ruhr University. Committee for the Defence of Democratic Rights and Freedoms   78
Russian Soviet Federative Socialist Republic (RSFSR) Criminal Code
　Article 26   28
　Article 70 ('anti-Soviet agitation and propaganda'; 'treason against motherland')   2, 32–4, 47, 51, 53–4, 175
　Article 120 ('corruption of minor')   55
　Article 121 (criminalization of sodomy)   34
　Article 130 ('fabrication and dissemination of libellous inventions')   163
　Article 172   160
　Article 176 ('criminal prosecution of a person known to be innocent')   194
　Article 190-1 ('systematic circulation ... of false statements which defame the Soviet state or social system')   25–6, 51, 54–5, 109, 152
　Article 224 ('unlawful possession of narcotics')   3, 17, 28, 51, 136, 175, 178
　Article 224-1 ('with intent to sell or sale')   41, 240 n.7
　Article 224-2   43
　Article 224-3   22, 34, 36, 40–3, 65, 94, 142, 161, 203
　Article 224-4   40–2
　Article 306-5   40
Ryazanovsky, Savely   39, 65
Rybakov, Anatoly   170

Sadovnik, K.P. 222
Sapunov, I. 22, 28
Scammell, Michael 83, 86
Scandinavian philologists 79–82
Schacke, Lene 80
search witnesses 16–21, 40, 42, 43, 67, 144, 164, 175–7, 212, 215, 216, 220, 223
second culture 8
Sedletsky, V. 143
Semyonov, Vladimir S. 78, 83
Shalman, Yevgeny 92–3, 100
Sharymova, Natalya ('N. Kononova') 75–6
Shchekochikhin, Yury Petrovich *131*, 169–72, 177, 183–4, 187, 189–91, 207–8, 230, 237–8
Sheinis, Viktor 200
Shistko, V.I. 50, 55, 65–6, 69, 163, 173–4
Shlemin, Vladimir Vladimirovich 167, 193, 211, 218, 219, 224
 and Azadovsky's retrial 173–4, 178, 180–2, 186, 212, 216
 explanatory report of 222–3
Shumov, O.K. 219
Slavinsky, Yefim 4, 209–10
 1981 Jensen's letter to 79–80
 with Chalsma *115*
 conviction of 239 n.7
 response to Jensen's letter 80–1
Slavinsky Trial 9–13, 27, 38, 61, 68–9, 81, 175
 Ivanov's article on 47–9, 174
Smirnova, Natalya Borisovna *129*, 173, 175, 181
sodomy 34
Soroka, Oleg 171
Soviet Union
 in 1960s and Khrushchev thaw 2–3, 13, 58, 235, 236
 in 1970s and 1980s 1–2, 169
 1970s mass exodus 73
 adversarial relations between intelligentsia and the state 1–2, 7, 75, 137
 collapse of 186, 195
 'Era of Stagnation' 3, 181, 200, 236–7, 239 n.4
Sozzani, Maria *133*

Spangenberg, Kaj 80, 85
Sperling, Vibeke 85
Spitsyna, Alyona 65
Sputnik Bureau of International Youth Tourism 58–9
Starovoitova, Galina *132*, 190–1
Steffensen, Eigil 85
Stepashin, Sergey 197, 200, 231–2, 237
Stern, Joseph Peter 84
Storck, Joachim Wolfgang 82–3, 86
Strugatsky, Arkady 170
Strugatsky, Boris 170
suicide attempts 18, 108, 150–1
Sukharev, Alexander 171–2
Supreme Soviet Commission for the Rehabilitation of Victims of Political Repression 196–201, 227
Susuman labour colony (ITK-5)
 administration's provocations and harassment 148–151, 154–7
 delay in transfer to 91–4
 history of 96
 infirmary stay 151–3, 156
 Lepilina's visit and marriage 140–2
 life at 135–40, 142–50
 release from 156–7
 transfer to 94–106
Switzerland 82–3, 86

Teslyuk, Ensign 154–5
Tkachyov, A. 27, 35
Tkachyova, Zinaida 17–18, 35, 40, 113, 160, 206, 221–2
Tolkunov, S.V. 207, 213
Toporov, Viktor 9, 29
Toporova, Zoya 26
transit prisons 97–9
Tsakadze, M.G. 56, 222
Tsekhnovitser, Yury 18
Tsvetkov, N.A. *129*, 173, 174, 176, 179, 180

Ulyanovka (US-20/2) labour colony 44, 107–13
underground poets 8
United Kingdom 83–4
University of Bremen. Research Centre for East European Studies 4

UPK. *See* Criminal Procedural Code
USSR. *See* Soviet Union

Vanag, Zigrida   18, 26, 29, 39, 92, 109
Vasilyev, V.I.   212
Vasilyeva, Katya   141
Vera Mukhina Higher Secondary School
    of Art and Industry   12, 27,
    50–1, 65, 68, 76, 163, 173, 191,
    231
Vinnichenko, N.A.   225, 230
Volodin, E.V.   167, 212, 217, 219, 220,
    222
Voluntary People's Guard. *See druzhina*

witnesses. *See also* search witnesses
    KGB agents as   174, 182
witness examination and testimony
    Azadovsky's retrial   174–83, 212
    Azadovsky's trial   66–7
    Lepilina's trial   42–44
Writers' Union   60, 64–5, 74, 85, 90, 149
    Azadovsky's membership   173, 192
    rejection of Azadovsky's
        membership   55–6

Yakubovich, A.E.   *129*, 173, 175, 178,
    183
Yampolsky, Isaak   27
Yanovskaya, Genrietta   15–16, 23, 26, 65,
    92, 108–9, *117*, 140–1, 157
Yatkolenko, I.V.   210–11, 217–20,
    225–6
Yegorov, Boris   27
Yeltsin, Boris   195, 196, 199, 233
Yermakov, V.D.   219
Youth Communist League
    (Komsomol)   43, 59–60

Zamyatin, Yevgeny   46
Zamyatkina, Major   17, 18
Zarubin, V.V.   142
Zborovsky, Sergey   18
Zhmaev, Alen   9, 11, 58
Zhuk, Vadim   23
Zigalenko, Georgy   178
Zilbershtein, Ilya   71–2
Zilitinkevich, Sergey   91–2, 95, *130*
Zionist   153–4
Zolotaryov, Yury   135
Zoshchenko, Mikhail   7, 46

www.ingramcontent.com/pod-product-compliance
Lightning Source LLC
Chambersburg PA
CBHW062125300426
44115CB00012BA/1813